HUMAN
BEHAVIOR
IN THE
SOCIAL
ENVIRONMENT

HUMAN BEHAVIOR
IN THE
SOCIAL
ENVIRONMENT
A SOCIAL SYSTEMS APPROACH
(Sixth Edition)

Irl Carter

ALDINETRANSACTION
A Division of Transaction Publishers
New Brunswick (U.S.A.) and London (U.K.)

First Aldine Transaction printing 2011
New Material this edition
Copyright © 2011 by Irl Carter

This book is printed on acid-free paper that meets the American National
Standard for Permanence of Paper for Printed Library Materials.

Library of Congress Catalog Number: 2010040840
ISBN: 978-0-202-36398-1 (Cloth) 978-0-202-36400-1 (Paper)
Printed in the United States of America

Library of Congress Cataloging-in-Publication Data

Anderson, Ralph E.
    Human behavior in the social environment : a social systems approach /
Ralph E. Anderson and Irl Carter.
        p. cm.
    "Sixth Edition."
    Rev. ed. of: Human behavior in the social environment : a social
systems approach / Ralph E. Anderson and Irl Carter with Gary R. Lowe.
5th ed. 1999.
    Includes bibliographical references and index.
    ISBN 978-0-202-36398-1
    1. Social systems.   2. Social institutions.   3. Human behavior.
I. Carter, Irl. E.   II. Title
    HM586.A54   2011
    301—dc22

                                        2010040840

Dedicated to the memory of

Ralph Anderson (1928-1997)
and
Diane Anderson (1931-2008)

Nobody would choose to live without friends
even if he had all the other good things.
—Aristotle

Table of Contents

Acknowledgments

I am deeply indebted to the people mentioned here for their support and advice during the preparation of this edition of *Human Behavior in the Social Environment.*

To Dr. Irving Horowitz and Mary Curtis, for their support and guidance, and to the Transaction staff. It is an honor to be associated with a publishing house with such a distinguished record in the social sciences, and a commitment to scholarship, integrity, and truth.

To Dr. Bruce Curtis, Emeritus Professor, Michigan State University, and Joy Hilleary Curtis R. N., M. A., Emeritus Professor and Ombudsman Emeritus, Michigan State University, for their willingness to review the book and to contribute to sections of it.

To the staff of the Washington County, Minnesota, Public Library, and Marlyce Lee, former Branch Manager, for years of assistance. It is an invaluable resource, amazing, well-provisioned and helpful.

To the four K's of the Anderson family: Kim, Kyle, Kristi, and Kerry, for carrying on their parents' tradition of generosity and friendship.

To William R. McCarthy, poet and *anam chara*, and his wife Kathryn, great friends, for hours and days of companionship and inspiration at various coffee shops, New Year's and St. Patrick's day parties, and in Spain, Peru, England, Ireland, and who knows where, next?

To my family, for being there, and being who they are; and to Abby, Jacob and Sam, who are becoming the amazing people they will be.

And to Sharon Carter, who supported me (literally and figuratively) in recovering from a leg fracture during the months before this edition was completed. She bore with my spells of productivity and frustration, as she has for nearly forty years, and is as responsible for this edition as I am.

Irl Carter

Introduction to the Sixth Edition

*We will need, as Balzac said, "profound people," and not merely those who calcu-
late; radical minds and not merely technicians. Thus, we will need people trained
through doubt and questioning. The havoc caused by routine thinking and political
improvisation is clear enough today.*

Maurice Merleau-Ponty, quoted in Georgiou (2007)

This edition marks the thirty-seventh year since the first edition of this
book appeared. Then, systems theory was a relatively obscure set of sup-
positions and observations, and *social* systems had little recognition or
status; in fact, it was largely regarded as one more attempt to "scientize"
ideas about human behavior. Now, social systems is a theory accepted
widely in the social sciences and human service professions. Systems
theory is an acknowledged source of some of the most exciting ideas in
science, including the social sciences and the field of human behavior.
One theorist celebrates the "systems movement" (Georgiou, 2007:35).
That may be an overstatement, but clearly systems ideas have been fruitful (to continue the tree metaphor) and have become the *lingua franca*,
the common metaphor or model, across most academic, scientific, and
technical disciplines. Clearly the computer, in its infinite applications,
plays a major role in this.

This sixth edition is organic; its branches have spread and its roots
are deeper than in previous editions, but it is still the same tree. Those
of our readers who are familiar with preceding editions may notice
that we have dropped or revised some items, while adding others: in
particular, the section on phenomenology and its relationship to professional practice in the human services.

Our emphasis in this edition is less to carry the banner of systems
theory, than to encourage "systems thinking," meaning both to think systemically and to make explicit its implications for practice and praxis.

The theme of *caring,* in the previous edition, has expanded and deepened in this edition; here, we develop *empathy* as the key concept, as

elaborated in the Addendum to Chapter 2, a new section on application of systems thinking to professional practice. Empathy emerges as a central concept in the line of reasoning from Systems Theory to Phenomenology to Neuroscience to professional practice and praxis as we lay it out in that Addendum. It underlies all the human services, as the foundation on which personal commitment and professional practice are based.

Introduction

To my mind there must be, at the bottom of it all, not an equation, but an utterly simple idea. And to me that idea, when we finally discover it, will be so compelling, so inevitable, that we will say to one another, "Oh, how beautiful. How could it have been otherwise?"
—John Archibald Wheeler, quoted in Wheatley (2006)

Marvin Minsky has said that you need to understand something at least two different ways in order to really understand it. Each way of thinking about something strengthens and deepens each of the other ways of thinking about it. Understanding something in several different ways produces an overall understanding that is richer and of a different nature than any one way of understanding.
—Mitchell Resnick, quoted in Johnson (2001)

This book maps the territory of human behavior. It is intended to introduce students in the human services to ideas and theories that are fundamental to understanding human behavior. Students in social work, nursing, education, child development, and other disciplines that provide human services require an acquaintance with a vast body of knowledge about the behavior of humans. Today it is impossible to present enough information in one book to accomplish this.

In our teaching and in our students' learning, we found that we came nearest to accomplishing this task by writing this book and using it as a global map of human behavior. It designates the major levels of knowledge of human behavior and enables students to recognize the human systems that most concern them. It is designed to organize human behavior content into an understandable whole.

Along with most of our students, we have found this book useful as a large-scale map in a "survey" of human behavior. We know from our experience that its utility in any particular sector of human behavior may be limited; therefore, we provide "small-scale maps" in the suggested readings at the end of each chapter. These sources provide more detailed explorations of particular human systems. This book, however, serves to place knowledge of human behavior within a broad context to remind us that one's theory and one's practice are "a piece of the continent, and a part of the main," as the poet John Donne put it.

The manner in which this book and the more specialized resources fit together varies with the terrain. For example, a great many books and articles deal with organizations as systems, and it is fairly clear how the large- and small-scale maps of organizational behavior can be integrated. However, the integration of the two scales is less clear as they converge in the behavior of a person, where the relation of the part and the whole is always at issue. One recurrent question, for example, is whether a person should be regarded as the basic unit, a system capable of being subdivided, or only as a subsystem of some larger system such as society. Our intent is to demonstrate that these are all legitimate perspectives to be used selectively in accord with the system "level" being examined.

Our objectives in this book are to explain how our map is designed and to establish its utility. We have sought an "umbrella" theory under which various theoretical perspectives would fit, or—to shift the metaphor—a "skeleton" framework upon which various theories can be affixed and fleshed out toward a comprehensive theory of human behavior. In our experience, no single theoretical perspective can encompass all aspects of human behavior.

Courses in human behavior have had various organizing themes, including:

1. *Normal vs. abnormal behavior.* This perspective provides knowledge of individual and family dynamics, which is invaluable in understanding and dealing with behavior of individual persons, but is of doubtful validity when applied to groups, institutions, communities, and societies.

2. *Developmental patterns of the person.* This perspective includes groups, communities, and society, but only from the standpoint of their effects on the development of the person. Inherent in this approach is a view of the person as an "adjuster" or "adapter." Human behavior is seen as adjustment to social stresses. Intervention possibilities are dichotomized, *either* working toward helping the person to adjust to the social situation *or* attempting to change the social situation so that it would be supportive to the person.

3. *Social process.* This perspective emphasizes knowledge of the social and cultural patterns that provide the social context for development and behavior. Such understanding is essential to social planning, but omits the uniqueness of the individual, and the distinctiveness of lifestyles.

Each of these perspectives, as well as others, has served as a structuring theme for ordering knowledge of human behavior. Each enables scrutiny of various theories and hypotheses. However, each taken alone has limited applicability to the broadening base of human services. There has been an exponential increase of social science knowledge, which varies greatly in its quality and reliability. This increase requires a more comprehensive integrative framework than that provided by any of the previously employed organizing schemes. What is now required is an approach that will foster an integration of psychoanalytic, psychological, and developmental perspectives with the burgeoning discoveries from the many disciplines that study human behavior. We have found that social systems theory is that approach.

Social systems theory may be described as a "way of thinking," a "theory about theories," a "hypothesis about theories," which has evolved into a loosely knit body of theory. It is a particular form of *general systems theory,* which crosses physical, natural, and social sciences. Emerging findings in many disciplines buttress the validity of a general systems theory.

Social systems theory has these characteristics:

1. *It is comprehensive.* It offers greater potential for description and integration of seemingly disparate theories into a single framework than any other framework we know of.
2. *It provides suggestive leads* for all sectors of human behavior, even though it does not map all sectors adequately or equally.
3. *It has the potential to provide a common language* to various disciplines, both within and across disciplines. Students interested in psychotherapy, education, community development, and administration may find social systems theory a useful common framework. The psychotherapist may not be vitally interested in community development, believing that significant changes occur within individuals; the community developer may believe that significant changes occur only when groups act; while the administrator may believe that change is real only when it is structured and solidified in an institution or program. We believe that each is partially right and partially wrong. Like the proverbial blind men examining the elephant, each has part of the truth. Yet these three specialists can see relationships between and among their localities if they share a knowledge of social systems. Each might prefer her "home territory," but would be aware that it was "part of the main." They can recognize that interactions of persons, groups, and organizations are integrally related in a common system.
4. *Parsimony* is the final characteristic. Social systems theory allows the student to reduce the "blooming, buzzing confusion" of theories of human behavior and methods of practice to a framework that can

be mastered; the proverbial "Occam's razor" (the simplest answer may be best) comes to mind. Herein lies a danger, of course; through reductionism, the student may be content with the global map, flying from continent to continent, coast to coast, without encountering the precipices, mudholes, and arid deserts upon which many a theory has foundered. The systems approach cannot replace detailed knowledge of at least some particular sectors of human behavior. After all, people live through the processes of human interaction, not on maps.

This book describes a systems "skeleton" and then locates important human behavior concepts upon it. The instructors and students who use this book must flesh out the skeleton so that the approach will be directly applicable to the practice of each respective profession and the system or systems which is its preferred domain.

How to Use This Book

This book is a large-scale map, intended to be supplemented in each particular sector of human behavior by more detailed maps. We have used it this way with both undergraduate and graduate students. We have guided students through the courses in modular fashion, using selected theories and indicating where each more detailed theory meshed with the large-scale map.

The first two chapters acquaint the student with social systems theory. The essential characteristics of systems are introduced and explained. These concepts, which serve to draw the map, reappear in the subsequent chapters. They are the key ideas that together form the social systems approach of this book. The Addendum to Chapter 2, new to this edition, discusses the philosophy of phenomenology and the concept of praxis in relation to practice in the human services.

The subsequent chapters (3-8) are modules—each can be taught as a separate unit, with only the first two chapters as prerequisites. The present arrangement of the chapters is only one feasible way of ordering human systems, in descending order of magnitude. If instructors using this book prefer other sequences, the order can be altered. In this way, a course might be better integrated with other courses during the same term, or might better convey a particular theme being emphasized.

We have found it most useful to use other texts with this book to provide additional threads of continuity through the general map, to assure degrees both of latitude and longitude, and to provide a single small-map source for each human system examined. For continuity crossing all systems, in the past we have used *The Autobiography of*

Malcolm X, Tillie Olsen's *Tell Me a Riddle,* Ken Kesey's *One Flew Over the Cuckoo's Nest,* and Randy Shilts's *And the Band Played On,* among others. For specific systems, we have assigned Erikson's *Identity, Youth and Crisis* (1968) for the chapter on the person; Billingsley's *Black Families in White America* (1988); Erdrich's *Love Medicine* for the chapter on families, and Hall's *Beyond Culture* for the culture module. Again, many choices are open to the instructor.

Suggested readings, with brief commentaries on their particular usefulness, follow each chapter. The readings actually used will depend upon the instructor and students and on the clock and calendar time available. If students are unfamiliar with particular social systems (such as family or groups), the supplemental materials should be selected with this in mind. For students acquainted with particular systems, supplemental readings can give deeper insights into theoretical writings and related research. The listed films and videos may also be helpful to convey particular ideas, or as an opportunity for students to apply the concepts in analyzing the situation that is portrayed.

The glossary is designed for easy reference to the key concepts used throughout this book. The reader should consult the glossary because these are the definitions used throughout.

The book is (metaphorically) an open system. Each instructor may add or substitute books, articles, films, videos, computer-assisted learning, or other learning aids. This flexibility allows the book to be used in graduate schools, four-year colleges, community and junior colleges, and perhaps in-service training programs.

In other words, this book comes to you incomplete. It not only suggests that students and instructors add their own input to this study of human behavior; the book *requires* it. We hope that social systems theory will be a step toward an integrated body of social science knowledge that will reflect both the complexity of social forces and the uniqueness of the individual person.

1

Social Systems Theory

Everything flows; nothing remains.... One cannot step twice into the same river.

—Heraclitus

No man is an island, entire of itself; every man is a piece of the continent, a part of the main.... . any man's death diminishes me, because I am involved in mankind; and therefore never send to know for whom the bell tolls; it tolls for thee.

—John Donne, Devotions XVII

Theorie c'est bon, mais fa n'empeche d'exiter. (Theory is good, but it doesn't prevent things from happening.)

—Attributed to Sigmund Freud

Introduction: Providing Meaning to Theory

Reverend Donne's well-known passage expresses this book's theme, *social systems theory*. General systems theory (GST), which includes the narrower field of *social systems,* is a cross-disciplinary body of scientific thought that emerged during the mid-twentieth century.

This chapter will introduce the basics of the social systems approach to understanding human behavior. We will provide a brief overview of the scientific context that gave rise to systemic thinking and the particular version known as social system. We will define and discuss basic concepts, some of which include terms that may be new to you, such as *holon.*

We will also discuss familiar terms, such as *energy* and *organization,* but some of these terms will have new, important meanings.

The social system model that we present in these first two chapters provides organizing principles for this book. This model enables the reader to recognize similar or identical ideas (isomorphs) emerging from different scientific and philosophical ancestries and provides a scheme for classifying and ordering such related ideas. Most importantly, it provides a means to understand human behavior better and may point to new directions for professional practice (see Addendum to Chapter 2).

1

One systems theorist says:

> For decades, and even perhaps for 100 years, social science has been trying to describe, or hit, a moving target—nonlinear behavior. It has been scoffed at as "soft science," but this may no longer be the case. Potentially, these theories of nonlinearity indicate that [it] is more difficult to study nonlinear phenomena, tougher to pin things down. Entirely possible is the notion that social science has been doing the most difficult work in science. (Bütz, 1997:xviii)

The advent of computers has allowed testing of nonlinear hypotheses (e.g., of fractal geometry and so-called "fuzzy logic"). This has presented exciting (and frequently unanticipated) insights into commonalities among the natural (or "hard") sciences and social (or "soft") sciences.

At times, we will describe it as the social systems *perspective,* a philosophical viewpoint on the relationship of persons with their social environment. Occasionally, we will also refer to it as the social systems *model,* meaning that it is a hypothesis to be tested, primarily through its application to professional practice and praxis in various professions and disciplines. Since "person-in-environment" (or PIE, as it is abbreviated) is a central motif of social work and of other human services, the systems metaphor is particularly well suited to social work practice. Gordon Hearn first stated this connection:

> ... if the general systems approach could be used to order knowledge about the entities with which we work, perhaps it could also be used as the means of developing a fundamental conception of the social work process itself. (Hearn, 1969:2)

This conception is useful to other professions as well, for example, psychology, nursing, education, communication, and medicine. A generation ago, Auger stated that a systems approach enabled the nurse

> to evaluate the status of the person who is ill and the significance of changes that may or may not have occurred in patterns of behavior. This content will help the student to develop a broader concept of the relationship between health and illness, the wide variations of "normal" behavior, and changes that may occur as a consequence of illness and/or hospitalization. (Auger, 1976:x)

At the same time, Monge argued that a systems perspective provides the best theoretical basis for the study of human communication: "That perspective which incorporates the others is, until at least more information is available, the one best suited to guide us in our quest for knowledge about human communication" (1977:29).

A. Systems and Systemic Thinking

In most dictionaries the first meaning of *system* is "a set of things or parts forming a whole," "a complex unity formed of many often diverse parts subject to a common plan or serving a common purpose," or something similar. *Systems thinking* then means using the mind to recognize pattern, conceive unity, and form some coherent wholeness—to seek to complete the picture (which Ion Georgiou [2007] says is inherent and a driving compulsion in human consciousness). That which is called *system* comprises elements cohering in some intelligible way, that is, capable of being understood.

As humankind seeks to find order and the quality of wholeness amid disorder and meaning, thought is patterned and imposed on the world **as experienced by the observer** (see the discussion of this point in the Addendum to Chapter 2). This point is thoroughly and precisely presented by Georgiou in his book, *Thinking Through Systems Thinking* (2007).

Systems thinking includes those ways of thinking that seek to understand unity and connectedness of all life. A recurrent phrase that conveys this quality of coherence is, "hang together." Here are two uses of that phrase from quite different sources (emphases added):

> [H]e who wants to have right without wrong,
> Order without disorder,
> Does not understand the principles
> of heaven and earth
> He does not know how
> They *hang together.*
> —Chuang Tzu, poet-philosopher of Taoism

> *The doctrine that everything in the universe* hangs together *... runs as a* leitmotif *through the teachings of Taoism and Buddhism, the neo-Platonists, and the philosophers of the early Renaissance.*
> —Arthur Koestler, philosopher (1979:265)

Comprehension of the *part/whole* nature of life is the central tenet of systems thinking. From this flow the propositions of our social systems approach.

I. Essence and Ancestry: The Atomistic/Holistic Continuum

A social system is a special order of system within general systems. It is distinct from atomic, molecular, or galactic systems in that it is composed of persons or groups of persons who interact and mutually influence each other's behavior.

> [A] social system is a model of a social organization that possesses a distinctive total unity beyond its component parts, that is distinguished from its environment by a clearly defined boundary, and whose subunits are at least partially interrelated within relatively stable patterns of social order. ... *[A] social system is a bounded set of interrelated activities that together constitute a single entity.* (Olsen, [1968] 1978:228-229)

A. Polar Positions

Social systems exist at all "levels": persons, families, organizations, communities, societies, and cultures. It is important, both analytically and ideologically, to specify what should be seen as the "basic unit" of social systems. In order to explain adequately what we consider the "basic unit" of social systems, we must step back and review the theoretical positions that have emerged.

Within sociology there historically have been opposite positions on the designation of the primary social unit: "macro" vs. "micro," or whole vs. part. Macrofunctionalists, such as Talcott Parsons, tended to view the society as the primary focus and therefore to view the behavior of smaller human systems and their components as being determined by the society's needs and goals, i.e., the whole determines the actions of its parts. Simply put, people are determined by society. This is a *wholistic* viewpoint.

At the opposite pole were social behaviorists and social interactionists, such as Max Weber and G. H. Mead. They began with the smallest unit of the system, the behavior of the individual person. In this view, the acts of the individual persons tend to cluster into patterns; therefore the social system is constructed out of these patterns; i.e., the whole is the sum of its parts. Simply put, persons determine the society. This is an *atomistic* viewpoint. The wholistic view implied "downward" causality, while the atomistic view implied "upward" causality.

These two positions are important and powerful when applied to the task of deciding how to (or whether to) intervene in human behavior, as well as to explaining how change is achieved in the realm of human endeavor. Within social work education and practice, this duality has emerged as the historical distinction between casework and community organization, or as "individual change vs. social change." The social change emphasis is grounded in the macrofunctionalist view that behavior is primarily determined by the larger social systems: macro-systems such as society, community, or organization. Emphasis on clinical or individual change is based on the belief that society is constructed from the behavior of the person. This duality is inherent in other social/behavioral disciplines, most explicitly in the paradigm of "nature vs. nurture." This phenomenon of *polarity* will be a recurrent theme throughout the remainder of this book. Most significantly, it is this duality and its historical tension that gave rise to the necessity for an integrative tool such as the social systems approach.

B. Holon

We hold that both polar positions must be considered when examining human affairs. There must be attention to both the whole *and* the part. Our point of view is that each social entity, whether large or small, complex or simple, is a *holon*, a term we borrow from Arthur Koestler (who borrowed, in turn, from the Greek language) to express the idea that each entity is simultaneously a part and a whole. A social unit is made up of parts to which it is the whole, the *suprasystem,* and at the same time it is part of some larger whole of which it is a *component* or *subsystem.* Like the Roman god Janus, a holon faces two directions at once—inward toward its own parts, and outward to the system of which it is a part. What is central is that any system is by definition both part and whole (see Figure 1.1).

The individual person constitutes the apex of the hierarchy of organisms and, at the same time, is the lowest unit of the social hierarchy (Figure 8.1 conveys this idea). The concept of holon is particularly useful; it epitomizes a consistent theme in this book: *Any system is by definition both part and whole. No single system is determinant, nor is system behavior determined at only one level, whether part or whole.*

The idea of holon as used in this book extends Koestler's proposition of whole/part relationships to include certain corollaries:

1. The systems approach requires the specification of *a focal system,* which is the system chosen to receive primary attention. Another way of saying this: the choice of focal system identifies the perspective from which the observer views, and analyzes, the system and its environment (see *perspectivism* in Glossary). In other words, "from where I sit. ..."
2. The idea of holon then requires the observer to pay attention to both the components (*subsystems*) of that focal system and the *suprasystem* of which the focal system is a part (or the *significant environment* to which the focal system is related), in order to fully understand it.

In Figure 1 (parts a-d), diagrams of a family are useful to explain the concept of a focal system. If the family is viewed as a holon, attention must simultaneously be given to both the family's members and to its significant environment such as schools, community, work organizations, other families, and neighborhood. To focus only on the interactions among family members (family as suprasystem) ignores the family's interactions with larger systems (family as subsystem).

Social systems theory may be described as "contextual," "interactional," or *perspectivistic.* The latter term connotes that causation, or

Figure 1.1
Diagrams of a family system, (a) Family, (b) Family as a whole: looking inward,
(c) Family as a part: looking outward, (d) Family as holon (part and whole).

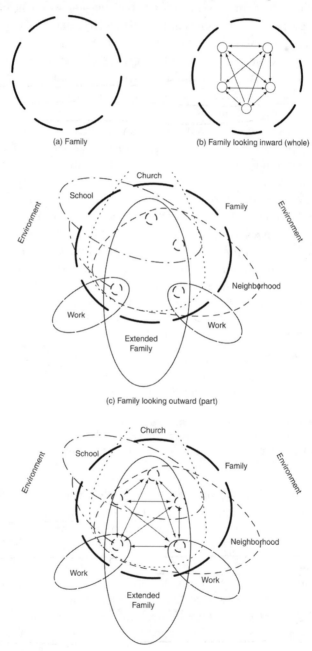

(a) Family   (b) Family looking inward (whole)

(c) Family looking outward (part)

(d) Holon (part and whole)

the significance of an event, is relative to the focus one has at the time of assessment; that the interpretation one places on events depends upon where and who one is and the perspective one has upon the focal system. As an example, recall in your own experience when you witnessed a situation and someone else who witnessed the same event described it very differently (the classic film *Rashomon* portrays the same events as seen by four different people; the more recent film *Vantage Point* (2008) employs a similar technique). It is the same in larger social/historical contexts: as events are viewed by other observers or at other times, meanings are often likely to change. Social systems theory is "holonistic," requiring

1. specification of the focal system and its boundaries;
2. specification of the units or components that constitute that holon;
3. specification of the significant environmental systems; and
4. specification of one's own position relative to the focal system.

This is the process that Georgiou (2007) calls "intuiting" the "identity" of the system. It is also what some systems theorists take as the "emergence" of the system; that is, when an observer sees systemic characteristics, the system "emerges" (see Addendum to Chapter 2). This process can be called *mapping*. One example is the use of "ecomaps" in family systems approaches to understanding and helping families.

Components and environment find their meaning in their effects on the focal system and, conversely, the focal system finds meaning in its effect on its component parts and its environment. To define a family and its components, one asks, e.g., is the father/husband present or absent? are grandparents or other extended family members present? what is their significant environment, a middle-class suburb, or a Brazilian *favela*? Who is the observer, and what is her/his role: Is she a "member of the wedding," caseworker, or police officer? Is he the family's therapist, patient's nurse, or community's organizer? Such a perspectivistic view is philosophically consistent with the basic metaphor drawn from Einstein's theory of relativity, that *perceptions of events are relative to the position of the observer.*

II. Energy/Information: The Necessary Element

Consistent with the atomic metaphor introduced earlier, we suggest the basic "stuff" of a system is *energy.* Metaphorically, as atoms and molecules are composed of energy, so also are social systems. The question becomes: Is energy an inclusive enough concept to denote the life of a

Energy is the information or resources
exchanged btwn persons or groups
that activates the system

8   **Human Behavior in the Social Environment**

social system? We suggest it is, if, borrowing from physics, the broader meaning includes both *information* and *resources* as "potential energy." The nature of both information and resources includes the capacities to activate or mobilize the system and to serve as energy sources.

> While most readers would have no problem in conceiving of coal or petroleum as energy forms, the present argument requires that we also regard human beings, human behavior, social groups, and assemblages of social interactions as energy forms. Similarly, mental processes located in the brain, writing on paper, and sound waves in the air are also energy forms. The inclusion of all these different kinds of things as energy forms is legitimate because all of them meet the definition. (R. Adams, 1988:15-16)

Monane agreed: "System action can be understood ... as the movement of energy/information (1) *within* a system and (2) *between* a system and its environment" (Monane, 1967:1-2). To disqualify information as energy is to deny its reality; information is nothing if it does not provide potential for action. Information *"is ingested as energy to the same extent that food fulfills biological needs"* (Bütz, 1997:136). The same author emphasizes that human beings use symbols to encapsulate their experiences and to communicate that experience to others—and that our symbols are "self-referential." That is, we constantly communicate our symbols not only to each other, but to ourselves, constructing reality and constructing self (see the discussion of self, neuroscience, and mirror neurons in the Addendum to Chapter 2). Bütz (1997:131) ingeniously uses an illustration of the Mobius (or Moebius) strip, a strip of paper that is given a half-twist and then the ends are joined, so that it forms a continuous, one-faced strip—an unending loop. By this, he means that our experience is always simultaneously both internal and external, a continuous dialogue (or dialectic) between self and the world. Information is the content of this dialogue. This is a fundamental example of what we later describe as a *feedback loop* (in this case, a literal, paper loop).

What occurs in and between social systems are "transfers of energy/information" between persons or groups of persons. The energy in this dynamic process is not directly observable; its presence is inferred from its effects upon the system and its parts. There is some disagreement among system theorists as to whether energy is a valid concept for social systems. Without getting into this intellectual debate now, we define energy as "capacity for action," "action," or "power to effect change."

It is important to understand that *energy* and *information* are not identical, but that they are complementary and inseparable in living systems: both are necessary although neither is sufficient. Energy must be structured in order to be useful; information, just as its root meaning implies, gives form to the energy. All systems carry information and instruction, in some form. We will occasionally use "energy/information" to convey the relation of the two or, rarely, just "information."

The exact nature of human energy is undetermined and depends in part upon the particular system being examined. Within a person, we refer to *psychic energy* (the energy of the psyche, or personality); we could similarly refer to the social energy of a family, group, organization, or community. In these instances, energy means the system's capacity to act, its power to maintain itself and to effect change.

Energy derives from a complex of sources including the physical capacities of its members. These sources include social resources, such as loyalties, shared sentiments, and common values, and resources from the environment. Energy sources for personality systems could include food; the physical condition of the body; intellectual and emotional capabilities; emotional support from friends, family, or colleagues; cultural and religious sanctions for one's beliefs and activities; recognition of one's status by society and one's colleagues in an organization; and perhaps most important, one's own sense of worth and integrity.

A. Entropy and Synergy

1. *Entropy.* There are some fundamental concepts necessary to an understanding of energy as the term is used in social systems theory. The first is *entropy,* the tendency of an undisturbed system to move toward an unorganized condition, characterized by decreased interactions among its components; this is followed by decrease in usable energy. *Entropy* is a measure of the quantity of *energy not available for use.* Some common expressions that convey this concept are: "He's not performing up to his potential," and "What a waste of talent."

Entropy is a concept from physics that is applied metaphorically, not literally, to social systems. This limitation was recognized early by the general systems theorist Ludwig von Bertalanffy:

> Physical processes follow the second law of thermodynamics ... they proceed toward increasing entropy, that is, more probable states which are states of equilibrium, of uniform distribution and disappearance of existing differentiations and order. But *living systems* apparently do exactly the opposite. In spite of irreversible processes continually going on, *they tend to maintain an organized state of fantastic improbability;* they are maintained in states of non-equilibrium; they even develop toward increasing differentiation and order, as is manifest in both the individual development of an organism and evolution from the famous amoeba to man. (Bertalanffy, 1967:62; emphasis ours)

2. *Synergy.* The second concept is *synergy,* which refers to increasingly available energy that results from heightened interaction among a system's components. Expressions of this might be: "She's got it together, and look at the results," and *E pluribus unum* ("Out of many, one"). An open system need not deplete its energy but, in addition to importing energy, may actually compound energy from increased interaction among its parts. *Synergy* (working together) occurs in open, living systems (and thus in social systems). Ruth Benedict, an anthropologist, first applied the idea of synergy to social interaction. She used it to denote the amplification of goal-directed activity where there was a fit between persons' individual goals and the goals of their culture. As with *entropy,* we again emphasize that the concept of synergy should not be used literally with regard to social systems, but rather as an analogy.

For example, it may be apparent that one organization is becoming increasingly static and predictable while another organization may be increasingly unpredictable and fluid, with internal shifts in concentration of energy and powers that result in "dynamic growth." One example was the seeming contrast between IBM and Apple early in their rivalry; IBM was the established company, Apple the brash upstart. A current example might be Yahoo vs. Google, or Microsoft vs. Google. The analogy we have introduced would be applied by describing the first organization described above as somewhat *entropic* and the second as more *synergistic.* This same analogy could be applied to a person as well: rigidity and maintenance of psychological defenses could be evidence of entropy, while absorption of new stimuli and constant adaptation to the environment, with stimulation of new attachments and ideas, could be evidence of *synergy.*

III. The Four Basic Energy Functions

Systems require energy in order to exist. In our view, there are four basic energy functions that are essential to carry out a system's *purposes.* We simplistically diagram these four energy functions (see Figure 1.2) in order to illustrate the interrelatedness of energy functions and to demonstrate their applicability to all human systems.

A. Functions of Securing Energy (SE and SI)

The first pair of functions (cells SE and SI) pertains to *securing* energy, as opposed to *expending* energy to achieve goals (cells GE and GI, discussed below). SE represents the function of securing energy from *outside* the system (*negentropy,* discussed later in this chapter);

Figure 1.2
Four energy functions.

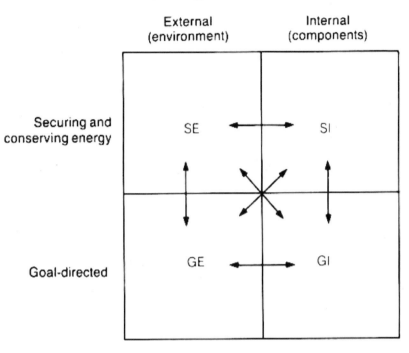

S: Securing
G: Goal
E: External
I: Internal
See Glossary for definitions of terms.

that is, from the environment. The SE function inevitably involves GE as well, since the importation of energy occurs as a transactional process between the human system and the environment. SI denotes securing energy from *inside* the system, from one or more component parts of the focal system. A variety of outcomes is possible in the performance of SE and SI functions. The SE function is well-illustrated by the fossil fuel situation now facing industrialized nations. If less fuel is available externally (e.g., oil from the Persian Gulf, Russia, or China) to supply national goals, more must be conserved and secured internally (SI function) through domestic oil, wood, coal, biomass, natural gas, wind power, or solar energy. An example occurring in a social system during the recent national financial crisis would be for family members to become unemployed (as many parents have). This would result in all members "pitching in" to pool resources. Fathers might work at home or provide child care while mothers work (illustrated by the comic strip "Adam@home"), children's earnings (e.g., a newspaper route) might become family income, and everyone might have to "make do" with what they have (witness newspaper and magazine articles about shopping at thrift stores, growing gardens, and lowering home thermostats).

If internal system energies are in short supply and energy from the subsystems is critically needed, energy-consuming frictions and conflicts among subsystems must be prevented or reduced. ("All right, break it up! We have work to do.") If, instead, the focal system has a surplus of energy available from its components, then the system can tolerate diversion of energy into subsystem conflicts ("Oh, let 'em fight it out! They need to let off steam."). Such conflicts between components may be, in a choice between focal system goals, the lesser of two evils: diversion of energy to suppress one subsystem may be preferable to allowing the subsystem to go unchecked. One example of this process is the operation of defense mechanisms (see discussion of Freudian theory in Chapter 8): suppression of impulses or wishes may be preferable to allowing them free expression, which in turn could endanger the "survival" of the personality. On a larger societal scale, a national policy of racial domination is another example: the amount of energy required to maintain segregation and second-class citizenship for a racial minority (United States) or a racial majority (South Africa) was great, and thus dysfunctional for the attainment of some goals. Continuation of such a system *(morphostasis)* might take priority for the privileged because of fear of the anticipated consequences of changing it *(morphogenesis)*.

When a system is in danger of being destroyed or radically changed, system components may pool energies. Pulling together, tightening the ranks, and forgetting past differences may be found in the family, city, or nation when circumstances or events threaten continued existence. In foreign policy and war, the often-repeated mantra by members of Congress is "Politics ends at the nation's shores" (which may or may not be true in the current contentious political environment).

B. Functions of Goal Attainment (GE and GI)

The second pair of basic functions (cells GE and GI of Figure 2) pertains to the *use* of energy, that is, the *purpose* to which energy is applied.

One characteristic of living systems is the purposefulness of activities. They operate in a *goal-directed* manner. This pair of functions together may be called *goal achievement* or *goal attainment*. As in the first pair of functions, this pair is performed both internally (GI) and externally (GE), and both are interrelated with SE and SI.

GE refers to goal-directed activity outside the system. The system must carry on transactions with the environment to achieve its own goals as whole and as part. It must achieve as much reliability and control over the linkages between system and environment as possible; this is the function of "intelligence" as Piaget (See Chapter 8, The Person) and Georgiou (See Addendum, later) describe it. One example is the "vertical integration" of corporations (like Microsoft), which purchase other companies to reduce competition (often referred to as "mergers and acquisitions"), to assure supplies of raw material, or to control and enlarge the market for their products. In the case of Microsoft, this has been a risky strategy that provoked antitrust actions by the federal Justice Department—an example of a suprasystem (the U.S. government and Europe as well) placing limits on the energy controlled by a system that seeks to control its own environment. Current examples are the controls placed on banks and other financial institutions by the federal government as a condition of receiving "bailout" funding, and the effort to enact legislation curbing unwise (and apparently sometimes illegal) financial behavior.

GI refers to goal-directed activity inside the system. Here energy is employed to subordinate the subsystems to the goals of the focal system in order to be consistent with the nature of the system and the environment. The declaration of a state of martial law in a nation is an example of goal-directed activity within the system. Because system survival is supposedly at stake, energies are directed inward to reduce or eliminate disorder. An example: professional organizations require their members to align their goals and behaviors with the goals and patterns of the organization; if members violate the rules, they are subject to expulsion or disciplinary measures. Social workers are regulated by a code of ethics and subject to sanctions by the National Association of Social Workers; psychologists are monitored by the American Psychological Association. A family system that holds a goal of educational achievement might direct energies to control a member who neglects education as a goal, for example, denying use of the family car, or suspending a child's allowance until grades are satisfactory.

C. *Interrelatedness of the Four Energy Functions*

It should be emphasized that these four functions (SI, SE, GI, GE) are not separate; a system performs all of these functions at the same time, although not equally at any particular moment. In any exchanges between whole and parts, all elements receive some energy and have some goals met. The reciprocal nature of the transactions and exchanges should be kept in mind. If one function is always dominant, the other functions are neglected, to the detriment of the total system. For example, the family system that concentrates energy only on the SE function through securing and importing energy from the external environment may experience internal disintegration. This might happen if a parent (or parents) devotes excessive time and energy at work, to the detriment of internal family functions, and does not spend time with children, support them, play with them, or discipline them. The phenomenon of "latch-key kids," children who arrive home after school to an empty house because the parent (or parents) work and have no other afternoon care, might be an example. A parent may not have a choice: survival of the family may depend upon the efforts she (or he) exerts at work; but all parties may pay a price (bear in mind the unpredictability of human systems, however; the children may be resilient enough to cope adequately). There have been a number of proposals to subsidize employers who provide day-care for employees' children, and subsidizing good day-care facilities at affordable prices at convenient locations (SE). This could reduce workers' stress and anxiety (SI) about their children's care, allow them to be more stable and productive (GE), and assure that children receive predictable, professional care that would allow them to become productive adults (GI), thereby benefitting the society.

IV. Organization: The Sufficient Element

Just as energy is the basic "stuff" and the *necessary* element of a system, organization is the *sufficient* element. Even if energy is available in and from outside a system, if there is a total absence of organization, then there is a total absence of system. Absence of organization equals entropy. To be a social *system* means to have at least some degree of organization; the word *organization* refers to the grouping and arranging of parts to form a whole in order to put a system into "working order." System organization secures, expends, and conserves energy to maintain the system and further its purposes.

The cybernetic concept of organization distinguishes between "high" and "low" organization. The degree of the system's intrarelatedness, that is, the degree to which components' actions affect each other, indicates the level of system organization. For example, in a highly organized system, such as the family portrayed in the novel and movie *The Great Santini* (based on the author's own family), the components are strongly interdependent; what one member does is crucial for others. The founding of a social system, that is, the delineation of a new entity from its environment, can generally be expressed in the familiar phrases, "Let's get organized," and "Let's get it together." The first action of the components of a burgeoning system must be to put randomly distributed energies in order. If this task of energy organization is not accomplished, then the system will fail to develop.

The Constitution of the United States is a real-life example of the notion of organization and its necessity for ensuring systemic operation. In short, the Constitution is a document that organizes component systems in such a way as to create a suprasystem of both government structure and sociopolitical behavior. The Preamble sets forth the general purpose for forming a new system and then specifies system goals:

> We the people of the United States, in Order to form a more perfect Union, establish Justice, insure domestic Tranquility, provide for the common defense, promote the general Welfare, and secure the Blessings of Liberty to ourselves and our Posterity; do ordain and establish this Constitution for the United States of America.

Following this introduction, the various articles and amendments of the Constitution specify the conditions of intrarelatedness of the components (states and individual persons) to the larger system (federal government). The goals of the national system as specified in the Preamble are, and must be, congruent with the goals of its components. It was precisely this organization and interrelatedness that were at issue in the Civil War (or the War Between the States, as secessionists defined it).

Organization is not synonymous with higher levels of complexity. That is, "A complex society is not necessarily more advanced than a simple one; it has just adapted to conditions in a more complex way" (Farb, [1968] 1978:13). A personality with complex defenses is not necessarily better or worse than an "uncomplicated" personality, but certainly the two function differently. Complexity or simplicity is not the issue; the measure of the effectiveness of a system's organization is its ability to fulfill the system's goals, as well as the goals of its components (See discussion of "effectiveness" and "efficiency" in Chapter 5, under "Goal Direction"). Effective organization not only enables the internal energies of the system to be generated and purposefully used, but also enables the system to secure energy from the environment (i.e., SI and SE functions).

Disorganization of a system—whether person, family, or neighborhood—does not mean totally *unorganized;* it means not *sufficiently* organized. The system's energies are not in working order; the components of the system do not stand in sufficient relatedness to one another. Energy is randomly distributed and expended; the system is tending toward a state of entropy.

Organization is apparent in the human personality. It is present in Freud's personality subsystems of *id, ego,* and *superego;* as he envisioned it, this triad must work in harmony (with the ego being domi-·nant) in order for a person to function effectively in a social context. Following Freud, Erikson's ([1963] 1993) formulation of *identity* is an expression of an *organizing* principle that enables the components of the personality to "get it together" in order to fulfill the goals of the person. Central to Erikson's formulation is the notion of a person creating an identity for herself or himself, as opposed to experiencing *identity diffusion.* Identity is defined as personality components working together as a whole, while identity diffusion refers to lack of integration among personality components. A person who is schizophrenic is, in essence, a disorganized system.

We can also see the importance of organization when it is applied to the family system. Families with problems are generally disorganized families, and the reasons for this disorganization can emanate from internal sources and/or external forces:

1. The goals of one or more members are in opposition to system goals.
2. The elements of organization (e.g., communication, feedback, and role expectations) are disrupted or unclear.
3. Energies from within the system are not available or not sufficient for the demands on the system,
4. The family is not adequately organized to obtain additional energy from outside its own system.
5. The environment (the suprasystem) exercises a disorganizing influence on the family system (e.g., oppression or economic downturn).
6. Energy is denied or not available from the suprasystem (e.g., unemployment or having welfare benefits cut off).

The dimension of organization—the fact of organization—is characteristic of all social phenomena that can be designated as social systems. If there is no organization present, there is no system, and it is unorganized. If organization is insufficient or dysfunctional for the goals of the system, the system is disorganized. Organization means the structuring of the units within a system: the ordering of the energies of the component parts in some fashion that results in a whole.

V. Causation, Feedback Loops, and Chaos Theory

A social system contains a causal network that is not linear. Causation is multidirectional, multiple, and mutual. A change in any part of the causal network affects other parts, but does not determine the total network. In other words (as we said earlier), behavior is not determined by one holon but rather by the interaction and mutual causation of all (or many) of the systems and subsystems, that is, by holons of differing magnitudes.

It is not useful to seek to understand human behavior through searching for *linear,* one-directional cause-effect relationships. Consequently, it serves little purpose to ask "why" persons do what they do. A "why" question demands a causal explanation, a "because" response. A more useful inquiry is "how," or in what way something happened. A current example is "global warming;" This wording implies that the burning of carbon fuels is the major, if not the only, cause of climate change. A more accurate description might be "global climate change," or "radical climate change," either of which recognizes that the causes may not solely, or mostly, be due to a single factor. Flatulence by cattle, for example (though usually said in jest), changes in the earth's ozone layer, and deforestation in the Amazon basin are also possible contributors. That is, "A causes B causes C" is less likely than "A interacts with B to produce AB, which changes both A and B, and results in C, which is partly A, B, and AB, and possibly AC or BC." Certainly, this is a more complex description, but it is also closer to reality, particularly the reality of human relationships, that is, *systemic* relationships. This more complex view of causality is the core idea in *nonlinear dynamic systems.* This retroactive influence on initial causal factors is called a *feedback loop* (see Glossary) and is characteristic of complex systems, including human systems at all levels. As the name of a 2010 romantic comedy suggested, "It's Complicated."

Developments in the study of fractal geometry, in "fuzzy thinking," and in *chaos theory* place great emphasis on the role and importance of feedback for systems. Fractals are geometric shapes that resemble forms found in nature (look up the "Mandelbrot set," e.g.); the basic idea is that systems (and parts of systems) such as crystals, leaves, and coastlines proliferate in forms that are based upon "exquisite sensitivity to initial conditions." This means that each new form or development in a system is highly sensitive to the previous condition of the system, and to feedback as the new development occurs; so sensitive that the slightest variation

A causality from a system perspective

will affect the evolving structure, making the outcome unpredictable. The classic expression of this is that the flutter of a butterfly's wings in Brazil affects weather in Texas; surely an overstatement, but it makes the point. This sensitivity to feedback confirms the principle of indeterminacy in systems: that only averages or aggregates can be predicted with any assurance. Weather forecasts are an excellent example of the use of systems theory in science. That is, local forecasts are less valid than those for an entire region or continent, and are frequently altered as unexpected developments occur. The analogy to social systems is that developments in human systems are unpredictable also and highly sensitive both to the system's history and to current feedback as new developments occur.

The term "fuzzy thinking" (Kosko, 1993) is not meant to describe what students do (or professors, or politicians, either). It describes the application of feedback to industrial and scientific instruments and machines. The basic idea is that instead of simple binary decisions ("on or off," or in computer terms, "1 or 0") gradations of judgment can be made automatically by the device itself: for example, "cold-cool-medium-warm-hot" by stovetops or crock pots, "intermittent-slow-fast-medium" by windshield wipers, or a combination (slow-warm then fast-warm then slow-hot, for a furnace, e.g.). Japanese corporations have been particularly innovative, and hold most of the United States patents on fuzzy logic applications in electronic and household equipment, e.g., washing machines that use constant feedback to adjust water temperature, to sense the type of dirt in clothing, to choose the amount of detergent and softener to use, to monitor the length of time needed to clean the fabric, and even the direction the fabric is moved: horizontal spin, vertical agitation, and combinations of other motions (a 2010 Sears ad showing four male dancers making the moves is a funny example). Another example is automobiles that self-correct stabilization, sense the proximity of other vehicles, and apply brakes with appropriate force (though recent recalls by major manufacturers illustrate that the feedback cycle can be defective). The relevance here is that the theoretical and practical significance of the feedback cycle in systems, and the uses of it, have become much more sophisticated during the last generation.

Chaos theory is a confusing name for complex ideas. Its importance to human systems, however, requires that we make an effort to understand the fundamentals of the theory. The fundamental concept in chaos theory is *order* vs. *disorder.* As discussed earlier, entropy describes a condition in which energy is completely dispersed (randomly distributed) and is not available for use by the system or its components. That is *disorder,* completely flat, unorganized, and undifferentiated, in other words, *chaos.* This use of the word chaos is somewhat difficult for most of us, because we think of piles of refuse, like the aftermath of a tornado or hurricane (or a typical teenager's bedroom; see the comic strip "Zits," e.g.). But in chaos theory, chaos is better pictured as a pile of sand, or a beach, or a bag of marbles, made up of inert, disconnected particles. Living systems exist at the opposite extreme; they lump and clump (and sometimes bump) energy into concentrations: systems and subsystems, which are maintained only by great effort and only by intense energy exchange internally and with their environments. In chaos terms, this is *order:* "order [is] departure from maximum entropy" (Bailey, 1994:243). The effort required by living systems to maintain order means that they constantly live "on the edge of chaos" (Capra, 1996).

Ilya Prigogine (1917-2003), a Russian-born Belgian chemist, won a Nobel prize for his work on the subject. He founded the "Brussels school," which has analyzed the dynamics of complex nonlinear systems. During forty years of research, Prigogine determined that living systems are able to maintain their high level of disequilibrium by importing energy and exporting entropy. Importing energy is, in the arcane language of GST, *negentropy,* or negative entropy. Another way to describe this process is that living systems are *dissipative* structures (Prigogine and Stengers, 1984); they dissipate, or export, entropy from the system; they "get the lead out." An example would be a person whose internal conflict drains energy, or ties up energy, who resolves the conflict by interacting with a therapist or a treatment group; this then releases the person's emotional (psychic) energy for freer, more productive living. Another example in an organization would be the restructuring of a department so that employees who are "dead-ended," unstimulated, unhappy, and unproductive are encouraged to interact with other units, or are moved to them; the department's entropy would be replaced by new flows of energy in the form of new ideas, new alliances, and new challenges.

The way in which systems accomplish negentropy, or dissipation, is through feedback. As part of the feedback cycle, the system and its components modify their relationships to each other; in other words, they adapt their structures to accommodate (see Glossary, and discussion of Piaget's theory in Chapter 8) this feedback. In this sense, exchanges between the system and components are more influential than the system's exchange with the environment; this is a modification of earlier thinking about system, and is largely attributable to Prigogine's work. This does not change the fact that *both* the components and the environment influence the system, however.

Conclusion

Social systems theory emerged during the twentieth century as an effort to bring more coherence among the disparate theoretical fields in the social sciences. It is a way of thinking and ordering theory and knowledge with the goal of "putting the pieces back together," rather than continually to pare social phenomena into ever smaller units of inquiry. It permits the observer or analyst to recognize different levels within the same phenomenon at the same time, and to understand the workings of the whole as well as the parts, as they occur. While this may make analysis more difficult, it also makes it more likely to be accurate, and closer to life.

Arthur Koestler, one of the pioneers of system thinking and the origi-nator of the term *holon,* provides the final words of this chapter:

> Looking inward, the person is a self-contained, unique whole, looking outward as a dependent part. No man is an island, he is a holon. ... (Koestler, 1979:303)

Suggested Readings

Adams, Richard.
    1988 *The Eighth Day.* Austin: University of Texas Press.
        "A study of human society," " applying social evolution concepts that have originated elsewhere." Compatible with our approach.
Bailey, Kenneth D.
    1994 *Sociology and the New Systems Theory.* Albany: State University of New York Press.
        An attempt to reconcile sociological and systems concepts as they developed in the decades of the seventies and eighties.
Bütz, Michael R.
    1997 *Chaos and Complexity: Implications for Psychological Theory and Practice.* Washington, DC: Taylor and Francis.
        Recommended for the advanced student of systems theory who wishes to apply the concepts to professional practice.
Capra, Fritjof.
    1996 *The Web of Life: A New Scientific Understanding of Living Systems.* New York: Anchor.
        Clear, understandable, thorough, and engaging. Theory is applied at all levels, atomic, physiological, social, and terrestrial.
Georgiou, Ion.
    2007 *Thinking Through Systems Thinking.* London: Routledge.
        Georgiou identifies a theory of knowledge that derives solely from systems theory. He argues that phenomenology is compatible with systems theory, which is consistent with our own emphases on *perspectivism,* choice of *focal system,*

and *boundaries*. It is a highly sophisticated argument, for systems scholars, and demands careful reading. This is an original and significant contribution to systems ideas.

Jervis, Robert.
1997 *System Effects: Complexity in Political and Social Life.* Princeton, NJ: Princeton University Press.
The author applies systems ideas to political processes, with clear perception of their congruence, or lack thereof. Chapter 4, "Feedback," is an excellent review of this concept.

Koestler, Arthur.
1979 *Janus: A Summing Up.* New York: Random House.
Koestler's final conception of holon and its application.

Richardson, George P.
1991 *Feedback Thought in Social Science and Systems Theory.* Philadelphia: University of Pennsylvania Press. A history and critique of the concept of feedback in the natural and social sciences. Not for the beginner.

Skyttner, Lars.
2005. *General Systems Theory.* Singapore: World Scientific.
A comprehensive overview and update.

Van Geert, Paul.
1994 *Dynamic Systems of Development.* New York: Harvester Wheat sheaf.
Detailed, complex exploration of a model of "nonlinear dynamic systems," for the advanced student of systems. This Dutch author's humor lightens this dense, challenging subject. How *do* you make wooden shoes out of concrete?

Literary Sources

Forster, E. M.
1989 *Howard's End.* New York: Vantage Books.
This symbol-laden novel with its oft-quoted theme, "Only connect," beautifully describes the systemic properties: "Only connect the prose and the passion, and both will be exalted, and human love will be seen at its height. Live in fragments no longer."

Mailer, Norman.
1993 *Executioner's Song.* New York: Modern Library.
Mailer's biography of murderer Gary Gilmore in novel form is an excellent portrayal of the complexity of a person's part/whole aspects interacting across the range of systems: family, group, organizations, communities, and society.

Films and Videos

We know of none that directly address the content of this chapter. We suggest that it would be useful to view several variations of computer programs that demonstrate fractal geometry, e.g., the Mandelbrot set, to observe the general idea from systems theory that fantastically complex systems may evolve from simple premises, and that systems are "exquisitively sensitive" to small variations in their starting conditions. The sheer beauty and complexity of the designs will prepare you to envision systems in a different way.

2

Aspects of Social Systems

Man is related to everything that he knows, And everything is both cause and effect, working and worked upon, mediate and immediate, all things mutually dependent. A bond that is both natural and imperceptible binds together things the most distant and things the most different.
—Blaise Pascal, 1658

Whether an order is formed or not depends on whether or not information is created ... the essence of creating order is in the creation of information.
—Ikujiro Nonaka, quoted in Wheatley (2006)

Introduction: Energy—Evolutionary, Structural, and Behavioral

As introduced in the previous chapter, *energy* and the *organization* of energy are the prime characteristics of social systems. We now discuss in more detail aspects of social systems that follow from these prime characteristics.

All systems are composed of energy interchange. One way to describe this basic energy interchange is to employ the constructs of *evolution, structure,* and *behavior* of social systems. *Structure* refers to those processes of energy interchange in which change is slowest and of longest duration and thus appear to the observer to be static. Those processes that change slowly over time but are not apparently static (that is, they move faster than structural but slower than behavioral changes), we label *evolutionary* aspects. *Behavioral* processes are of relatively faster tempo and shorter duration. For example, a structural change in the family may be from extended family to nuclear family over centuries; evolutionary change may be from traditional nuclear family to single-parent families over decades in the last century; and behavioral change includes a particular family's functioning during its life cycle. This distinction between energy interchanges is important as we explore the "stuff" of social systems. Our focus will begin with the evolutionary process basic to all viable social systems.

I. Evolution of Social Systems: Change and Maintenance

In reality, change and maintenance are not diametrically opposed. Systems never exist in a condition of complete change or complete maintenance of the status quo. At any given time, systems are both changing and maintaining themselves. The balance between change and maintenance may shift drastically toward one pole or the other, but if either extreme were reached, the system would cease to exist. As philosopher Alfred North Whitehead said, "The art of progress is to preserve order amid change and to preserve change amid order." This is similar to Erikson's "bipolarities" of personality growth and Piaget's "assimilation" and "accommodation" (discussed in Chapter 8).

A. Steady State

Steady State is a systems concept borrowed from physics; it appears to be the most adequate term available to describe a "particular configuration of parts and relationships which is maintained in a self-maintaining and repairing system. ... It is a state in which energies are continually used to maintain the relationship of the parts and keep them from collapsing in decay" (Laszlo, 1972:37). This is consistent with our discussion of living systems maintaining themselves in a state of high disequilibrium.

Steady state occurs when the system is "in balance"; the system maintains a viable relationship with its environment and its components, and its functions are being performed in a way that ensures its continued existence. The concept of steady state applies to all social systems. The word *steady* is somewhat confusing because it implies some kind of fixed, static balance, but in systems theory it means a *dynamic* balance and is always changing to some degree. Von Bertalanffy called it a "flowing balance," perhaps the most accurate description; like the metaphor of a river, similar to Heraclitus' view, at the beginning of Chapter 1.

We realize that the use of the word *state* in its singular form also is confusing. However, the concept involves a series of states in which the system, as a complex of components, adapts by changing its structure. It is somewhat the same, but not exactly the same, from one time to the next. The steady state is modified (perhaps along with the system's goals and the system's purposive, self-directed efforts) to maintain the system's integrity. A social system that is in steady state is characterized by a sufficient degree of organization and complexity, and by sufficient openness to the environment.

Steady state is introduced here as an alternative to the more familiar term *equilibrium* and the less familiar term *homeostasis*. The two latter terms have meanings similar to steady state but with important differences. In both instances, they denote a fixed balance in which some particular adjustment is maintained, and the structure of the system is unaltered (or is not altered significantly). An example might be a person during a particular period of life, e.g., late adulthood, in which change is relatively minor, but there is still some change. Steady state does *not* include a fixed balance: the system may find a new balance and new structure; in some instances the new steady state might be radically different from the previous one.

The three terms may be illustrated by analogy to transportation, using the human body and the means of transportation to represent a system. Equilibrium is like a teeterboard: balance can be achieved, but the limits of being in balance are narrow. Very little movement is possible on a balanced teeterboard, and the balance is sensitive to changes in the environment, such as wind or movement by the occupants.

Compared to equilibrium, homeostasis denotes a somewhat more variable balance; that is, the system's balance may change within narrow limits; balance is maintained by movement and includes encounter with the environment. Homeostasis may be illustrated by a motorcycle. The motorcycle rider has some latitude in controlling his or her vehicle's movements and remains upright by opposing centrifugal force (leaning into a curve) or by altering the machine's center of gravity on a banked curve by tilting the machine. Within some limits, which are determined by the weight of the machine, wind velocity, speed, and road angles, the bike is maintained in balance.

The various states of movement and balance experienced by the space shuttle dramatize what is meant by the notion of *steady state*. The shuttle is transported slowly, by feet per hour, to its launch pad; then hurled into space by powerful rockets at increasing velocity; held in space by centrifugal force, traveling 17,000 miles per hour relative to the earth; and finally descending to earth in a long, controlled fall. It changes its configuration during each of these periods: first, simply cargo to be transported, then an appendage of the huge fuel tanks, then a space ship and cargo carrier, and finally a glider (labeled a "flying brick" by some astronauts). Throughout, it is a vehicle for moving people and machines, but it significantly (and radically) changes its mode of movement and its actions.

The two tendencies involved in balance are *morphostasis* (structure maintaining) and *morphogenesis* (structure changing). Again, no system reaches either extreme, although it may tend toward one pole or the other. In order to continue to survive, all systems must maintain a shifting balance between status quo (morphostasis) and change (morphogenesis) and likewise a balance between order and disorder.

Another important distinction between steady state, equilibrium, and homeostasis is the significance of *stress*. Equilibrium demands a minimum of stress and disturbance and seeks minimal interchange with the environment. Homeostasis also requires minimal stress and disturbance but does allow moderate interchange with the environment. Steady state may involve a high degree of stress; social systems may prosper from stress and disturbance; they are maintained in a condition of high disequilibrium, "on the edge of chaos." In fact, human systems tend to *seek* situations that are stressful as a means to achieve synthesis and wholeness. You may be experiencing stress as you are learning these systems concepts. You often experience some degree of stress as you pursue your studies, but you *choose* to expose yourself to this stress, presumably because you believe that it will ultimately lead to an affirmative future. More than likely, you have encountered this book as a consequence of actively seeking to acquire information/energy as you seek a new steady state for your system.

Interchange is essential to the existence of steady state. Equilibrium implies closed and static systems, homeostasis implies open and static systems, and steady state denotes open and changing systems (see Table 2.1). In essence, what we mean by steady state is the "identity" of the system, its continuity with the previous states through which it has passed, its newly emerged elements, and the states through which it will pass in the future. This is analogous to the human personality, as it progresses through stages, but remains identifiable. A familiar French

Table 2.1   Comparison of Equilibrium, Homeostasis, and Steady State

	Equilibrium	*Homeostasis*	*Steady state*
Stress	Least possible	Minimal	Optimal and necessary
Structure	No change	No change	Wide possibility of change
Interchange with environment	Least possible	Minimal	Optimal and necessary
Openness	Closed	Minimal	Open

saying can be translated as "the more things change, the more they remain the same." If one explains that from a social systems perspective, the idea of steady state will be clearer.

B. Transition (or transformative state; Emergence)

It could be said that *transition states* occur more often than steady state (the lives of many of us might testify to that!). One of Prigogine's major points is that open systems "at the edge of chaos" react to stress or to new stimuli that require adaptation by transforming themselves to significant degrees; he called this *bifurcation*, meaning "branching"; other theorists identify such change as *phase transformation; "a system moves from a previous order to a new and more complex order by virtue of a chaotic transitory period"* (Bütz, 1997:16).

> At times, a single fluctuation [may] shatter the preexisting organization. At this revolutionary moment ... a "singular moment" or a "bifurcation point"—it is inherently impossible to determine in advance which direction change will take: whether the system will disintegrate into "chaos" or leap to a new, more differentiated, higher level of "order" or organization. (Prigogine and Stengers, 1984:xv)

A restatement of this is that "some models teach that life is not order, but flux, and that stability lies somewhere between bifurcations, the edge of chaos, and chaos" (Bütz, 1997:113). Capra elaborates the same point:

> According to Prigogine's theory, dissipative structures not only maintain themselves in a stable state far from equilibrium, but may even evolve. When the flow of energy and matter through them [this is the meaning of "dissipative"] increases, they may go through new instabilities and transform *themselves* into new structures of increased complexity. (Capra, 1996:89; emphasis ours)

Prigogine's work revolutionized systems thinking. He and other systems theorists no longer regard steady state as the most natural or desirable condition of living systems—indeed, change/flux/bifurcation/transformation/transition is now seen as the "normal" condition of complex systems. For example, in describing the self, clinical psychologist Michael Bütz says, "The transitory self represents those briefly ordered periods of an individual's life, such as steady states. This self is the consummation of a *self-organizing* process that occurs at the edge of chaos or following chaos, and precedes another encounter with [a] novel stimulus that would call for a new adaptation" (Bütz, 1997:114; emphasis ours). In other words, change is normal. (Self as a self-organizing process is consistent with the discussion in the Addendum to this chapter.)

Another, crucial aspect of bifurcation or phase transformation is that systems' adaptations are accomplished by *altering relationships between components of the system;* another way to say this is that the *components* alter their relationships to each other and to the suprasystem.

The adaptations in phase transformation can be subtle and unpredictable, as Malcolm Gladwell described in his bestseller, *The Tipping Point* (2000). His case studies were of products that "took off" such as Hush Puppies shoes, epidemics of sexually transmitted diseases, and breast cancer awareness among women. He concluded that the explanations of such surprising successes lay in three key factors: "The Law of the Few," "The Stickiness Factor," and "The Power of Context." The "few" were a small number of people who could spread information rapidly, with credibility, to another, larger group of influential adopters. "Stickiness" is a quality that makes a product, concept, or idea attractive to people; it is often unconventional, unexpected, and contrary to conventional wisdom. "Context" means the milieu in which the event occurs; again, often unexpected, and can be a "minute" change in social groups and social environments. At bottom, Gladwell's observations do not seem likely to help prognosticators, but rather explains what has already happened. The relevance to our discussion here is that, like the legendary butterfly in Brazil (previously discussed), extremely small events or factors may have surprisingly large and unpredictable effects, and phase transformations can catch us by surprise.

The major point of the "Prigogine revolution" is that systems **transform themselves**; it is their *own components* that reorganize to accomplish the transformation. This is the meaning of *self-organization* and *self-development*. "Change is not controlled or imposed by a source outside the system. Rather it is the connection of the elements in the system or their interaction with the environment that create *[sic]* a different composition" (Bütz, 1997:16). We recommend Steven Johnson's 2001 book, *Emergence* (see the bibliography at the end of this chapter) as the clearest, most useful (and entertaining) source for this set of ideas.

C. Emergence and Complexity

As Johnson (2001:65) wryly said, the last few years have seen the emergence of emergence; that is, the idea of *emergence* has recently been the most discussed facet of systems theory. Another theorist says that General Systems Theory should now be called "The Theory of Emergence."

Why? The most obvious answer is that there has been a chain of events leading up to this point. First, we now live in a computerized world (most readers of this book know this more intimately than their elders); computers have provided immense capabilities to analyze phenomena that were previously beyond human ability to interpret (even to recognize, sometimes), and systems theory proved its usefulness in exploring the nature of these complex phenomena. Second, these analyses have revealed an unexpected complexity in the systems analyzed; linear causality is inadequate to explain or analyze the intricate and powerful feedback mechanisms. Third, planners and managers of social systems (and the material components of the systems) needed to understand, explain, and to guide the development of systems in their respective fields. Globalization of warfare, commerce, and social and economic development, require data in quantities that were inconceivable seventy years ago, even though such developments began during World War II.

Johnson (2001:21) said that in the last decade of the twentieth century, "...we stopped analyzing emergence and started creating it. We began building self-organizing systems into our software applications, our video games, our art, our music. We built emergent systems to recommend new books, recognize our voices, or find mates." He continued, "Up to now, the philosophers of emergence have struggled to interpret the world. But they are now starting to change it" (ibid., 21).

New questions came into being. How can we recognize the emergence of a system? How can we create it and/or control it? The issue was defined as *complexity*. One example is the United States' so-called "health system," which is not a system at all, but a loosely organized, internally competing jumble (if not jungle) of institutions, policies, professions, industries, political interests, and consumers. Faced with unsustainable costs to both consumers and government, what kind of system should be created (emergence)? What are the key elements to be preserved, and which elements are to be eliminated (complexity)? What are the complex effects on the insurance industry? On the national economy? On welfare costs? What are the political realities? Similar questions obviously are relevant to the economic crisis of the first decade of this century, and were addressed in the major health insurance legislation passed in 2010. All are relevant to members of the social professions who may use this book.

II. Structural Characteristics

This discussion of structural characteristics is related to the preceding sections, especially the discussion of holon and organization in Chapter 1, and to the immediately preceding section regarding change in structure as a means of adaptation to bifurcation or phase transformation.

A. Boundary, Linkage, and "Open" and "Closed" Systems

In order to be identified as distinct from its environment, a system must have some limits, that is, locatable boundaries. Consistent with our view that energy or activity is essential to social systems, we define a boundary as being located where the intensity of energy interchange is greater on one side of a certain point than it is on the other, or greater among certain units than among others. The intensity of energy transfer between units within the boundary is greater than the intensity of exchange across the boundary. For example, members of a family are distinguished not only by blood relationships, but also by frequency or intensity of personal contact. A neighbor would usually be considered outside the boundary, but may become "a member of the family" by participating in family activities and sharing emotional ties of the family. A household pet may be "like one of the family." An adopted child is another example of a person not related by blood who crosses the boundary and is incorporated by the family (or creates a family by being incorporated). One criterion is who "comes home for Christmas."

Boundaries can be identified only by observation of the interaction of the parts of the system and the environment. Some boundaries are visible because of their impenetrability, for example, the rigid personality that permits little modification by the environment. Some religious orders have boundaries defined clearly by behaviors such as dress, marital status, and allegiance to group beliefs. The Old Order Amish are set apart by dress, modes of transportation, and styles of beard. The fact that boundaries may change is evidenced in the Roman Catholic church by changes in nuns' habits and by changes in some members' beliefs about, e.g., birth control, and roles of women in some aspects of ritual. That women may not become priests is an example of a boundary.

It is important to distinguish between the location of a boundary and its nature. Boundary does not necessarily mean barrier. A social system may have a readily discernible boundary and yet be very open to transfers of energy across its boundary (e.g., the boundary of male-female).

Some social agencies survive by drawing clear boundaries (e.g., they serve teenage pregnant women, but do not provide abortions). Another example is the boundary between generations, which has become an important tenet in systems approaches to family therapy.

Other boundaries are difficult to identify because interchange is frequent and intense across the boundary. An important concept here is the *density* of the boundary: the degree to which energy and information penetrate the boundary, that is, its permeability.

No single interaction defines a boundary; more than one criterion is involved in being "American," for example. Such behaviors as paying taxes, voting, and acknowledging "American" values and responsibilities are some criteria to be considered. "Love it or Leave It" is still voiced by some who challenge the patriotism of dissenters. The distinction between "illegal immigrant" and "legal immigrant" is important regarding eligibility for some welfare and medical services, as well as the right to remain in the country. During the Vietnam war, the issue of amnesty for draft evaders raised the question of such boundaries in a tangible and dramatic form, so much so that we now have a "volunteer army." Hospitals have boundaries between medical personnel and patients, and there are boundaries between physicians and nurses regarding procedures each can perform; however, the licensed Nurse Practitioner can now assist in minor surgeries, write prescriptions for drugs and therapy, and perform other activities traditionally reserved for physicians; the boundaries have modified in significant ways. There are boundaries between what married partners and domestic, same-sex partners are allowed to do, e.g., make legal and medical decisions for the partner, or be a dependent on a partner's health insurance policy; again, these boundaries have changed in many states and localities in recent years (see the Family and Person chapters of this book).

In the opening decade of this century, due in particular to the September 11, 2001, destruction of the World Trade Center in New York, the status of Muslim Americans was questioned by some non-Muslims. The American Muslim community itself has struggled with its identity as Americans, its identification with Islam, and how to respond to questions and accusations by non-Muslims. This is perhaps similar to the experience of German descendants or Japanese *Issei* and *Nissei* (immigrant and American born) during World War II, or contemporary Jews who may be ambivalent concerning United States' policies toward Israel, e.g., regarding settlement on the West Bank, or military intervention in the Gaza Strip. What are the boundaries in these instances (see, e.g., the reference to Rachel Coorie at the end of the Addendum to this chapter)?

When systems exchange energy across their boundaries they are *linked* or have *linkage* with each other. Their linkage may be for a very limited and peripheral purpose or may constitute a vital linkage, e.g., a family's association with a work organization. A family's memberships in social clubs and civic groups may be important links to community activity and resources. Their religious affiliation may be a vital social, emotional, and ideological link as well. A family's linkage with the military, e.g., while a member is deployed in Iraq or Afghanistan, can be crucial to family well-being; think of video links between soldiers and their families on special occasions (births, proposals).

Energy transfers by way of linkages are rarely, if ever, one way: *reciprocity* of energy, or true exchange, is present in virtually all linkages, The church, club, or industry draws energy from its linkage to the family, hence industry's willingness to contribute to families' welfare through Social Security, United Fund drives, mental health campaigns, or ecological improvements. Some companies provide services directly in support of family welfare (e.g., day-care, social services, and retirement preparation—see discussion of organizations' relationships to other systems in Chapter 5). So, similarly, religious organizations maintain their role as prime defenders of family and marital stability because these linkages are considered vital and central to the organizations' purposes and to ensure the continued existence and relevance of the organizations.

Open and *closed* are largely self-explanatory terms: a system or its significant environmental systems can be receptive or unreceptive to the movement of energy across their boundaries. In actuality, no system is completely open since it would then be indistinguishable from its environment, nor is a system ever completely closed. The following describes the importance of openness:

> [W]hen a novel situation arises that the system does not have an appropriate response for, it must open up again to incorporate enough energy and information for a transformative adaptation to occur. Different aspects of the system will have to begin searching for new information to accommodate these new changes in the system. (Bütz, 1997:119)

Examples of openness are the inclusion of "alternative medicine" in the curricula of medical schools, or the licensing of midwives as alternatives to physicians. These instances illustrate a degree of openness of the medical profession in response to societal needs and public requests. As noted on the previous page, Nurse Practitioners are licensed to perform many services previously reserved for physicians, in recognition of nurses' demonstrated capabilities, and society's need for additional highly trained medical personnel.

We must clarify our usage of open and closed: what we mean is "relatively more open" or "relatively more closed" than some other system or than some standard by which we are judging the system. A person is an open system but, from a teacher's or counselor's point of view, may be less open (or more so) than is desirable for the person's growth. For example, a child may be less open to interaction with peers than he or she "should" be and more open to interaction with parents than is expected at a certain age. Community organizers might wish for a social agency to be more open to inner city residents and less open to interchange solely with white, suburban, middle-class clientele. These examples illustrate that it is often not sufficient to generalize that a system is open or closed; it is frequently crucial to specify one's point of view (perspective) and to specify "open to what" or "closed to what." For example, systems theorists now state that a system is simultaneously open with regard to energy exchange, and closed with regard to its structure; that is, it maintains its integrity by regulating energy flow.

B. Hierarchy

Parts of systems are related to each other in various ways. One of these kinds of relationships is vertical or hierarchical, meaning that parts are arranged in the sequence in which energy is distributed, or the degree to which it is allocated among them. For example, parents in a family ordinarily have greater access to the family's income than do the children. Because they receive larger shares of public goodwill and public resources, and presumably promise more contributions to society's goals, state universities have an advantage over welfare and penal institutions in receiving public funds.

A second form of hierarchy is that of *power* and *control:* some parts control others by regulating access to resources or by regulating communication. For example, the executive officer of an organization has rank not only by title (status) but by virtue of controlling the allocation of responsibilities and resources. Another example is the power wielded by members of the White House staff, particularly the Chief of Staff ("Leo" in the television series "The West Wing") or Rahm Emanuel in the Obama administration, who derived his authority from the president by "having his back" and by enacting the president's agenda (for which he was chosen because of his previous experience both in the Clinton White House and as a member of Congress). The persons in these positions control access to the president, monitor his appointment schedule, and screen incoming information. The "gatekeeper" function is of central importance to a system; it is the locus of control of the flow of information and the crossing of system boundaries from both inside and outside.

A third form of hierarchy is that of *authority*. Some parts serve as sources of sanction and approval through acting as "defenders of the faith" (a phrase applied to the monarchs of England, whose status far exceeds their actual power). Religious institutions and schools serve this function. Within a family, part of the mother's role has traditionally been that of imparting and representing certain values of the society—hence Mother's Day has been observed with a certain prescribed reverence and respect.

A fourth form of hierarchy is a *fixed sequence* in which development must occur. Some events or functions must occur before others can be attended to. One example of this is Maslow's "hierarchy of needs" within each person:

> Needs or values are related to each other in a hierarchical and developmental way, in order of strength and priority. Safety is a more prepotent, or stronger, more pressing, more vital need than love, for instance, and the need for food is usually stronger than either. [A person] does not know in advance that he will strive on after this gratification has come, and that gratification of one basic need opens consciousness to domination by another, "higher" need. (Maslow, 1968:153)

The physiological development of the human organism follows a hierarchical sequence of emergence and integration. Freud noted this in his stages of tissue development. Similar forms of hierarchy are found in Erikson's developmental tasks and Piaget's cognitive stages, discussed in Chapter 8.

There are, then, several varieties of hierarchies. We will discuss hierarchy in one of the forms just described. We will discuss instances in which the hierarchy is one of control and power and in which the parts are dependent upon other parts for some vital resources. The relationship in these instances will be that of *subordination-superordination,* or *submission-dominance.* The hierarchies most often examined will be those in which control is exerted in a "chain of a command" (e.g., bureaucracies or communities with elected leadership) or the personality, in which ego functioning provides control and direction.

C. Autonomy: Autopoiesis and Self-Development

1. *Autonomy.* Literally, *autonomy* means living by one's own law, being self-governing, or independent. Living systems are distinctive by-virtue of having a significant degree of autonomy from their environments; there is an interactional boundary between the system and environment. There are feedback loops of energy/information exchange, communication, and organization that are exclusive to the system; that is, they exclude those "outside" the system. Capra's description of networks applies to all social systems:

> Whenever we encounter living systems. ... Whenever we look at life, we look at networks. ... The first and most obvious property of any network is its nonlinearity— it goes in all directions. ... In particular, an influence, or message, may travel along a cyclical path, which may become a *feedback loop.* ... Because networks generate feedback loops, they may acquire the ability to regulate themselves. (Capra, 1996:82)

Autonomy is achieved and maintained by feedback cycles that are continually initiated by the system. A developing child is encouraged to develop autonomy by parents, and the feedback cycle is positive; the child responds with independent behavior (e.g., in the toddler stage by saying "No!" and by refusing to control its eliminative functions). Succeeding positive feedback cycles encourage the growing child to practice the behaviors that our society, especially, expects of autonomous, self-governing adults. Some limits are placed on this, however, again, through the feedback cycle. Driving a car is a signal of adult status; but recklessness results in a curbing (literally and figuratively).

We should note that every system has some degree of autonomy (otherwise it wouldn't have an independent existence), but at the same time is constrained by its environment, by other systems at its own level, and by its own subsystems. This repeats what was said earlier about holonistic relationships and the fact that causation is mutual; each system is both a superordinate whole and a subordinate part.

2. *Autopoiesis.* Within the last quarter-century, research and writing on systems, especially by Ilya Prigogine, stress the autonomous, self-initiating behavior of living systems. Humberto Maturana and Francisco Varela at the University of Chile at Santiago (their ideas are labeled the "Santiago theory") coined the term *autopoiesis* to designate this autonomous behavior, combining Greek words that mean "self-made." In Ilya Prigogine and Isabelle Stenger's book, *Order out of Chaos*, the term is translated as "self-organization"; other authors refer to it as

self-regulation; it could be translated as self-creation or self-control. We prefer to translate it as "self-development," which allows us to engage in a bit of wordplay that conveys two meanings:

Est of identity

a.   *self-development* connotes both self-origination and ongoing self-modification by the system; and

b.   *self*-development, or development of the self, which connotes that a major ongoing task of the system is the establishment of its *identity*, its steady state(s), its character, and the traits that are characteristic of the system (see the discussion of self in the Addendum to this chapter), which are observed to be relatively constant during its evolution.

This "paradigm shift" (a hackneyed phrase that even its creator tired of) in systems thinking toward emphasizing self-development does not vitiate the mutual interaction and interdependence of part and whole. Instead, it deepens our understanding of the nature of systems and their relations to suprasystems and subsystems. Instead of focusing our attention at the boundary of a system at which transactions take place, it focuses attention within the system, to identify the purpose and effect of such transactions. The change in focus is consistent with our experience: that persons and groups of persons are experienced as autonomous entities, not merely as flows of interactions. There is a "there" there; an initiator and shaper of experience that does not simply respond to flows of energy and information, but that selects and evaluates in order to create a self. This brings systems theory closer to phenomenology, to our experience of ourselves and others; perhaps to an existential psychology of consciousness as discussed in Chapter 8 and the Addendum to Chapter 2. One definition of phenomenology is:

> A method of exploration that primarily uses human experience as the source of data and attempts to include all human experience without bias. ... Phenomenology is the basic method of most existentialists. (Corsini and Wedding, 1989:597)

This shift in focus permits systems theory to "come down from its ivory tower" and to deal in direct experience, not only in "bloodless categories." It is consistent with our position in Chapter 7, "Families," that "a family is to be construed as patterns of relatedness as they converge in a person." From a phenomenological or existential viewpoint, this could be said of all systems

D. Differentiation and Specialization

The terms *differentiation* and *specialization* are similar but not identical. As we use it, differentiation means "dividing the functions," that is, assigning functions to certain parts and not to others. Specialization adds the further stipulation that a part performs only, or predominantly, a particular function. Differentiation is not the same as, but is always related to, allocation or distribution of energy. For example, assigning particular societal goals (GI function) to the federal Department of Health and Human Services is not the same as providing the necessary appropriations. Income maintenance for the elderly, as provided for in the Social Security Act, cannot be realized without the collection and allocation of necessary revenues; the perennial debate over Social Security funding illustrates this very well.

Differentiation may apply to any of a large number of aspects of system functioning, There is differentiation by age, with regard to earning income for the family. Typically, in middle-class families, adults are expected to earn, teenagers are expected to provide their own spending money, and children are not expected to be self-supporting. Elders hope to have at least some degree of adequate income.

As society becomes more complex, it becomes necessary to differentiate functions. Modern professions such as social work and psychology have come into being as part of the evolution of particular societies, to deal with problems of social welfare, health, and problems in social relationships. This is described well by Catherine McDonald (2006: Chapter 2) as part of modernization.

There are several other aspects of differentiation that merit discussion. As a social system becomes differentiated, at some point the need arises to integrate and to establish communication among the differentiated parts: e.g., between schools and social work, and lawyers and physicians. The greater the degree of differentiation, the greater the degree of internal exchange of energy/information that likely will be necessary.

Differentiation may be reversible; a system may reorder its structures to adapt to new information from its environment, e.g., tainted food from another country may lead to tighter screening of imports; a community may create new programs for immigrants, like Hull House in Chicago, or programs to assist Asian immigrants, in Vancouver, B.C. The medical "community" acts similarly by creating specialties, e.g., family practice or the nurse practitioner. Social work has also differentiated by licensing clinical social work.

There are levels of differentiation according to the stages of development of the social system; the more complex, the more fully the functions are differentiated among the parts; this leads to discussion of specialization. As noted earlier, specialization means exclusivity of function—as a popular song puts it, "I can handle this job all by myself." Professions stake out their territories, their boundaries; who shall administer medication, who shall give legal advice, who shall approve adoptions, who is an expert witness in court. In that sense, professions are specialties, but they are not completely specialized, in that all of them are performing integrative SI and GI functions in the society.

The extent of occupational specialization in modern society has become problematic. As Darwin and later scientists demonstrated, the usefulness of specialization is always dependent upon particular environmental conditions. When these conditions shift, highly specialized adaptation may no longer be functional. Similarly, if technology replaces or supersedes a specialized occupation, the previous workers are no longer valued or needed (e.g., telephone operators, service station attendants, and, increasingly, bank tellers and postal clerks (with sometimes unfortunate social effects).

As with differentiation, specialization is necessary to perform functions, but certain dangers also arise. One such danger has been referred to as "tyranny by specialists," when people are divided into expert and ignorant, able and unable. As the physician may tyrannize the patient, so may the auto mechanic, electrician, or plumber tyrannize the physician. An indication of such tyranny is found where the expert assumes the matter is too complex for the nonexpert to make decisions; this may happen in social work as well. There is another danger of overreliance on specialization, which is that as specialties proliferate, so do areas of ignorance by others; ignorance then, increases commensurate with specialization.

Others have stressed that greater specialization leads to greater dependence on the products of other groups and the greater importance of systemic linkage. It is risky to specialize completely. Systems may have to rely on other systems that do not perform adequately: the family upon the school, or the school upon the family, e.g., In order to reduce risk, systems integrate vertically, both upward and downward. Examples include "mergers and acquisitions" among corporations, to assure access to suppliers and raw materials, and integration of hospitals with satellite clinics, specialized practicioner groups, and "minute clinics." Thus we come full circle to hierarchy as an aspect of structure.

III. Behavioral Aspects of Social Systems

Behavioral aspects are those interchanges that are of shortest duration and fastest tempo. Three of these seem to us most significant: They are related, but not identical, to the basic energy functions, and they are the subfunctions that seem to be most important for this book.

A. Social Control and Socialization

Social control and socialization occur in all systems and can have the purpose either of securing energy for the system from its components (SI) or of achieving goals (GI, GE). This process of securing energy or expending it to achieve goals can be done in either a coercive or cooperative fashion. The system can secure energy or achieve goals coercively either by threatening the component's survival and functioning or its goal achievement, or cooperatively by supporting the component's goal and encouraging its harmony with the system's goal. An example of this is the "gentle persuasion" that a religious organization can apply to its members to summon their efforts in supporting the system's goals, such as a building fund, yearly budget, or attendance at a revival. Or the religious organization may employ coercive means—excommunication or expulsion from membership—if the member interferes with its goals by refusing to rear children in the faith, failing to contribute financially, or violating its ethical standards.

Coercive control is usually labeled "power" (see the discussion of power in Chapter 5, under "Power and Control"). Traditionally, the helping professions have espoused cooperative approaches, holding up the value of "self-determination," but in practice, decisions are sometimes made for clients. When these decisions are forced upon the client and fulfillment of the client's own goals or the client's access to needed resources is threatened, the professional person is using power and is an agent of coercive social control.

Socialization is the induction of persons into the social system's culture or way of life, whether the system is a family, group, community, organization, or society. A bargain is struck: the system offers support or noninterference with the person's goals as long as the person's behavior is consistent with the system's goals. The purpose of socialization is to get the work of the system done; the more successful the socialization, the less control is necessary, because the person's goals will be harmonious with or identical to the system's goals. A certain degree of aggressiveness is tolerated and sometimes valued in our society if it is expressed in approved ways (football, military action, or self-defense, e.g.); but if we interfere with society's functioning by threatening people's lives, disrupting transportation, or preventing police or firefighters from performing their jobs, we are liable to be controlled in some manner consistent with our "offense."

B. Communication and Feedback

Communication is discussed in Chapter 3, "Language," in regard to symbols and language and in the appropriate chapters for functions of communication in communities, organizations, and families. Here we wish only to point out the necessity of communication and energy transfer in systems. As described above, when a system undergoes bifurcation or phase transformation, the relationships among its components are restructured; this is accomplished by exchanging information (communication) and energy. One of the results is altered communication; so communication is both cause and effect of the change.

Organization depends upon effectiveness of communication (think of the frequent question, "Didn't you get the memo?"). We often think of communication as conveying emotional warmth and bringing components together. It may, but it may also alienate and separate people by its content. The point is that *communication* is the transfer of energy to accomplish system goals. The effect of communication depends upon the context in which it occurs. For example, "You're under arrest!" hardly encourages affection; it expresses control. Professionals who say they "communicated" with clients usually mean that positive affect was conveyed. But the professional and the client also communicate when the communication conveys control.

Systems develop means to send and receive information. Feedback is the primary means by which systems accomplish self-direction and seek goals. Feedback is a term that has been bankrupted in popular usage. "Give me your feedback" or "I really want your feedback" are corruptions that, at best, deal with only one side of feedback. Feedback is not, as the popular definition suggests, merely the echo received in response to one's actions, like a radar blip. In cybernetics and systems thought, feedback includes not only the echo but the adjustment made to the echo. It is "feed" and "back"; a newer way to put it is "feed forward."

Feedback loops are the means by which systems accomplish adaptation and self-direction. Feedback has been referred to as the secret of nature's activity, that is, adaptation and self-direction in natural systems. It refers to the process of interaction whereby information is received and processed; behavior is validated or changed. Feedback enables a system constantly to monitor and adapt its own functioning, which is the means to steady state.

The use of the terms *positive* and *negative* in describing the nature of feedback varies among systems authors. Some view positive feedback as that which impels behavior in desirable directions and negative feedback as discouragement. Others describe negative feedback as characteristic "of homeostasis (steady state) and therefore [it] plays an important role in achieving and maintaining the quality of relationships; positive feedback, on the other hand, leads to change, i.e., the loss of stability or equilibrium" (Watzlawick, Beavin, and Jackson, 1967:31). Still others, including the authors of this book, label *feedback as positive if it confirms or encourages existing behavioral patterns. Negative feedback, then, discourages or invalidates current behavior.* The confusion about "negative" and "positive" is likely to continue; we suggest just bearing in mind both the popular usage and the technical usage.

Feedback operations and mechanisms are familiar to people in the human services. Some commonly encountered concepts are "reaction formation" and "overcompensation"; "looking-glass self" and "generalized other"; "positive reinforcement"; "unconditional positive regard"; "cycle of poverty"; dynamic modeling; and deviation-amplifying, deviation-counteracting, and deviation-reducing mechanisms.

An example of deviation-amplifying feedback is the following: an immigrant to the United States speaks English poorly, and his employer concludes that he is probably not very intelligent (think of the stereotypical "Dumb Swede," ancestors of both authors of this book). He is treated as though he is not, and he responds with lowered performance in order to "get along." His behavior confirms the employer's opinion, so the employer gives him less attention and less demanding assignments. When he is evaluated, it is confirmed that he does not perform as well as other employees. His employer continues to regard him as less capable than other staff. Eventually, he quits or is let go

This example serves to illustrate the differing uses of the terms "positive" and "negative" feedback. As this worker is confirmed in and accepts the negative status, it becomes a central element of his conception of himself. Each time, he receives further recognition of being inadequate or unwanted, that is, "positive" feedback. It is "positive" since it validates his self-conception. In this instance, "negative" feedback would be information that impels him to reappraise himself and change sufficiently to cause others to revise their expectations of him. Since such change is more difficult than remaining the same, the first adaptation to this sort of negative feedback is to accentuate the familiar patterns of adaptation. One example of this feedback cycle is Malcolm

X's encounter with Mr. Ostrowski, who discouraged Malcolm's interest in becoming a lawyer. (Malcolm X, 1966) Again, the point is that feedback processes are not simple causal chains; they are complex cycles of mutual interactions.

Feedback is an integral part of all teacher-student relationships or all counselor-client relationships, as it is of all human relationships. In part, therapy consists of interpreting signals from the client and "feeding back" carefully and skillfully chosen responses that are neutral, positive, or negative to stimulate behavior that is consistent with the goals of the two-person therapeutic system (or group treatment system, or milieu). Usually, the client similarly interprets and feeds back to the therapist.

C. Adaptation

The feedback cycle could be considered identical to adaptation, but adaptation is discussed separately here to emphasize two points. First, adaptation is viewed by some theorists as being of paramount importance because systems must adjust to their environment. While it is true that there must be adjustment between systems and environment, adjustment must be made by *both* system and environment, not by only one of them. Capra (1996) calls this *coevolution* of the system and its environment; this concept is a major revision in thinking about Darwinian evolution.

Second, adaptation takes two forms: *assimilation* and *accommodation.* These are discussed in Chapter 8 in the section on Piaget. These two terms indicate whether the system accepts or rejects the incoming information without any change on the part of the system (assimilation), or whether it modifies its structure in response to the incoming information (accommodation). In reality, systems do both of these at the same time in some mixture; as with other polarities, no system does one or the other exclusively.

We have now completed the introduction to systems terminology, in these first two chapters. In the next section, the Addendum, we will present some advances in systems thinking, and applications of the concepts in these chapters to practice in the human services and social work, with emphasis upon the demands upon the self of the practitioner, and her or his intellectual preparation for practice.

IV. Addendum: Philosophy, Practice, and Praxis

We create each other. This simple premise is the basis of human services and allied professions. The final section of this Addendum explores the implications of phenomenology and systems theory for professional practice (or *praxis*).

Systems thinking and phenomenology

A profession must articulate a philosophy which underwrites its practice, in order to receive sanction and legitimacy. This section presents a "creative synthesis" of the philosophy of *phenomenology* and its implications for practice in social work and the human services.

Within the last decade, there have been significant new contributions to phenomenology: among them Dr. Ian Georgiou's 2007 book, *Thinking Through Systems Thinking*. Georgiou's brilliant, original work establishes a philosophical base for systems theory and the human services. In addition, the rediscovery of Edith Stein's work in phenomenology bridges the gap between systems theory and human services practice (the Appendices are brief biographical notes regarding Stein and Paolo Freire).

It might be more accurate to describe these advances as "systems thinking" rather than systems theory. The title of Georgiou's book is a clever play on words: (1) critiquing systems theory, "thinking it through," and (2) thinking *by means of* systems theory. In both senses, it is systems thinking that is the focus of this Addendum.

Our first concern is *how we think and how we know*: questions of epistemology. Our second concern is with *the thinker*; what is a *self* and how does it come about? Finally, in this Addendum, the question is how we apply these ideas to practice.

Consciousness in phenomenology

We must distinguish between terms, here. "Mind" is too imprecise and leads to confusion: by "brain" we mean the physical organ, and by "consciousness" we mean awareness as most persons experience it. Phenomenology defines consciousness in the same sense. Phenomenology is defined as "the study of consciousness as experienced by a person," and from the *perspective of one person*, as discussed earlier in Chapter 1, in the Summary at the end of Chapter 7, and in the Glossary.

Edmund Husserl (1859-1938) was a professor in German universities, "one of the most important and influential philosophers of the twentieth century" (Sawicki, 2005:2). He published *Logical Investigations* in 1900, marking the beginning of phenomenology, which "has been central to the tradition of continental European philosophy throughout the 20th century" (Smith, 2008:2). The existentialists Jean Paul Sartre and Martin Heidegger, e.g., acknowledged their debt to Husserl, who said that a person's awareness of phenomena in the real world is not

INTERNAL SCHEMAS

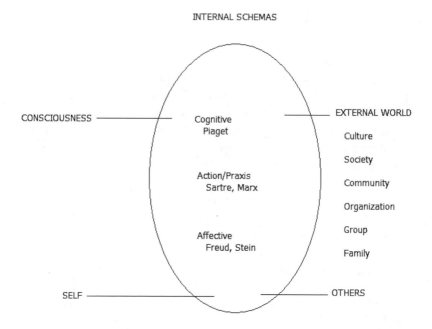

direct or first-hand, but rather as mediated by the person's consciousness. For Husserl, the essential fact was that consciousness **must** seek information about the external world, and **must** interpret it. Georgiou says that consciousness is "hungry" to engage external phenomena and "*throws itself* onto them, *grasps* them, *invades* them ... *battles* with them" (Georgiou, 2007:122). Sartre said that consciousness "critiques" information from its interaction with the environment, and tests it, and then the result can be regarded as "knowledge." You will note that this resembles scientific methodology—and rightly so—but which came first, human consciousness or scientific method? Scientific method, then, is an objectification of the operations of our consciousnesses. This diagram is intended to convey that relationship; the meaning of the diagram will be discussed in the section on "Self," later.

Structures exist within consciousness to interpret external phenomena and facilitate responses to them; for now, we will only suggest that these structures are similar to Piaget's *schemas*, described in Chapter 8 of this book. We will refer to *schemas* rather than structures, from this point onward.

Systems thinking is one such schema: "Systems are *tools of understanding* devised by human minds for understanding situations" (Vickers, 1983, quoted in Georgiou, 2007:64). Husserl and later phenomenologists concentrated on cognitive schemas; Edith Stein supplemented this with affective (emotional) schemas, as did Freud when he discussed "complexes." Sartre and other existentialists stated that consciousness must **act** *in its social environment* or the self is not "authentic." Sartre borrowed Marxist terminology: such action is *praxis*, which will be discussed below.

Consciousness fits perceptions of external phenomena into these schemas and, in Husserl's term, "intuits wholes" (systems). It critiques any systemic characteristics in phenomena and, when a whole/system is identified, this perception amounts to the *emergence* of the system. This emergent "snapshot" is the means by which consciousness engages the external world.

Consciousness then must repeatedly critique phenomena (by analogy, going from still photo to streaming video) about the identity and characteristics of the system, including the system's boundaries and behavior. (Calcagno, 2007:66) This is the operation that Piaget identified as "intelligence," a biologically-based capability intended to help the human being adapt to its environment. Since an object is never understood in its entirety in one observation, consciousness must construct a "holographic" picture of it, a composite model, like an MRI (magnetic resonance image), slice after slice. Husserl said that the task of phenomenology is "infinite," because consciousness must continuously critique systems as they emerge and persist.

Recently, some theorists have said that systems theory *is a theory of emergence*—that is, again, in Sartre's terminology, critiquing a system so that consciousness can act intelligently toward it. Think of television's doctor "House" who, in every episode, tries to fit a patient's symptoms into a diagnosis that makes sense and can be treated. House's search continues until his internal schemas match the external evidence and the patient is healed (we hope). Dr. House does this because he must; he is driven to understand the phenomenon that is presented to him and to act upon it: and so it is with consciousness. In Husserl's phenomenology, it is this craving that is the essential characteristic of consciousness.

Self

Each person's consciousness is unique, based upon one's experience and one's interpretation of those experiences. Phenomenology maintains that a person develops a "self" only by interacting with others (see the concepts of "looking glass self" and "generalized other" in Chapter 3).

Sartre and other phenomenologists deny that the Freudian "ego" or any "I" or "me" exists. In their view, "self" is a useful construction built from consciousness's reflections upon its own experience, its encounters with others and with the external world. One might ask, to paraphrase an old saying, "If a self grew in the woods and no one saw it, would it exist?" As Earnshaw (2006:86) stated, "we are only aware of being, or have consciousness, through, or because of others. Until I am aware that I am perceived by an other, I do not have consciousness, therefore my consciousness is utterly dependent upon the presence of the other." Piaget stated that the self is the outcome of this feedback cycle—that a person learns to know her self when acting upon the environment, and the environment only becomes known because of the person's actions upon it. (Zelazo, *et al.*, 2007:405) Piaget said "The person is a *Träger* [bearer] of himself or herself and of all those people who helped form the individual . ... One cannot have a self without others . ... Likewise, other people need us in order to grow and develop" (Calcagno, 2007:128). In other words, **we create each other.**

Empathy

In Figure 2.1, above, affective/emotional schemas are placed directly between Self and Others. This does not imply that the self-other relationship occurs only through affective/emotional schemas to the exclusion of cognitive or action schemas. Rather, the diagram conveys that the content of the self-other relationship is greatly, and fundamentally, affective/emotional. Certainly ideas and actions are conveyed in this relationship; for example, a parent-child relationship teaches both parties about the roles of each, and about the boundaries of actions of each (shared tasks, decision-making, and household rituals, e. g.). "Emotions are central ... because they are the principal processes in which selfhood is constructed" (Oatley, 2007:383).

Edith Stein, a protégé of Husserl, was the first phenomenologist to identify feeling (*Einfühlung*) as a component of consciousness. She recognized "empathy as a structure of consciousness that permits us to enter into and know the minds of others" (Calcagno, 2007:789-79). Sartre agreed with Stein regarding the primacy of emotion, in his *Sketch for a Theory of the Emotions*: "In [Sartre's] view, we are bound to other people by the fact that ... our consciousnesses are revealed to us through the very recognition of other consciousnesses" (Earnshaw, 2006:155). Certainly, if Freud is to be believed, emotions are the deepest, most powerful elements of the feedback cycle—constituting the various complexes (e.g., Oedipus and Electra) that he identified.

We cannot directly experience others' emotions: instead, we infer from their behavior, as interpreted by our own internal schemas: "what we directly perceive is intentional or meaningful behavior—expression, gesture, and action—not mere physical movement" (Zelazo, 2007:82). We interpret others as like ourselves (until proven otherwise). We respond as though we were experiencing what the "other" is experiencing: feeling what the other is feeling. According to Stein, this constitutes empathy. As discussed below, our brains are "hard wired" to respond to these interpretations by imitating them—an astounding finding by neuroscientists that seems to confirm Stein's theory of empathy.

Neuroscience and the neural basis of empathy

> Leslie Brothers, a psychiatrist-neuroscientist and author of *Friday's Footprint: How Society Shapes the Human Mind*, has demonstrated that the brain's structure predisposes us to be socially oriented. Newborns experience a form of empathy, and at six months, well before they can speak, infants experience advanced socially oriented emotions like jealousy. (Rock and Schwartz, 2008:4)

Earnshaw commented that

> ... what can be said about consciousness ultimately depends on how it matches up with neuroscience. ... there may yet be work done which would bring together the existentialist views of self, being and consciousness and contemporary work in cognitive neuroscience. (2006:139)

The "cognitive revolution" of the later twentieth century (McGovern and Baars, 2007) and current theorizing about the brain coincide with the development of computerized analysis of the brain and of instruments that are sensitive to extremely small physical phenomena. The field of brain studies was brilliantly discussed on public television's "Charlie Rose" show in early 2010 in a series of programs that included conversations with a number of scientists from related fields.

Twenty years ago, Dr. Giacomo Rizzolati and his team, of the University of Parma, Italy, discovered "mirror neurons" in the right temporoparietal junction (abbreviated as "rTPJ") of the brain. This encouraged other scientists, among them Dr. Vilayanur Ramachandran, who wrote "The Neurons That Shaped Civilization," a work which underscored the significance of these findings.

These neurons facilitate imitation of another person: enabling a person to adopt another's point of view. This feedback cycle is theorized to operate as follows: (1) Abby observes Sam's expression; (2) this stimulates Abby's mirror neurons, which interpret Sam's expression in terms of Abby's own experience of, e.g., sadness; (3) Abby's neurons initiate imitation of Sam, triggering an "empathic" response, e.g., feeling sad herself, and perhaps crying and/or reaching to touch Sam. Ramachandran refers to these as the "Gandhi" neurons, in that they perceive the needs of others and stimulate an empathic response. If this theory is correct, then the old adage, "monkey see, monkey do," might be rephrased as "monkey see, monkey *be.*" Again, we are "hard wired" for empathy.

Implications for the human services

We say in the Family chapter (p. 159) that family is best studied from the perspective of a particular person, as *"patterns of relatedness as they converge in a specific person."* Similarly, now, we state that *the self is a lived convergence of relationships,* a center of a web of human attachments. While this relatedness does not fully provide an *identity* as Erikson described it, it does provide consciousness with sufficient information, experience, and experience of empathy, to construct a meaningful and substantial self.

It is this self that a human services professional employs in practice and praxis. This self must be competent enough to provide to others opportunities to possess selves. *We create each other.* It requires a self to create a self in others; demonstrations of empathy, knowledge, and commitment.

We return to Sartre's use of "critique," referred to earlier in this Addendum. He presented us with a question: What is the purpose of critiquing our experience and knowledge, if not to act upon it? Earnshaw (2006:88) said that " 'to be,' in Sartre's view is 'to act', it is to perceive a lack in the world and to want to effect a change," which seems to derive from empathy. Sartre said that the person who does not act is not *authentic*, that is, is not acting from her present self, nor acting in accord with a desired future self (a desired steady state). The person must be *engagé,* engaged with life and her environment, and be fully committed; philosopher Søren Kierkegaard gave marriage as an example of such commitment: "till death do us part."

Praxis

Applying one's critiques to make change, Sartre called **praxis,** a term borrowed from Marxian philosophy. It is virtually impossible to find an agreed upon definition of praxis among theorists. The most common element is "putting theoretical knowledge into practice"; Marx defined it as "a willed action by which a theory or philosophy becomes a social actuality," and added that only through praxis can a problem be resolved. Cohen (2000:97), recognizing the variability of definitions, commented that "The social significance of praxis is what actors make it, no more and no less." Similarly, one theorist referred to praxis as "situated creativity," meaning that praxis occurs in specific situations, and the actor, as agent, has some latitude in what is done. Another theorist distinguished between practice and praxis: "practice refers to how actors make what they do happen ... praxis refers to what goes on when we act." This is about as clear a definition and distinction as can be found.

Praxis involves "agency," acting as an agent on behalf of someone or something; this includes putting the actor/agent's knowledge, skills, and talents to work for a "client" system (whether person, family, organization, etc.). Anthony Giddens, sociologist, referred to "social agency"; Margaret Mead referred to "social praxis." Catherine McDonald refers to "human agency." Social workers and other allied professionals are "change agents," actors on behalf of change or, more accurately, of client systems in need of change internally or in their environments.

Sartre emphasized that praxis must be "revolutionary," in the sense that McDonald describes social change that must occur in Western society. Sartre said that praxis requires "Dirty Hands," the title of one of his plays, sacrifices that sometimes entail dubious ethical choices.

An example of an attempt at social change was Paolo Freire's *conscientizacion* in Brazil, which developed from a number of theoretical sources, among them phenomenology and existentialism. Freire (see Appendix for personal information) was described as the "most well known educator of our time." He devised and tested an educational system and an accompanying philosophy of education that involved "a praxis approach to education," including a deepened awareness of the learners' own reality—socially, politically, and economically, and encouraged "critically reflective action based on practice" (Gerhardt, 2000:11). His efforts at reform had mixed results when he was in charge of Brazil's department of Education, because of societal upheavals, but his influence has been profound.

The practitioner

In the following subsection, we will discuss skills and personal qualifications in each of several human services activities. McDonald comments that

> Human agency actively contributes to and is important in institutional-level processes which after all are, for the most part, *human* processes, and the agency of social workers is no exception. ... social workers are *already* contributing with proposals being made, suggestions put forward, and arguments developed about how social work should be undertaken in the contemporary environment. (McDonald, 2006:135)

For the following discussion, the activities of social workers and allied professions are described as the following processes: awareness, analysis, action, assessment, advocacy, and accountability. While these do not seem revolutionary, their importance lies with the practitioner who performs them. We will discuss each, briefly.

1. *Awareness*. Social workers are "utility infielders," generalists (except for clinical social workers, perhaps) who must command a wide range of information. This book, e.g., is intended to assist in providing this range. Awareness comes through a variety of educational training, work experience, and life experience. The latter can come from local, national, or international exposure to diverse populations, cultures, and social arrangements. The objective is to understand and appreciate the values of each, while recognizing the limitations of each (including one's own cultural niche): and further, to recognize the strengths and needs of each. It is hoped that empathy with the living conditions of each culture and smaller systems is the outcome.

Beyond this, knowledge of societal patterns of service provisions and institutional structures is required, and the societal ideologies and material limitations of each setting, as well. This permits, at a minimum, comparison with one's own society.

Not least is one's exposure to how people live their lives in each locale. What accommodations are made, and the rationales for them, are part of understanding personal, family, and community characteristics.

The crucial question is whether workers can step outside their own "frames" in order to partner effectively with the systems they work with, and the degree of empathy they possess for these systems. Means to acquire this include work experience, volunteer experience, living in a "foreign" setting, or examining one's own cultural experience thoroughly and critically.

2. *Analysis*. Again, a systems approach provides a basis, along with advanced study of each system level, for research into the energy functions of each: the GE, GI, SE, and SI functions. What energy flows function well, which inadequately, and what accounts for the deficiencies and sufficiencies? What interventions might be effective, if any are required? What resources exist or can be developed among the components? What intervention styles are appropriate to the system? What communication networks are used?

This activity requires knowledge of organizations, communities, families, and persons that comes from advanced training, as well as first-hand experience. It requires a suspension of judgments on the values and living styles of the population being served or researched.

The crucial questions here are whether the worker has skill in research, in program design, and in intercultural communication, and whether the worker has objectivity toward the client system. Can the worker collaborate to utilize or increase the capacity of the client system for self-analysis? What further professional training, perhaps in another professional field, will prepare for this (e.g., political science, sociology, second language, photography or video techniques, writing skills, educational techniques, and technology)?

3. *Action.* Experience in action modes is essential, acquired through experience in a system equivalent to the level selected for *praxis*. The worker needs to be aware of her own style (aggressive, laid back, analytic) and resources (e.g., physical strength, patience, tolerance for opposition or ambiguity, and temperament)—that is, knowledge of the worker's own action system. What is the style of intervention practiced or accepted by the client system (are women allowed power? Must actions be couched in indirect terms rather than straightforward (in other words, diplomacy)? What resources are present in the system or its environment—financial, emotional, political, historical, and personal relationships) and how accessible are these to the worker and the person(s) or groups who will carry on the action? What ideology or cause exists to sustain the action? Can the worker articulate, or encourage the client system to articulate, a rationale for action and a calculation of the probable costs to the participants?

The questions involve endurance, effectiveness, and motivation, on the part of all participants and on the part of opponents and resisters. What in the worker's or the participants selves requires this action—what rewards will motivate, and are the activities and results consistent with self? What steady state(s) is desired by participants and worker(s)? At what price to one's integrity and sense of self?

4. *Assessment.* The worker, and the participants as well, must have criteria for success, and one hopes, agreement on most of them. Where do these criteria derive from: within the client system, from a leader or leaders, from the ideology of the environment, from a particular population (the poor, immigrants, an ethnic group, a social class, or abused women or children, e.g.)? Whose agenda is being "pushed," and at what cost? What long-term cost/benefit (both financially and socially) are worker and participants willing to pay (in case of divorce, imprisonment, political or community antagonism)? What instruments and techniques will be used in the assessment, and who is equipped to utilize them?

The questions are: how skilled is the worker at conducting an assessment or how skilled is the worker at developing or recognizing the talent within the client system? Who is capable of interpreting the results, and in communicating them to the desired audience most effectively? Is the process aimed at developing the talents of the client system? What additional resources might be needed that the worker can secure? That is, what connections does the worker have, and what access to outside resources, to make the process and the results public? Is the worker credible to outside sources, and knowledgeable about the procedures to secure them—what linkages with other systems, and what linkages exist for the client system?

5. *Advocacy*. The emphasis here is less on a client system with a situation needing direct or near-term intervention, than with systems in the environment which possess resources—financial, ideological, or cause-oriented—that may be brought to bear on a larger stage. Fund-raising, publicizing needs, information, or lobbying political organizations or government units, are examples. What experience, education/training, personal attributes (temperament, communication style, and vocabulary appropriate to the system that is approached, e.g.), and understanding of the needs and requirements of the systems being solicited (and the persons in key positions) are necessary?

What are the worker's credentials and credibility both with the solicited source and with the client system she represents? Does the worker have experience with foundations, government agencies, volunteer and community organizations, so as to be able to identify with and communicate to, the systems being approached? What are the worker's and client system's willingness to compromise, to satisfy, funders or sanctioning agencies—what standards must be maintained personally and professionally to protect integrity? What trade-offs are acceptable?

The questions here include the worker's or client system's acquaintance with a network of organizations, groups, and communities involved. What political, social, and financial networks must be negotiated for the present approach, and for future contacts? How genuine is the worker in her personal style; is she credible personally as well as professionally? What are her communication skills in writing, presentations, in electronic media, and in one-to-one conversations? These skills come with experience—sometimes hard won (or lost). This experience can come from mentors, from "second chair" experiences, or from observations while working in a solicited system. It requires time, patience, and willingness to fail with equanimity, and wisdom to leave the door open to future contact. What aspects of self are at risk; is the worker or client system aware of this? What rewards are necessary for satisfaction?

6. *Accountability*. The bottom line—did the job get done, on time and on budget? That is one way to frame the issue. More broadly, was the client system represented well—were the goals achieved? Did the client system benefit from achievement of the primary goal(s), and from secondary goal(s) such as self-development, increase in capability, morale, and affirmative recognition? Was the emotional, financial, and social cost acceptable? Was the likelihood of future efforts increased? Who benefitted—client system, broader systems, subsystems such as community institutions, employers of clients, children of clients, the funding agency, and the worker (in increased competence and credibility)? Were professional standards maintained—did the worker represent his profession well?

The questions here are the worker's appreciation of the stakes involved for all parties. Was the result equitable for all parties or only some? What issues remain to be dealt with in the future? Does the worker have the skills to provide accountability? Is the capacity for self-examination established or strengthened among the client system, worker, and related systems?

Accountability requires a range of skills, as noted in the earlier activities. Financial accounting, public accountability for personal and professional conduct, legal standards for use of resources, liability for actions taken, all require command of professional standards, which will be assessed by both private and public audiences. The worker should prepare, and prepare client systems, for such auditing, and for public presentations to promote or defend the actions taken. Communication skills are at a premium in this regard.

Conclusion

The daunting list of activities and requirements of the worker is intended as a preface to discussion of the systems in the chapters that follow, to emphasize the range of knowledge necessary to effective practice and *praxis* with these systems.

Central to practice and praxis is the practitioner, the professional person's individual perspective, knowledge, experience, talent and, fundamentally, his or her capacity for empathy. These requirements go beyond technical skills; they extend to the practitioner's motives, which are developed and revealed by one's engagement with life. What explains the practitioner's self? The theorists just discussed suggest that self derives from the people you relate to—the desire to be like someone significant in your life, or to help others who are similar to someone you know or are close to, who has needed help. In short, someone for whom you had or have empathy.

Suggested Readings

Calcagno, Antonio.
    2007 *The Philosophy of Edith Stein.* Pittsburgh: Duquesne University Press. Recommended as an introduction to Stein's thought, particularly for students or first-time readers of Stein.
Earnshaw, Steven.
    2006 *Existentialism: A Guide for the Perplexed.* New York: MJF Books. Excellent text for the beginning inquirer about existentialism. Accessible and highly useful.
Ford, Donald H., and Richard M. Lerner.
    1992 *Developmental Systems Theory.* Newbury Park, CA: Sage. This is *the* book to begin with to construct a complete theory of systems practice in the human services. A thorough review of systems concepts with promising leads for practical applications. For our present purposes, we recommend Chapter 4, "The Person as an Open, Self-Regulating, Self-Constructing System" (that about says it all!).
Georgiou, Ion.
    2007. *Thinking Through Systems Thinking.* London and New York: Routledge.
    This is a brilliant work, without precedent regarding the philosophical implications of system theory. His exposition of phenomenology is precise and accurate. The serious student of phenomenology and systems theory is strongly encouraged to engage the book in its entirety.
Gerhardt, Heinz-Peter.
    2000 "Paolo Freire (1921-97)." Paris: UNESCO: International Bureau of Education. Relatively brief but informative publication detailing Freire's life and career, emphasizing his activism and theory of social change.
Johnson, Steven.
    2001. *Emergence: The Connected Lives of Ants, Brains, Cities, and Soft ware.* New York: Scribner.
    A brilliant, enjoyable, and thorough presentation of the newest theoretical developments regarding self-developing systems. The theme is that decisions by groups of lower-level actors create patterns in suprasystems such as flocks, swarms, and cities.
Kauffman, Stuart.
    1995 *At Home in the Universe: the Search for Laws of Self-Organization and Complexity.* New York: Oxford University Press.
    Pioneering discussion of chaos (or complexity) theory, in particular, the emergence of order, self-organization, and phase transitions. Assumes basic knowledge of systems theory.
Kosko, Bart.
    1993 *Fuzzy Thinking: The New Science of Fuzzy Logic.* New York: Hyperion. The author is described as one of the leaders of "fuzzy logic" in systems. This book is in part autobiographical and anecdotal, relating the process by which he and others recognized the need for, and developed, fuzzy logic. Very useful as an introduction to the subject and its use in various fields, including manufacturing.

Luhmann, Niklas.
1995 *Social Systems*. Stanford, CA: Stanford University Press. The author says: "This is not an easy book. It does not accommodate those who prefer a quick and easy read, yet do not want to die without a taste of systems theory." He's right, of course; it's also over six hundred pages. The introduction is entitled "Paradigm Change in Systems Theory," an accurate description of what Luhmann accomplishes here. He is undeniably one of the most original systems theorists.

Mingers, John.
1995 *Self-Producing Systems: Implications and Applications of Autopoiesis*. New York: Plenum.
The foreword describes this book as "a much-needed reference on autopoiesis. ... It took me stage by stage through a clear and easy-to-grasp understanding of the concepts and ideas." This is the definitive book on the subject, intended for advanced students.

Sawicki, Marianne.
1997. *Body, Text, and Science: The Literacy of Investigative Practices and the Phenomenology of Edith Stein*. Dordrecht: Kluwer.
Authoritative study of Stein's work, with some passages in both English and the original German. Highly recommended.

Smith, David Woodruff.
2004 *Mind World: Essays in Phenomenology and Ontology*. Cambridge: Cambridge University Press.
Definitive and comprehensive. Highly recommended for serious study of phenomenology.

Thompson, Evan, and Dan Zahavi.
2007. "Philosophical Issues: Phenomenology," in Zelazo, *et al.,* pp. 67-87.
A brief, informative discussion of the major issues in phenomenology; recommended for a "newbie" on the subject.

Zelazo, Philip David, Morris Moscovitch, and Evan Thompson, eds.
2007. *The Cambridge Handbook of Consciousness*. Cambridge: Cambridge University Press.
This is the "bible" of consciousness. At almost 1000 pages, it is hardly a "hand" book. It is exhaustive and authoritative. Recommended for the serious scholar.

Literary Sources

Malcolm X (with Alex Haley).
1966 *The Autobiography of Malcolm X*. New York: Grove Press.
This moving autobiography exemplifies all levels of human systems and a person's interactions with them. It demonstrates how systems affect the person and how a person can influence wider systems. The authors have used this as a major text in the course. The movie, starring Denzel Washington, is well done, but obviously omits much of the book.

Mandela, Nelson.
1994. *Long Walk to Freedom*. Boston: Little, Brown. An autobiography.

Warren, Robert Penn.
1946 *All the King's Men*. New York: Harcourt, Brace, Jovanovich.
Written by a former poet laureate of the United States, and loosely based on the later years of political boss and governor Huey Long of Louisiana, this novel has as one of its fundamental themes the "web" of consequences that follows from human actions. "What goes around comes around"—or one can view it systemically: all actions reverberate, and affect the rest of the system, in unpredictable ways.

Proust, Marcel.

1913. *Remembrance of Things Past.* Better translated as *In Search of Lost Time.* It is highly regarded as *the* novel of the twentieth century, the first modern novel. The theme is memory and loss; it is the self and the consciousness of the protagonist that is central.

Film, Video, and Play

Mindwalk (1990)

This unusual video is pure systems philosophy, voiced by three fine actors: Liv Ullmann, Sam Waterston, and John Heard. The setting is Mont Saint-Michel, the mystic castle and island on the Atlantic coast of France. They explore the setting along with the ideas. Thought-provoking, even if a bit didactic. Directed by Bernt Capra, it is a showcase for the ideas of his brother, Fritjof Capra, author of *The Turning Point,* and *The Web of Life.*

My Name is Rachel Corrie (2005)

This controversial play portrays an activist who was killed while protesting Israel's policies toward Palestinians. Directed by actor Alan Rickman, it has frequently been performed internationally. "You may disagree with Rachel Corrie's politics, but this play is about an activism that goes deeper than politics." (Royce, 2009)

Rifkin, Jeremy.

"Empathic Civilisation." (RSA Animate). London: Royal Society for the Encouragement of Arts, Manufacturers and Commerce. (www.theRSA.org).

This short lecture is illustrated by humorous animation—a hand madly wielding a marker on a white board. Delightful and insightful, it presents and elaborates on the ideas expressed in the Addendum, above. Available on YouTube, also.

3

Culture and Society

Men commonly feel according to their inclinations, speak and think according to their learning and imbibed opinions, but generally act according to custom.
—Sir Francis Bacon

The noblest study of mankind, is Man, says Man.
—James Thurber, *Further Fables for Our Time*

Introduction

In the twenty-first century (of the Christian or Common Era), we are faced with a cultural crisis and a crisis of cultures. From the viewpoint of our own culture, we face the necessity of adjusting to the presence and the power of other cultures to which we must relate in new and unaccustomed ways: as economic partners and competitors, as societies in which many of us live, study, and work for periods of time, and as places that are depicted (however briefly) in international news stories as locations of events that profoundly affect us. From the viewpoint of all cultures, technology presents us with pictures (both still photos and live television) of a small planet in a vast space, and poses the question, "Can't we all live together?" How to preserve the highest values of each culture (whether of a society, community, ethnic or racial group, or a family) while recognizing the validity of others is perhaps the major question facing us. The answer will almost certainly be given within the present century. The election of an American president who is biracial, African-American, born in Hawaii, and lived in Indonesia as a child may provide some indication. Championship golfer Tiger Woods, also biracial, was raised as a Buddhist, as he mentioned in a public apology for personal lapses.

This chapter explores human behavior at the broadest, most general level—that is, as a species. We will examine ideas from a number of disciplines, ideas that seem particularly pertinent to human services and social systems theory. These disciplines include biology, sociology, linguistics, psychology, ethnology, communications, and especially anthropology.

A. Definitions

First, we should explain how we use the terms *culture* and *society*. To be consistent with social systems theory, we use the term *culture* in two ways. First and generally, culture refers to those qualities and attributes that seem to be characteristic of all humankind. Culture denotes those things unique to the species *homo sapiens* as differentiated from all other forms of life. Humans, by contrast to all other species, evolve and adapt primarily through culture rather than changes in anatomy or genetics. We employ this general usage of culture to underscore the notion that the human evolutionary timetable is unique in that it is through culture that the human is immediately affected by and subject to the evolutionary principle of natural selection. Sociobiologists have derived formulas of cultural diffusion and demise based upon maximization of selected cultural traits through breeding and mate selection. This approach is hotly disputed as lending itself to a theory of cultural (or racial) superiority. In general, we can say that a culture survives if it can accommodate to changing conditions. One reason for the decline and near disappearance of some Plains groups of American Indians is that the buffalo (bison) were exterminated by white hunters and there was no adequate substitute. Another example might be the demise of Western, industrial cultures as we know them, if supplies of cheap petroleum decline midway through this century—would American culture survive the demise of the private automobile, cheap energy, and cheap food?

Humans are social beings, uniquely possessing culture. Cultural forms may be changed, synthesized, radiated, and extinguished, but biological change of the human species proceeds at a far slower pace. Consistent with this broad definition, we view culture as a macrosystem.

A *society* refers to a group of people who have learned to live and work together. Society is a holon, and *within* the society, "culture" refers to the way of life followed by that population. This, then, is the second usage of culture—that which binds a *particular* society together, and includes its manners and morals, tools, and techniques. To repeat, culture may refer to either of two levels: that which is characteristic of the species, and that which is characteristic of some specific population within the human species.

One must be careful in identifying a culture. For example, "Western culture" includes American society, French society, Jamaican society, and American Indian society, each a culture with distinct subcultures within it. Similarly, one must be careful in generalizing "Muslim" culture, which includes Iraq, Indonesia, and Pakistan.

B. The Nature of Culture

Culture is a group phenomenon. While individual persons may originate ideas or behavior, they do not create cultures alone. Cultures evolve from the interactions of persons with others, and a person's belief or behavior becomes part of a culture when it is *externalized* and *objectified*. Externalization is the process by which ideas are presented to others and become accepted as part of the culture. Once the ideas are built into a culture, and act upon the people within the culture, they have been objectified as part of the external world: "This world as an objective reality manifests itself most unmistakably in its coercive power, in its capacity to direct behavior, impose sanctions, punish deviance and at the extreme, destroy human life" (Wuthnow et al., 1984:39).

Television is an excellent example of externalization and objectification. The television set itself is an objectified conception of human communication, and the concepts (in picture or word form) presented on its screen are another layer of objectification. There is yet a third layer of objectification. Having become reality, television acts upon us, emotionally and physically:

> Recently, Toronto media critic Morris Wolfe created the concept of "jolts per minute"—or JPM's—to describe how TV shows hit us. ... [W]e interpret gestures, postures and expressions on TV with a kind of sub-muscular response, expressed in muscle tone and stress factors. ... [W]e store their relevant effects in our neuromuscular system ... precisely what Hans Selye called stress. (De Kerckhove, 1995:11-12)

Bear in mind the operation of mirror neurons that was discussed in the preceding chapter. The brain adopts behaviors that it observes in others. Does television, then, have "coercive power" or "capacity to direct behavior," and so forth? That is precisely the question posed regarding the effects of television (and movie) violence on children. It is the "Frankenstein" question, here applied to culture (or "cyberculture"): Does that which we create have the power to destroy us? One tentative answer is that by Robert Putnam in Chapter 4, on community, regarding the power of television to destroy community.

A culture evolves as each person encounters four "poles":

1. *One's own body,* or somatic process, which includes the biological constitution and genetic endowment.
2. *Other persons, or society;* this encounter can be described in such terms as the feedback cycle, "looking-glass self," and "generalized other," discussed later in this chapter. This includes the behavior of others as mediated by symbols and interpretations.
3. The *material world of nonhuman objects,* experienced as Piaget described them (see Chapter 8); this world exists independent of each person, but must be interpreted by each. It includes tools and other objects created by humans, as well as the natural environment.
4. The *universe of socially constructed meanings,* which must be interpreted by each person. This includes language, customs, and institutions.

These "poles" are similar to Erikson's description of the three processes of organization: ego processes, somatic processes, and social processes (see Chapter 8). This can be diagrammed as a spiral, in which the self evolves within a field that has the four poles just described (see Figure 3.1). This conception can, by analogy, be pictured as an atom evolving in a dynamic field. As one atom evolves in interaction with its environment, it changes, as does the environment; simultaneously, other atoms interact with the first, and with their environments, of which this atom is a part. Thus, cultures evolve simultaneously with their components, the persons who inhabit them. In this process, objects, artifacts, conventions, and language (layers of meaning) accumulate, but some are dropped or modified; these elements are part

Figure 3.1
Evolution of Self in Culture.

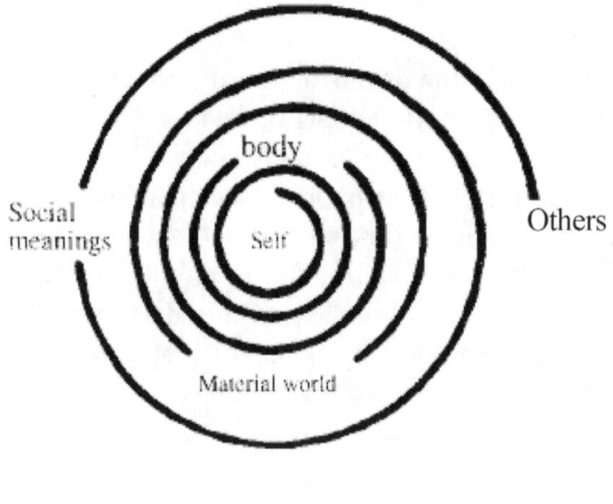

of the culture only as long as they are employed by someone who inhabits the culture.

The spiral in Figure 3.1 might be seen like the path of a pinball as it caroms across the playing surface of the pinball machine, bouncing from one pylon to another, sometimes "hung up" at one spot and sometimes suddenly hurled toward another. Is a person similarly determined by the forces of society?

Can a person transcend the playing field, escape culture and its poles? Can a person be "beyond systems"? Apparently not. Contrary to Abraham Maslow's conception of the "self actualizing" person who transcends culture and Lawrence Kohlberg's similar view of the most advanced stage of moral development, Erikson's psychohistories of persons such as Gandhi, Luther, and Jefferson indicated that these creative people externalized and objectified (and internalized) the most universal values of their respective cultures, but did not escape them (see our discussion in Chapter 8). At most, they experienced other cultures sufficiently to internalize significant values of those cultures also.

As in the examples Erikson analyzed, cultures change through the actions of persons whose ideas and behavior "fit" the culture, and were adopted by the culture because (as Erikson said) these new ideas and behaviors solved a problem for the culture (see Chapter 8) and hence were adopted.

Change can also occur as a result of cataclysm, either physical, as in famine, war, epidemic, disaster (the "four horsemen of the apocalypse"), or economic collapse. It can also change as a result of a "paradigm shift" (Kuhn, 1970) in fundamental understandings by those in the culture; one example is secularization, as occurred in Western societies; another is scientism, as believed in the "modern world" and discussed later in this chapter. The acceptance of Freud's views constituted such a "paradigm shift" in Western cultures, grounded in the two examples just given, of secularism and scientism.

The two major sections following deal with, first, those aspects of culture that are uniquely human; and second, dimensions by which culture can be analyzed.

I. Species and Culture: Unique Aspects of the Human Species

Human beings have certain attributes in common regardless of time or place. For our present purpose, we will generalize these attributes under four headings; (A) the capacity to think, (B) the family as a human universal, (C) language/communication, and (D) territoriality.

A. The Capacity to Think

The capacity to think is perceived as humans' most distinctive attribute, as witnessed by the identification of our species as *homo sapiens,* "thinking man." The first unique characteristic is the capacity for conceptual thought, or employment of the true speech, which is only another way of saying the same thing. The capacity to think and communicate thoughts sets humans apart from most other forms of life. However, it appears that humans are not unique in this ability. The language of dolphins, e.g., has been decoded by means of computer; it appears whales have an elaborate set of sounds, consisting of songs and "whistles" by which they communicate over long distances; and higher primates can communicate in sentences by using signs for words, and can fashion tools (unfortunately, sometimes to attack each other).

Gross impairment of the capacity for thought in humans is a grave matter. Much of child rearing is devoted to the refinement and development of this capacity (as is apparent in the discussion of cognitive theory in Chapter 8). Perpetuation of tradition and use of tools is dependent upon members of the culture having the capacity to think.

Humans are unique in that not only can they think, but that they can externalize the thought process itself, possibly in three ways. An implication of the viewpoint expressed earlier about culture is that each thing created by humans is an externalization of human thought and, in some particular way, reveals some aspect of the human thought process. As discussed later, tools are amplifications of human capacities, and the tool that comes closest (at least so far) to fully externalizing human thought is (1) the computer. We can discuss the human brain as a computer, but this is backward; the computer is an externalization of the brain and nervous system, and a comparatively inefficient copy, at that. Scientists have constructed computers from mechanical switches, vacuum tubes, transistors, silicon chips, and magnetized film. They are now experimenting with living cells as material from which to construct computers. Should this prove successful, human beings will have externalized human thought through (2) the creation of biocomputers. Fancifully, one way is through human reproduction; every baby is, in a very limited sense, a human biocomputer. (3) The third way for humans to externalize their thought processes would be through cloning (Aldous Huxley's novel *Brave New World* raised this possibility generations ago). The implications and possible dangers to human culture have been expressed by science fiction writers, notably Isaac Asimov, who raised the fundamental question: What is distinctively human about human thought?

B. The Family as Human Universal

We devote Chapter 7 to the family, but discuss it briefly here as part of culture. Family is both cause and result of culture. It is the basis for transmission of cultural attitudes toward caring, as discussed later in this chapter.

The family is biologically based and is the primary social (and socializing) unit. The *fact* of the family is a constant; the *form* of the family is variable. Anthropological studies have demonstrated convincingly that although the family as a primary socializing unit is a universal phenomenon, there is no "normal" form. As ethnologists have learned about the mating, reproducing, and rearing patterns of a range of species, they have uncovered a number of factors that seem to influence the pairings and groupings of various species. These factors include:

1. The number of offspring per mating—the reproductive rate.
2. The length of the gestation period, which influences the number of matings.
3. The length of the period of the immaturity of the young, expressed in ratio to total life span.

As the first factor reduces (smaller number of offspring per mating) and the other two factors lengthen (gestation and length of time of immaturity), pair bonds and family rearing of the young increase. Among humans, the existence of the family is, of course, a necessary element for the development of culture because culture is transmitted from one generation to the next through education—not through the genes (though this is still a debatable point).

The cultural form of family must never be confused with the biological norm of the family; the cultural forms vary tremendously between cultures and between subcultures within the same culture. The nuclear family, consisting of the biological parents and their offspring, is only one of these forms, and not the most prevalent among the forms in the world.

It is an understatement to say that the status of laws regarding same sex marriage in the United States is confusing. Opposition to legalizing same sex unions is largely based on religious grounds. As of April, 2010, such marriages were legal and performed in five states (Connecticut, Iowa, Massachusetts, New Hampshire, and Vermont) and the District of Columbia; the issue was being debated in twenty other states and some American Indian tribes (the Coquille tribe in Oregon allows them). The city of San Francisco was the first governmental unit in the country to recognize same sex marriage; the first state was Massachusetts, on November 18, 2003. Some states authorized same sex marriages, and then reversed the law (in California, such marriages between June 16 and November 4, 2008 are legal and continue to be recognized). Other states (about nine) recognize "civil unions" or "registered partnerships," which provide the benefits of marriage, such as joint insurance coverage, the right to make legal decisions (e.g., medical or end of life decisions), and inheritance. Where legally sanctioned, such unions provide all or most of the rights of traditional marriages.

At least seven other nations (Belgium, Canada, the Netherlands, Norway, South Africa, Spain, and Sweden) accept same sex marriages. In December, 2009, the Federal District (Mexico City) of Mexico legalized them also. Israel and the Netherland Antilles (the Dutch half) recognize these marriages but do not perform them. Twenty other countries, half in Europe, provide civil unions and registered partnerships. In Argentina, Australia, Venezuela, and several states in the United States, some political subdivisions perform same sex marriages. Same sex unions are being debated in fifty other countries.

When same sex marriages are legally sanctioned, recognition of new family forms presumably must follow, with new definitions of filial responsibility, divorce, inheritance rules, and custody provisions for any minor children (e.g., it is becoming more common for lesbians to choose artificial insemination in order to bear children, and adoption by same sex couples is increasingly permitted). The form of the family is influenced by the culture in which it exists; in turn, the family form influences the culture. The human family, then, is a system, a holon, and it has a simultaneous existence as part and whole. Its form organizes the energies of the family members, and it must engage in transactions with its supra-systems. An Iowa lawyer who represented same-sex couples in their successful challenge to state law, said, "Go and get married! Live happily ever after. Live the American dream" (St. Paul *Pioneer-Press*, April 4, 2009).

The following is an example of how cultural aspects influence the family system. Our economic system, with its accent on production and distribution of goods achieved through the standardization of organization of energies, requires a mobile work force. Adaptation to this single cultural artifact has been extremely stressful to the form of the family during the past generation and has been amply discussed in both popular and technical literature. (See our discussion of this subject in Chapter 7.) The cultural bind experienced by emigrants from Appalachia and by

African-Americans from the South is a prime example. (Stack, 1996) To seek and find gainful employment required a move to an industrial city. The nature of the mutual obligations between the emigrants and those who remain behind, especially those obligations to family, required the emigrants' presence at certain times of need. As these occur, the emigrant may decide to "take time off" to "go down home." This is a phenomenon also noted among American Indians, many of whom return to their home reservations to be with family and tribe, periodically and for varying lengths of time. During the economic downturn of 2007-2010, many workers returned to their families when they were laid off; this included Mexican citizens and other legal or illegal immigrants who were in the United States.

C. Language/Communication

Etymologists broadly define language as any transfer of meaning, but general usage refers only to spoken and written messages. Appreciation of the universality in the broader sense—that is, any transfer of meaning—is particularly important. Persons with troubles often have difficulties because they rely on nonverbal means of communication; therefore it is essential to be attuned to unspoken and unwritten language. A person may express feelings and ideas with signals (a shrug, bowing one's head, throwing up one's hands) rather than with consensual symbols of communication. Consequently, such ideas as "body language" become important.

There are explicitly arranged language forms other than spoken and written verbal messages. A driver's exam for persons who are illiterate may use colors and sign shapes rather than the printed word. American Sign Language uses a combination of stylized gestures, and signals for specific letters and words, which are a significant part of what is increasingly recognized as "deaf culture." Transients ("hobos") developed a more or less standardized set of signs that were chalked, painted, or scratched on walls, posts, or fences to inform others about what to expect at particular homes or businesses; a stick-figure cat meant, "Kind-hearted woman lives here"; a hieroglyph resembling a broken-leg chair with a cross on top meant, "Food here if you work" (Richards and Associates, 1974). Urban gangs use hand positions to signify comradeship, and wear identical colors; in fact gang fights and some killings are attributed to nonmembers' wearing colors that have been appropriated by the gang.

The key to nonverbal language is the consensus of meaning attached to symbols and their manipulations. An important aspect of socialization into a new system is to become acquainted with such symbolization and learn the attached meanings. Excellent examples are the sometimes subtle and complex, silent or audible signals exchanged at auctions, and the elaborate (and often humorous) motions employed by baseball coaches.

There are also implicitly understood conventions and symbols that require even more consensual agreement than the explicit symbols. The initiation of a social transaction between equals can be signaled by the shaking of hands, an embrace, or mutual acknowledgment of deference, such as bowing or the removal of hats. Rituals are evident in candidates' political debates; a candidate who wishes to appear cordial will grasp an opponent's hand with the right hand, and grasp an elbow with the left hand. The culturally conditioned "embracer" learns very quickly in a "handshaking" culture that the meanings of gestures are culturally relative and are not universal. The media had a brief "field day" over whether, when they met for the first time, First Lady Michelle Obama or Queen Elizabeth was first to put an arm around the other; the issue was familiarity vs. respect.

Communication seems to be present in other life forms, as noted earlier. The dancing flight of the bee and the singing of birds to announce territorial prerogatives to other members of their species are well-known. Many animals have elaborate "dances" or drumming as mating rituals. Such phenomena seem distinguishable from human language in respect to the thought and meaning signified. The evidence thus far is that such animal behaviors, operating from instinct, evolved for purposes of species survival.

Etymologists have an interesting time with cross-cultural comparisons of word meanings, and in the process, provide interesting insights. For example, in his fascinating book *The Story of Language* ([1966] 1984) Mario Pei dealt with the symbolism of color and how symbols vary from one language to another and one culture to another. Why are we "blue" when depressed, "yellow" when cowardly, "red" when radically inclined? In Russia, red is beautiful, and both "red" and "beautiful" have the same word root. White is the color of purity and innocence (and surrender) to most European cultures, but to most Asians, it is the color of mourning and death. In the Russian civil war, the Reds had a gigantic psychological advantage over the Whites because of the symbolic overtones. This kind of information carries implications for attempts to understand racial conflicts. Those who launched the "Black Is Beautiful" campaign in the 1960s were attuned to the cultural importance of color symbolism. How much racial prejudice is attributable to the cultural artifact of color symbolism is unknown, but it appears to be an important factor. In considering language and thought as species characteristics in humans, the thesis propounded by Whorf and Sapir is worthy of note. Their hypothesis was that language structures reality; the form and variability of the language determine how members of the culture will view reality and structure their thoughts (Whorf, 1956). This hypothesis is generally accepted. In developing his thesis about territoriality and its importance to people, E. T. Hall analyzed the words listed in the Oxford Pocket Dictionary and found that 20 percent of them referred to space and spatial relations (Hall, 1969:93). In American culture, "war" words are common: e.g., "it impacted him," she was "blown away."

There is a close, demonstrable relationship between culture and language. This relationship is not necessarily causal in either direction. As often cited, modern English and American language structures attend closely to the passage of time, and to gender. Tenses are of utmost importance, since time is so essential to aspects of these cultures, and gender distinction is considered essential. Some cultures and languages make no provisions for tenses or gender, e.g., Mandarin (Putonghua)—the precise measurement of time is (or was, historically) of lesser importance in these cultures, and gender is interpreted from the context of the sentence.

La Barre presented intriguing facts and speculations about language as symbolic communication. He accepted Whorf's hypothesis and stated that the structure of reality is, much of the time, merely *imputed* to reality by the structure of our language. As soon as the human infant learns to speak any language at all, it already has a "hardening of the categories," or "they are different, this we know, for our language tells us so" (La-Barre, 1954).

La Barre observed that language is so flexible that a word can put into semantic equation any two disparate objects in the universe. If the society accepts the equation by consensus, semantically it becomes reality; if the individual does this without societal consensus, the person may be labeled schizophrenic and thus not attuned to reality (the person may, alternatively, be a creative genius, of course, such as Ireland's James Joyce). Another alternative is the deliberate use of "plastic words," words borrowed from science, but denote little in factual content (D. Schwartz, 1997:37); they are the "hamburger helper" of conversations: words such as "project," "function," "model", "system" (yes, even that one), "needs", "information," and "communication." The popular way to describe these words is as "buzz words," often intended only to convey that the speaker is "with it," "'hip" to cultural trends, and "cool." Other usages creep into the language because influential persons or media personalities use them; for example, "comprise" is often used incorrectly, when what is meant is "compose" or "include." "Regular" becomes "on a regular basis," and "now" becomes "at this point in time."

La Barre (1954:266) said "A psychotic's truth is one *'I'* make it, and cultural truth is what by unwitting vote 'we' make it; but ultimate truth still remains in the outside world of that which is." Robert Merton expressed the same idea in his Thomas theorem, "If [persons] define situations as real, they are real in their consequences" (Merton, 1957:421). Hence the significance of "politically correct" language, an effort (occasionally strained) to eliminate conscious or unconscious bias such as sexism, racism, or classism from the culture by altering perception. A "mailman" is now a "letter carrier"; a "policeman" is a "law officer." A new generation learns the new usage, and the culture is changed, perhaps, to at least some small degree.

D. Territoriality

Territoriality refers to the tendency of people (as well as other species), in their social systems, to seek and maintain a territory. Some authors deal with territory as primarily spatial, while others stress the interactional aspects. The definition of spatial and interactional territories is a paramount feature of any culture.

One simple example is the definition of territorial elements as squared or rounded. It seems that this choice is simultaneously determined by other features of the culture and is a determinant of culture, as well. "Home territories" within a given culture give clues to other aspects of the culture. A sedentary and specialized culture with much differentiation of function tends to organize living and work spaces in squares with specialized uses. The square house has its bedrooms, bathrooms, kitchen, living room, den, and so forth. The nomadic, unspecialized culture lives in round houses (igloo, wigwam or tepee, yurt, or round hut) without specialized compartments. Arranging territories in squares tends to close boundaries. A newspaper columnist said that a "cube farm" is slang for cubicles, work spaces created by the temporary and movable partitions used in many organizations (Wilbers, 1998). The squares are mutable as necessary; some have curved walls, to avoid squareness. "Prairie dogging" is "when someone yells or drops something loudly in a cube farm, and people's heads pop up over the walls to see what's

going on." The "Dilbert" daily cartoon is a rich source of such organizational behavior. Some workplaces are large, open spaces without
walls, "industrial" or "warehouse" in style, in which workers have areas,
rather than enclosed spaces; the usual intent is to convey an atmosphere
of creativity and fluidity; a sort of "workplace in the round."

The spirit of equality, fidelity, and camaraderie embodied in the
King Arthur legend is symbolized by the "table round." Formal dining tables are usually rectangular, while tables in small, intimate bars
are round. Youths' expressions of dissatisfaction with the impersonal,
highly structured role relations and specialized functions of bureaucracies were expressed in the 1960s epithet "square," which had been
used in African-American culture even earlier, to denote someone who
wasn't "hep" (which later became "hip"). Dictionaries show that the
meanings attached to "square" by immediately preceding generations
were "just," "fair," and "honest," as in a "square shooter" or a "square
deal." These meanings reflected the primary purpose of the impersonal
bureaucratic system—to protect the person from unjust and arbitrary
decisions. Negotiations at the end of the Vietnam War were delayed for
months over whether the talks would be conducted over a rectangular
table or a circular one. In part, this symbolized crucial differences in
cultural traditions and beliefs. Schools continue to be built with round
lunch rooms, and with "pods" to facilitate (or to make manageable)
communication.

Relationships are symbolized by diagrams intended to concretize
interactional territories (Figure 3.2). The components in Figure 3.2a are
arranged in a vertical hierarchy and each component (person or department)

Figure 3.2.
A typical representation of a bureaucratic structure is depicted in (a).
A typical sociogram is represented in (b).

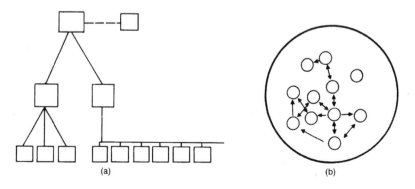

(a)   (b)

is designated by title or role rather than by name. These labels designate specialization and differentiation. In Figure 3.2b, the components would be labeled by name (or number, to protect the innocent); the hierarchy here is represented in the horizontal plane and conveys positive, negative, and absent patterns of relatedness. Each diagram is illustrative of interactional territorial arrangements and relationships.

It is hypothesized, then, that all systems have a territorial dimension. This territory may be spatial or interactional; it probably is a "sense of territory," and is congruent with the particular culture. Territoriality refers to the cultural ways people locate themselves in their universe and establish the boundaries of their various human systems.

II. Analytic Dimensions of Culture: Qualities of a Society

Definitions of culture abound and frequently conflict. The definition given by Edward Tylor in 1871 was as good as any: culture is that complex whole that includes knowledge, belief, art, law, morals, custom, and any other capabilities and habits *acquired by a human being as a member of society.*

Rather than choosing a definition of culture from the myriad that have been offered, or trying to formulate another, we will discuss six dimensions of culture. The first five of these dimensions are expansions on what Jerome Bruner termed "the five great humanizing forces" (Bruner, 1968:75ff.): tool making, social organization, language, management of the prolonged human childhood, and the human urge to explain the world. We add another: social relationships. These dimensions are definitive aspects of any culture. One can approach the analysis of culture through examining these dimensions regardless of the time, place, or kind of culture being studied. In regard to a *subculture* within a culture, such as a peer group or professional culture, certain of these dimensions may seem less applicable; but each of the five seems applicable to some extent. Here, we are viewing culture as the ways of doing, being, and explaining, as they exist in each particular system.

A. Tools

Tools are amplifiers of human capacities, whether the tools are invented or synthesized. They fall into three classes:

1.   Amplifiers of *sensory capacities;* for example, microscopes, telescopes, telephones, television, clocks, spectacles, radar, conch shells, and "mind-expanding" drugs (such as peyote, in some cultures).

2. Amplifiers of *motor capacities,* for example, hammers, wheels, the lever, rockets, and automobiles.
3. Amplifiers of *reasoning and thinking capacities,* for example, mathematical systems, logic, the abacus, the computer, and the chalkboard (a major educational invention, in its time).

Tools include devices, objects, and procedures that are extensions of human natural capacities. The crucial, most important aspect is not the tool itself but rather its function, that is, the use to which the tool is put. A hammer is generally assumed to be of use to pound nails and, if it is a claw hammer, to remove nails as well, but it can also be used as a lethal weapon or to prop open a door or window (or for any other use that a five-year-old can think of). Books generally are assumed to be for the purpose of reading, but they can also be used to press flowers, impress people, to level the short leg of a table, or as a prop to be carried to make an impression, e.g., a politician carrying a Bible. Understanding the tools of a culture includes, therefore, not only understanding their seeming intrinsic or built-in purpose but, more importantly, their purpose for the user. Some years ago, one of the authors worked on a small Indian reservation where electricity was available and each household had been given a refrigerator, but preserving food by refrigeration was not then part of that culture's way of life. The refrigerators were used for other purposes—for decoration in a few instances—but mostly for storage. They were perceived as attractive boxes with a door; the "built-in purpose" was not the purpose of the users. A current example is the function of unused exercise equipment as clothing racks or end tables; they function to maintain an air of potential, if not actual fitness. Wearing sports clothes for everyday wear may be another example.

Peter Farb, a cultural anthropologist, analyzed the evolution of cultures in a remarkably readable book. One of his theses was that a new tool or technique must have a counterpart in social organization or knowledge to become functional. He used the example of the introduction of the horse into two quite different cultures. The first of these cultures, a hunting tribe, mounted the horses and used them to pursue the bison. This amplified human motor capacities, making them much more efficient hunters, and the horse rapidly became central to the culture. The second culture merely slaughtered and ate the horse; it had no function in that culture (Farb, [1968] 1978:129). A more homely example might be the personal computer in some homes, used by adults only for word processing, while their children use it for games, net-surfing, watching a video, or jointly performing course assignments with others, each in their own home. The same generational difference may also be true for cell phones and camera phones (see the comics page "Zits" for frequent illustrations).

Tools, then, are a key dimension by which a culture may be analyzed. They extend the uses of energies within the cultural system toward fulfillment of the system's goals. It may be equally significant and analytical of a culture that certain tools do not exist. For example, the absence of written languages, or of the wheel, was significant in some North and Central American Indian cultures. In another example, what does it mean that Europe and Japan have more cell phones *per capita* than the United States, and that users in those societies have access to greater bandwidth at higher speed than most Americans?

B. Social Organization: Society and Roles

All cultures, being social systems, have organization. As previously stated, the structure is not fixed, and any analysis of structure is like a still photograph. At the moment of analysis, the social organization of a culture is not what it has been, nor what it will become. It is structured in the sense of a system of interacting elements, and any change in one element or single pattern of relationships affects all other elements directly or indirectly.

The theory of evolution, in its essence, describes the increase of complexity, whether from simple to complex biological organisms or from simple to complex cultures. The social organization of an evolving culture becomes more complex because of an increased volume of relationships among the various elements of the culture. A "stagnant culture" is one in which the relationships are static and interaction of the cultural elements is unchanging. Some have postulated that bureaucracy appears as an organizational structure when society reaches a given state of complexity, regardless of the form of government. The bureaucracies of ancient China, Rome, the Roman Catholic church, the Russian monarchy, and most recently Western democracies and Communist states can all be cited as illustrations. Bureaucracy seems to have as a major function the reduction and containment of forces that may lead to change. As such, bureaucracy is probably used as a "buffering" device by all complex societies. The systems term *equifinality* (see Glossary) applies to this phenomenon; Beer defined it as "the proven ability of certain open systems to reach the same characteristic result, despite differences in initial conditions, and despite different rules of conduct along the way" (1981:191).

Certain important concepts related to social organization are commonly employed. These are the interrelated ideas of *social class, status, and role.* All societies have schemes of ordering human interaction and ways of defining and communicating expected behaviors. As with definitions of culture, many theorists have proposed hypothetical social class structures. Perceptive observers have identified life-styles, socioeconomic indices, and values that differ among social classes. Columnist George Will, e.g., decried the popularity of denim trousers.

English sociologist T. H. Marshall believed that there are three aspects operating to define social class: economic status, social status, and political power (Marshall, 1964). When the groupings of these three coincide (multibonded), then social class is visible. If the boundaries between the social classes are clear, closed, and institutionalized, the result is *caste.* The idea of social class suggests a group consciousness on the part of members, both of their own social groups and other groups, and of their general position in the social hierarchy. Actor Michael Caine observed that the class structure in England is a burden that he does not feel in the United States. In the United States, the existence of social classes is largely denied, by asserting that almost everyone is "middle class"; in such an instance, Marxist theorists would presumably suggest that this is a "false consciousness" that obscures class members' real positions in the societal hierarchy.

Some researchers and writers suggest the emergence of a permanent "underclass" in American society, made up of those who persist in poverty for several generations (e.g., Zinn, 1997). Approximately 39 million persons lived in poverty in the United States in 2008, approximately 13 percent of the population; this is an increase of 6 million since 2000. A third of these were children, age 18 or under. About 9 percent of Caucasians (non-Hispanic), 12 percent of Asian-Americans, 23 percent of Hispanics (of any race or nationality) and 25 percent of African-Americans, lived in poverty. The unemployment rate for African-Americans was 10.1 percent (historically, always about double that of Caucasians); Hispanics; 7.6 percent, Caucasians, 5.2 percent; and Asian-Americans, 4.0 percent. The length of unemployment was 12 weeks for African-Americans; 10 weeks for Asian-Americans; 8.8 for Caucasians; and 8.4 for Hispanics.

Median annual income for Asian-American households was about $66,000; for Caucasians, $55,000; for Hispanics, $39,000; and for African-Americans, $34,000. Not having health insurance (15.4 percent, nationally) was highest among Alaskan and Hawaiian indigenous populations, at 31.7 percent; followed by Hispanics, 30.7 percent; African-Americans, 19.1 percent; Asian-Americans, 17.6 percent; and Caucasians, 10.8 percent. Such figures lend support to the existence of an "underclass," composed not just by race, but in other measures, also, by access to higher-quality education, geographic location, and quality of housing. These figures have been relatively constant for decades.

Role relates to and derives from status. Role is the total of the cultural expectations associated with a particular status (male/female, professional, elder/young, minister/lay person, e.g.) including the attitudes, values, and behavior. The complexity of a status is manifested partly by the complexity and differentiation of role expectations. Bureaucracy is one of the organizational forms devised to reduce this complexity. In a bureaucracy, the role often becomes more important than the person occupying the status, but it is only through occupying the status that the person can assume the role. In systems larger than the family, continuity depends less on the characteristics of the person and more on the role being occupied. Compare, e.g., the differing personalities among the Presidents of the United States during your lifetime.

Role expectations, then, are defined by the culture and its components, and incorporated by the persons filling the role. A culture may allow greater or less latitude in deviations from the expected behaviors. Certain cultures rigidly define role behavior, but more often the rigidity or flexibility of role definition is dependent on what else is transpiring within the system.

In a dynamic, open cultural system, role occupants constantly seek flexibility of role definition with or without the encouragement of the culture. As the cultural system is threatened from either internal or external quarters, strings are drawn more tightly on the expected role behaviors. One dramatic example is the behavior of students in Beijing's Tienamen Square in May and June 1989; their behavior was proscribed so severely that many were killed, and others hunted by means of nationwide searches. This was part of a series of student demonstrations beginning in 1985, and is part of a pattern of cultural change involving a contest for power between the Communist party, the army, and a new managerial middle class (Woodruff, 1989). Students, some of whom have traveled or studied abroad, represent this new class in China. It is apparent to any visitor to Europe and many Asian countries (both the "big tigers" and the "smaller tigers") that there has been massive economic change within the last forty years, with profound change in the roles of women and youth, particularly. The popular movie "Slumdog Millionaire," set in contemporary India, portrays both the rise of middle-class professionals and the persistent, extreme poverty that still remains. It is not accidental, of course, that many American technical and computer-related firms have "outsourced" their technical support functions to India and other Asian countries.

All persons occupy a complex of roles: parent, child, worker, voter, and worshipper, for example. The total number of roles is influenced by the quantity of networks they are involved in. At any given moment, a person is likely to be more actively fulfilling one role than another, but carries them all at once, nevertheless. When a person experiences excessive conflict in fulfilling varying role expectations, or if society judges the person to be failing in this respect, the person and the society both have troubles.

A contemporary example is the strong expectation for a work role. Work is quite narrowly defined as contractual employment, profession, or own business, and it is expected that each adult, unless certifiably disabled or past an arbitrary age, will fulfill such a role. The work role is fused with the economic role. Even though members of the society accept the prescribed role expectations, a significant number are not able to fulfill the agreed-upon role if there are insufficient jobs, or if they have insufficient qualifications for the jobs. The culturally prescribed remedy is to attempt to generate more jobs (i.e., work roles). The un-employment figures cited above indicate that such remedies have met with mixed success; the Obama administration claims some success as a result of "stimulus" funds provided by the government to both private and public employers. Another culture might seek to broaden the defini-tion of work (e.g., paying women for "mother's work") or to separate work from economic participation (e.g., Social Security or a guaranteed income). This is the larger meaning to the health insurance legislation passed by the Obama administration in 2010—to assure that nearly all citizens have health insurance coverage regardless of employment or unemployment. European countries and Canada are most frequently cited as models in this regard.

If any significant minority of the members of a society (some have suggested 10 percent is sufficient) do not do what the consensus requires for a length of time, the system is in difficulty and the survival of the culture is in question; or it may undergo phase transformation. In such instances, energies of the system must be devoted to maintaining the organization and redefining the expectations of those in the particular status. In the latter years of the Vietnam War, a significant minority refused to fulfill the expectation for military service. Subsequently, the draft was terminated. It may not be clear for a generation or more what effects the revolt of Beijing's young, educated elite against the regimentation and militarism of China's culture will have, although the ruling elite have made significant adaptations within the last decade, such as allowing more access and openness in use of the internet (despite the disagreement in 2010 between Google and the Chinese government which led to Google's removal of its Chinese headquarters to Hong Kong). Almost certainly there will be further profound effects.

C. Language

Here again we refer to language in its broadest sense, that is, as *transfer of meaning* between systems and between subsystems. The structure of language strongly influences the content conveyed. Knowing what a culture considers important enough to symbolize and communicate is as important as knowing the methods of communication. The *Amelia Bedelia* series of children's books is an amusing and instructive introduction to the ambiguities in our use of language, and not only for children; "jump in the car," e.g., has an unorthodox meaning for Amelia.

Language is composed of symbols (authors' note: "comprised of" would be the wrong usage here) and the meanings are learned and transferred through social interaction. *Symbolic interaction* refers to this process. The communication of symbols and their meanings represents the major form of transaction between human systems. Most of the work of the symbolic interactionists is built on the insights of George Herbert Mead and Charles Horton Cooley. Mead stated that we do not simply respond to the acts (including speech, of course) of others; rather, we act on *our interpretations* of their intentions and judgments (again, refer to the discussion of mirror neurons in the Addendum to Chapter 2). Gestures are an important kind of symbolic communication, and we respond to the meanings not necessarily as they are intended, but as we interpret them. When a gesture has a common meaning (some measure of consensus), Mead termed it a linguistic element—a significant symbol. Common examples include the kiss as an expression of affection; the drawn-back, clenched fist as threat of aggression; the smile as an expression of pleasure; and the frown as an expression of displeasure. Because of the consensus of meaning, we attribute the quality of pleasure to the smile of a baby even though it may be an expression of gas in the stomach.

The term *generalized other* is central to Mead's formulation. This refers to a generalized stance or viewpoint imputed to others that one uses to evaluate one's own behavior. A person responds not only to others who may be present, but to the general expectations of one's reference group (that is, a group to which one belongs or wishes to belong).

Another key concept in symbolic interaction is *self* (see the discussion of the concept of self in the Addendum to Chapter 2). The self is seen to be composed of the *I* and the *Me*. The *I* is the impulsive, spontaneous, and unorganized part of the self. *Me* is the incorporated other, derived from other persons via the feedback cycle. The *I* energizes and provides propulsion, whereas the *Me* provides direction, in other words, controls function. These are similar to, but in important ways different from, Freud's id and superego. The emphasis here is on social rather than intrapsychic functioning.

The *looking-glass self* is Cooley's construct and refers to the idea that we interpret what others think of us. It involves the following sequence: (1) the imagination of our appearance to others; (2) the imagination of their judgment; and (3) a self-feeling in response to this imagined judgment (e.g., pride or mortification).

The symbolic interactionists go far toward explaining the process of transfer of meaning. Their formulations demonstrate that meaning derives from interaction between the sender and receiver, both verbally and nonverbally. These are forms of the feedback cycle. If there is insufficient feedback from outside the focal system, then an assessment of one's appearance and judgment of it must be projected from inside. For example, the paranoid person is not able, or is not allowing self, to participate in this feedback cycle with outside systems and must rely on his or her own imagined judgments. As Philip Slater put it, "Without air we die, without love we turn nasty, without feedback we go crazy" (1974:49). The same can occur in nations that are cut off, with feedback projected from within, which therefore become isolated and chauvinistic. This may have been part of the dynamic of China in 1989, as its army killed its own citizens; it may have been reacting to its own internal feedback, due to millennia of cultural norms of order and centralized control. The same may apply to North Korea, another relatively closed society. What is meant by "modernization" and "democratization" is, in part, increased openness across traditional or authoritarian boundaries.

Language is a means of setting and maintaining cultural boundaries, as well as a major means of organizing the energies of the system. Subcultures universally employ their own jargon and argot. One of the major tasks of socialization into a subculture is to become acquainted with the special language. Certainly the subculture of social work is an example, with such jargon as "person in environment," "personal-social needs," "relationship," and "intervention." Another example is the American Psychiatric Association's standardized nomenclature, in the *Diagnostic and Statistical Manual* (e.g., in the current fourth edition, DSM-IV), which facilitates communication among psychiatrists, and between other professions and psychiatrists. The special language of a subculture may serve to exclude others from participation in the culture. Youths' abbreviated internet and cell phone texting is an example, often portrayed in cartoon strips (see "Zits," e.g.), of exclusion of parents from the topics being discussed.

IMHO	In my humble opinion
LOL	Laughing out loud
MOTOS	Members of the opposite sex
ROFL	Rolling on the floor laughing
SHID	Slapping head in disgust
404	I don't know
2MI	Too much information
POS	Parent over shoulder
IRL	In real life

and "emoticons":

:-)	Smiling
:->	Winking
:-{	Unhappy
:-D	Laughing
:-x	Keeping a secret
#|8>)#	An author of this book

Because it prevents interaction, this "linguistic collusion" is an effective way to close a boundary.

The importance of screening and interpreting symbols in working with people is abundantly clear. Much of the literature of the helping professions, for example, is devoted to making the reader sensitive to the possible meanings of symbols received from the person being helped. Theodore Reik's idea of "the third ear," in which the therapist's own emotional reactions give clues to unspoken messages being sent by the patient, is a time-tested example. Another example is psychological testing, especially "projective" tests such as the Rorschach, Thematic Apperception, or House-Tree-Person tests. In these tests, the responses of the subject are interpreted in order to provide clues about the subject's personality structure and what treatment methods may be most useful.

In these instances, between the professional person's reception (input) of the symbols and response (output) to them, the interpretation (processing) that occurs is formalized and takes on the character of scientific problem-solving—or at least, this is what professional schools hope their graduates are capable of doing.

In each profession, some standardization of language and symbols is necessary, and thus each theoretical approach, such as psychoanalysis, behavior modification, or family therapy must devote much energy to training professionals in some standard terminology (and so must social systems theory). This is necessary so that the results of professional efforts and the theoretical elaboration of them can be conveyed in some common language. The history of psychiatry is replete with examples of attempts by Kraepelin, Freud, and others to standardize terminology (see Menninger, 1963: Chapters 1 and 2, and Appendix). A major problem for each of the developing helping professions has been the training of professionals to apply the same labels to similar phenomena so that terms have some consensual meaning—that is, so that one psychiatrist's "schizoid" is not another psychiatrist's "passive-aggressive." Television's "House" series illustrates almost weekly the difficulty in arriving at accurate nomenclature for a given phenomenon. Despite such efforts as the American Psychiatric Association's standard nomenclature (DSM), however, serious disagreements on interpretations of symbolic behavior do occur within that profession. Reportedly, DSM-V, a newer version which is currently being drafted, may have a new category that will identify problems in relationships rather than in individuals. Consensus of meaning with a high degree of precision is difficult to achieve: if it were not, books like this would not need a Glossary.

D. Child Rearing: Management of the Prolonged Human Childhood

Anthropologists, sociologists, and psychologists have exhaustively researched forms of child rearing in various cultures. Although most of these studies focus on the family system, many deal with other educative and socializing social systems as well. The management of the human's prolonged childhood is a major task of any culture and, as such, must fit with other aspects of the culture and interact with these. As a culture becomes more complex and differentiated, so too does child rearing, and other social provisions appear. There are numerous examples in the recent evolution of United States society. As the economic system required greater mobility, the extended family began to dissipate (see the discussion of this in Chapter 7). This was accompanied by the advent of the baby-sitter. Demands of the economic system and shifts in role definition of women have lead to growth of day-care centers, the emergence of the "househusband" (in two comic strips, "Sally Forth," and "Adam@Home," e.g.), and demands for federal legislation to support wider availability and higher quality of day-care centers.

Social institutions such as day-care facilities for children and elders are accompanied by changes in family functions, but this is not necessarily equivalent to family breakdown. These new systems arise to realize more effectively the complex of values of a culture. Usually, certain values are in conflict with certain other values, leading to tension and strain within the culture. The historical development of the public school is an excellent illustration. The belief that a certain amount of formal education should be the right of every person developed over centuries in a number of places, particularly Western Europe. This was related to values such as "equality" and "the importance of knowledge." An informed citizenry became a national system goal in the first half of the nineteenth century. As the belief became a cherished value held by a significant portion of the components of the system, provisions were implemented such as the "common school" in the 1850s. The public school as a child-rearing social subsystem (if not a sub*culture*, almost) has continued to evolve, becoming more complex and differentiated. The continuing controversy over the transmission of culture, manners, and morals through education about sexual behavior and sexually transmitted diseases (STDs), and whether this should be a family or school responsibility, exemplifies the process of culture change and the inherent value conflicts. Concern about portrayal of violence in television and movies, and its effect upon children, as well as the issue of prayer in public schools, are other examples.

E. The Human Urge to Explain the World

As noted in the discussion of consciousness in the Addendum to Chapter 2, humans crave, and are compelled to find, order in the world they experience. This explains Georgiou's theory that the mind must *intuit* order in the phenomena it is observing. This major dimension of culture is often overlooked or minimized. Much of the energy of a culture system is expended in this effort to find meaning and to institutionalize it. Religion, philosophy, science, government, and superstition are some of the means. This quest to explain the unexplained can be viewed as an integral aspect of the adaptation of a system to its environment. In our present-day, "advanced" cultures, science continues to be the dominant means of exploring, explaining, and changing our world (scientific method, empirical observation, and inductive reasoning are, of course, highly valued only in certain cultures). It is dogmatically believed that the scientific method or technology can solve all important problems. The George W. Bush administration was heavily criticized for its subjugation of science to the beliefs of "faith organizations," e.g., with regard to abortion and stem cell research, supposedly for political purposes. But major religious organizations in this culture have historically engaged in social problem-solving in the "scientific" way (e.g., the Charity Organization, Societies of the late nineteenth century). One denomination, of course, refers to "Christian science." Another organization promotes the use of "Scientology" among its members.

F. Social Relations: Caring

Cultures are marked by the style in which they conduct social relationships. For example, Japanese culture is marked by a high degree of formality, and specificity about interactions and obligations between roles. Confucian ethics were based on the concept *jen,* translated as "human-heartedness," "love," and "magnanimity"; this Chinese character denotes what is common, or shared, between human beings. "Filial piety" (*hsiao*) begins with respectful affection toward one's parents, one form of *jen*. Relationships between parent and child, family and community, and ruled to rulers were spelled out in detail.

A game that has been widely used to sensitize persons to cultural differences separates participants into two "cultures" and then requires them to interact; one culture is exclusively oriented toward acquisition, the other toward sharing and communication. The results are often confusing to participants, and hilarious. Perceptive analyses of Western cultures, particularly that of the United States, suggest that ours is a "commercial" culture in which material gain is foremost and people are treated instrumentally, that is, as means to an end. Buber's philosophy described the difference between an *I-Thou* relationship, a complete, open, and mutual relationship between persons, and an *I-It* relationship, in which the other person is treated as an object (Buber, [1937] 1947, 1965), "Thou" is intended to convey the sacredness of the other person's being, a reflection of the divine.

> An animal does not need to be confirmed, for it is what it is unquestionably. It is different with man … . he watches for a Yes which allows him to be and which can come to him only from one human person to another. (Buber, 1965:17)

Many writers have observed that our culture is largely characterized by *I-It* relationships, and a lack of validation of each other; a more recent observation by feminists particularly, but not exclusively, is that our culture generally lacks *caring* among its members.

Caring "involves both an emotional disposition and caring labor. Care has been defined as '*a species activity that includes everything that we do to maintain, continue, and repair our 'world' so that we can live in it as well as possible*'" (Joan Tronto, quoted in Kimball, 1995:153). Caring, then, is a dimension of culture as much as tools and language; it preceded them both. Illich defined culture as "the sum of rules by which the individual came to terms with pain, sickness and death, interpreted them, and practiced compassion toward others faced by the same threats. Each culture set up the myths, the taboos, and the ethical standards needed to deal with the fragility of life" (Ivan Illich, quoted in D. Schwartz, 1997:84). Note that he is describing *empathy* as a basis for culture.

A feminist critique states that caring is largely delegated to women by a male-dominated society. Wood (1994) agrees, but adds that caring arises from a situation of subordination which is not confined to women. She cites studies of ethnic groups, and in particular, African-Americans, that support this thesis: "regardless of sex, individuals and groups who occupy subordinate status display a responsive orientation to others characterized by deference, attentiveness, awareness of needs, under-standing of perspectives, moods and intentions, and responsiveness" (ibid.:100). However, she cites examples in which caring occurs outside subordinate statuses. She suggests a more constructive way in which caring may become part of men's behaviors: psychologically as part of a "dynamic autonomy" ... . defined as "an awareness of one's own desires, plans, motives, and viewpoints and those of others ... thinking and acting independently and thinking and acting cooperatively or in relationship with others ... . a person may recognize and accommodate someone needing care without 'losing self'" (ibid.:109). This describes moral, cognitive, and identity development at a mature level, as they are described in Chapter 8. Also, as noted in discussing Gilligan's ideas in Chapter 8, this emphasis on autonomy as a basis for caring may be more acceptable to men.

Wood describes a second means to inculcate caring as a cultural ethic in the chapter, "The Cultural Imperative: Creating a Culture That Values Caring." She outlines a program that includes government actions, inno-vations in business and industry, educational institutions, and parenting, which through "synergetic change" (ibid.:156) could "restructure how our society evaluates and teaches its members to think about caring, men and women, and the essence of public life" (ibid.:157).

The Peckham Experiment in a London suburb previous to World War II (D. Schwartz, 1997:79-81), was an experiment in "retribaliza- tion" and "social network intervention." The experiment began with two physicians who explored why people did *not* become ill: "they made the great leap of going beyond individual factors to examine the character- istics of a community and to try to do something about individual health by focusing on the strength and viability of the community" (ibid.:80). They founded a health center with a range of services, similar to a com- munity center, which encouraged wide interaction among members of the community. They documented the improved health of individuals, and the concept gained attention; ironically, the war intervened, and the experiment was not repeated.

Conclusion

All professions and disciplines concerned with human behavior now recognize that culture must be taken into account and understood. The concept of culture has become politicized as an instrument of change in the past two decades by, e.g., feminists, racial minorities, ethnic groups, and organizations for deaf persons; they have called attention to the vitality and integrity of their own subcultures and have influenced "mainstream" culture. A powerful example of a redefinition of our culture is this indictment:

> What is a rape culture? It is a complex of beliefs that encourages male sexual ag- gression and supports violence against women. It is a society where violence is seen as sexy and sexuality as violent. In a rape culture women perceive a continuum of threatened violence that ranges from sexual remarks to sexual touching to rape itself. A rape culture condones physical and emotional terrorism against women *as the norm.* (Buchwald, Fletcher, and Roth, 1993: vii)

Obviously, changes in our thinking about culture have implications for the human services. "Diversity" has become the key word (sometimes a "buzz" word) in attempting cultural change in order to reflect the experi- ence of less powerful groups and individuals; to reflect the mosaic of cultures that is the United States. Without an awareness of the power and legitimacy of culture, it is very difficult to assist, care for, teach, or learn from anyone whose cultural experience is different from one's own.

The pioneering anthropologists tended to study cultures markedly different from their own; these were so-called "primitive" cultures. Lack of familiarity allowed them a measure of objectivity in reasoning from symbolic behavior to related meanings, but even so, they were frequently confounded by what they observed, or inaccurately inferred meanings derived from their own cultures. Margaret Mead said that her field studies were conducted so that Americans might better understand *themselves*. Some have observed that to be able to see one's own culture, it is first necessary to experience a foreign culture. This is true for the simple reason that one's native culture becomes "normal," "sensible," "natural," and "right." Moreover, *it feels* natural; it feels natural to shake hands, to smile when pleased, to bathe frequently, and to be informal; but, of course, all these conventions are peculiar to particular cultures. An example of cultural misunderstanding is the finger-thumb "OK" sign in America, which is an obscene gesture in Germany. Other examples are that one does not touch the top of another's head (to pat a child, e.g.) in Asian cultures: that is a sacred spot; likewise, one does not show the sole of one's foot to another, in Thailand; that would be an insult.

How one applies the concept of culture depends on one's vantage point, what one is prepared to see, and perhaps most important, the knowledge that is used to interpret one's observations; this book was written with the conviction that systems theory can assist in such interpretation. Visualize the three-dimensional atomic model as a system and then consider the study of culture. If you are within a system, you can see some components well, others less well, and others not at all. If you are outside the system, your perspective may help you better see the "big picture," but the further away you are, the more danger there is of reductionism, oversimplification, and misinterpretation.

To understand best a culture in any of its forms (e.g., a tribal society, an ethnic group, a peer group, or a profession), observers must strive for objectivity if they are themselves components of the system, or strive for involvement if they are outside the system. Social work, nursing, and other professions have increasingly emphasized the need for greater understanding of and greater involvement in the "client system," whether it be family, organization, neighborhood, community, or culture. Internationally, the current relationship of Western societies to Islamic societies is described as a "clash of cultures" (mistakenly, according to many experts, who point to agreement on many values), with disagreement over crucial issues, including art and free speech:

> The Danish newspaper Jyllands-Posten ... said it was defending free speech in 2005 when it printed 12 cartoons of Mohammed, one in a bomb-shaped turban, setting off protests and the torching of Western embassies in several Muslim countries. (Yahoo News, March 14, 2010)

Similarly, disagreement over domestic social issues has been described as a "culture war." The practitioner must understand these issues and the underlying values, in order to be effective.

Suggested Readings

Farb, Peter.
1968 *Man's Rise to Civilization as Shown by the Indians of North America from Primeval Times to the Coming of the Industrial State.* New York: Dutton.
In this very readable book, with its foreboding title, Farb illustrated how cultures evolve.

Hall, Edward T.
1977 *Beyond Culture.* Garden City, NY: Doubleday Anchor.
Hall's synthesis of his own research and the research of others, and his theorizing about culture.

De Kerckhove, Derrick.
1995 *The Skin of Culture: Investigating the New Electronic Reality.* Toronto: Somerville House.
The title is from McLuhan's comment, "In the electric age, we wear all mankind as our skin." His ideas are provocative and, while descended from McLuhan, are perhaps more accessible.

Van Maanen, John,
1988 *Tales of the Field.* Chicago: University of Chicago Press.
A practitioner's guide to methodological and conceptual issues in ethnography, the study of culture in the field. Witty, wise, and useful to the student of cultures. It surveys most of the major works of cultural field studies.

Literary Sources

Curtis, Bruce.
2008 *Like Ordinary People.* East Lansing, MI: Little Stronach Press.
Ostensibly a biography of the author's mother Josephine (1903-2007), this book is a superb example of the intersection and interaction of all the systems discussed in this text. The subtitle, "An Illustrated Iowa Social Biography ..." indicates Dr. Curtis's background as a historian of American culture, and researcher and teacher of gender studies. This is that rare scholarly work written with insight and humor, grounded in the author's personal experience in the region, which he describes with familiarity. It could appropriately be listed after each chapter in this book.

Dorris, Michael.
1987 *A Yellow Raft in Blue Water.* New York: Warner.
A novel of American Indian culture related through the experiences of grandmother, mother, and daughter, who move through life together. Vine Deloria, Jr., said it "shows us the humorous, ironic side of reservation life as it has rarely seen portrayed."

Erdrich, Louise.
1985 *Love Medicine.* Toronto, New York: Bantam.
This is a powerful novel of a complex American Indian family and rich culture, in which meanings become evident only after the fact, in the understandings of others. The stories of some of these characters have been continued in subsequent novels.

Films and Videos

Capitalism: A Love Story. (2009)

Michel Moore's latest jeremiad about the collusion of government and greedy corporations and their assaults on the economy, laid-off employees and their communities, and on foreclosure of people's homes. He proposes an alternative to unbridled capitalism.

The Cutting Edge: Portraits of Southeast Asian Adolescents in Transition (1983)

Portraits of three Asian refugees: Hmong, Vietnamese, and Lao. Each describes scribes the survival of his culture in the new United States setting. Music, instruments, costumes, and rituals are part of the background.

Dreams on Hold (1986)

This documentary examines the growing gap between rich and poor in the United States, and the shrinking middle class. Underemployment and the need for two paychecks in a family are examined. The implications of employment of mothers of young children are discussed.

Farewell to Manzanar (1976; made for television)

Superb portrayal of the internment of Japanese-Americans during World War II. Pictures well their plight as acculturated Issei, Nissei, or Sansei (first, second, or third generation) Americans; their humiliation by their chosen country, and their dignity.

Gandhi (1982)

British and Indian cultures, and the transformation of both by a powerful set of ideas embodied in one person, vividly portrayed. The dramatic events convey well a sense of how cultural change occurred.

Maids and Madams (1986)

Apartheid in South Africa viewed in the relationship of the black household worker and the white employer. More than a million black women were economically bound to such jobs. The psychological battle for dominance was waged in intimate settings in white homes.

Powwow Highway (1989)

A small, unpretentious film that is a gem. Believable characters, plausible plot. A unique film in that contemporary American Indian cultures are presented accurately, sympathetically, and with humor.

The American Future: A History (2009; BBC Worldwide)

This series, presented on public television by Simon Sharma, focuses on four aspects of America's future: water, war, moral fervor, and immigration/cultural issues. The latter hour is revealing about our values and our legislation (prophetic, considering Arizona legislation in 2010 mandating that law enforcement officers examine anyone whom they suspect might be an illegal immigrant).

4

Communities

... when community falls, so must fall all of the things that only community life can engender and protect: the care of the old, the care and education of children, family life, neighborly work, the handing down of memory, the care of the earth, respect for nature and the lives of wild creatures.
—Wendell Berry (quoted in D. Schwartz, 1997)

Under the seeming disorder of the old city ... . is a complex order. Its essence is intimacy of sidewalk use, bringing with it a constant succession of eyes. This order is all composed of movement and change... an intricate ballet in which the individual dancers and ensembles all have distinctive parts which miraculously reinforce each other and compose an orderly whole.
—Jane Jacobs, quoted in Johnson (2001)

Introduction

As a perceptive writer put it, "Yearning for community seems to have become a modern preoccupation. It is as if everyone were thirsty and always dreamed of water" (D. Schwartz, 1997:43). A text on community labeled community a *catachresis,* meaning "there is no literal referent for [it]; that its definition comes apart ... as soon as we begin to articulate it. ... We can neither say what we mean ... nor mean what we say" (Godway and Finn, 1994:2). *Is* community dead?

I. Community as System

Probably the most difficult systems to define with precision are the community and the small group (which will be discussed in Chapter 6). The term *community* has become too common, with broad and vague applications. It is frequently employed to impute commonality of interest to what, in fact, are disparate groups of people, e.g., the "intelligence community," the "community of elders," the "Latino community," and the "faith community." Biological scientists and ecologists refer to the "eco-community." Possession of one common defining quality does not in and of itself form a community. For some, a definition of human community must include nonhuman and nonliving elements as well. Over sixty years ago, conservationist and ecologist Aldo Leopold "proposed enlarging 'the boundaries of the community to include soils, water, plants, animals, or collectively, the land.' The implication of this deceptively simple shift is that humans must change their role from conqueror of the community to citizen" (Lind, 1994:128).

The destruction of much of the city of New Orleans in 2005, and the fouling of the Gulf of Mexico and the adjoining Louisiana coastline in 2010 are both instances in which the conception of an eco-community has been violated. The first violation was the long-time destruction of coastal wetlands which could have ameliorated damage to New Orleans and other coastal communities, and to wildlife, and second violation occurred by either accidental or neglectful drilling practices in the Gulf, which threatened the fishing industry and aquatic wildlife of the Gulf. The effects of these violations will persist for generations, with dire effects on all members of the ecological community.

Both communities and organizations are macrosystems as contrasted with the microsystems of persons, families, and small groups. Both are intermediate (or "mediating") systems between society and the small groupings in which intimate affective transactions occur. Sociology has found it difficult to define and distinguish among community, organization, and society. The major distinction between community and organization, historically, is: "A community is held together by feeling and sentiment, primarily, while an organization is sustained by 'rational' considerations, usually explicit in formal contracts, usually written" (Tönnies, 1957). Edith Stein similarly said, "The community is not founded or produced by an act of free will like [an organization], which is convened or disbanded at will ... The community grows out of the life of a group of individuals " (Calcagno, 2007:39).

Because the community is at the interface between society and microsystems, it is of concern to all social disciplines and professions. The family is a person's primary field of interaction during childhood; in adulthood, the other major field of interaction is community, or at least significant sectors of community. Such sectors include the financial, commercial, religious, educational, social, and legal institutions in which the person participates. Community is simultaneously a subsystem (or component) of society and *is* a society itself. To the individual, the community represents the culture and shapes persons' lives; in turn, community is affected by individual persons who can change the community. Consistent with our stance on adaptation and accommodation (Chapter 2), we place importance upon mutual causation here; the citizen and the community influence each other with family, small group, and organizations as intermediaries.

A. Kinds of Communities

Communities differ in several respects. First, Tönnies described them as being held together by two sorts of bonds—*gemeinschaft* and *gesellschaft*. A *gemeinschaft* community is characterized by implicit bonds that relate all community members to the others. These bonds include common values and beliefs, mutual interdependence, respect, and a shared sense of status hierarchy. Symbols may indicate these shared ties: for example, the United States flag, which symbolizes patriotism and common values (note, e.g., how many automobile dealerships display multiple flags). Rules regarding relationships are not formalized but rest in cultural traditions and complementary social expectations rather than written codes or contracts. An American Indian tribal community may be an example, in that behavior often is greatly influenced by tradition and culture; however as tribes have "modernized," they too have become somewhat more formalized with Reservation Business Committees (as required in the federal 1934 Indian Reorganization Act) and parliamentary structures. Yet, there remains for many a *gemeinschaft* feeling of place, such as for Roland Lussier, who wrote this as a sixth-grader in Northern Minnesota:

> There is no place better than the Indian reservation. It's so beautiful, the land is covered with dark green pine trees and other kinds of trees. At dawn we can watch the sun, and we will see beautiful colors around the sun. We are proud of our reservation and we thank God for giving it to us. (Brill, 1974:56)

A *gesellschaft* community is characterized by bonds that are both formal and specific. Community members relate to each other through formally structured relations within community institutions such as work organizations, professions, schools, courts, and civic organizations.

A second way that communities differ from one another is in the degree of attachment to a specific location. This variable can also be used to determine specific types of communities, but the reader should keep in mind that these categories, like all typologies, are ideal and not real. In reality, attachment to place or location is more or less present in all communities. Tönnies described *place* and *nonplace* communities:

1. *Place communities.* Tönnies also called this kind of community a "locality." One form of community organization has been called "locality development" (Cox et al., 1987). This type of community has also been called a geographic or spatial community. It is based upon a common habitat and occupation of adjacent (or nearby) properties.

Examples of place community are neighborhoods, reservations, villages, and cities, and in some instances, states (often symbolized by sports teams—Go Hawkeyes! Go Ducks!).

2. *Nonplace Communities.* Tönnies also called this community a "mind" community, which "implies only cooperation and coordinated action for a common goal," without reference to "place" (Hillery, 1968:77-78). Examples of nonplace communities include religious communities and professions. A spirited debate continues among sociologists as to whether "social networks" are nonplace communities. Are YouTube and Facebook really communities?

Beginning with Barnes's study of the social structure of a fishing community in Norway, researchers have found social networks a fruitful topic of study. His definition of social network is useful:

> Each person is, as it were, in touch with a number of other people, some of whom are in touch with each other and some of whom are not. Similarly each person has a number of friends, and these friends have their own friends; some of any one person's friends know each other, others do not. I find it convenient to talk of a social field of this kind as a network. The image I have is of a set of points some of which are joined by lines. The points of the image are people, or sometimes groups, and the lines indicate which people interact with each other. (Barnes, *1954:127*)

The diagrams in Figure 4.1 represent Barnes's ideas. The fact that it was a fishing village may have influenced Barnes's choice of the term network rather than other possible terms, such as "web." In Barnes's view, a network consists of the relationships between pairs of people (or dyads), an atomistic view. Later theorists have applied network concepts to larger social groupings. Barnes's definition is perspectivistic: each person has a unique social network defined by the person's dyadic relationships. In most current usages of the term, social network is synonymous with nonplace community: This is the sense in which it is used in discussing "networking" as a technique for changing the personal and working conditions of women, or for job hunting.

In a social work context, Eilene McIntyre defined a social network as consisting of "a set of people all of whom are linked together, but

Figure 4.1
Diagrams of unbounded networks.

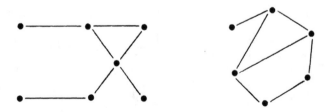

not all of whom know one another. This inclusion of indirect links differentiates a network from a group" (1986:422). All such networks are not necessarily socially desirable. For example, illegal drug distribution is often carried out through such a social network, and organizations such as Al Qaeda are similarly constructed.

Virginia Hine noted the emergence of "segmented, polycephalous, ideological networks" (abbreviated to SPIN), which were loosely organized alliances with bonds based on strongly held ideological bonds (Hine, 1982:4-5), including terrorist organizations. She believed that this was a new form of hierarchical organization; it functioned effectively and did not collapse in the face of opposition. This may be the nature of terrorist cells, such as Al Qaeda. The model she observed has in fact become common in "movement" organizations such as gay rights and feminist associations. E-mail, Facebook, YouTube, and Twitter, e.g., permit distribution of information to large numbers of people simultaneously at low cost, a necessary factor in most such organizations. Such ties are referred to as "loose coupling"; at the same time, observers discuss the "strength of weak ties" in such loose couplings. Our discussions of boundaries in Chapters 1 and 2 are relevant here, in that linkages can be intense for limited periods of time, for specific purposes. This is very similar to the descriptions of women's mutual support groups or networks, in feminist literature. To the extent that they are stable and function as significant environments for their members, such networks qualify as nonplace communities.

3.   *Kinship.* As Tönnies described it, this third kind of community is one in which members have blood relationships. An example might be an American Indian reservation, a barrio, or community as portrayed in the movie, *The Milagro Beanfield War,* or an Amish community. It might also include immigrant groups that, though geographically dispersed in the new country, still support each other; examples include Chinese communities that comprise members in Hong Kong, Vancouver (Canada), and San Francisco, and Vietnamese (or Lao or Hmong) communities that include Los Angeles, Minneapolis-St. Paul, the Philippines, and Vietnam. It is common for more affluent members of such communities to remit money to their less prosperous relatives in the "home" country (e.g., Jamaica, Cuba, Haiti, or Mexico). Barnes's definition of social network includes both a "networking," goal-oriented social system (which might also be viewed as a loose-knit organization) and kinship networks.

As mentioned, these categories are not exclusive. Nonplace communities and social networks have some geographic connection, even though members may never convene in one location at one time (indeed, cannot, in the case of refugees and those left behind) and do not consider physical location to be a primary or constant factor. For instance, the "academic community" does not reside in a single location, although it does have ties to college campuses. Similarly, the "scientific community" and the "medical community" have ties to laboratories and other research facilities. A "community of believers" usually has connections with temples, synagogues, churches, or shrines, but exists independent of these, as well.

Other examples of nonplace communities, such as the traditional occupation of barbering, are protected from intrusion by custom or by law, as symbolized by the striped pole and the barber's license. Another example is the academic community's jealous protection of academic freedom, as when a professor went to jail rather than reveal a secret vote on whether to give another professor tenure. Academic freedom, also, is a highly abstract and symbolic territory that some persons will defend with their liberty, if not their lives. It is not unusual for reporters to choose jail rather than revealing the names of their informants. In some cases, they risk their lives to preserve freedom of information—see the movie "Veronica Guerin," based on a real reporter killed in Ireland in 1996; the deaths of reporters who are targeted by drug gangs on the Mexican-U.S. border; Judith Miller of the New York Times, who spent two and a half months in jail; or the movie "Nothing But The Truth" (2008) a fictional depiction in which a female reporter sacrifices her professional life, and her family, for the same principle.

A third way in which communities differ is in the breadth of activities, interests, and needs that they encompass. The place community encompasses virtually all human interests and needs; the nonplace community is usually concerned with one, or few, of these. Almost every kind of human activity, in one form or another, is to be found in Chicago, for example, or nearly any city or small town, while the nonplace "business community" or "academic community" concerns itself with a narrower range of interests and needs, even though members are widely dispersed.

II. Definition of Community

We suggest the following composite definition. Community is a population whose members:

1. consciously identify with each other,
2. occupy common territory,
3. engage in common activities, and

4. have some form of organization that provides for differentiation of functions, which allows the community to adapt to its environment, thereby meeting the needs of its components.

Its components include the persons, groups, families, and organizations within its population and the institutions it forms to meet its needs. Its environment is the society in which its exists and to which it adapts (and which it also modifies) by energy exchange, and other communities and organizations outside itself that impinge upon its functioning. We discuss the energy functions in the following section.

A. Energy Functions

1. *For Components/Subsystems.* The functions the community performs include the maintenance of a way of life or culture (in the second usage of "culture" in Chapter 3). Wallace Stegner described this in *Where the Bluebird Sings to the Lemonade Springs:*

> A place is not a place until people have been born in it, have grown up in it, lived in it, known it, died in it—have both experienced and shaped it, as individuals, families, neighborhoods and communities, over more than one generation. Some are born in their place, some find it, some realize after long searching that the place they left is the one they have been searching for. (1992:201)

Another important function is the satisfaction of common needs, interests, and ambitions. A striking example of the recognition of common interests and needs was Malcolm X's redefinition of the community to which he belonged. He found common interests and needs unexpectedly in a new community:

> That morning was when I first began to reappraise the "white man." It was when I first began to perceive that "white man," as commonly used, means complexion only secondarily; primarily it described attitudes and actions toward the black man, and toward all other nonwhite men. But in the Muslim world, I had seen that men with white complexions were more genuinely brotherly than anyone else had ever been.
> That morning was the start of a radical alteration in my whole outlook about "white" men. (Malcolm X, 1966:333-334)

Further, the members of a community must be aware of its "we-ness"; There must be a social consciousness or "sense of community." This assists the community to meet the social identity needs of the persons who are its components. The community must provide for them opportunities to engage in personal growth, similar to Erikson's description of ego identity (see Chapter 8).

Erik Erikson and Karen Homey, both psychoanalysts, and Harry Stack Sullivan, a social psychiatrist, recognized the importance of the social environment, including the community, in providing a milieu for the evolution of the person. They were a distinct minority among early psychoanalytic theorists in the importance they placed upon the social environment.

Many communities are unable to provide opportunities to develop work identities because of lack of jobs. The national unemployment rate in the spring of 2010, was 9.5-10 percent; some areas were higher (see discussion in Chapter 3, Culture). While some social theorists and policymakers accept this as an inherent risk in a capitalist industrial society, others regard this as unjustified damage to the community as a system and to its members. Michael Moore's film, "Roger and Me" (1989) detailed the devastating effects of unemployment on workers in Flint, Michigan. Many communities in the "Rust Belt," from Michigan to Pennsylvania, seem permanently damaged.

We do not yet know the effects of such failure by society and the community to provide adequately for their members' identity needs, although the effects of previous economic depressions are known to some degree. Some suggest that we now see the effects of economic marginality in a rise in violent criminal behavior (though that may not be true in the current negative economic situation), and in the institutionalization of an illicit drug trade whose participants number in the hundreds of thousands. Some writers suggest that the effect of such societal neglect may be to produce severely alienated persons and groups who turn to authoritarian ideologies for security and as a means of participation in some form of community. This may, e.g., be related to the arrest, in April 2010, of a group of "militants" in Michigan who stated they wanted to start an insurrection against the government, starting with the killing of policemen. Erich Fromm, Hannah Arendt, and other writers on "alienation" stated strongly that such alienated groups are breeding grounds for fascism (Arendt, 1962; Fromm, 1942, 1955; Giner, 1976:138-144). The burgeoning of paramilitary militia groups in the United States, and violent incidents such as the Oklahoma City bombing of a federal building may reflect a societal turn toward absolutist, extremist, or anarchist ideologies.

Other components such as families, organizations, and groups must also be able to identify with and find common cause with the community's way of life in order that their energies may be used to meet the community's needs, Alexis de Tocqueville, the French nobleman who so accurately described the United States and its future in 1831, identified three characteristics of community groups who came together to solve problems they held in common: "First, they were groups of citizens who decided they had the power to decide what was a problem. Second, they decided they had the power to decide how to solve the problem. Third, they often decided that they would themselves become the key actors in implementing the solution" (McKnight, 1995:117).

The term *common cause* was adopted as the name of a national citizen's action organization that explicitly recognizes the necessity to involve citizens and to draw upon their energies. This organization mobilizes energy in the form of funds and lobbying activity from its citizen-members to attain agreed-upon goals. It meets the definition of a system, specifically a social network, or nonplace community, in this respect; its website illustrates a contemporary means of linkage of such nonplace communities.

2. *For Environment/Suprasystems.* A community must also meet the needs of its environment in order to survive. It is clear from "central place" theory in geography and economics that place communities function as parts of hierarchical, relatively stable economic and political systems, and that alterations in one community affect other parts of the region as well. The rise of Chicago ("that toddlin' town, the town that Billy Sunday could not shut down") as a major industrial and railroad center affected the commercial and social development of communities within its region. It became, as poet and historian Carl Sandburg put it,

> Hog butcher for the World,
> Tool maker, Stacker of Wheat,
> Player with Railroads and the Nation's Freight Handler.
> (Sandburg (1955:442-443)

Smaller communities nearby adapted, sometimes unwillingly, to Chicago's emergence as a trade center, both supplying and being supplied by Chicago's services and industries. Communities unsuited to adapt to new economic and transportation networks, or unable to compete with new centers of power, declined or ceased to exist.

> Clearly, the pace of modernization in rural Jefferson County, and in Iowa generally, depended not only upon time, but upon place as well. Like thousands of little settlements in Iowa and nationwide, County Line was a temporary town, at the mercy of an ever-changing economy. (Curtis, 2008:126)

In the American West in the last few decades, "boom towns" arose as the demand for minerals or new sources for oil increased; some have failed to prosper; "boom and bust" cycles have been common for high technology areas, such as "Silicon Valley," as well.

Religious communities, as examples of nonplace community, have also been confronted with the need to adapt to their environment. Within the Roman Catholic church, some orders that formerly were relatively removed from society have become socially active, performing less specifically religious tasks, such as teaching and social service. A few orders have disbanded as their members have returned to lay status, some members in order to marry and others to carry on secular work as part of their religious commitment. The Roman Catholic "community," however, maintains some clear boundaries. Priests and nuns are still forbidden to marry (except when released from their vows), and procreation is still defined as the purpose of marriage. In another example of boundary-setting, the pope banned priests from holding elective office, which caused strong reactions from some Latin American priests who subscribed to Liberation Theology, which calls upon priests to participate in the civil community to fulfill their responsibilities in the religious community. In 2010, the boundaries of the church are being tested as government and lay persons protest the Church's (and the Pope's) alleged failures to discipline some priests who molested children.

The history of Utopian communities is replete with examples of those who attempted to isolate themselves from the social environment and thrive as closed systems, unsuccessfully. Without energy exchange with the environment, a system is certain to become entropic and die. Amish communities in Pennsylvania, Indiana, Iowa, and other states have survived by maintaining energy exchange with the environment in certain carefully limited ways; this is an excellent illustration of boundaries that are relatively more closed than other communities but still open to exchanges of energy.

American Indian reservations are examples of communities that were excluded from the general society and experienced entropy. In recent years, economic and social development by the tribes (in part funded by casinos operated by about a quarter of the tribes) have opened the boundaries somewhat. While "white" society may wish to remove the boundaries entirely (through "assimilation" or relocation policies, particularly in the 1950s), American Indians have consciously encouraged maintenance of open, but clearly recognizable, cultural boundaries (e.g., reintroducing their traditional language to both adults and children), especially during the past half-century. From a systems perspective, the assimilation policy was unworkable because it would have required only the Indian societies to accommodate (to change their *schemas*—see Chapter 8), after which white society would assimilate them. A systems perspective would indicate that mutual accommodation would be necessary, and each culture would have to both *accommodate* and *assimilate*. The Indian Child Welfare Act of 1978 is an example of accommodation by the larger society, by recognizing the historic treaty rights of tribes as sovereign nations, with the corollary right to control adoptions and foster care placements of their children.

In general, the functions that a community performs for its environment are the energy functions described in Chapter 1, *giving, getting, and conserving* energy. The community supplies energy to its environment and its components in the form of persons and products to be used by those systems. For example, a community may supply students for higher education who become leaders while also supplying political support for organizations outside the community and taxes for state and national governments.

President Reagan's "new federalism" explicitly stated that communities and states were required to supply too much of their resources to their suprasystem, the federal government, handicapping their efforts to meet the communities' own needs and those of its components: organizations, families, and persons. President Reagan, both Bush presidents, and President Clinton agreed in principle that too much has been taken by an overgrown federal bureaucracy. However, in the opinion of many liberals (reinforced in part by the economic downturn of 2007-2010), only the federal government can be trusted to redistribute these resources equitably because communities and states are more vulnerable to pressure groups and more likely to deny resources to the powerless and disadvantaged. This liberal-conservative debate will continue for the foreseeable future; it illustrates the need for an energy exchange that meets the needs of each, among suprasystem, system, and components, if all system levels are to function satisfactorily. A large part of the debate also, of course, is over the definition of "satisfactory" functioning, and which functions should be performed at what system levels. It seems likely that the community system will be the arena in which a great deal of this controversy will occur during the new century. President Obama's experience as a community organizer in Chicago will, no doubt, provide a distinct perception of the needs and resources of communities. His approach to the health insurance legislation passed in 2010, creating state-based insurance pools, seems to be a middle road between the two polar positions.

B. Aspects of Community Systems

1. *Evolutionary Aspects.* The first cities were burial places to which wandering tribes returned at certain times to perform ceremonies that ensured the stability of the universe. From that symbolic beginning, place communities evolved to encompass all human needs and functions. Max Weber contended that the city had its genesis in the market. Thus, a city is a settlement with a resident population that regularly satisfies economic and social (including spiritual) needs for energy exchange through the device of a local market. We could combine these speculations by saying that cities began as locations that were sites of seasonal rituals, which became permanent market sites as agriculture evolved.

The character of a particular community is determined by its relationships to other communities and the society within which it exists, by the characteristics of its components, and by its own preceding steady state. The Lynds' Middletown (Muncie, Indiana) evolved toward being a satellite in the regional system of New York City, because decisions about industries were increasingly made outside Middletown (Lynd and Lynd, 1929, 1937). When Theodore Caplow and associates reexamined Middletown fifty years later, they found the major change to be the degree to which the federal government determined economic and social conditions. Increasingly, cities depend upon the federal government for resources to carry out their responsibilities. This has been epitomized by the acceptance of federal "stimulus" funds by local communities and states in 2009 and 2010, and acceptance of funds for construction projects and extension of unemployment benefits. Even some governors and state legislators who oppose stimulus funds, in general, have accepted them as a practical matter of securing resources.

Some believe that microchip technology, most importantly the computer, will enable us to adapt to change, by increased efficiency in use of resources (better planning and development, e.g.), in order to retain the viability of local communities. Transportation, a major concern at the local level, may benefit, e.g., by allowing employees to work at home rather than commute. Federal funding is available to make broadband internet communication more available to rural communities thanks to global satellites. Large numbers of people compose on computers at home, utilize libraries via computer, correspond with workmates in other parts of the country and overseas via e-mail and satellite, and research subjects, many using Google, on the (literally) World Wide Web. McLuhan's (1965) "global village" is a "virtual reality"; another way to describe it would be a nonplace or "mind community."

How a sense of community will be maintained in what observers call "mass society" is not clear; some are optimistic that such communication will enhance individuality, rather than detract from it.

Divisions of social class or status, ethnic or racial heritage, religion, or ideology continue to frustrate efforts to strengthen a sense of "the commons" shared by all inhabitants. The shape taken by cities of the future is being determined by the experiences and crises in cities today. Many wonder whether the continuing exodus from central cities to the suburbs is a permanent trend, especially given a potential long-term shortage in petroleum fuels. Like other systems, cities are subject to multiple factors that influence growth and decline.

Today, ghost towns that were formerly company-owned mining camps (one of the authors was born in one), small farming villages, or fishing villages attest to the alternative of disintegration for the community that does not have, or does not use, resources to adapt. Currently, in both Canada and the United States, the future of the family farm is in doubt. According to a member of Congress, "In North Dakota and parts of northern Minnesota, it is feared up to *half* the farmers will close their operations. The "ag" sector is a vital part of our region's economy, not just for farming families, but for residents of our towns as well" (Minge, 1998). The Midwest lost 3 percent of its population in the first half of the 1980s. In the eighties, half the small-town gas stations in Iowa closed; nationally, over 150 hospitals in small towns closed, and at least that many more were threatened; smaller school districts closed throughout rural areas. In the economic crisis of 2007-2010, many smaller banks failed. Churches closed; retail stores were replaced by shopping malls, Wal-Mart, Shopko, Costco, and K-Mart. A farmer in Saskatchewan, Canada, told a researcher:

> Tell the people that they're going to have to start supporting the family farm. Make sure you put *family* farm in there. We don't want corporate farms. Co-ops are okay but we don't want huge corporations in here. Let the families stay out there. We want the community to stay there. (Lind, 1994:120)

Harry Caudill's classic book, *Night Comes to the Cumberlands* (1963), painfully illustrated the process by which rural Appalachian communities became the lowest level in a hierarchy of industrial power, subject to decisions made by corporations in Pittsburgh, Detroit, and New York. Many communities have turned to tourism as a major source of revenue (e.g., Central City, Colorado; Bayfield, Wisconsin; Gatlinburg, Tennessee; Victoria, British Columbia; Kyoto, Japan; and Beijing and Shanghai, China). Las Vegas, Nevada, was founded as a tourist location.

Still other localities are seeking survival through developing a "retirement industry," specializing in housing, goods, and services for the expanding population of active elders. The same principle of adaptation applies to nonplace communities. Certainly the history of Christian and Muslim sects or denominations illustrates the evolutionary process of such nonplace communities.

2. *Structural Aspects*

a. *Boundaries.* The boundaries that separate communities from larger and smaller social units—the so-called vertical hierarchy—are often difficult to establish precisely. Minnesota's Red Lake Reservation is, by United States treaty law, a sovereign nation. For a time, visitors to the reservation were (formally) required to have a Red Lake passport to enter legally. As one entered the reservation, one encountered signs like this:

> Warning. This is Indian land. No trespassing. No fishing, hunting, camping, berry picking, peddling or soliciting without authorized permit from Red Lake Tribal Council Office. Violators and trespassers will be prosecuted under Federal Law 86-634. (Brill, 1974:22)

In some communities, the internal structure may comprise relatively autonomous bodies such as corporations that function as private, independent governments. Rochester, New York, is the home of Eastman Kodak; Detroit to Ford, General Motors, and Chrysler; "silicon valley" to high-tech industries in California; Rochester, Minnesota, to the Mayo Clinic and hospital; and Redmond, Washington, to the Microsoft Corporation. Whether federal intervention in the form of "bailouts" will curtail the autonomy of some of these "mega-corporations" remains to be seen, but the power of communities to influence these corporations are not likely to increase. Corporations can move; cities cannot.

Boundaries within the community include those between institutions that differentiate tasks. These horizontal boundaries include, for example, the uniform worn and the choice of specific colors and tasks. Firefighters' gear is adapted to their task, but it also distinguishes them from police. Their distinctive gear says, "We fight fires. We don't baptize children with our hoses, pick up garbage with our trucks, or fight off mobs with our axes and poles!"

Sometimes the boundaries between differentiated institutions are not so clear: Are parochial schools entitled to public funds? Should schools provide sex education? Should police conduct drug education programs? Should health clinics perform AIDS testing and should they be required to report the results to state or federal agencies? These continue to be controversial questions in many communities.

b. Institutions. The differentiation of functions through the assignment of functions to specialized subsystems leads to the emergence of institutions within communities. Such institutions usually originate in several communities in slightly different forms. Since the community is a holon between society and microsystems such as families and ethnic groups, it contains fundamental system processes such as socialization and social control, embodied in religious institutions, schools, and police; these institutions are prescribed in modern, industrialized cultures. The form the institution takes in a particular community depends upon the community's components, its previous steady states, and its environment (an institution is a holon also). Our society prescribes that education shall be performed by formal schools (with the notable exception of home schooling), but the form of the school varies from community to community. It may be a one-room country school or an urban elementary school; it may be single-sex or coed, private or public, and may be a "magnet" or "charter" school. The mode of instruction may be the Montessori method or the traditional "3 Rs"; the instructional equipment may be slate blackboards or satellite television and lasers.

Certain communities evolve distinctive institutions. Pine Mountain Settlement School in Kentucky began the "Little School," a forerunner of the national Head Start program. Significant portions of the War on Poverty of the 1960s were modeled on the Mobilization for Youth program in New York City; hot lines and youth crisis centers originated in a number of cities at about the same time; in California, Berkeley's Shanti Project was a model for services to AIDS patients. Internationally, several Austrian communities are known for their Children's Villages, a unique response to the need to care for orphans. The process originates as a recognized need that is unmet by existing institutions; the community (or some influential component) differentiates a new institution to incorporate the new service.

Some institutions almost escape our notice because they exist in most communities, but their functions are overlooked. Examples are taverns or bars (pubs are more visible in British and Irish communities), e.g., Small's Bar, which Malcolm X protected by confessing; this was an important institution in Harlem's social structure, as were the nightclubs Malcolm frequented. Think of bars as settings for radio and television shows, e.g., "Cheers" (based on an actual bar in Boston) and "How I Met Your Mother." The laundromat serves a socializing function in many neighborhoods. Restaurants and coffee bars (now including McDonald's) serve a similar function, as portrayed on television series such as "Friends," "Frasier," and "Seinfeld." One author points out, "In the eighteenth century, some of the most basic discussions about the formation of the government of the United States and its Constitution occurred in inns and taverns" (McKnight, 1995:118). In eighteenth-century England, penny newspapers, made available in coffeehouses, were the first mass news organs.

Community institutions pose special challenges, as well as support, to social workers and other professionals acting as change agents, because institutions are social systems and seek to maintain themselves. This may be done by modifying structure and function to better fulfill community needs (*morphogenesis*). However, as systems, they also seek to remain the same (*morphostasis*). Thus, institutional provisions generally lag in meeting emergent community needs. As Thorstein Veblen wrote in 1899, "This process of selective adaptation can never catch up with the progressively changing situation in which the community finds itself at any given time" (Boguslaw, 1965:150-151).

c. Social class and caste. Studies of social stratification have substantiated social class or status groupings in most communities. Hollingshead's *Elmtown's Youth* is among the most ingenious of these studies and has been a fountainhead for other community studies. Differentiating characteristics found by researchers are income, life-style, and access to services. The recent history of the United States indicates a widening gap in income (and presumably in social class). In 2007, the median household income was slightly over $50,000. The top 2 percent had incomes over $250,000. The top 6.4 percent received one-third of all income. The top 20 percent received half of all income. The middle-class maintained its position by having two income-earners.

As noted in Chapter 3, communities differ in their cultures. Diagrams of class structure (or, more usually, socioeconomic status) vary from a diamond-shaped structure, with most persons in the middle class, to an extreme pyramidal structure, with either very few poor in some wealthy suburban communities or very few wealthy in some Appalachian communities (see Figure 4.2).

Another differentiation between communities may be that of *caste*. Most would deny that caste exists in the United States. If it is defined as an impermeable boundary, a status assigned by virtue of some characteristic beyond a person's control (e.g., skin color, gender, national origin, or age), it might be an accurate description for the status of some Latinos, Asian-Americans, African-Americans, and American Indians. The election of President Obama in 2008 may signal that such boundaries have become somewhat more permeable in the most recent generations.

Figure 4.2
Diagrams of class structure (1: higher, 2: middle, 3: lower socio-economic class).

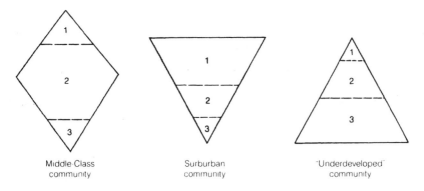

Middle-Class   Surburban   "Underdeveloped"
community   community   community

d. Social networks. We have placed this discussion of social networks between the sections on structural aspects and behavioral aspects of community systems because in reality it is difficult to describe social networks.

Some theorists maintain that neighborhoods are simply social networks that have a base in a particular locality. Opposing theorists maintain that neighborhoods are not synonymous with social networks and have different dynamics. The opposing positions are similar to the distinctions between place and non-place communities—that is, must a community (or a social network) be based in a particular location? One test of the answer is whether computer "bulletin boards," Facebook, YouTube, or other networks through which people exchange information can be considered real networks; the important criteria being the significance the exchanges have to the participants, the breadth of the content of the messages (especially whether content is personal), and duration of the relationship.

Social networking has become popular as a vehicle for "consciousness raising" among disadvantaged populations such as women, gays and lesbians, and racial or ethnic minorities. Such networks emphasize awareness of commonality among the members and often stimulate awareness of their disadvantaged status and the societal dynamics that underlie it. Further, the network provides support (the networks are often called "support groups") to members that consists of both emotional support and suggestions for immediate action. The "Move On" organization has been very effective politically in promoting liberal causes, through online communication, fund-raising, and advocacy; it has been emulated by other networking organizations. Support groups for rape and assault victims, and feminist groups in general fit this description.

3. *Behavioral Aspects*

a. *Social control.* The purpose of social control is to maintain the system, not necessarily the status quo. Values and goals may be maintained by a community's network of institutions; these may act on behalf of the entire community or on behalf of some group or special interest. In nonplace communities, control may be exerted by formal or informal sanctions. In nursing or teaching, e.g., sanctions may include loss of professional license, or the employer may be sanctioned so that no member of the profession may work for that employer.

Persons in a community may hold interlocking positions: the same family may be represented on the library board, the zoning commission, the board of directors of a bank, and operate a large business. This may lessen centralized control, or may increase it. Lynds' *Middletown* study found that commercial leaders had a great deal of social control; Caplow and his associates (1982) found the same fifty years later.

A related aspect is "community power." Hunter's *Community Power Structure* (1953) found that the most powerful persons in Atlanta were heads of large commercial enterprises, e.g., banking and finance. Other leaders included professional men and a few officers of government and labor unions. A small number among the persons who were identified made up the "power elite."

Domhoff and Dye (1987) summarized three methods by which the networks of community power structures can be constructed—the positional, the reputational, and the decisional.

> A Positional analysis uses printed public information available in libraries and other archives to establish the leadership interlocks among profit, nonprofit, and governmental agencies. ... A Reputational study ... is based upon the personal opinions of a wide range of people who are interviewed about who the key people and organizations in the power structure are. ... A Decisional mapping of a power structure is based on case studies of the people, organizations, and pressure groups. ... In effect all three methods generate a list of people and their connections. ... (Domhoff and Dye, 1987:9-12)

Community researchers have described models of decision-making that range from the bureaucratic, pyramid model in which decisions were made "at the top," to "mutual adaptation" models in which decisions were made by consensus in a participatory, decentralized fashion. These two models are related to the argument between "elite" and "pluralist" theorists. In these decision-making studies, it was found that the political subsystems played important, but not necessarily dominant roles. Instead, decisions were made by informal or private subsystems differentiated by social class, organizational position, or the kind of institution being represented. The informal decision-making structure was often as influential, or more so, than the formal (including political) structures.

  b. Socialization. Socialization is essential to the life of a community. If new members are not socialized into the community to supply new energy (*negentropy*), it becomes entropic. Acculturating the newcomer is often a community concern. Some communities have attempted to socialize nonconformist subcommunities that reject established community values, specifically norms of productivity, health, and dress, or perhaps ethnic or racial characteristics. In the face of such "deviations," communities attempt to apply social control in the form of jail sentences, compulsory socialization (e.g., enforcing truancy laws or mandatory work programs for welfare recipients), expulsion or simply avoidance or social isolation. Expulsion took the form of "warning out" as early as the sixteenth century in England and was perpetuated in the United States. Persons likely to become recipients of public assistance were told to leave the county.

  New institutions arise to perform new functions, just as public schools were created to socialize millions of European immigrants and Project Headstart was intended, in part, to socialize racial minorities. In Vancouver, British Columbia, e.g., new organizations, funded by the Canadian government, were created to socialize immigrants, particularly refugees, who entered the society and who now constitute significant minority populations in Canada's largest cities. Their presence has added to the rich diversity of the Canadian population.

  There are less formal means of socialization: parades and Fourth of July or Victoria Day celebrations socialize citizens into wider patriotic values. Formal ceremonies may mark induction to the community: the Jewish Bar or Bat Mitzvah, Christian baptism, freshman hazing, the "hooding" of new Ph.D.s, and naturalization ceremonies are examples. Such rites of passage symbolize the socialization of a person into a new status within a system. Another example is drumming and singing in Ojibway (Chippewa or Anishinabe) culture.

> A small boy may grow up standing at the edge of the drum circle. A circle of three or more intense, somber, sweating men. … There are times, in the afternoon or early in the evening, when a young boy may be permitted to kneel between the men and beat on the metal edge of the drum with a stick. Then one day when it is time, he will have the courage and the confidence to drum on the white surface, straighten his body, lean forward, and make the sound. It is time to become a man. (Brill, 1974:82)

Social networks can be highly significant in socialization in organizations and communities. Newcomers usually find that the most important task is to join a social network that reliably describes the norms, mores, and sanctions of the system. Everyone who has entered a new school, new job, or new community, or who has changed status within a system can probably remember the process of finding such a network (or failing to find one). Junior high school and high school are legendary settings for such transitions; stuffing freshmen into lockers, or hazings still occur, though less frequently, perhaps, than in past generations.

As noted earlier in this chapter, networks function as sources of information and as efficient distributors of information. Nonmembers of networks often have less information than members of the network about matters that are equally important to both. Networks are typically more fluid and have fewer fixed roles than groups, organizations, or communities; thus, it may be easier to fit into a network and both to give and get energy (in the form of information). Networks often serve as "welcome wagons," assisting newcomers to find niches for themselves in new systems and to learn the "lay of the land." Networks are less demanding than organizations or institutions, since they are partial and cannot offer either a full set of societal roles or complete roles. As illustrated in Chapter 6, "Groups," centrality in the flow of information is often synonymous with leadership roles; thus networks are often the "farm teams" or "out-of-town tryouts" for more established systems. On occasion, a network functions as the embryo of a developing system in which network participants are the charter members. This has been the pattern for organizations that socialize, develop, and induct women into leadership roles in their communities, e.g., Junior League, university women's clubs, women's health clinics, and Children's Defense Fund. United Way and Chambers of Commerce, along with community organizations such as Rotary are a common training ground for the socialization of community leaders of both genders. The Masonic Lodge and the Knights of Columbus also perform such functions for their members and communities.

c. Communication. Communication is a highly important aspect of system behavior in communities. Certainly, institutions such as churches, businesses, and schools carry on some communication, but both inside and outside these institutions, the most frequent and significant communication activities occur between persons face-to-face and through public media such as newspapers, television, radio and, increasingly, the internet. In early British, American, and some Sioux (Dakota and Lakota) communities, this function was performed by the town crier or its equivalent. Billboards, soapboxes (more common in England than the U.S.), loudspeakers, sirens, pamphlets, classified advertisements, and targeted internet ads and e-mails are all means of communication used and controlled by segments of the community to impart symbols of the community's way of life. In contrast, bumper stickers, T-shirts, stylized hand movements by gang members, and cell phones in automobiles tend to be communication devices used for individual expression.

As philosopher and educational reformer John Dewey suggested, "The essence of community is communication, for without communication there cannot be that interaction by which common meanings, common life, and common values are established" (quoted in Ross, 1955). Communication is one form of energy exchange; it is a vital process, and cannot occur if components are isolated or are unable to interact. The result would be entropy or disintegration.

Social networks, discussed earlier, have communication as their major function. They have both *instrumental* (goal-oriented) and *affective* (emotional) functions, but networks perform primarily as conveyors of information, rather than suppliers of material needs or intermediary systems that negotiate survival. That is, social networks identify groups, families, neighborhoods, or even communities within which primary needs can be met; but the networks themselves do not meet the primary needs. However, to the extent that a network evolves a culture in which members do meet each others' needs (e.g., a women's group in which members become "family" to each other), it may *become* a system, better identified as a group, organization, or (in the sense we use it later) a family. This distinction may seem minor, but it is necessary to clarify focal systems and whether or not something is a system. In this respect, a network may be seen as an interlocking set of roles with relatively specific functions, compared to groups or communities that are broader in their functions. In other words, social networks resemble groups and communities in some respects while resembling organizations in other respects.

C. Professions as Nonplace Communities

An established profession claims for itself, and is recognized by society as having, responsibility for a symbolic territory or domain. Almost by definition, when a group carves out for itself a societal function or some part of the society's stock of ideas, it becomes established as a profession or licensed trade. When the societal function of instructing the young was delegated to and assumed by teachers, the next logical step was the formation and protection of territory by professional teachers' organizations. The same is true of medicine, nursing, law, and the clergy, the so-called classic professions. It can be said as well of social work, a "newer" profession.

The major commonality among the professions is that they are formally legitimated by society to bring about change that is beneficial to the society and its components, as well as to maintain the society. Despite their seeming conservatism on occasion, professions do promote change as well as maintenance. If a profession refused to allow change, that could be harmful to a society and could signal that the profession might lose its societal sanction. An example might be a refusal by physicians to accept changes in the provision of care to elderly or the poor, to defend their incomes; a refusal of college professors to accept public accountability through evaluation of their performances, or pharmacists' refusal to sell means of birth control, for religious or moral reasons.

Professional licensure symbolizes societal acceptance and sanction for a professional territory: "Each profession has a specific or core function and in a sense holds a monopoly on this function. ... However each profession shares with all other professions in society what Hiltner called a 'village green,' a common area that is peripheral to each profession" (Boehm, 1965:642). Clearly, social work, nursing, psychiatry, education and law enforcement, among other professions, share a village green that is socialization and social control.

Historically, social work has concerned itself more with change among microsystems (persons, families, and small groups) than with change among macrosystems (organizations, communities, and society), but it has dealt with societal and community change as well, although these arenas have also been the domains of other professional groups such as political scientists and sociologists. Social work has enlarged its territorial claims in the past half-century, and boundary disputes between professions within the same institution are common. Examples are social work and law within the juvenile court, social work and psychology in mental health institutions, and social work and educators in schools. There are boundary disputes between home economists and family counselors, between nurses and physicians' assistants, and between teachers, guidance counselors, and school psychologists.

There are other characteristics of community that distinguish a profession: a common system of values and ethics (way of life, or culture), a group identity that holds the allegiance of the members, and social control and socialization within the profession. All of these characterize professions as nonplace communities. The most accurate way to define a profession may well be to define it as a social network, that is, a set of interlocking roles organized for relatively specific goals that are set within expressly stated, idealized goals of "service to society" and the sanctity of the persons being served. Professions are organized for specific purposes, with limited bonds between members, and are largely dependent upon affiliations between a limited number of members who are loosely connected to some larger system (looser, presumably, than their connections to family or friends). Professions often lack a sense of "community" that is sufficient to mobilize their members to joint action, and usually resemble organizations as much as communities. Some professions exercise a significant degree of social control typical of organizations, with power to disbar or "defrock" practitioners; but do so only rarely. Most professions have relatively weak powers of enforcement.

III. The Community in Critical Condition

The community is the subject for sharp (and productive) debate, and the outcome of the debate is crucial for community theory. It can be viewed in systems terms as a systems crisis, with two fundamental systems questions to be answered: (1) What is the focal system: the society, the community, the family, or the person? (2) What should be the relationships of subsystems to the community; what should be the balance among them?

There is general agreement that communities in the United States are threatened, and many are in decline, or defunct: "Gloomy tendencies toward social entropy are all too visible in wide areas of American life today" (Sullivan, 1995:180). Observers blame many factors. Harvard's Robert Putnam and his associates studied local communities in Italy; they found that the communities that thrive are "civic" communities, with strong traditions of citizen participation and vital subsystems in which residents are deeply involved, including choral groups. In "The Strange Disappearance of Civic America," Putnam isolated the factor most responsible for the decline of community:

> The culprit is television. ... Most studies estimate that the average American now watches roughly four hours per day (excluding periods in which television is merely playing in the background). ... TV viewing is strongly and negatively related to social trust and group membership, whereas the same correlations with newspaper reading are positive ... more detailed analysis suggests that heavy TV watching is one important reason *why* less educated people are less engaged in the life of their communities. (Putnam, 1996:46-47)

Putnam believes that we should "consider how technology is privatizing our lives ... to ask whether we like the result, and if not, what we might do about it. Those are questions we should, of course, be asking together, not alone" (Putnam, 1996:48; see also Putnam, 1995).

One ideological solution to the problem is offered by *communitarianism,* a philosophy of community that stresses the "social compact" or "social contract" between persons and the society, and the mutual obligations that community members have to each other. "Communitarians think of themselves as searching for solutions that go beyond both the market and the state" (Wolfe, 1995:128). Communitarianism attempts to avoid the extreme individualism and lack of social obligation of classic liberalism and, at the same time, to avoid some of the oppressive features of community. This is similar to progressivism, presumably a middle ground between liberal and conservative viewpoints; in general, an approach favored by President Obama.

The communitarian viewpoint is attractive, in that it reestablishes community as the focal system in the effort to bring a sense of belonging to the atomized society of the United States, and to emphasize mutual obligation among its citizens. However, there are three counterpoints to the communitarian conception. First, there is a preoccupation with self in our society; Bellah, *et al.* (1985) described individualism as our society's "first language." Lasch (1979) labeled ours a "culture of narcissism." Lichterman described "personalism" as seeking "self-fulfillment and individualized expression, 'growth' in personal development rather than growth in purely material well-being. ... The self lives with ambivalence towards, and often in tension with, the institutional or communal standards around it" (Lichterman, 1996:6). A feminist critique (Weiss, 1995) maintains that this personalist or individualistic conception is directly at odds with women's experience, which is more commonly characterized by connection to multiple systems and caring, as described in the writings of psychologist Carol Gilligan (1982) and others (see Chapter 8). Second, a feminist critique says that the community espoused by communitarians overlooks the presence of disadvantaged groups, and the effects that recognition of these groups would have on the definition and behavior of communities. Gays and lesbians, for example, often suffer community disapproval (Bawer, 1996; Bull, 1994).

> [C]ommunitarians fail to note that the separated self of liberalism reflects the reality of men more than women [and] may also be more reflective in many Western cultures of those who are white and /or heterosexual than of those who are Black and /or homosexual ... feminists not only recognize a broader range of social forces that influence identities than do communitarians, but they also find that these forces have a deeper impact than is generally acknowledged by communitarians.... (Weiss, 1995:166-167)

Further, according to this critique, the communitarian conception of community neglects the family in its various forms, and in doing so, implies that the heterosexual, patriarchal family is the norm (Weiss, 1995:174). At the same time, children are absent from the census of this community; this is a critical omission, from a feminist viewpoint. They want a redefinition of community that recognizes women's lives and their concerns, including their children, as "public" and not merely "private" issues. One way to put this is that women want a place at the conference table, not just the kitchen table.

A third counterpoint is, "There's little that anybody could find fault with [communitarianism's] basic theme of social responsibility. Its weakness lies not in its intentions, but in its misreading of what is going on in the world. … no amount of moral exhortation can recreate the idealized existence in intimate and familiar connection to a single town or neighborhood" (W. Anderson, 1995). Most Americans are "multilocal," relating to two or more geographic communities: the city in which one works, and the suburb in which one lives, e.g.; or the community in which one lives with a new partner and children, and the community in which one's older children and former partner live.

The Internet has become a "virtual community" for some computer users via "chat rooms," social networking sites such as Facebook and YouTube, as well as one-to-one simultaneous or "time-shifted" conversations. This pseudointimacy sometimes blossoms into face-to-face friendship—or its opposite; there is also the danger to children who are contacted by predators. The "Web" is a powerful tool for activists of all political and ideological persuasions: both liberal and conservative groups mobilize thousands of messages to Congress instantly. A longtime community activist says:

> It's about being able to keep track of government programs and pending legislation. … It's about emailing a message to a Congressperson on Tuesday and getting a response by Wednesday afternoon. It's about creating networks among organizers in their own neighborhoods and communities who go online to maintain contact with each other even when they're not in a position to meet. (E. Schwartz, 1996:176)

Conclusion

A community:

1. is a system intermediate between society and "microsystems";
2. has a consciously identified population characterized by a sense of belonging, that is, it is aware of itself and is part of its members' identities;

3.   is organized and engaged in common pursuits;
4.   has differentiation of functions;
5.   adapts to the environment through energy exchange; and
6.   creates and maintains organizations and institutions to fulfill the needs
      of both subsystems and suprasystems.

To find or keep a place for themselves in a "postmodern world,"
persons and groups of persons seek to create or maintain communities
in many ways. The following perceptive comments appeared in a local
newspaper:

> All these developments create a confusion of new connections, new identifications
> … In an era when communication is no longer rooted in place, sermonizing about
> voting or serving on juries offers no solution. The real question is how to develop
> and sustain lasting ties in the absence of proximity, how to find intimacy in a world
> where borders no longer exist. (W. Anderson, 1995)

Suggested Readings

Fellin, Phillip.
  1995 *The Community and the Social Worker,* second edition. Itasca, IL: Peacock.
      The author uses a systems approach to analyze community and to describe pro-
      cesses within it. The book could be used as a "large-scale" text for this chapter.
Fowler, Robert Booth.
  1991 *The Dance with Community.* Lawrence: University Press of Kansas. Fowler
      identifies the crucial elements of the debates regarding community: feminist, com-
      munitarian, new age thinking, and contemporary Christian ideology. He identifies
      with existentialism: Community is "a calling, a struggle, a journey."
Hardcastle, David A., Stanley Wenocur, and Patricia R. Powers.
  1997 *Community Practice: Theories and Skills for Social Workers.* New York: Oxford
      University Press.
      This is a masterwork, all 450 pages. If it isn't here, you probably don't need to
      know it. Chapter 5 on documenting the life of a community and Chapter 10 on
      using networks are exceptional. Their "Field Force Analysis" of community is
      highly useful.
Putnam, Robert.
  1996 "The Strange Disappearance of Civic America." *American Prospect,* Winter.
      Putnam identifies the sources of the decline of community.
Selznick, Philip.
  1996 "In Search of Community." In *Rooted in the Land,* edited by William Vitek
      and Wes Jackson. New Haven, CT: Yale University Press.
      Selznick, along with Robert Putnam, is an indispensable resource regarding the
      state of community and what may reverse its decline.
Sheehy, Gail.
  2003 *Middletown, America.* New York: Random House.
      Sheehy, a former student of Margaret Mead and author of *Passages* and other
      best-selling books on adult life, interviewed surviving families of persons killed
      in the September 11, 2001 attacks. The setting is the New York City suburb,
      Middletown, New Jersey, the city with the largest number of victims.

Literary Sources

Keillor, Garrison.
  1985 *Lake Wobegon Days*. New York: Viking.
  Created by one of the nation's finest humorists, this fictional community portrays "Midwestern," small-town values subtly and sometimes hilariously. Lake Wobegon is a vehicle for social criticism and profound observations about contemporary America.
Lee, Harper.
  1960. *To Kill a Mockingbird*. Philadelphia: Lippincott.
  Now fifty years old, the novel is truly an "American classic." The interwoven strands of community are seen through the eyes of a young girl. Secrets that bind the townspeople together are gradually revealed. The rigid rules of racism in the southern town are well portrayed. The movie is powerful, but omits subtler aspects of community.

Films and Videos

The Amish: Not to be Modern (1985)
  Rare film of a community that maintains a significant degree of separation from the world. Photographed over four seasons, capturing the daily life of people who preserve rural traditions. Narrated by Amish persons themselves, with four-hundred-year old Amish hymns, handed down orally, as the soundtrack.
High School (1968) and *High School II* (1994)
  Frederick Wiseman's documentaries are always profound and provocative. These two, a generation apart, are revealing studies of community through one of its institutions.
The Hutterites: To Care and Not to Care (1984)
  The Hutterites have preserved a completely communal life-style for nearly five centuries. While they live simply, they employ modern technology such as computers, but not for personal comfort.
The Last Picture Show (1971)
  Set in a small Texas town in the 1950s, it is very well acted. The lives of the residents are interwoven in ways that only gradually reveal themselves. Bittersweet and poignant. The demise of the movie theater is a metaphor for the loss of a *gemeinschaft* way of life in small towns.
Matewan (1988)
  A fictional depiction of life in a mining community. A union organizer enters the community; his methods are a case study of organizing tactics. Portrays elements of community and conflict.
The Milagro Beanfield War (1988)
  Rituals and binding ties in a Mexican-American community are well portrayed in this film, based on the novel. Cultural pride and vitality sustain them in their battle with the large landowners who control the water supply.

5

Organizations

Given the expectation that organizations will take a relatively narrow band of interests and pursue them unremittingly, our reluctance to enshrine organizations as the social and moral centers of the new society may seem more intelligible.
　　　　　　　　　　　　—Scott Adams, *The Dilbert Principle*

So pervasive is the power of the institutions that we have created that they shape not only our preferences, but actually our sense of possibilities.
　　　　　　　　　　　　—David B. Schwartz,Who Cares? Rediscovering Community

Introduction

Modern societies are organizational societies. Human service professionals have been slow to recognize and take this into account in their appraisals of human behavior. We notice the effects that the organizations that employ us have on our practice and our own lives, but tend to overlook the influence that organizations have on the persons we serve. Organizations constitute the fabric that connects the person and the society and have, to a significant degree, replaced communities and families as mediating (or intermediary) institutions in society. Social systems theory enables the reader to appraise and evaluate the influences that organizations have on human behavior (see Oshry, 1995).

The nature of organizations has been insufficiently understood, and even the most knowledgeable organization theorists admit that there is no single definitive theory. However, W. Richard Scott (1998) reviewed theories of organizations, and concluded that there has been substantial change in recent years:

> The structural level of analysis became prominent in the 1960s and continues to be heavily utilized by sociologists. The ecological [systems] level was the last to develop, emerging in the late 1960s, but it is this level that is associated with much of the intellectual excitement and energy that have characterized the field during the past three decades. (W. R. Scott, 1998:16)

We begin with a workable definition of organization. The sociologist Talcott Parsons's statement is clearer than most:

> Organizations are social units (or human groups) deliberately constructed to seek specific goals. Corporations, armies, schools, hospital, churches, and prisons are included; tribes, classes, ethnic groups, friendship groups, and families are excluded. Organizations are characterized by: (1) divisions of labor, power, and communications responsibilities. ... (2) the presence of one or more power centers which control the concerted efforts of the organization and direct them toward its goals .... [and] (3) substitution of personnel. (Parsons, 1960:17)

Sociologist C. Wright Mills defined an organization as "a system of roles graded by authority." Members of organizations are not expected to exhibit their full range of behaviors, but only those that are necessary or useful to the purposes of the organization, that is, goal achievement. In other words, persons are to perform according to their assigned roles, not according to their personal wishes. These roles must be *coordinated* so that they can combine to achieve the system's goals. They must be *differentiated, hierarchical* (in power, or sequence, or both), and have some functions taking priority over others, although the ranking in the hierarchy can change from one occasion to another.

Taken together, Parsons's and Mills's definitions provide a description of organizations that includes the following elements: (1) an organization is a social system whose purpose is the achievement of specific, explicit goals. In order to accomplish this, its members must (2) confine themselves to a relatively narrow range of behaviors intended to fulfill this purpose. The members (3) exercise power over each other, in the form of authority and hierarchical control, to (4) assure compliance with the system's goals and adherence to the members' prescribed roles.

The principles of bureaucracy, as delineated by Weber, are:

1. *division of labor* and specialization of tasks;
2. *hierarchy of position;* each officeholder or employee is supervised by a higher authority;
3. a consistent *system of generalized rules* to assure coordination of tasks and uniform results (that is, effectiveness), through, e.g., a manual of policies and procedures;
4. *impartiality* toward members of the organization as well as those being served, in the conduct of the organization's activity, at all levels;
5. *secure employment* within the organization, based on objective criteria and impartial evaluation;
6. machinelike *efficiency;*
7. *separation of career and personal life,* so that the organization's control is limited to work-related matters;

8.   positions are filled by persons *qualified* by training and/or experience specifically for that position; and
9.   transactions are *reported* in a form that can be recorded and properly stored.

I. Theories of Organization

We will present five major theories of organizations (1) the Classical model, (2) Decision theory, (3) Human Relations theory, and (4) Conflict theory, followed by (5) the Systems model. Interwoven with these are Handy's conception of organizational "cultures," which are consistent with our discussion of microcultures in Chapter 3. Following these, we briefly discuss three alternatives, person-based, power-based, and patrimonial organizations.

The order of presentation here is deliberate; in our view there is a continuum that extends from the abstract principles that underlie the *rational systems perspective* through the more complex *natural systems perspective,* in which the organization is personalized, to the *open systems perspective,* which embraces complexity. The latter stresses intensity and mutuality of the organization's relationship to its turbulent environment while it also incorporates the main aspects of the other two perspectives. Another way to state this is that in the rational systems perspective, the organization itself is the focal system; in the natural systems perspective, the components (members) are the focal system(s), and in the open systems perspective, both of the other perspectives are taken, along with the organization's relationship with the environment; it is *holonistic.* That is, the difference between the perspectives is the *level* of the focal system: the open systems view allows the analyst to shift the level of analysis from one focal system to another. A third way to state the differences is that the first perspective treated the organization as a relatively closed system; the second treated the organization as having permeable interior boundaries (internal openness); and the third treats the organization as open to both components and environment.

A. Rational Systems Perspective

Scott's definition of this rational systems perspective is: "Organizations are collectivities oriented to the pursuit of relatively specific goals and exhibiting relatively highly formalized social structures" (W. R. Scott, 1998:26). Both models discussed under this heading share these characteristics. One difference is that the classical model focused on the *structure* in which decisions and actions were taken, while decision theory focused on the *goals* being sought within the structure. The two are interlaced: they are warp and woof of the fabric that is an organization, two dimensions of the same entity. Another difference is that the classical view aimed at complete rationality, while decision theory is realistic enough to recognize the impossibility of complete rationality, and aims for maximum feasible rationality at a given time, regarding a given decision, and within a given set of circumstances. Nonetheless, the general perspective is the same: organizations operate with rationality as their prime directive, and strenuous effort should be made to achieve it.

1. *The Classical Model.* The classical model is sometimes called the "machine theory" because the organization was viewed as a machine with interchangeable parts and clearly identifiable operations, and members were treated as cogs and gears in that machine. The emphasis was on mechanical regulation, control, and rationality, which are characteristics of this model. Principles of this formal organization include (1) *division of labor,* with each unit performing certain tasks; (2) *pyramid of control,* with each unit subordinate to one above it in the hierarchy; and (3) *unity of command,* that is, centralized control emanating from the top of the pyramid (see Figure 5.1). We will discuss this model further in Section I, C, The Bureaucratic Situation.

In Handy's conception, a bureaucracy is a "role culture." Its structure is a "Greek temple," with a relatively shallow pyramid of control at the top, and supporting vertical columns. Each "pillar" or department has its assigned function, and reports to the triangle of power at the top. Coordination is performed by the triangle, made up of a relatively small number of people. "Role prescription" is more important than individual personalities. The major source of power in this culture is *position power,* the status the person holds. Rules and procedures are

Figure 5.1
Diagrams of the classical model.

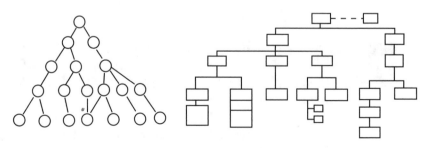

the major elements of the culture. This structure operates well in a stable environment—its role occupants can feel secure; however, its adaptability is limited.

This has been the most visible model, from the Roman army to modern bureaucracy. The fact that this form of organization (e.g., the Roman Catholic church) has survived thousands of years indicates how effective it can be at achieving goals and ensuring compliance. However much we denigrate "bureaucracy," in fact it freed societies from traditional patriarchal, autocratic rule. Bureaucracies (ideally) embodied rules that were just, based on merit, and administered impartially. Henry Ford based his assembly line on the rationality of this model. Social historian Lewis Mumford said that organizations arise from the human need to create regularity in the world (see Chapter 3, Section II, E, The Human Urge to Explain the World, and the Addendum to Chapter 2):

> Behind every later process of organization and mechanization one must ... recognize primordial attitudes, deeply ingrained in the human organism ... . for ritualizing behavior and finding satisfaction in a repetitive order that establishes a human connection with organic rhythms and cosmic event. Organization Man is the common link between the ancient and modern type of megamachine: that is perhaps why the specialized functionaries, with their supporting layer of slaves, conscripts, and subjects—in short, the controllers and the controlled—have changed so little in the last five thousand years. (Mumford, 1970:277)

2. Decision Theory. Decision theory is concerned with the achievement of rational decision-making *whenever possible.* This theory recognizes that there is, in addition to the horizontal differentiation by task, a vertical hierarchy or differentiation by "levels of decisions" that are made. This differentiation is made on the basis of *power* (i.e., whose decisions are binding upon whom), and distinguishes between policymaking and policy implementation. In this theory, power consists of access to, and control of, information that is sufficient to formulate policy, and the ability to get others to carry out the actions necessary to implement the policy. Perhaps most important is the qualification "whenever possible."

This theory holds that human behavior in organizations is best described as "intendedly rational" (Simon, 1945:196). It recognizes the nonrational aspects of decision-making in organizations. It also emphasizes "search behavior," the concept that an organization does not seek endlessly for perfectly rational behavior but instead seeks satisfying (sometimes called "satisficing") solutions that are "reasonably good" or "acceptable." If tension or conflict between components and the organization cannot be completely resolved to everyone's satisfaction (and it rarely is), the organization may need to find another solution. The solution may be to coerce members into agreement, to modify the organization's behavior, or to accommodate the difference in order to arrive at a compromise that does not fully satisfy anyone, but permits continued movement toward a mutual goal.

Decision theory recognizes the inevitability of tension and conflict; it states that tension and conflict occur not only over personal factors but also over organizational issues. That is, conflict is sometimes nonrational, but it is often rational and concerned with decision-making. Further, decision theory recognizes a necessity for organizational differentiation in order to make decisions and accomplish tasks. Differentiation need not lead to a fixed hierarchy, since organizational structure, leadership, and decision-making can change according to task.

3. *Task Culture.* Handy's (1985) conception of task culture is exemplified by the development of the space program by NASA, which was accomplished by "modular" work structures and assignments. Units were formed as needed and disbanded as particular subprojects were completed (the movie *Apollo 13* portrays this reshaping of boundaries during an extreme emergency). This can perhaps best be represented by a grid. The "matrix" organization embodies this culture. The organization assembles the appropriate resources and expertise at the appropriate intersections of the grid. Expertise is placed at the intersections where projects occur; a premium is placed on expertise, and power flows from these temporary locations. The organization and its temporary subunits are united by specific tasks, in the short term, and by a sequence of tasks accomplished, in the long term. This is a highly adaptable organization.

B. Natural Systems Theory

> Rational systems theorists emphasize the normative structure and so focus on decision—designs or proposals for action—as if they were the principal outcomes. Natural systems theorists stress the behavioral structure and are more interested in examining what is done rather than what is decided or planned. Commitment and motivation loom as more salient variables. (W. R. Scott, 1998:58)

Scott identifies two varieties of natural systems theory: (1) *social consensus,* "a view of collectivities as composed of individuals sharing primarily common objectives," exemplified by human relations theory, and (2) *social conflict,* which "views social order as resulting from the suppression of some interests by others. Order results not from consensus, but from coercion, the dominance of weaker by more powerful groups" (ibid.).

1. *Human Relations Theory.* Human relations theory arose in reaction to "machine" theory. It is exemplified by Elton Mayo, Kurt Lewin, and, indirectly, the philosopher John Dewey. It stressed the *informal* structure and the emotional, nonrational motivations that operate in organizations. It emphasized such processes as communication, participation, and leadership. Japanese organizations' motivational programs for workers, such as saluting the company flag, singing the company song, and other means of encouraging a corporate spirit and corporate identification (a pattern followed by Wal-Mart), are variations of human relations theory. They presumably increase productivity and decrease alienation through greater participation and involvement in the corporation by employees. Another means used by some American corporations to encourage a sense of participation has been employee stock option plans (ESOPs), which supposedly permit employees to see themselves as owners. Given what has happened to many corporations during the early years of this century, including bankruptcy, insolvency, layoffs, and reduction or elimination of employees' pensions, these stock option plans were at best risky and, at worst, were worthless.

The best known studies issuing from human relations theory were the Hawthorne studies, including the Bank Wiring Room study (Mayo, 1945; Roethlisberger and Dickson, 1947). The results of these studies showed conclusively that the classical theory was inadequate to explain behavior in organizations. Clearly, other factors besides rational, impersonal calculation determined the workers' production.

These studies found that the highest motivation for one group of workers was neither money nor working conditions but rather what is now known as the "Hawthorne effect"—the fact that they were a special group being researched! The general conclusion that sets this theory apart from the machine model is that workers do not function as separate, distinct units organized in linear chains, but rather as members of groups to whose norms they adhere. The influence of the small group became readily apparent.

Adaptations of human relations theory included Maslow's "hierarchy of needs" to explain motivation and behavior in organizations (Maslow, 1968). In this view, needs are hierarchical, with "safety" needs (adequate food and physical protection, e.g.) and "security" needs (medical care, income assurances in case of illness, e.g.) being fundamental. Psychoanalyst Karen Horney had earlier anticipated this description of needs. If these fundamental needs are filled, a person progresses to fulfill "higher" wants/needs: "social" needs, including contact with others and membership in groups; "esteem" needs for positive regard by others, and one's own positive feelings about self. If all other needs are satisfied, a person then progresses to the "highest" need, which is *self-actualization,* the fulfillment of one's potential as an individual.

Scott places human relations theory within the "natural systems perspective," in which the "goals pursued become more complex, diffuse, differentiated, and subject to change; participants are viewed as motivated by their own interests and as seeking to impose these on the organization" (Scott, 1998:26). His definition of an organization from this perspective is:

> Organizations are collectives whose participants are pursuing multiple interests, both disparate and common, but recognize the value of perpetuating the organization as an important resource. The informal structure of relations that develops among participants provides a more informative and accurate guide to understanding organizational behavior than the formal. (ibid.)

2. *Conflict Theory.* Conflict theorists, who include Karl Marx and Max Weber, represent in some respects a synthesis of theories; they recognized both formal and informal structures, and their interaction, as significant. They agreed with the classical theorists that the attempt to achieve goals through rational, impersonal structure is important; they also recognized a necessity for the organization to meet the human, personal needs of its components. However, conflict theory does not place primary emphasis on the human, emotive factors; instead, this view stresses the importance of the work setting and the influence of the technology that is used, not the human, emotive factors. This gave rise to the study of the "sociotechnical" aspects of industry, the interaction of persons with technology (often called cybernetics). In contrast to the classical, machine theory, conflict theory pictures organizations as open systems; that is, the structure of the organization varies according to the environment and the technology employed.

The major difference from the previous theories is that conflict theory states that conflict within an organization is inevitable. Conflict theory "sees the organization as a large, complex social unit in which many social groups interact . . . . The various groups might cooperate in some spheres and compete in others, but they hardly are or can become one big happy family" (Etzioni, 1964:41). Conflict theory resembles social systems theory because it recognizes the components within the organization, the tension that inevitably exists between components, and between components and the organizational suprasystem. Like systems theory, conflict theory does not view conflict as a "problem," the resolution of which will restore equilibrium. Conflict is an inherent characteristic of organizations; indeed, one administrative or organizational development strategy may be to induce conflict deliberately in order to stimulate change (analogous to the use of paradoxes in psychotherapy, or stimulating patients' awareness of inner conflict through psychoanalysis).

Conflict may have positive effects; it may force a confrontation that leads to a test of power and the possibility of significant change. The history of nearly any organization reveals successive tensions and conflicts whose resolution (or nonresolution) contributed to its present condition. Some of these conflicts could be viewed as "healthy" because they restored vitality or resolved issues that had retarded the organization's development. Conflict theory, then, like social systems theory, portrays organizations more realistically than either the classical or the human relations theory alone.

C. Alternative Principles of Organization

We have discussed two of Handy's "cultures" previously, role culture and task culture. Here, we continue with his other two cultures followed by discussion of other principles of organization.

1. *Power Culture.* Here authority and control derive from a powerful person, often the entrepreneurial founder. Rules and procedures are less important than employees' connections with those who are powerful at the center. The organization depends upon trust and face-to-face relationships. Handy pictured this as a web, with power emanating from the center, delegated through intermediaries to the periphery. This kind of organization can be flexible and can react quickly to threat or opportunity, but it is limited by the central figure's managerial style ("style" is apt in the movie *The Devil Wears Prada*, e.g., based on a real fashion magazine editor). Success may be endangered, also, because *gemeinschaft* qualities may be difficult to maintain in a larger organization. It is frequently a competitive, "tough" climate, and judgments about effectiveness or worth can issue quickly from the center (television's *Mad Men* comes to mind). Staff must be very alert to changes in the environment because of the organization's reliance on other organizations for resources, both finances and clientele, and perhaps upon government (another organization) and the public for goodwill and support. Examples include a treatment facility begun by an entrepreneurial social worker to serve developmentally disabled clients, and a clinic founded by a medical specialist to serve Alzheimer's patients. In this type of organization, staff must be very alert to changes in external resources or clientele.

2. *Person culture.* This is similar to the power culture in that both are based upon personalities, but the person culture is decentralized. In some respects it resembles the task culture in its fluidity and adaptability. It is best represented by an aggregation of independent professionals who share a single location, whether law firm, medical practice, or university department. Here each individual is a nodal point: thus there may be no single center. Universities are largely made up of such "kingdoms"; a university president once described a university as "a bunch of prima donnas united by plumbing."

Handy said the structure is as "minimal as possible," and that a "cluster" may be the best description, or perhaps "a galaxy of individual stars" (Handy 1985:195). Control is minimal, except by consent. Individuals have a great deal of autonomy, either because of their expertise and the demand for their services elsewhere, or because they are tenured in their position (as with professors or partners in a law firm).

> The kibbutz, the commune, the cooperative, are all striving after the person culture in organizational form. On the whole, only their original creators achieve any success. Too soon, the organization achieves its own identity and begins to impose on its individuals. It becomes, at best, a task culture, but often a power or a role culture. (ibid.:196)

He added that there are many persons who prefer a person culture, but find themselves in other settings. For example, the stereotype of professors is that they are person-oriented, working in a role culture; that they do what they must (e.g., committees), and teach when they must, to retain their positions in the organization, but that they view the organization essentially as a base upon which to build their own careers and carry out their own interests (ibid.). To the extent that the stereotype is true, this behavior has been supported by the increasing reliance of universities and colleges on faculty to secure outside resources, largely through research grants. But this phenomenon is two-edged: as the institutions' dependence upon entrepreneurial faculty increases, so does the institutions' need to monitor and control their performance. Accordingly, there are efforts throughout the nation (and internationally) to abridge the independence of professors in the name of "accountability" and "fiscal flexibility," through post-tenure peer reviews, fixed-term appointments, and an increasing proportion of "non-tenure track" and temporary appointments.

The resolution of issues of "intellectual property," that is, whether a professor's or researcher's ideas belong to that person, or to the institution, are also vitally important; the issue is being pressed in the name of securing financial resources for the institution. The traditional person culture of universities may be ending as universities become "corporatized," that is, as they have become role cultures (under centralized control by a university president, state Board of Regents, or state governor, e.g.) or task culture (as departments are dismantled and faculty are shifted into *ad hoc* research or instructional units). The implications of this for universities as "knowledge organizations" are enormous. The issues illustrate the power of organizations and institutions, and the nature of our organizational society.

3. *Patrimony.* Are there realistic alternatives to large-scale bureaucracies? Weber thought the (unfortunate) alternative was *patrimony,* that is, control by persons (apparently males; notice that *matrimony* has a much different cultural meaning) rather than by laws and regulations. Patrimonial control is one in which decisions are the leader's prerogative (a variation of power culture). The leader appoints friends and loyal supporters and delegates patrimonial powers to them. Although Weber favored bureaucracy because of its norms of equity and impartiality, he recognized that bureaucracies are likely to become cumbersome and immobile, that means tend to become ends, and that such organizations tend to be self-perpetuating.

As Weber observed, perhaps all organizations are a combination of bureaucracy and patrimonialism, formal and informal. The Constitution of the United States established ground rules enabling the coexistence of the two. The presidency exemplifies the patrimonial aspect. A president appoints those loyal to him and his cause, those who have aided in his attainment of the office. For example, John Kennedy appointed his brother to the office of Attorney General. Richard Nixon appointed his campaign manager to the same position. Jimmy Carter appointed loyal supporters (referred to as "the Georgia Mafia"); presidents Reagan, Bush, and Clinton followed the same pattern. President Obama chose his close colleague in Illinois, Rahm Emanuel, to serve as his White House Chief of Staff, and Valerie Jarrett, a longtime friend and confidant of the Obamas, as one of three Senior Advisors. Such appointments are at the discretion of the president, and are usually personally close—a useful role in Washington, since as one president said, "if you want a friend in Washington, get a dog."

A strong symbol of the patrimony of the elected executive is the presidential pardon, which allows the officeholder to make an independent, legally binding decision that does not require legal precedent or any justification. President Lincoln pardoned deserters. President Ford pardoned Richard Nixon, and President Carter granted amnesty to those who fled the country to avoid the draft during the Vietnam War. President Clinton issued, among others, a controversial pardon for a person who had fled the country to escape prosecution. President George W. Bush issued fewer pardons than most of his predecessors.

The "new entrepreneur" business owner is another example of patrimonial organization. The business is operated with authority remaining firmly in the hands of the owner(s). Promotions, bonuses, and status are the means used to foster employee loyalty. The owners can employ and discharge employees as they see fit without recourse or appeal (except as a court may find illegalities). This contrasts with the bureaucratic situation, in which procedures for hiring and firing are thoroughly detailed, often complex, and slow; and conditions for promotion and salary advancement are carefully spelled out.

An organization's movement from bureaucracy to patrimony (or perhaps power culture) may be exemplified by General Electric's former chairman, "an intense, powerful man" who "spearheaded a gut-wrenching change" in the company, slashing thousands of jobs;

> Like him or not, Jack Welch has succeeded in sweeping a major American company clean of the bureaucratic excesses of the past and transforming a paternalistic culture into one that puts winning in the marketplace above all other concerns. Like it or not, the management styles of more U.S. companies are going to look a lot more like GE. (*Business Week,* 1998)

4. *Other Alternatives.* Alternatives to large-scale bureaucracies have been attempted by some organizations, with decentralized structures such as autonomous work groups that allow freedom and control to line workers. Such attempts have drawn heavily on research done following World War II by the Tavistock Institute in England; these studies indicate that greater productivity and reduced alienation are best achieved by autonomous work groups. Other efforts have focused on redesigning jobs ("job enrichment," job enlargement") and restructuring to permit greater self-determination by workers. In a few instances, U.S. companies have permitted workers to participate in management decisions. In Europe, this has long been practiced as "codetermination" or "industrial democracy."

In the Japanese model ("Theory Z"), trust is fostered by companies' commitment to lifetime employment for each employee (although this has been modified greatly in recent years as the nation's economy declined); in case of a recession, companies aggressively looked for new markets or new products while workers perform other duties (including janitorial services) until the financial situation improved, meanwhile keeping their jobs. This is more difficult in companies with unionized employees, unless the union agrees to the modifications of their contract. Faced with a serious recession and international competition, Japanese corporations have transferred employees to other cities or countries, causing hardship for employees' families. One couple sued the husband's employer for nearly a quarter-million dollars for "emotional pain of separation and traveling-expenses" (Coleman, 1998).

> As companies have diversified and expanded overseas, branch offices and subsidiaries have proliferated. Bosses say they need to move trained employees around to spread their expertise and give them wider experience. The trend, which is increasing as juvenile delinquency is rising and Japanese youth seem more troubled, has some people alarmed that companies are breaking up families at the expense of children and society. (ibid.)

The "groupness" of the work situation is encouraged by workers sharing space without walls; interaction is not only encouraged, it is demanded, consistent with Japanese culture. Permanence of employment and group solidarity result in absence of (or at least lessened) alienation, since "people committed to long-term relationships with each other have strong commitments to behave responsibly and equitably towards one another" (Ouchi, 1981b:34).

> Intimacy, trust and understanding grow where individuals are linked to one another through multiple bonds in a wholistic relationship. ... The Japanese show clear evidence that wholism in industrial life is possible. (Ouchi, 1981b:54-55)
>
> It is a consent culture, a community of equals who cooperate with one another to reach common goals. Rather than relying exclusively upon hierarchy and monitoring to direct behavior, it relies also upon commitment and trust. (ibid.:83)

This resembles a community, clan, or tribe, with strong communal ties. In this instance, organizational culture mirrors the wider culture. There is some question as to whether the society and culture are changing, and whether the organizational culture must change accordingly.

Humanization and improving the "quality of work life" are complex undertakings, involving recognition of more facets of the person than simply the employee's role as a production unit in the industrial system. Paradoxically, it may well require the person to give up some freedom and independence (randomly distributed energy that tends toward entropy), to assume new obligations of mutuality (negentropy or synergy) with management and other workers. Some observers suggest that we are witnessing the breakdown of bureaucracy and that it will be supplanted by a task culture of temporary, shifting structures. The chances of unemployment and alienation would seem to be increased for many employees, unless opportunity for retraining and personal growth are commensurate to risk.

One hypothesis is that larger size generates a greater variety of subsystems. Organizations, unlike families, may outlive the original members (though, of course, family generations may outlive *any one* organization). Because organizations can replace components and learn from experience, it may be true that the longer an organization lives, the better its chance for survival, although in the present economic circumstances, the daily news often features long-standing companies succumbing to market failures.

> Organizations may take a long time in order to realize their cognitive frame should be changed ... . the first reaction of the US automotive industry to the entrance of Japanese rivals in the US market was to blame its difficulties "on the government, on unfair trade, on brickheaded workers, on snooty American consumers, and ... on the "congenital sickos" in the media. ... Only after years of irregular and dwindling profits was it realized that Detroit's view of a reasonably predictable world and competitive advantages built on economies of scale had given way. (Fioretti and Visser, 2006:504).

Many have observed that the changes previously discussed (decentralization, or humanization of the workplace) are more cosmetic than real, and that organizations tend to perpetuate their ways with as little change as possible (morphostasis). When pressed, governmental organizations "reorganize"; industry becomes "lean and mean" and "downsizes." Millions of American workers have suffered this fate in the last three decades and, since 2007, the losses have accelerated. Some analysts have suggested that organizations are being short-sighted by reducing their productivity to the point that it may be difficult to recover.

For significant organizational change to occur, there must be modification in both internal and external aspects, especially goals. Contentions over plant closings during the last generation provide an instructive example (see Michael Moore's early movie, *Roger and Me* for a humorous take on a very serious subject). Corporate industry, in its pursuit of its profit goal, may determine that a particular production facility is not contributing to profit and decide to close that facility to move production to another location in which labor and raw material are cheaper, often to a "third world" or "developing" country. Other interests and organizations, such as labor unions, have been strongly affected by the relinquishment of the secondary goal, i.e., the provision of employment. For example, IBM has grown its operations in India from 15,000 to 100,000 in the past five years. Within the first ten days of his administration, President Obama initiated legislation to make it easier to form and join unions, as part of his effort to revitalize the economy and protect workers. Efforts have been made to block closures of plants or to develop other ways to maintain employment (see Michael Moore's recent film *Capitalism: A Love Story*). Similar dynamics operate with the closing of a prison or a hospital, as regards the impact upon the surrounding community or neighborhood.

The pace of change in an organization is nearly always controversial. The last several presidential elections, especially that of President Obama, indicated public dissatisfaction with the lack of change in the federal bureaucracy; civil rights reforms were occurring too quickly for some and too slow for others; tax reforms were occurring too slowly (one reaction was the "tea bag" protests across the country beginning in mid-April, 2009, expressing dissatisfaction with what were regarded as excessive taxes). Elections since 1968 have frequently been interpreted as "mandates" against centralized federal bureaucracy; in part, a societal reaction to the Vietnam War.

One reason for organizational change is the rapid diversification and expansion of major corporations and a rapid acceleration of "megamergers." According to a highly regarded management expert, the new multinational corporation (MNC):

> ... does not fit the traditional organization structure of the multinational corporation, with a central top management to which management of subsidiaries reports, It requires, rather, a *system* approach, in which one body coordinates autonomous managements that do not report to one another.
>
> A major requirement is the ability and willingness to adapt to different cultures and to work with people of different habits and traditions. [It] is not only transnational, rather than multinational; it is, above all, transcultural. And it is an idea whose time has come. (Drucker, 1982:192; emphasis ours)

Thoughtful analyses including some by science fiction writers (notably the late Isaac Asimov in the *Foundation* series) suggest that governments of the future may not be nation-states. Instead, international conglomerates may rule, and perhaps more rationally. It may well be that unless national governments become equally adaptable, other organizations may absorb what we now recognize as "governmental" functions. The United Nations recognized the insufficiency of information on multinationals and their activities and formulated a code of ethics for multinational enterprises.

D. The Bureaucratic Situation

The term *bureaucratic situation* was coined to describe the "total environment" provided by large organizations (Presthus, 1962:4). We use it in the same sense, knowing that not all organizations are characterized by what is often derogatorily referred to as "bureaucracy." Bureaucracy is a phenomenon that has its roots in ancient societies, as said earlier. It underwent morphogenesis with the emergence of the modern nation state, contemporary with industrialization.

The classic principles of bureaucracy as Weber described them were intended to protect the integrity of the offices and the officeholders at all levels. Like the feudal contract between lord and vassal, which spelled out mutual obligations, these bureaucratic prescriptions detailed the rules for interactions. "Authority is strictly circumscribed and confined to those directives that are relevant for official operations. The use of status prerogatives to extend the power of control over subordinates beyond these limits does not constitute the legitimate exercise of bureaucratic authority" (Blau, 1956:29). It is not so easy to limit the power of one's superiors in bureaucracy, however. We have the examples of Nazi Germany, the Soviet Union, Watergate, China, and the abuse of prisoners at Guantanamo during the second Bush administration to remind us of the potential for abuses of bureaucratic power. In the Watergate, Iran-Contra, and Whitewater investigations during the Nixon, Bush, and Clinton administrations, respectively, bureaucratic power was also employed to prosecute crimes. The bureaucracies of the Justice Department, the Office of the Independent Counsel, the courts, and legislative committees were brought to bear.

Such rationality as is demanded by rules and regulations is unrealistic, as the human relations school pointed out. There are limits to rationality. The basic commitment to the organization is only partially rational. It inevitably involves emotive factors such as loyalty and sentiments about the worth of the organization and about oneself as part of it. Such commitments, values, and feelings do not originate with the organization. They must begin in other systems, with the socialization provided by family, school, and community: socialization toward such qualities as reliability, commitment, sacrifice, and the ability to subordinate oneself to larger systems. It is also true that personal integrity and the courage to confront organizational pressures have the same origins.

1. *Bureaucratic personality.* Many writers have described the effects of bureaucratic organizations on the personalities of their members. Some have suggested a "bureaucratic personality"; it (a) is accustomed to shifting between social units, especially the family and the organization, (b) has high tolerance for frustration and the ability to defer gratification, and (c) has the urge to achieve material and symbolic rewards (achievement orientation). Etzioni added:

> The major credit for this convergence of personality and organizational requirements
> ... must go to the modern family and the modern educational system, both of which
> produce the type of person who will make a good organization man. The middle-class
> stress on the values of punctuality, neatness, integrity, consistency, the accent on
> conformity, and above all, achievement, are the foundation. ... (Etzioni, 1964:110)

An organization rewards the kind of personality that puts the organization's goals above its own. To the extent that the organization can enforce this, it has power over its members.

Scott (1998) cites feminist criticisms of bureaucracy: that it "feeds the dualism of private-expressive and public-instrumental selves and worlds" (Glennon, 1979) and that "[t]he organizational forms and discourse of bureaucratic capitalism institutionalize modes of domination that recreate the very patterns of oppression that feminism arose to combat." These critics point to the priority that bureaucracies give to "masculine" virtues and values (see discussion of Horney's and Gilligan's views in Chapter 8): inequality, hierarchy, impersonality, aggressiveness, competition, and independence. These differ from "women's values," which are egalitarian, personalized, nurturant, and relational (W. R. Scott, 1998:5). On these bases, feminist critics assert that the fundamental characteristics of bureaucracy as Weber described them are

> gender-biased not only in their application for criteria for appointment and promotion but, more fundamentally, in their choice of criteria—in their conception of what is entailed in creating a rational system for supporting collaborative action. Contemporary organizations are said to be modeled on military systems and sports teams. (ibid.)

Whether this is less true of human services or social work organizations is debatable. The criticism may be most applicable to large, public social welfare and health bureaucracies; whether it applies to smaller, or private health and welfare organizations depends on the particular organization and its environment.

2. The term *organizational climate* defines a narrower aspect of the organization's functioning, including the morale of its employees, the degree to which effort is rewarded, and the aggressiveness with which the organization pursues its goals. "Climate" also includes attitudes toward women, in at least two respects. First, as employees or executives, e.g., the "glass ceiling," meaning that women can see the upper levels of the organization, but are barred from rising to them (this issue arose during the 2008 Presidential election with regard to Hillary Clinton). Second, as victims of sexual harassment, which the Supreme Court defines not as "intersexual flirtation" but as "'behavior so objectively offensive' that it creates a hostile work environment for the victim" (El Nasser, 1998). Sexual harassment lawsuits frequently describe such "hostile work environments" experienced by women who object to sexual harassment or who file complaints: they are subjected to insults by the aggressor, their work is unfairly evaluated, or they are shunned by other

personnel (all means of social control) (see Reardon, 1995; see also the 2005 film *North Country*, about women in Minnesota mines).

Many female entrepreneurs leave corporate positions to start their own businesses:

> Professional women say they're leaving corporate jobs because of advancement barriers, scant help balancing work and family, and a desire to pursue an entrepreneurial goal. ... An unprecedented number of professional women are taking the same initiative. The number of female-owned businesses is growing at nearly twice the national average. ... "The rise in women entrepreneurs is one of the big demographics changing our society," says Lynn Neeley, president-elect of the United States Association for Small Business and Entrepreneurship. (Armour, 1998)

Women-owned (50 percent or more ownership) enterprises continue to outpace male-owned start-up businesses; as of 2006, there were over ten million such women-owned businesses. Nearly half (48 percent) of all privately-owned businesses were owned by women. Between 1997 and 2006, such women-owned businesses increased 42 percent, and were projected to generate over one trillion dollars in revenue. They employed about 19 million persons. These firms diversified into all industries, with the fastest growth in construction (30 percent), transportation, communications, and public utilities. The fastest growing states between 1997 and 2004 were Utah, Arizona, and Nevada (these were among the states with the greatest growth in the general population). In Europe, women were in the majority in these general occupational categories: health and social services, community and social services (this probably includes teaching), and hotels and restaurants; an additional category was "distribution" (presumably this included retail sales). The same general pattern would seem true for the United States, as well. The nations in which the number of women in businesses came closest to parity in 2004 were Poland, South Africa, and Finland. With regard to the proportion of women in business, the United States was seventh of the twenty-nine nations surveyed. Federal law in the United States requires that "certified women-owned businesses receive at least 5 percent of all federal contracts; the actual number is less than 3.2 percent.

3. *Alienation.* Much writing (both popular and academic) and research has been devoted to describing the dehumanizing influences of our institutions and organizations (consider the novel *Darkness at Noon,* the writings of Franz Kafka, the movie and novel, *One Flew Over the Cuckoo's Nest,* the Angelina Jolie movie, *The Changeling* (2008), and the George Clooney movies, *Michael Clayton* (2007) and *Up in the Air* (2009). In the effort to structure human interactions in large organizations to conform to criteria of efficiency, objectivity, and merit, the

needs of individual persons have been relegated to the background. Alienation, referred to at various points in this book, is a product of dehumanization. This is also an example of conflict between goals of component and system, and of system and suprasystem. Consequences of such conflict are many, and manifest themselves in shoddy products and negative attitudes, whether at the fast-food counter, in professional services, or an automobile factory:

> I can just look at a car and see all kinds of things wrong with it. You can't do that because you didn't see how it was made. I can look at a car underneath the paint. It's like x-ray vision. They put that trim in, they call it. The paint and all those little pretties that you pay for. Whenever we make a mistake, we always say, "Don't worry about it, some dingaling'll buy it." (Laughs.) (Terkel, 1975:229)

Classical organization theory assumes that rational behavior in organizations prevents alienation. Human relations theory perceives alienation as inevitable; this is similar to entropy, in that organizations will degenerate into randomness and disorganization if the members' personal needs are not tended to. Both conflict and decision system theorists suggest that some degree of alienation is inevitable.

> Outrageous as it may seem, the fact is that a new value system dominates America. The organizational imperative, while originally a subset within the context of the overarching social value system, has now become the dominant force in the homogenization of organizational America, displacing the more individualistic values of the past. (W. G. Scott and Hart, 1980:52)

Corporate domination of our society has been described as "the new feudalism." If these warnings are correct, we face a crisis in the degree to which organizations are responsive to the needs of human beings within them and the degree to which these persons are manipulated for the good of the organization. The economic crisis of 2007-2010 underscores the jeopardy in which employees and families are placed by the misbehavior of financial organizations and the failure of government departments to regulate these organizations' behavior (see Michael Moore's film, *Capitalism: A Love Story*).

Further, there is concern about whether organizations are responsive to social needs, for example, Toyota's reluctant acknowledgement of braking problems, Exxon's handling of the catastrophic oil spill in Alaska's Prince William Sound, the behavior of tobacco companies in promoting the sales of tobacco and in withholding information about the dangers of smoking (see the 2006 satirical film *Thank You For Smoking*), and the operations of banks and other financial organizations with regard to risky and irresponsible fiscal manipulations that triggered the 2007-

2010 global economic crisis. In the past, government regulations have constrained corporate contributions to political candidates and their campaigns; in 2010, however, the U.S. Supreme Court saw fit to lift most of these restrictions because corporations are deemed to be "persons" and have the same freedom of speech as individual citizens.

There are, of course, examples of corporate responsiveness to concerns about public health and safety: voluntary recalls of defective products, and introductions of safety features that are not required by law. In another example, some corporations cooperate in pledging five percent of their profits to charitable causes (e.g., Target). Other corporations and foundations support public radio and public television (e.g., Newman's Own), and support public service information. A significant number of companies participate in programs to train welfare recipients and the unemployed. It would be unfair to characterize most corporations as irresponsible or unresponsive, but unfortunately, such negative behavior is not uncommon.

4. *Burnout.* Many theorists and organizational specialists have studied the phenomenon of burnout among members of organizations. Burnout is defined as:

> . . . a debilitating psychological condition brought on by unrelieved work stress, which results in:
> a.   depleted energy reserves;
> b.   lowered resistance to illness;
> c.   increased dissatisfaction and pessimism;
> d.   increased absenteeism and inefficiency at work.
>   (Veninga and Spradley, 1981:6-7)

Burnout may be considered a particular, internalized form of alienation. Clearly, burnout is a serious and, in some extreme cases, life-threatening condition. Women are susceptible to burnout because they (a) are often placed in monotonous jobs with little opportunity for promotion, (b) have no leisure time because of domestic chores and child care, in addition to their full-time jobs, and (c) have limited social contact off the job because of work and family demands, and sometimes feel isolated and lonely because of the demands on their time.

Veninga and Spradley identified five stages of burnout, beginning with an initial period of satisfaction with the job ("the honeymoon"), followed by a second stage in which the characteristics previously listed (energy depletion, etc.) begin to be evident. The worker is not necessarily aware of the symptoms in this stage. In a third stage, the symptoms become chronic and begin to interfere with the person's functioning at work and at home. In a fourth stage, the worker becomes obsessed with the problem and burnout dominates his or her life. If the worker progresses as far as the fifth stage ("hitting the wall"), it is impossible to function on the job and the person's life deteriorates in significant ways.

There is no inevitable progression through the stages. People have highly individual patterns, sometimes moving in and out of burnout, depending upon their own resources, the resources available to them from their environments, and upon whether they find ways to relieve the chronic stress contained in the job. Change can come about in true systemic fashion by altering the job, the environment, or the person's perception of the job or of herself or himself. At times, however, the only available course is to find another, more compatible organization.

We should note that satisfaction among employees appears to be higher than dissatisfaction, according to most polls. Most workers appear to be relatively satisfied with the tangible and intangible benefits of their jobs. Membership in labor unions, e.g., has declined to about 15 percent of the work force, although major unions currently are making strong efforts to recruit groups that are traditionally nonunionized, e.g., women, professionals such as physicians and professors, secretaries, and low-wage manual laborers. The purpose is, of course, to redistribute power in work organizations.

Another means of altering the job, the environment, or the perception of self, is *networking*. A worker may find other workers experiencing similar problems, and they may be able, through group action, to generate mutual support or, further, to effect change in the organization. These were elements that fostered the development of labor unions. Among other benefits of unions, they may combat a sense of isolation and powerlessness. Movies and television series portray dysfunctional work settings; television's *The Office* is one example, and the movie *Nine to Five* (which became a short-lived musical on Broadway in 2009) showed not only some hilarious means of achieving change (including tying up the boss as a prisoner) but also some serious efforts at reduction of burnout including "flextime" (allowing workers to vary their hours), more individualization of work space ("flexiplace"), and day care for employees' children. These are sometimes supported by corporations and federal legislation. Often, efforts to humanize organizations take the form of decentralization: less emphasis on specialization by workers, reducing units to smaller scale, or restructuring decision-making processes to allow employees to have more influence in determining their own fates and that of the organization. Quality circles, discussed later in this chapter, exemplify an attempt at constructive use of feedback cycles.

II. The Systems Model of Organizations

An open systems perspective is less concerned with distinguishing formal from informal structures; instead, organizations are viewed as a system of interdependent activities. Some of these activities are tightly connected; others are loosely coupled. All must be continuously motivated—produced and reproduced—if the organization is to exist. The arrival of this perspective has triggered the elaboration and elevation of levels of analysis. (W. R. Scott, 1998:28)

Large organizations are similar to society as a system: they have specialization, hierarchy, and authority, and they socialize their members in similar ways. The systems model avoids some of the limitations of the preceding models; it agrees with decision theory that the goal is not perfection. It goes one step further by stating that goal-seeking behavior (GE, GI) is not always the primary behavior of a system since exclusive attention to goal attainment leads to neglect of other essential functions of the system (see discussion in Chapter 1). The systems model stresses a wider context of decision-making and organizational behavior than is pictured in other theories. Like conflict theory, it takes into account environmental influences as well as the influence wielded by components. Conflict is better explained by the systems model in that it recognizes the inevitability of conflict not only within and between components and subsystems, each of which holds to the legitimacy of its own goals, but between a system and its environment. James Miller, a systems theorist and former college president, stated the systems point of view:

No decision is entirely rational or satisfactory, a fact which can give administrators some solace. There is no perfect, rational solution to most administrative problems. The higher the echelon, the truer this is of the issues which confront it. The dimensions along which many decisions must be made are incommensurable. Human lives are incommensurable with money. Money is incommensurable with time. Time is incommensurable with professional excellence. Yet all of these are in scarce supply to a given organization and trade-offs among them must be decided upon. (Miller, 1972:79)

Control is also pictured differently in the systems model. Like goal attainment, control is exclusively pursued only to the detriment of other functions and, at times, other functions do take precedence. The fact that power, control, and the influence of the environment may vary from time to time requires the use of a flexible model of organization. The systems model accounts for such variant adaptive forms.

A. Communication

More than seventy years ago, in his influential book on executive functions, Chester Barnard stressed the importance of communication (appropriately, since he was president of a telephone company): "In an exhaustive theory of organization, communication would occupy a central place, because the structure, extensiveness, and scope of the organization are almost entirely determined by communication techniques" (Barnard, 1938:91). A more contemporary text also emphasizes communication: "Organizations are information-processing systems, One of the most vivid metaphors or images sees the organization as a *brain*. … This imagery captures the idea that organizations capture and filter information, process it in terms of what it has already learned, interpret it, change it, and finally act on it" (Hall, 1996:169).

In order to focus people's attention on specific goals and activities, organizations must monitor and set parameters for communications. This may become as detailed as prohibiting personal phone calls and use of E-mail for private correspondence, or as broad as requiring that all correspondence with external systems be reviewed (and perhaps censored), e.g., during secret military operations or in prisons. Such measures may also be used by one unit to protect its turf from some other unit. One means of controlling content and intent is the practice of submitting drafts of documents to committees or superiors for review before issuing them. Supposedly, organizations are exemplars of efficiency in communication, because they control the channels through which information flows. This is done hierarchically and by restricting the range of content; that is, information passes through various gatekeepers (supervisors, editors, legal advisors, policy analysts, and sometimes "spin doctors") before it is allowed to flow onward or outward to its intended audience. The White House and other federal departments are noted for such behavior. The most recent Bush administration was notable (the Vice-President, in particular) for its tendency to maintain as great a degree of secrecy as it could maintain. President Obama promised "transparency"; however, requirements of "national security" will continue to conflict with "the public's right to know," on occasion.

Researchers have identified certain standard patterns of communications networks: These are recognizable in general systems theory as feedback loops. Each network formation may be functional in a particular organizational setting, for a particular purpose. If centralized decision-making is important, then unidirectional communication, restricted times, and controlled volume may be the preferred modes. If open participation with widely shared decision-making is the organizational style, then bidirectional communication, accessibility at all times, and uncontrolled volume might be the appropriate choices.

The nature of the organization is a factor in the style of communication chosen. Hall says, "Communication is most important ... in organizations and organizational segments that must deal with uncertainty, that are complex, and that have a technology that does not permit easy routinization. ... The more an organization is people and idea oriented, the more important communication becomes" (1996:171). However, technologically sophisticated organizations require precision in communication also; replacing a "thingamabob" in a computer or handing a surgeon a "whatchamacallit" probably won't suffice. Learning the "lingo," cant, or jargon of an organization is another way of mapping the territory. Systems thinking may help to cut across disciplinary fields, in this respect, even though it has jargon of its own (see Georgiou, 2007).

Probably the most common means of communication in organizations is the infamous and universal *meeting*. Hall comments:

> While meetings are quite valuable, it is obvious that time spent in meetings is time not spent on other activities. When I have a day filled with meetings, I have a day when I will not get any research, writing, or preparation for classes accomplished. (ibid.:186)

It is a rare member of an organization who will not sigh in agreement. One executive and organizational expert seriously suggested that all meetings be conducted standing up, in order to shorten them (and they did, in his organization). Much depends upon the goals for the meeting. Solidarity or consensus may be achieved, but precise communication may be a less likely result—hence another infamous, universal device: the memo, whether on paper or in digital form. One news story illustrates the problem; in 2008, U.S. State Department computers were overwhelmed as a result of employees writing memos and sending copies to everyone in the Department. In response, the Department sent a memo to all employees directing them to cease this practice—and then requested that this memo have "the widest distribution possible"! The ability to write clearly and concisely is highly valuable in organizations; columnists in newspapers' business sections regularly suggest methods to accomplish this. On occasion, it is perhaps equally valuable to write ambiguously and with circumlocution. Former Chair of the Federal Reserve, Alan Greenspan, was a consummate practitioner of this, and admitted (after his retirement) that it was deliberate. One is not likely to find a guidebook for this practice; done skillfully, this can communicate that the author is wise in the ways of bureaucracy. Again, as mentioned previously, the *Dilbert* cartoon is a rich source of examples.

B. Goal Direction

Goals have various functions: (W. R. Scott, 1998:286-287): (1) *cognitive,* to guide decision-making and action; (2) *cathectic,* or motivational, to psychologically "hook" members and external systems into participation; (3) *symbolic,* to gain support by capitalizing on people's views of the organization, and to secure legitimacy and resources; (4) *justification* for organizational actions; and (5) bases for *evaluation* of organizational functioning.

What *is* an organizational goal? One definition is that a goal is a particular characteristic of a steady state that the organization attempts to achieve. In this sense, a goal may be expressed by an ideal or myth, sometimes expressed by an advertising slogan ("Better living through chemistry," "If you find a better car, buy it!" "We never stop working for you," "When you care enough to send the very best," "The King of Beers," or "Quality is Job 1.") or by a rational, projected set of specific objectives—that is, it may be "highest quality service to the client" or "caseloads of 20, using short-term treatment, that will increase agency clientele by 15 percent." One company changed its motto from "Best in the World," to "Best *for* the World," no small shift in its implied goals. The goal expressed by either of the latter statements is a desired future condition (steady state) of the organization in which its declared purposes would be fulfilled. These goals guide the organization in its activity; they either encourage or discourage specific actions undertaken or contemplated by the organization. This is similar in some regards to the "ego ideal" of the person, and to the self toward which one strives in Sartre's form of existentialism, or Maslow's self-actualization; this has been described as the *syntality* of an organization, similar to a personality.

An emerging theme within the last thirty years has been "organizational learning," which is analogous to ego functioning in the person: the ability to adapt by securing information both outside and inside the organization and sharing it among all components (Argyris, 1994). Sidney Winter, an economist at the Wharton School at the University of Pennsylvania, described current events as "disintegration of the vertical organization of firms. ... We are downsizing. It is all captured by a common theme: repackaging. We are shifting packages of economic activity into new smaller units. The folk model of organizations as top-down and centralized is out of date" (Kauffman, 1995:245).

Two aspects of goal attainment should be distinguished: *effectiveness* refers to the degree to which the organization achieves its goals; *efficiency,* refers to the amount of energy and resources necessary to achieve a goal. The former is part of the GE and GI functions of systems; the latter is part of the SE and SI functions. Efficiency in an organization requires reduction of conflict ("friction") within the organization; thus some internal control of the utilization of energy is necessary for goal attainment.

Goals are not static. Goals can be *displaced* (i.e., other goals can be substituted for them); the most frequent form of this is making ends of means. For example, efficiency in public welfare expenditure is purported to be a means to effective service to clients and society, but all too often efficiency by cutting welfare spending becomes an end in itself. "Social workers may be directed by their supervisors to provide therapeutic casework services but be evaluated primarily on the basis of the number and timeliness of their visits to clients and the correctness of their calculation of budgets" (W. R. Scott, 1998:347). Another example is the accusation by many university students, especially undergraduates, that universities have displaced education with publication and research, resulting in absentee professors and lower-quality instruction by teaching assistants (not always true, of course).

There are other forms of goal change. One is *goal succession,* in which an organization achieves its initial goals and establishes new ones; or the goal disappears and the organization turns to new goals. Examples of this include those private welfare agencies that began as adoption agencies in an era when there were more children available for adoption than now, and whose successive goals have become the treatment of emotionally disturbed children or family treatment. Definitions of social problems shift with startling rapidity; this is one result of "the turbulent environment" in which social service agencies exist, and to which they must rapidly adapt. Both Christmas Seals and the March of Dimes established new goals after attaining their original goals, the supposed elimination of tuberculosis and polio as major health hazards.

There may also be *goal multiplication.* The Red Cross, which began as a service to soldiers on the battlefield, broadened its goals to include services to soldiers' widows and orphans, then to disaster relief and to visiting political prisoners. The Boy Scouts have, in recent years, broadened their former goals of camping, crafts, and character development to include ethical leadership for adult leaders, and family support through family life education; 4-H has expanded to urban settings. There are, of course, advantages and disadvantages to such goal multiplication. Among possible advantages are that synergy of goals may increase the effectiveness of an organization; staff recruitment may be easier because they enjoy variety;

and because a wider range of contributors may be motivated to support the organization. Possible disadvantages include shortage of energy to accomplish tasks, conflict between goals, and a dilution of focus.

C. Differentiation

Differentiation is the prime sociological characteristic of modernization. Modern societies are societies of differentiated organizations, and these organizations differentiate internally to carry out their purposes more effectively. For example, education has become the domain of organizations grouped under the rubric of "schools." These in turn have differentiated along dimensions of age and function: preschool, elementary, middle, and high school. Secondary schools have differentiated into technical, vocational, college preparatory, and general. Postsecondary education has community colleges to prepare students for specific occupations, colleges for general higher education, and universities for occupations designated as professions.

Differentiation of tasks within an organization may have disadvantages. If workers do not see and understand others' activities as complementary to theirs and horizontally related to them, each employee may become nothing but an isolated, "inert piece of machinery." They must "keep in constant relations with neighboring functions ... not lose sight of [their] collaborators, that [the worker] acts upon them and reacts to them" (Durkheim, 1968:43). Differentiation may lead to isolation of the components of an organization (e.g., in offices and factories where there is little exchange between clerical and professional staff; between workers and management; a university with rigid departmental boundaries; or between physicians and laboratory staff). Some factories, e.g., Volvo and Saab in Sweden, employed "autonomous work groups" in which a group of workers produces a car, and each worker performs a variety of tasks; the outcome is a shared group product, with less differentiation or specialization. United States industries originated "quality circles" fifty years ago; the idea was then adopted by Japanese industry, and reimported to the United States during the 1980s

The quality circle consists on average of a half-dozen employees, headed by a supervisor, who constitute a natural work group. As group members, they are charged with pinpointing quality problems and developing effective solutions to them. ... For example, the fourteen members of a quality circle at the Kariya plant of Nippon Denso examined leaky auto radiators and determined how to produce a 100 percent leak detection rate. Nippon Steel sliced its liquefied petroleum gas consumption by 5.3 percent over a four-year period as a result of quality-circle suggestions each year. (Larwood, 1984:402)

D. Power and Control

 Organizations generate power; it is the inescapable accompaniment of the production of goods and services; it comes in many forms from many sources; it is contested; and it is certainly used. (Perrow, 1986:265)

Organizations must ensure compliance in achieving specific, narrow goals and therefore must apply some kind of control—the use of power. One characteristic of organizations as distinct from other systems is the explicitness of power: it is largely visible and institutionalized.

Robert Dahl defined power: "A has power over B to the extent that he can get B to do something B would not otherwise do" (1957:201-215). Emerson elaborated this: "A's power over B is (1) directly proportional to the importance B places on the goals mediated by A, and (2) inversely proportional to the availability of these goals to B outside the A-B relation" (cited in W. R. Scott, 1998:304). Such power is based on "manipulating rewards and punishments important to the other person" (ibid.).

Force should not be taken to mean only physical force: moral force or Gandhi's "Truth Force" qualify as well. Since power is an energy function, it is finite; energy expended (through GE or GI functions, for example) to influence the behavior of others may deplete the system's power potential.

Power is the system's *potential* to achieve its goals by the application or deprivation of energy to another system or component. The degree of effectiveness of power depends upon the extent to which the focal system is affected and the extent to which the goal is achieved. Power must be measured by its objectives, not merely by the magnitude of its effects. President Obama's achievement in securing health insurance legislation in 2010 was a demonstration of power—in persuading (or arm-twisting, or offering "incentives")—that presidents must demonstrate in order to govern effectively. Commentators were probably correct, that if he had not been able to do this despite determined opposition, his entire presidency would have been weakened.

Power and control are similar except that control suggests narrower and more precise goals than does power. Further, power may have effects other than control. The application of power could release control ("the truth shall set you free," e.g., is a good psychoanalytic principle). Etzioni stated the importance of control:

> The success of an organization is largely dependent upon its ability to maintain control of its participants. All social units control their members, but the problem of control in organizations is especially acute. Organizations as social units that serve

specific purposes are artificial units. They are planned, deliberately structured; *they constantly and self-consciously review their performance and restructure themselves accordingly.* (Etzioni, 1964:58; emphasis ours)

The objective of power and control is *compliance,* the cooperation of a system or component in achieving the goals of the system. Organization theorists have focused primarily on two aspects of organizations: structure and compliance. Understandably, managers of organizations devote more attention to compliance—how to assure the desired results—than to any other aspect of organizations.

There are three forms of control, as Etzioni describes them, each of which fits with a particular kind of organization: (a) physical control, employed by *coercive* organizations, such as the military or prisons, which use threat and punishment; (b) material rewards such as goods and services, used by *remunerative* organizations, in which members calculate the benefits they will receive; and (c) symbolic rewards, employed by *normative* organizations, which use moral involvement and social acceptance as means of control, which tend to encourage high levels of commitment to the organization by its members. Symbolic or normative rewards are in many ways the most significant, because one's sense of identity and the value one has is derived from symbolic interaction with others (as noted in Chapter 3, Section I, C, Language, and in the Addendum to Chapter 2). Symbolic rewards are most likely to be used by the systems with the least physical control or material rewards—religious institutions are the prime examples. In this light, professions such as nursing, social work, or education can be regarded as means of social control: through the deliberate use of symbols, they assist institutions such as schools, hospitals, prisons, or the military to secure compliance (SI and GI functions).

Organizations whose overriding purpose is social control are examples of "total institutions," a phrase coined by Goffman in his classic work, *Asylums* ([1961] 1973). He described a total institution as an organized agency of society in which a large number of like-situated persons, cut off from the larger society for an appreciable length of time, together lead a formally administered round of life. These systems are composed of two groups variously called staff and patients, guards and inmates, keepers and kept. This is descriptive of such organizations as workhouses (remember *Oliver Twist?*), prisons, mental hospitals (for example, the movie *One Flew Over the Cuckoo's Nest,* based in part on a Veterans Hospital in California), the military (the movie *A Few Good Men*), and, in some instances, boarding schools. The experience of American Indian children who were reared in federal boarding schools is particularly relevant: socialization into "American" culture was the primary goal. They were often denied contact with their tribal cultures: denied the right to speak their own language, denied their tribal dress, and denied contact with their families and tribes for extended periods of time.

Generally, the purpose of a total institution is to socialize or resocialize the population with which it works, This is done by the staff through a two-step process designed to change the "structure of self" of their charges. The process begins by changing the person through external definition, usually by (1) divesting the person of socially defining symbols and characteristics (e.g., the "GI" haircut in army basic training and personal clothing); (2) using clothing to symbolize distinctions between inmates and staff (e.g., separate uniforms for guards and inmates, and "street clothing" for administrators; or hospital gowns for patients, as opposed to the green or white clothing of the medical staff); and (3) severing links with outside systems that tend to support and validate previous identity (again, the experience of American Indian children in boarding schools is an example). Thus, depersonalization and dehumanization are often the initial phase of experience within a total institution. Once a new, imposed definition has been established, the second step in the process is to see that the definition is internalized by the inmate (or patient, prisoner, or student) thus changing that person's "selfhood." In the case of American Indian children, forced socialization was often unsuccessful. Many children rejected the imposed "American" identities and were denied their own personal and tribal identities; many suffered identity problems, along with difficulties in being reabsorbed into their own tribal cultures. The objective of power and control, again, is to ensure compliance with the organization's goals; but power has limits, even in total institutions.

Coser differentiated "greedy institutions" from Goffman's total institutions on the basis that the latter were physically separate and used isolation as a means of control. Greedy institutions rely on voluntary compliance and loyalty. Status rewards are heavily relied on, and the higher the status, the higher the personal commitment of time and energy; one example was the extreme commitment of some personnel in the computer industry, for example, at Microsoft or at Dell computers, who worked eighty or more hours per week for long periods, developing new products. Some of the latter became "Dell-ionaires," amassing fortunes in company stock, then leaving to pursue their dreams as automobile racers or independent entrepreneurs.

E. Leadership

Leadership may be either formal or informal, and it includes power and control used to achieve organizational ends and to make means effective. *Command* is defined as the use of power to ensure compliance. Leadership is defined as a "continually creative function involving constant appraisal." Command derives from the organizational position, from the role and status, while leadership derives primarily from the personal characteristics of the leader. But leadership is not solely dependent upon these personal qualities: it also depends upon the context (the environment) in which it occurs.

Here is a simple, elegant formulation, which forms a typology of leadership:

1. The person *ahead* of the system through special accomplishment or creativity, e.g., Lincoln, Gandhi, Einstein, Lenin, or Freud.
2. The person who is *the head* of the system, given leadership through formal structural procedures such as election or delegation of authority, e.g., the president of the United States or a corporate chief executive officer (CEO).
3. The person who is *a head* of a system, one who situationally emerges with particular talents or qualities for determining and attaining systemic purposes. (Ross and Hendry, 1957:13-36)

In actuality, most situations of leadership will be some combination of two or three of these aspects. These three correspond to the dimensions of systems we use in this book, i.e., evolutionary, structural, and behavioral. Leadership, like power, may be horizontally as well as vertically hierarchical. Leadership occurs at all levels; organizations contain groups, and leadership emerges from these. In some organizations, such emergence of leadership at "lower" levels is deliberately cultivated; the usual manner in which this is done is to decentralize decision-making.

McDonald describes in detail the challenges facing social workers and the organizations they and their organizations face (2006). She suggests five strategies to be used by social work leaders to leverage new innovations:

1. *Taking what the system gives* … grasp unexpected opportunities … . know the system and take what it will give at any moment.
2. *Asking for more, settling for less.* …
3. *Maintaining ambiguity* … . makes it difficult for other institutional actors to orient what they do in response. …
4. *Trying five things to get one.* … have multiple courses of action plotted … . most will fail but a few will succeed. …

5. *Networking with other challenger groups who have no other coalitions ... .* (McDonald, 2006:211)

She also describes, in Chapter 8, "Entrepreneurial Social Work," ways in which social workers create new services and organizations, as innovations that can influence other, less satisfactory institutions and organizations. An alternative is to work within the established social welfare system, using social work skills in less traditional programs, such as welfare-to-work. She suggests that social workers will find opportunities to innovate within business corporations, as "occupational social workers." This is not new (see Carter, 1975, for nineteenth and twentieth century examples), but the newer model is for major corporations to hire consulting firms, many of which employ social workers to conduct managed care.

Conclusion

Organizations present significant problems for our society, as well as providing means to deal with other, serious societal problems. Large business organizations may provide a model for federal programs, when they decentralize and allow local administration of services. However, it is an open question whether corporations will develop a "social conscience" sufficient to allay some of the very problems that their activities create: pollution, large-scale layoffs, removal of plants to other countries, inequitable tax write-offs, unsafe products, monopolizing local capital, and competing with smaller-scale, local businesses that have sustained communities for generations. The practices of large corporations and financial institutions, which led to the economic crisis of 2007-2010, lend urgency to answering this question; reliance on government intervention in a massive way, e.g., billions of dollars for "bailouts," raises other questions.

In the field of human services, the effects of privatization are yet to be determined, particularly in a time of economic crisis that has dire effects for large numbers of workers, their families, and dependents. Decentralization is an attractive idea; its implementation has an uncertain future. Returning responsibility for delivery of social services to local agencies ("devolving") may sound attractive, but it is clear that funding at local levels is inadequate to meet increasing needs, and that federal intervention will be necessary, in some form. Again, the structure and functions of these organizations will be critical to long-term viability of the nation's economy and society. We refer you to the quotation at the opening of the Introduction to this sixth edition. We need "profound" people in "profound" organizations.

Suggested Readings

Adams, Scott. *The Dilbert Principle.*
1996 *The Dilbert Principle.* New York: Harper Collins.
   Always a delight, and often too close to the truth, the daily "Dilbert" cartoon lays bare the inner torments of corporate America. Some ideas are inspired by submissions from the cubicles, probably using the company's E-mail.
Branch, Taylor.
1988 *Parting the Waters: America in the King Years: 1954-1963.* New York: Simon and Schuster.
   This historical account of the roots of the modern civil rights movement exemplifies the transitory shifts between community and organization.
Hall, Richard H.
1996 *Organizations: Structures, Processes, and Outcomes.* Englewood Cliffs, NJ: Prentice-Hall.
   This is a comprehensive, accessible text, organized in "reverse order," placing aspects of organizations first, and theory last, a useful approach. Well-organized and conceptually sound.
Handy, Charles B.
1985 *Understanding Organizations.* Harmondsworth, England: Penguin. 1993 *Understanding Organizations.* New York: Oxford University Press.
   "Jam-packed" with information; also entertaining due to Handy's selection of illustrations and excerpts. The "Guide to Further Study" is unique, a selection of the author's comments and musings on the subject. Highly recommended in paperback.
Hasenfeld, Yeheskel.
1983 *Human Services Organizations.* Englewood Cliffs, NJ: Prentice-Hall.
   This has been the most useful text for a course on human services organizations. It is comprehensive and thought-provoking.
Hasenfeld, Yeheskel, ed.
1992 *Human Services as Complex Organizations.* Newbury Park, CA: Sage.
   A highly valuable sourcebook; a companion text to Hasenfeld's earlier text, just described.
McDonald, Catherine.
2006 *Challenging Social Work.* Houndmills and New York: Palgrave Macmillan.
   No social worker should graduate without reading this book. It describes detail the organizational world in which social work exists, both a chilling and an exhilarating environment. She promotes radical changes in social work's mission.
Scott, W. Richard.
1998 *Organizations: Rational, Natural, and Open Systems,* fourth edition. Englewood Cliffs, NJ: Prentice-Hall.
   A remarkable book; this is the definitive overview of theories of organization; he regards an "open systems" theory of organizations as the most useful and comprehensive viewpoint. It includes detailed history and critiques of organization theories.
Senge, Peter M.
1990 *The Fifth Discipline.* New York: Doubleday.

While this is a management text, it is also a systems approach to organizations. He makes a convincing case that the "fifth discipline," which is systems thinking, underlies all aspects of management.

Literary Sources

Kesey, Ken.
  1962 *One Flew Over the Cuckoo's Nest.* New York: The Viking Press.
  The modern classic story of the round of life in a total institution. Loosely based on a real Veterans Hospital in California.
Solzhenitsyn, Alexander.
  1963 *A Day in the Life of Ivan Denisovich.* New York: Praeger.
  [1968] 1969 *Cancer Ward.* New York: Farrar, Strauss, and Giroux.
  1973 *Gulag Archipelago.* New York: Harper & Row.
  Any of Solzhenitsyn's novels/documentaries are worth reading as examples of "total" institutions and the survival of the human spirit within them.

Films and Videos

Barbarians at the Gate (*1993*)
  A humorous, true tale of the attempt by the CEO of RJR Nabisco to take over the company, with the help of American Express based on the book. Made for television; it won Golden Globe awards.
The Corporation (2005)
  Michael Moore's powerful indictment of the modern multinational megacorporation. While it omits some of the positive aspects of corporations, it still presents the negative effects on the environment and on people's lives, and identifies characteristics that justify labeling it a sociopathic "person" (The U.S. Supreme Court affirmed the "personhood" of corporations in 2010). Excellent history of the development of corporations over the last 400 years.
Enron: The Smartest Guys in the Room (2005)
  Based on the best-selling book, it portrays the fall of a highly successful corporation, due to the greed and manipulations of its top executives.
Roger and Me (1989)
  Michael Moore pursues the elusive chairman of General Motors, to discuss the closing of an automobile plant in his hometown of Flint, Michigan. Moore is a populist *agent provocateur,* satirizing and lambasting corporate America. The video vividly portrays community response to social disaster, and community decline. He pursued this theme in his 1997 Film, *The Big One,* also.
Up in the Air (2009)
  A consultant (George Clooney) whose job it is to terminate corporations' employees discovers, painfully, the high costs of his job, through his relationships with a junior colleague and with a woman with a similar job.
Welfare (1975)
  One of Frederick Wiseman's series of documentaries, it is among the best materials for the study of organizations. It portrays an unending purgatory for welfare recipients and staff in a Manhattan welfare office, a Kafkaesque environment in which clients and staff are both caught.

6

Groups

Introduction

The social group is a critical system to each person and, in particular, to the helping professions. As an arena of social interaction, the group has potential to provide for a range of human needs, which include:

1. a need to belong and to be accepted by others;
2. a need to be validated by others through feedback processes;
3. a need to share common experiences with others; and
4. opportunities to work with others on common tasks.

The human group is a social system that has received, and deserves, extensive investigation, because it is uniquely adaptable and can be put to an infinite number of uses in a huge variety of settings. The term "group" comprises those patterns of association and activity in which persons engage most of their "selves" from day to day. Its components are individuals and small constellations of persons (e.g., dyads and triads) and it is, in turn, a component of its environment. A group is more than simply an aggregate of individuals: it has a systemic wholeness. As Kurt Lewin phrased it, "The whole is different from the sum of its parts; it has definite properties of its own." (Note that we use the words "different from," not "more than.") The human group is a system distinguishable from its environment, has the characteristics and functions of a system, and provides the connection between its components and its environment. Like other social systems, groups are characterized by energy/information exchange to promote *synergy;* this term, originated by anthropologist Ruth Benedict, was applied to groups by psychologist Abraham Maslow.

From a social systems perspective, a cluster of persons can be considered a group only if it fulfills certain specific criteria of systems. Instead of assuming that aggregations are systems, each cluster should be examined to determine whether they do, in fact, have the properties of systems.

An example might be the ensemble of characters in the two popular television series "Friends" and "Cheers": in each series, the characters interact as a whole group on occasion, but some interact as dyads or triads; two couples were lovers who interact as a subset of the whole; and each interacts intimately at times with others who are not members of the usual "cast of characters." Do they constitute a group? A loose network? A fluidly structured aggregation? In other words, a gathering together of persons does not make a group. The expression "the group jelled" conveys a point in time or process when an aggregate of persons became an entity, a group, distinguishable from its environment (that is, it had an interactional boundary), and different from the sum of its parts.

This leads to the questions: What kinds of groups are there, and what are the significant properties of a group as system? The remainder of this chapter answers these questions.

I. Types of Groups

Small groups are distinctive among social systems examined in this book in that a group can be created for particular purposes: for therapy, self-actualization, support, problem-solving, goal achievement, or to influence larger systems as in community organization and social action. In practice, groups often fit into more than one of the types described below, simply because groups are such powerful instruments for change, and have a wide range of effects, both intentional and unintentional. Out of the incredibly wide range of types of groups, we have selected those that seem most common and useful for the human services.

A. Growth Groups, or Human Potential Groups

Growth groups, or human potential groups, are organized to further purposes of their members, usually *personal* growth, through provision of intensive group experience over a limited time span. Examples include

T-groups, sensory awareness groups, encounter groups, sensitivity training groups, and marathon groups. Other varieties of groups may also be considered in this general category, however: hobby groups, theater groups, art groups, book groups, recreation groups (swim clubs, softball teams, and bowling teams might even qualify, on occasion, if the physical activity is secondary to personal development; it is an elastic category). "Growth-oriented groups have as their focus the facilitation of an individual's passage through the normal developmental stages. There is no assumption of pathology. Rather, the person is interested in becoming more aware of himself or herself as a struggling human being" (Reid, 1997:11).

Growth groups tend to focus on expressive functions, to emphasize feelings and impersonal transactions. The norms include mutuality of support, openness, and disclosure. The group's powers of acceptance and validation are employed. However, it is essential that group leaders be competent to deal with the hazards of intensive group experience.

B. Therapeutic Groups, or Remedial Groups

Reid divides "remedial groups" (which we consider to be the same as therapeutic groups) into three kinds:

(1) *supportive treatment groups,* which "generally emphasize restoration,enhancement, or maintenance of each member's level and mode of functionor problem solving";

(2) *interpersonal growth groups,* which "focus on helping members gaininsight, growth, and change in their relationships"; and

(3) *intrapsychic growth groups,* which emphasize development of insight into one's own personality. (1997:12)

Therapeutic groups are structured to serve as vehicles for persons struggling with intrapsychic concerns. Often the group is open-ended and long-term, with members cycling in and out. Therapeutic groups usually have an expressive focus with leaders clearly differentiated from the group. Socialization and communication are emphasized. Group process may be subordinated temporarily to the need of an individual member.

C. Self-Help and Support Groups

Over the last sixty years, there has been a phenomenal increase in the incidence of persons who come together around a common personal concern; groups exist for virtually every such concern. Self-help and support groups differ primarily in the amount of direction the leader or facilitator provides.

> The role of the worker is to encourage sharing, risk taking, and mutual problem solving. He or she may ask members to speak directly to one another, may focus the discussion, and may limit story telling. ... The worker helps members explain their situations, offer suggestions to others, provide support, and learn from each other. (Reid, 1997:11)

Self-help and support groups differ from therapeutic groups in that members of self-help and support groups are not seeking (at least overtly) personal psychological insight or growth. Sharing experiences and ways of coping are vehicles for mutual help—self and other, helping and accepting help. In self-help groups, professional direction is usually not wanted, although in some circumstances, a professional helper may convene a group or sponsor it. The focus is either on participants working on a kind of personal problem they share with the other group members, or joining together to influence external systems to provide resources or recognize members' needs and rights (e.g., a battered women's group, or a group of neighbors in a community who seek better policing or better housing, or a feminist group). Such groups are:

1. a source of immediate support, where the knowledge that the meeting will take place every week provides a safety net in itself, e.g., Alcoholics Anonymous;
2. a place to recognize shared experiences and the value to be derived from these, e.g., a writers' support group;
3. a way of reducing isolation and loneliness, e.g., an elders' group in a senior center;
4. a source for a new perspective on personal problems, e.g., parents of autistic children, caregivers of Alzheimer's or AIDS patients;
5. a place to experience power of personal situations with the capacity to change and have an effect on these, e.g., divorced or divorcing persons; and
6. a source of friendship, e.g., a group of singles who meet regularly to attend social or recreational events.

Although some self-help groups may be largely task-oriented, sentiment is an ever-present factor.

Some self-help groups originate locally, whereas others are national organizations with local face-to-face chapters. Alcoholics Anonymous, Alanon, Ala-Teen, and Weight Watchers fit the cultural penchant for mobility, in that members who migrate to different geographic locales can immediately affiliate with a local chapter in their community.

Such groups evolve their own leadership in order to pursue specific goals, often the protection of civil rights, or social and cultural values that are threatened. Such groups include survivalists, white "militia," and white supremacists, whose avowed purposes are to defend themselves and their values, by violence if necessary, against those whom they define as enemies. Some "Tea Party" members, as well as members of other groups, publicly brandish guns (some loaded) to signify their willingness to resort to violence in defense of "liberty."

D. Consciousness-Raising and Social Action Groups

Consciousness-raising has its roots in radical social/political philosophy, e.g., the use of Paolo Freire's (1983) *conscientizacion* philosophy (see Appendix A) in which literacy training among low-income groups was accompanied by discussions about political structures and personal involvement in social change. One objective of such groups is *cognitive restructuring, self-examination of one's behavior and reactions.*

> ... cognitive restructuring can play a key role in helping group members to gain control over their environment ... by encouraging women to:
> 1. recognize patterns of self-protection, self-blame and self-effacement from the past, and to articulate the reasons behind the need for such behaviour;
> 2. express distress and anger at the extent to which direct, honest self-expression has been denied them ...
> 3. recognize such behaviours and cognitions as survival mechanisms, rather than pathological disturbances. (Butler and Wintram, 1991:66-67)

Groups that fit this category include:

1. *Social advocacy* groups, which promote and support activism, e.g., gay rights groups, HIV/AIDS patient groups, advocates for accessibility for handicapped persons, feminist groups, or tenants rights groups.
2. *Empowerment* groups, which combine elements from other types of groups (e.g., self-development, advocacy, and specific problem) while focusing on increasing each member's self-awareness, confidence, and capacity to gain control of their lives. Examples include groups for victims of domestic abuse, childhood sexual abuse, sexual harassment, or for persons who are overweight, anorexic, or bulimic, as well as self-discovery groups.
3. *Task Groups*. Task groups most often are part of organizations, but may exist independently. They assume, or are assigned, specific tasks to accomplish, within a specified time period. Task groups include committees (appointed for a fixed term or for as long as needed), work teams (e.g., the autonomous work groups described in the preceding chapter), and volunteers who accept responsibility for completion of a specific goal (e.g., fund-raising). Reid (1997:12) points out that "While not normally thought of as a form of treatment, task groups can have significant therapeutic value," but this is rarely their primary intent,

of course. In the authors' experience, personal dynamics of at least one member are often involved. As a community organization text states it, "all group interactions have a *task* and a *process* dimension, and *task groups of all kinds must attend to both in order to succeed* (Hardcastle, Wenocur, and Powers, 1997:264).

Aside from individual persons carrying out their assignments, task groups are probably the most common means of accomplishing tasks in our society, especially in organizations. It is a rare organization participant who is not a member of at least one task group. Productive participation requires sufficient personal development to initiate ideas and defend them, to maturely consider others' contributions apart from one's personal relationship to them, to assume leadership if necessary, and to be able and willing to subordinate oneself to the general will of the group if necessary. Thus task groups are adult enterprises that children learn by participating themselves, usually in school, youth organizations and clubs, or through their religious affiliations.

F. Cliques and Coalitions

This topic is an example of the difficulty in choosing a level of analysis when defining and analyzing systems. Some *ad hoc* groups operate within organizations without legitimation, as cliques, coalitions, or cabals (depending upon one's viewpoint). Most administrators or managers can provide examples of such groups, which challenge the formal leadership of the organization and coalesce around one or more issues. They may have a base of legitimacy as members of a committee, or by virtue of their positions (as supervisors, or lower-level administrators, e.g.); or, instead, they may have *power* by virtue of controlling certain resources internally (the majority of votes on an important committee; knowledge of Robert's Rules of Order; or knowledge of decisions made in the past) or through connections to external sources of energy (e.g., funding sources, or as members of the labor union that represents the organization's work force).

Such groups usually are time-limited: they dissolve with their goal satisfied (or unsatisfied); achieve power and become the leadership themselves; or simply fade as circumstances change (the current leader departs, the organization changes, or members of the clique drop out or leave the organization, e.g.). It is difficult to predict or generalize about the evolution of such groups.

Most people who work in organizations have observed such cliques, participated in them, or opposed them. We do not imply that such groups are necessarily wrong or unjustified; e.g., they may champion the cause of an employee (or group of employees) who has been wronged, like the once-famous *Willmar 8* (the name of a movie about them), a group of women employees at a bank in Minnesota who, for several years, protested the treatment they received. Groups might also protest illegal practices or inept management in the organization; e.g., a group of faculty members might advocate unionization as a means of "saving the soul" of a university from a "corporate mindset."

II. Dimensions of Groups

There are as many kinds of groups as there are group leaders, observers, and therapists (and perhaps members, since each has a unique personal perspective). Rather than attempt a comprehensive taxonomy, we will discuss a few important dimensions that have been used to classify groups. These dimensions are here discussed as polarities. Any given group, at any given time, theoretically could be placed at some point on each continuum.

A. Instrumental versus Expressive

This continuum is similar to others that are frequently used: "task vs. sentiment," "goal achievement vs. group maintenance," "task-oriented vs. group-oriented." The distinction is usually understood as being between a particular, articulated, time-limited objective and a diffuse, unarticulated, enduring and supportive group climate. Further, the distinction is usually taken to imply that a "goal" or "task" is adaptive, that is, related to the environment, whereas "expressiveness" or "sentiment" is related to interactions among components of the group. The distinction is best understood as a distinction between two desirable steady states toward which the group could move. The first steady state is one in which some fairly clear, specific objective would be accomplished. The other state is one in which the objectives are fairly diffuse and nonspecific. Consequently, instrumental or expressive activities are intended to move the group toward one of these two steady states. Perhaps "adaptive versus integrative" would be equally accurate: "The social system, in its organization ... tends to swing or falter back and forth between two theoretical poles; optimum adaptation to the outer situation at the cost of internal malintegration, or optimum internal integration at the cost of maladaptation to the situation" (Weisman, 1963:87).

These are polarities and are not mutually exclusive. The "adaptive" steady state focuses more attention on goals and tasks but also deals with integration, although to a lesser extent. The "integrative" steady state, similarly, does not exclude some adaptive activity. For example, the U.S. Supreme Court (indeed a powerful group) must spend some time mediating between the Justices' personal feelings at times (Woodward and Armstrong, 1981; Lazarus, 1998). A sensitivity group must make decisions about meeting dates and when termination should occur. Another example is Reginald Rose's play (and movie) *Twelve Angry Men* (in its original and later versions), which illustrates the successive steady states of a jury as it alternately focuses upon the court's demand for a verdict and the members' personal needs (Rose, 1955). It is this variability that makes "group" difficult to characterize, in contrast to the family, which is predominantly integrative, and the organization, which is predominantly adaptive.

Groups resemble both communities and organizations; a community comprises groups and shares their indeterminate character. We suggest this guideline: The greater the breadth of influence that a group has upon its members and the more diffuse its goals, the more it resembles a community. Groups resemble organizations to the extent that they are aimed toward specific goals.

B. Primary versus Secondary

This polarity describes the importance that the group has for its members. The afternoon (or morning) neighborhood coffee klatch in members' homes or at a coffee shop, and the Wednesday afternoon or Saturday morning gathering of golfers at "the 19th hole" are good examples. It is predominantly (if not purely) expressive. If it is highly significant to its members, it is a primary group; but if it has relatively little importance to them, it should be considered secondary (one shouldn't forget, of course, that the group may be more important to one member than to another). This criterion is the breadth of influence the group has upon its members and particularly its influence upon their affective functioning. Another way of saying this is that if members react to each other as role occupants rather than as persons, it is a secondary group. As these roles become more formalized, the group becomes more goal-specific and narrows its range of influence; thus, the closer the group comes to being an organization.

C. Narcissistic versus Generative

This polarity applies to the self-gratification of one or more members versus a wider commitment to the *group's* goals; this is similar to Freud's pleasure and reality principles, and is related to Erikson's crisis of "generativity *vs.* stagnation" (see Chapter 8). The importance of this dimension of groups is that it explains the ability (or inability) of some groups to survive; that is, a concentration solely upon members' needs violates the principle that no single function can be concentrated upon to the complete exclusion of others. If members are unwilling to adapt, the result could be an inability to alter relationships (and therefore structure), resulting in a closed, morphostatic system. By contrast, a generative system, like a generative person, would engage in mutually constructive interchange with its environment and among its components.

McClure reports that

> One member described an essential characteristic of generative groups when he related that the desire was always for the group's success rather than any individual achievement that might be gained by association with this project. One characteristic that indicated the enormous trust and safety that existed within the group was the childlike atmosphere that was created in many of the meetings. Members were able to suspend their adult behaviors and recapture the creativity, curiosity, and wonderment of childhood. (McClure, 2005: 233)

The polarities discussed above indicate that groups have important properties of systems: adaptation, integration, goal-seeking, structural maintenance, and structural change.

III. Aspects of Group as System

A. Evolutionary Aspects

Analysis of any specific group requires attention to its evolution. This is true because groups and families are more dependent upon specific persons than are other systems and are thus more likely to be affected by changes in personnel. By contrast, organizations are usually deliberately designed to minimize dependence upon individual persons. Formation and disintegration of a group are more likely to occur during a single member's lifetime, and therefore can be observed and analyzed by a single observer. Accordingly, in literature about groups, more attention has been paid to "process" (behavior) and to problem-solving (goal attainment) than to structure. Research on groups has focused mostly on the dynamic balance (or steady state) of the group. In group work practice, it has been almost a dogma that all aspects of groups are subordinate to the maintenance of steady state. In our discussion of other systems, we have had to establish that they are systems and that steady state is a valid term to apply to them; with groups, the problem is the converse—so much has been researched and written on the group as a system, and on group equilibrium or steady state, that the task instead is to establish that any other aspect of the system is of equal importance.

B. Steady State

> The group is like an organism—a biological organism. It forms, grows, and reaches a state of maturity. It begins with a set of constituent elements—individuals with certain personalities, certain needs, ideas, potentialities, limitations—and in the course of development evolves a particular pattern of behavior, a set of indigenous norms, a body of beliefs, a set of values, and so on. Parts become differentiated, each assuming special functions in relations to other parts and the whole. ... As a group approaches maturity it becomes more complex, more differentiated, more interdependent, and more integrated. (T. Mills, 1967:13)

This is a detailed way to describe a group's steady state. More general ways are to describe its "identity," or its "culture." Mills described groups as having some of the same qualities that Erikson described in persons. Groups have "personality" or "syntality," similar to the personalities of individuals. It might be accurate to say that each group possesses its own culture, a microcosm of the larger culture. Without its own culture (or microculture) the group would not be a system but merely an aggregate of individual persons.

a. Norm, consensus, and bond. A group establishes norms through consensus. One definition of *norm* is:

> It incorporates a value judgment. It is a rule or standard to which the members of a group are expected to adhere. A set of norms introduces a certain amount of regularity and predictability into the group's functioning. (Northen, 1988:33-34)

In groups, if successful, individual persons' norms tend to converge into a group norm. This was illustrated in the classic Bank Wiring Observation Room study, in which workers had explicit expectations about the production norms and pressured others to conform. Another example is the group norm of supporting their "buddies" among soldiers or their "partners" among police officers. As cartoonist Bill Mauldin stated in *Up Front,* combat units "have a sort of family complex."

> New men in outfits have to work their way in slowly, but they are eventually accepted. Sometimes they have to change their way of living. An introvert or recluse is not going to last long in combat without friends, so he learns to come out of his shell. Once he has "arrived" he is pretty proud of his clique, and he in turn is chilly toward outsiders. (Cartwright and Zander, 1960:165)

The norm is cooperation; the underlying consensus is survival, whether in World War II, Vietnam, Iraq, Afghanistan, or the streets of an American city.

Consensus is agreement regarding goals, norms, and roles. When such agreements and satisfactions of needs bind members to the group, the group has "attractiveness" or "valence," and the result is cohesiveness of the group. Such cohesiveness gives rise to solidarity. The Polish labor union Solidarity obviously included this meaning in its name. For a decade after the union was declared illegal, Solidarity's members exhibited sufficient cohesiveness to prevail over the government of Poland, to be declared legal again, and to function as part of the government; the head of the union, Lech Walesa, became President of the Republic of Poland.

With the establishment of norms and consensus, a group is well on its way to having forged a *bond* between its members. Grace Coyle described group *bond* as having three levels:

1. conscious purpose, for example sociability or friendship;
2. assumed or unavowed objectives, such as achievement or status, ego-expansion, courtship (especially among adolescents), and class rise;
3. unconscious purpose, including sanctioned release of aggression, escape from reality, and sublimation of erotic impulses. (Coyle, 1948)

Consensus and cohesiveness, then, are *expressive, integrative,* and *primary* aspects of the group and are essential to supporting goal direction.

b. Goal attainment. In contrast to consensus and cohesiveness, goal attainment is *instrumental, adaptive,* and *secondary.*

Group "purpose" means any ultimate aim, end, or intention, or, as we define it in the glossary, a desired steady state of the group. Group *objective* or *goal* usually refers to some specific end that is instrumental to the purpose. We use "goal" to mean both those ends the suprasystem assigns to the group and those ends sought by the group itself.

"Locomotion" is the name given to group goal pursuit by Kurt Lewin and the group dynamics theorists. It means that a group moves within its environment to achieve goals; the goals are mutually defined by the group and its relevant environment. Goal-directed behavior affects group consensus and cohesiveness. It may disrupt expressive, integrative norms and force members to choose between instrumental and expressive behaviors.

2. Stages of Evolution. As a group seeks to establish its steady state, it moves through various stages of dynamic evolution, as discussed in the following section. "Social scientists have, for decades, grappled with the issue of sequence and order in a group's development .... there is no agreement as to how many stages exist and what these stages actually look like" (Reid, 1997:56). Here is one very general, abstract view that describes stages as feedback loops within groups:

1. The group adapts to its environment; in response to this adaptive behavior, members develop activities, sentiments, and interactions. These adaptive components are the group's external system.

2. The group develops activities, sentiments, and interactions beyond the necessary adaptive behavior, through its goal-oriented behavior; these become the internal system.
3. As the internal system elaborates, it develops bond, cohesiveness, norms, roles, and statuses.
4. In feedback fashion, [external] adaptation is affected by the environment and the developing internal system.
5. The group, in turn, modifies the functioning of its members. (Weisman, 1963:87)

In Table 6.1, we present our own, generalized scheme of group development. Our scheme focuses on the internal development of the group; little reference is made to the environment, since it is difficult (if not impossible) to generalize about the myriad environments in which groups exist. It is designed to acquaint the reader with a wide range of aspects of group development—in reality, no single group exhibits all these aspects or this exact sequence of stages. We encourage the reader to apply this scheme to actual groups, bearing in mind that a systems view of groups includes "looping back" to other stages, and not a strict, sequential set of stages. None of these phases is presented here as discrete or absolute.

a. Phase I: E pluribus unum. During this first major phase, exploration of each other occurs among the members. Members probe each other, testing for security and support, and look primarily to the leader for direction, rather than to other members. Eventually, in successful groups, members agree to tolerate each other's thoughts, feelings, and behaviors, although there may be some reluctance, initially. Here is how an experienced group leader describes it:

> Handling the multifaceted intricacies of groups requires embracing their complexity. To do this requires the leader to move beyond the linear, rational thinking of cause and effect and into the nonlinear realm. Ultimately, recognition of nuance occurs as an intuition or a felt sense of the whole, a willingness to trust the "inner voice," the images and fantasies that arise from the unconscious. Unlike more reasoned interventions, responding to the group with a felt sense will more likely entrain the leader with the group. (McClure, 2005:120)

Such tolerance permits open discussion of the group's emerging culture, i.e., the way we do things. Some sense of "we-ness" must emerge: "Until that collection of autonomous individuals begins to feel some allegiance to the collectivity and finds some way to work together on a common goal, a group has not yet formed" (Hardcastle et al., 1997:265).

Carl Rogers identified and described the phases of encounter groups. His phases are similar to our generic outline here. Rogers described "patterns or stages," the first five of which fit within our first major stage. They are (1) "milling around," (2) "resistance to personal expression," (3) "description of past feelings," (4) "expression of negative feelings," and (5) expression of personal feelings (Rogers, 1970:15-20). Discussion of symbols and meanings may take the form of tentative exploration of what structure is possible for the group, what "freedom" means in this group, and how others interpret what the leader says. The interpretation that members arrive at determines the group's "valence," or attractiveness. Members begin to share their "life space" (Lewin's term) to permit others to enter their interactional, personal territory, their "bubbles." This first stage is similar to Tuckman's (1965) stage of *forming*. Leaders of women's groups reported that

> ... women's groups should experiment with as many different pursuits, activities and exercises as possible, in order to connect with the totality of women's lives and selves. ... Our own trials and errors, and statements that women have made, have taught us that trips out and visits, the opportunity for fun, laughter and enjoyment, are just as central as psychotherapeutic exercises and sociopolitical discussions. (Butler and Wintram, 1991:42)

b. Phase II: Control phase. In our second major phase, the emphasis shifts from "inclusion" to "control." In this control stage the member asks: Now that I have decided to be a member of the group, what power will I have in it? Who is in charge and how do I find this out? What does the group want of me?

One text (Corey, *et al.*; 1982:91-93) describes a stage following the preliminary testing of each other by members, a stage in which members are engaging in productive, mutual activity. This is labeled the "working stage" and has the following characteristics: (1) a focus on the immediate interactions; direct and meaningful interaction, including confrontations; (2) free communication among members; the group becomes an "orchestra," listening to each other and working productively together; (3) self-disclosure is the norm; (4) members know each other through feedback and learn to trust the feedback; and (5) group cohesion is increased as they become "a trusting community." This second phase is similar to Tuckman's stage of *norming*.

Rogers's stages 6-10 are not applicable to all types of groups but illustrate evolution in encounter groups. In these stages, immediate interpersonal feelings are disclosed; a "healing capacity" develops; members are willing to risk, resulting in self-acceptance and change; "facades" begin to be discarded, and the member receives feedback, both positive and negative.

Table 6.1 Synthesis of Stages of Group Evolution[a]

Phases	Cognitive aspects	Affective aspects	Behavioral aspects
I. E. pluribus unum Components' goals predominate Affiliation (approach-avoidance) Commitment	Discussion of symbols, meanings Attempt to find common meanings, symbols Limited agreement on symbols, meanings, norms	Checking for feelings, values of others; "valence" Expression of feelings Development of group bond; satisfaction of individual's feelings; group values emerge	Observes behavior of others; tentative participation Interaction and reaction in overt behavior; territory shared Beginning of modification of behavior to conform; mutual accommodation; locomotion
II. Control phase Group goals predominate Socialization Social control ↘a Stability (internal)	Internalization of developing group culture; accommodation of schemes Standardization; acceptance of group views; subordination of idiosyncratic views Enforcement of group views, codes and stated purposes; "right thinking" and developed symbol systems	Same as cognitive Subordination of idiosyncratic feelings; reinforcement of those that "match" others' Enforcement of group values; statements expressing solidarity and allegiance; traditions	Roles defined and agreed to Group prescription of behavior; reduction of deviance; differentiation of roles and territories Rituals, offices, hierarchy

Group goal direction (external) ↘a; Intimacy; cohesiveness	Problem solving; decision making; thought exclusively focused on goal and means to achieve it; "brainstorming" — Exchange with each other to the exclusion of non-members; "private" group views, beliefs, actions	Elevation of values that support goal; devotion to them, excluding other values, both personal and group — Devotion to each other, to exclusion of ties with "outsiders"	Focus on specific group goal; sacrifice and joint effort — Group rituals and culture concretized and protected
III. Conflict phase — Components' goals predominate	Dissensus on norms, goals, evaluations; selectiveness of evidence used against group members	Disaffection; return (or maintaining) to predominance of individuals' sentiments; "hidden-agendas" predominate	Antagonistic behavior; violation of roles, territories, boundaries; violation of rituals, hierarchy
	Loop to earlier phase or move to terminal phase		
IV. Terminal phase — Disintegration (into subgroups or complete disassociation)	Maintenance of divergent views; ideological combat	Hostility; defensiveness; feelings of betrayal, anger	Alliances; power struggles; 'splitting' from the group; 'betrayal' to outsiders
Termination (planned or by agreement)	Reinforcement of belief of worth of group; attempt to analyze "meaning" of the group	*OR* Feelings of guilt, rejection because of termination; warmth toward other members	Open communication about termination; displays of sentiment; approach or "flight" behaviors

[a] Arrows indicate that these subphases may be reversed in sequence.

The notable difference between our scheme and Rogers's is that he deals little with group goal attainment. This is understandable since his encounter groups were oriented toward relatively diffuse goals, and achievement of goals beyond group process were of minor importance.

c. Phase III: Conflict phase. Phase III can occur at any point in the group process. It does not necessarily follow Phase I or II. It is similar to Tuckman's stage of *storming.* Conflict can occur at any point, and it is a crisis in the life of the group: the group will either loop back to an earlier stage (similar to regression in individual persons) to resolve the issue or at least deal with it in some fashion so that the group can proceed. Rogers described well some of the most intense encounters that take place in groups:

> *Confrontation.* There are times when the term feedback is far too mild to describe the interactions that take place ...
> *Norma:* (loud sigh). ... Any real woman I know wouldn't have acted as you have this week and particularly what you said this afternoon. That was so crass!! It just made me want to puke, right there!!! And—I'm just *shaking* I'm so mad at you,—I don't think you've been real once this week! ... I'm so infuriated that I *want to come over and beat the hell out of you!!* (1970:31-32)

After this, this group could have disintegrated or reverted to an earlier stage. However, if norms are established permitting resolution and continuation, positive resolution can occur. One example is the full expression of negative feeling to another member, which may lead to a deeper understanding and acceptance between the two members. Rogers called this "the basic encounter." Butler and Wintram described values in women's groups that promote integration even through confrontation:

- a belief that all contributions should be considered and if not used, then appreciated;
- a belief that mutual support is an effective buffer against stress and oppression;
- a belief that confrontation should be communal;
- the validation of efforts by members to change their behaviour, attitudes or lifestyle;
- a belief in sisterhood and collective action. (Butler and Wintram, 1991:85)

If norms have not developed, and positive outcomes are not forthcoming, however, conflict may result in disintegration and termination. Coser observed that "not all conflicts are positively functional for the relationship, but only those that concern goals, values, or interests that do not contradict the basic assumptions upon which the relation is founded" (ibid.:80). If members of one of the groups Rogers described did not take a healing role or offer mutual support, the conflict could indeed affect the basic function of encounter groups. The group might terminate or break into subgroups as indicated in the disintegration subphase of our Phase III. Northen described several attempts to resolve conflict that include:

> *elimination,* that is, forcing the withdrawal of the opposing individual or subgroup, sometimes in subtle ways. In subjugation, or domination, the strongest members force others to accept their points of view. ... Through the means of *compromise* ... each of the factions ... give up something to safeguard the common area of interest. ... An individual or subgroup may form an *alliance.* ... Finally, through *integration* a group may arrive at a solution that is both satisfying to each member and more productive and creative than any contending suggestion. ([1969 e,] 1988:42-43)

The latter is an example of *synergy,* of course, and an example of integration as a basic system function. Ødd Ramsoy (1962), a Norwegian sociologist, investigated the conflict inherent between system and subsystem in social groups. He observed that a group as an entity must tend toward adaptation and integration if it is to survive. The members must always decide between choices that favor system, subsystem, or suprasystem. Ramsoy postulated that conflict between part and whole decreases as the integrative problems of the common inclusive system outweigh each subsystem's adaptive problems and goal problems. Ramsoy and others concluded that *conflict can be reduced through concentration on a superordinate problem* (e.g., manufacturing a war to allay internal conflict, as satirically presented in the 1997 movie, *Wag the Dog*). Such conflict may provide an occasion for restoring a balance between adaptation and integration in the system's steady state. As an outcome of group process, it means that the components (individual members) and the system (the whole group) may have synergistically satisfied needs and goals. That, indeed, is the height of achievement for any system. We do not intend to minimize the existence or the (sometime) usefulness of conflict in systems, but no system endures with conflict alone, rather than cooperation (synergy), as its predominant mode of activity.

  d. Phase IV: Terminal phase. As indicated in Table 6.1, Phase IV represents a terminal phase, which may have one of two general out-comes: (1) disintegration or (2) a planned, or agreed-upon termination in an affirmative manner. Disintegration is essentially a loop back to an earlier phase in which components' goals predominated over those of the

group: either to the beginning (Phase I) if fundamental issues were unresolved at the start, or to Phase III, in which conflict predominated.

Reid's description of group evolution is based on the life stages of
individual persons, and this phase is "death." He uses Kübler-Ross's
stages of death and dying to identify group members' reactions to group
termination. While these seem appropriate enough (denial, rage and
anger, bargaining, depression, and acceptance), they seem to omit the
most positive outcomes of group process: celebration, a sense of fulfillment and accomplishment, satisfaction, and sometimes merely relief.
Our Phase IV is more similar to Tuckman's *adjournment* stage, which,
like ours, contains both affirmative and negative possibilities. Reid says
of the worker's role in this final stage:

> [T]he worker needs to help each member examine his or her responses. The worker
> also needs to help the members evaluate how the group has evolved and how they
> have grown. ... And the worker needs to encourage the members to look to the
> future and apply what they have learned to the other systems in their lives. (Reid,
> 1997:72-73)

B. Structural Aspects

1. *Boundary and Autonomy.* As with all systems, the boundaries of a
group are determined by the activity of the group and its components,
through interaction among the members and with the environment.
Persons define themselves as members, and are defined by others as
being members of the group (boundaries are reinforced both internally
and externally). For example, separation into religious denominations
is largely a matter of individual choice in many societies, but segregation by race, age, or gender is usually prescribed by society. Here is a
discussion of the boundaries of women's groups:

> There are ... times when women's group process *reflects* what happens in society
> by way of jealousy or competition between women. Women learn not to value each
> other, are threatened by each other, are deeply afraid of being seen to be dependent
> on each other, and resort to manipulation to get some leverage in personal relation-
> ships. All of this demonstrates the profound internalization of oppression. How can
> this well-established pattern be broken down among women's groups? (Butler and
> Wintram, 1991:93)

Groups have greater or lesser degrees of autonomy from their environment. A delinquent group such as Whyte's ([1955] 1981) Norton gang
was relatively autonomous from its environment, with few direct controls
or supports. In 1987, the Los Angeles city attorney stated concern about
the lack of societal controls on gangs (i.e., their autonomy): "In a mood

of frustration, you feel like the only effective way to deal with street gangs is with a flame thrower" (Vigil, 1988:x). The group of workers in the previously mentioned Bank Wiring Observation Room study was much less autonomous, being subject to a high degree of control by the Western Electric company (Roethlisberger and Dickson, 1947). The boundaries of both groups were clear: the Norton gang's boundary was much less permeable. Other examples of permeability of boundaries is cliques ("clicks") among high school students, and Mauldin's description of combat units cited earlier in this chapter. A group, as any other system, must have discernible, locatable boundaries in order to exist.

2. *Differentiation, Hierarchy, and Role.* As previously noted, differentiation of roles occurs as part of elaboration in the evolution of groups. These roles are ranked by the group according to the usefulness of the roles for adaptation and integration. In addition, the person who fills the role is evaluated; members of the group may respond to either the role or the person, or to both. When group members agree on rankings, the group may be said to be stratified.

Some roles become standardized among groups and persist regardless of the person occupying the role. Some roles are common to most groups: a scapegoat, who is the recipient of group hostility; a clown or joker, who may be either the butt of humor or the donor, and who serves an important expressive function; a peacemaker, to whom the group turns for conflict reduction, an important integrative or social control function; an idol, who sets some moral or social standard for the group; and a critic, who may carry out social control by voicing group ideals and negative judgments.

C. Behavioral Aspects

Adaptation has been discussed under the section on steady state, earlier in this chapter. Here we only restate that all group behavior has some bearing upon securing and expending energy externally (SE and GE functions) whether explicitly designed to do so or not. All systems must provide some service or product to their suprasystems or environments, but systems cannot concentrate exclusively on the adaptive function to the exclusion of integration.

1. *Leadership.* An important component of adaptation is leadership, the most researched subject on groups. The two most commonly identified forms are the *task* (instrumental or adaptive) *leader* and the *social-emotional* (expressive or integrative) *leader.* The latter is sometimes

called the sentiment leader. In his study of groups, Homans observed several rules for leadership:

1. The leader will maintain the primary position.
2. The leader will live up to the norms of the group. The higher the degree of conformity, the higher will be the member's rank.
3. The leader will not give orders that will not be obeyed; "losing face" would result.
4. In giving orders, the leader will use established channels.
5. The leader will listen.
6. The leader will be self-aware. (1950:440)

Common expectations for the leader role, for example, are:

> ... leadership in a group may be at one time abrupt, forceful, centralized, with all communications originating with the leader, and another time, slow, relaxed, dispersed, with much communication back and forth between leader and followers. Each mode is acceptable, appropriate and authoritative, but each in different circumstances. (ibid.:419)

McClure described a crucial point in groups:

> ... when the group reaches a tipping point or is far from equilibrium, linear explanations fail. These unstable points of change are best described from a chaos perspective because change is not smooth or linear, but involves a sudden transformation in which a lower form of organization is replaced by a higher order. As I discovered, it is during these moments of high instability that leader interventions can have the most impact on the group. (McClure, 2005:19)

In other words, interaction between the leader and the group members and between the group and its environment determine (through activity that creates structure) which form of leadership is most functional for the group at any particular time. The leadership role need not, and usually does not, reside in only one person. Leadership tasks are usually, if not always, distributed among the members. Perhaps leadership is best defined as "the set of functions through which the group coordinates the efforts of individuals" (Katz and Bender, 1976:117).

Problem-solving has received prime attention in social group work practice. Mills described task leadership and decision-making in groups in a way that could also apply to organizations:

> The executive system is the group's center for assessment of itself and its situations, for arrangement and rearrangement of its internal and external relations, for decision-making and for learning, and for "learning how to learn" through acting and assessing the consequences of action. ... The executive system is the partly independent, autonomous center where information about the role-system ... is processed. (ibid.:93)

More accurately, it is an executive *subsystem* that primarily serves the function of goal attainment.

2. *Socialization.* Socialization is integrative behavior within the group that is intended to furnish energy to the group and to reduce the likelhood of conflict. The use of small groups to facilitate socialization is widespread, e.g., the pledge group in a sorority, basic training in the military, groups to prepare schizophrenic persons for employment, and groups to resocialize former cult members (who were previously socialized *into* the cult group). Much like the family, the small group can readily serve as a transition into wider systems. Socialization into the group itself is based upon some match between the person's needs and the group's offering; a good example is the frequent use of groups by adolescents for security, opportunities to make friends, and to learn the cultures of both youth and adult life stages.

The process of socialization may be of three kinds:

a.   *compliance,* in which the person conforms, but does not agree with the group's view;
b.   *identification,* in which members adopt the group's view because the group becomes part of their own identities;
c.   *internalization,* in which the group's view is adopted because it meets some personal objective, or resolves a member's internal or external conflict; that is, the group's view agrees with the member's view.

The adaptation of the person and the integrative behavior of the system must reach some mutually acceptable "bargain," or the process of socialization will fail.

3. *Social Control and Social Conflict.* The process of standardization is related to social control. A group achieves consensus or steady state by shaping its members' behaviors in certain ways. The application of sanctions in one form or another is social control. The major means of control is energy applied to, or withheld from, a member. One example is the traditional Robert's Rules of Order in formal meetings; if members do not conform to its usage, they may not be recognized (i.e., allowed any oral interchange with the entire group) or may be ejected from the group. A more subtle example is that new members of the U.S. Congress are expected to "be seen but not heard." The play and film *Twelve Angry Men* illustrated the various forms that social control can take in a group, from threat of violence to ridicule or "putting down" a member.

An important part of social control in groups is conflict, discussed earlier in this chapter, and the management of conflict. Probably the most complete statement concerning the dimensions and uses of conflict in groups is found in Coser's *The Functions of Social Conflict* (1964).

4. *Communication.* We previously defined communication as "transfer of meaning or energy" by any means. According to this definition, virtually all group activity could be considered communication, rendering the term so broad as to be meaningless. Rather, we mean communication intended to accomplish adaptation, integration, social control, or goal attainment (in other words, the SE, SI, GI, and GE functions) for the system.

Bales's interaction process analysis theory of groups (Bales, 1950) is based upon the analysis of units of communication into a few categories, such as "shows solidarity," "shows tension release," "disagrees," and "shows antagonism." Tabulating the number of units exchanged during a given time and their distribution by categories allows some index of group process to be derived. This has been a popular means of group analysis. Other theorists, especially those with backgrounds in information theory, have also focused on communication as the basic process in groups. Small group communication became a field of study in its own right, with a rapidly increasing body of literature that included descriptions of communication nets in groups, including the diagrams in Figure 6.1 (Shaw, 1981; Handy, 1985).

Communication is best carried out when members have significant freedom, and are not overwhelmed by communication's demands on them. Communication between group members is one powerful element of leadership. In addition, one purpose of communication in groups is to allow the group members to improve their communication skills within the group and then transfer these skills to other systems. An example is a group of single, pregnant young women and their parents. This group provided

> ... the means whereby families may learn new, more appropriate communication behavior. ... In some instances, family members learn how to communicate better

Figure 6.1
Diagrams of communications networks.

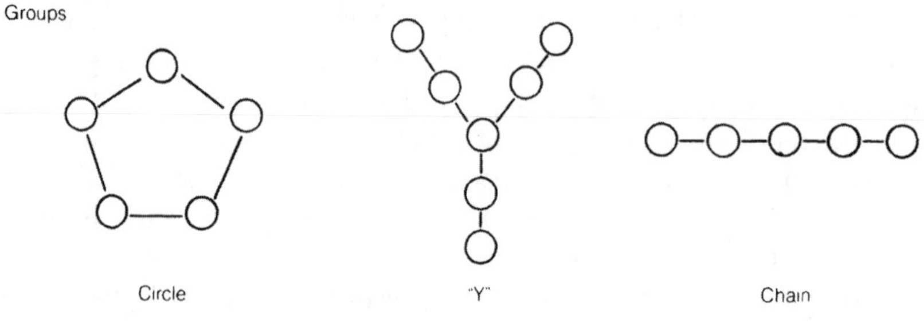

Groups

Circle   "Y"   Chain

when the therapists and the group decode messages that are sent and inappropriately received in a family system. In other instances, good communication among the therapists in the group's presence serves as a positive model. (Papademetriou, 1971:88)

One means of assuring that all members have opportunity to speak, and to be listened to, is the use of "speaking turns," periods of time during which each member is "given their own space," and other members give support and empathic responses. Among some American Indian tribes, passing around a "talking stick" has been a sophisticated means to achieve the same end, the recognition of every member's contribution.

Conclusion

It is clear from a wealth of research that groups are social systems. Furthermore, it is apparent that most group theory is based in systems thinking. Since group experiences are both natural and essential to social living, purposeful use of groups offers opportunities for people to come together to pursue mutual interests and goals. Those who work in human services must understand group phenomena and develop competence in working with groups in order to use wisely the fundamental and immense power contained in the human group.

Suggested Readings

Butler, Sandra, and Claire Wintram.
  1991 *Feminist Groupwork.* London: Sage.
    Excellent presentation and discussion of group work with women, thorough and insightful. They describe the social and psychological situations of women with precision and sensitivity.
Donigian, Jeremiah, and Richard Malnati.
  1997 *Systematic Group Therapy: A Triadic Model.* Pacific Grove, CA: Brooks/ Cole.
    This little book focuses on "the systemic nature of groups within the framework of general systems theory." It is clear, cogent, readable, compact, and (presumably) affordable; it is an excellent supplement to this chapter on groups. Its description of group process is generalizable to other groups.
Durkin, James E.
  1981 *Living Groups: Group Psychotherapy and General Systems Theory.* New York: Brunner/Mazel.
    Excellent attempt to reconcile social systems theory and other group treatment theories. Highly useful for the practitioner or teacher looking for stimulating ideas. Includes some case examples of the fit between the two bodies of thought.
Glassman, Urania, and Len Kates.
  1990 *Group Work: A Humanistic Approach.* Newbury Park, CA: Sage.
    The authors emphasize democratic values in the goals and conduct of groups. Their discussion of group stages is useful, and compatible with social systems theory.
Handy, Charles B.
  1985 *Understanding Organizations.* Harmondsworth, England: Penguin.
  1993 *Understanding Organizations.* New York: Oxford University Press.

Chapter 6, pp. 154-184, "On the Workings of Groups," is a fine, brief summary of knowledge about groups in organizations. As noted in Chapter 5, this is a unique book in its organization and excerpts.

Johnson, David W., and Frank P. Johnson.

1991 *Joining Together: Group Theory and Group Skills,* fourth edition. Englewood Cliffs, NJ: Prentice-Hall.

This book is truly impressive in its comprehensiveness and its inclusion of examples and exercises. Perhaps too large for a supplementary text.

Northen, Helen.

1988. *Social Work with Groups,* second edition. New York. Columbia University Press.

A newer edition of a classic text. Our comments on Roberts and Northen, below, are applicable here.

Reid, Kenneth E.

1997 *Social Work with Groups.* Pacific Grove, CA: Brooks/Cole.

Reid provides historical context for general group work. Much of what he describes is applicable to other kinds of groups. This is highly valuable, and is probably the best text currently for beginning group workers regarding group dynamics and process.

Roberts, Robert W., and Helen Northen, eds.

1976 *Theories of Social Work with Groups.* New York: Columbia University Press.

Excellent sections on historical development and thoughtful evaluation of current status of group work theories. They demonstrate explicitly that a systems approach is fundamental to virtually all theories of group work.

Literary Sources

Golding, William.

1959 *Lord of the Flies.* New York: Capricorn Books, Putnam.

Are human beings evil? Are we basically savage? These are Golding's questions in this famous novel, which portrays a Freudian triad of leaders. Provocative and disturbing depiction of a group of juveniles stranded on an island.

Films and Videos

The Full Monty (1997)

A small group of unemployed men in England find a unique way to cope with their common situation. Stages of group development are identifiable. Funny, and poignant in conveying their sense of loss.

Twelve Angry Men (1957; originally on television's "Studio One" in 1954)

Illustrates the interactive processes among jurors deliberating a capital case, and the shifts between individual and group goals; it demonstrates that a group is indeed different from the sum of its parts. There is also an updated version.

The More We Get Together (1986)

This video is primarily about working with very old, disoriented nursing home residents. Part II, "Three Stages of a Validation Group," demonstrates how to form a group with the goals of anxiety reduction, regaining social controls, and recovering sense of well-being.

7

Families

All happy families resemble each other; each unhappy family is unhappy in its own way,
     —Leo Tolstoy, Anna Karenina

As families go, so goes the nation.
     —Margaret Mead, United States Senate Hearing

Introduction

"Family systems theory" has been the predominant mode of analysis in family research and family treatment over the last half-century. As Burr says,

> Many of the concepts in family systems theory are the same as in general systems theory—for example, terms like input, output, feedback, rules of transformation, and boundaries. In addition, however, a number of concepts are primarily limited to the family-systems theory: individuation, mystification, paradoxical bonding, double bind, complementary and parallel relationships, metacommunication, rules and metarules, boundaries, openness, pseudomutuality, coalition, and triangulation. (Burr, 1995:85)

Since social systems theory lies between the "suprasystem" of GST and the "subsystem" of family systems theory, it uses some terms from both of the other levels, as was apparent in Chapters 1 and 2.

The family system is centrally important in defining social expectations and in providing resources necessary for growth, in every phase of the person's life cycle. Family is the only system that is inextricably interwoven with all other systems. As noted in Chapter 3, Section I, B, "The Family as a Human Universal," the family assumes, or is delegated, primary responsibility for socialization into the culture and major responsibility to ensure the survival of society and of humanity. However, it is not a unanimous opinion that families are responsible for the traits of their children. Rowe (1994) marshals research data to demonstrate that the "fit" between genetic endowment and cultural characteristics explains far more than family dynamics does. Whatever the outcome of this theory of *coevolution,* we should be cautious about heaping responsibility and blame upon families.

This chapter is entitled "Families" to emphasize that there is a wide variety of family forms. Use of the singular "family" and its implication of a single, normative form would perpetuate confusion and lack of precision when conducting "family analysis," "family policy," and studies of "family impact." Further, it would abet unrealistic and sometimes ideological efforts to enforce that norm as part of a political agenda, to the detriment of other families and children.

I. Approaches to Family Analysis

We will briefly examine selected approaches to understanding the family. Our intent here is to summarize those approaches that are most congruent with social systems theory.

A. Family as a System of Roles

The family as a system of roles is the predominant theme in the literature of family analysis. Roles embody cultural expectations for behavior, and the family is where these roles are learned and carried out. In classical psychoanalytic theory, the resolution of the Oedipal conflict depends upon the availability of constructive role models and the child's adoption of these roles. Families function through the use of roles that change during the family life cycle. Members may exchange roles, or import new roles to the family (children who are "computer literate" or cell phone and Twitter savvy, for example). Roles may be explicit or implicit, and *instrumental* (that is, goal oriented) or *expressive* (that is, emotional). Healthy families carry out roles that are appropriate to the members' developmental stages, their abilities, personal characteristics, and social and emotional needs; these factors change over time, of course. Disturbed families may have faulty perceptions of roles, may be incapable of performing appropriate roles, or may (for internal or external reasons, e.g., racism or excessive demands by employers of one or both parents) be forced to perform roles inadequately or destructively.

The family system of roles must be analyzed both structurally and functionally. Parsons's description of the family as a social system differentiated between instrumental and expressive role functions by gender (male-father as breadwinner and link to the environment, female-mother as social and emotional provider who integrated the family's members) did not apply to all families fifty years ago, and certainly not to the majority now. Many of Parsons's critics point to the fluidity of these roles within the changing family in the United States. Billingsley (1968) viewed such fluidity in African-American families as a source of strength. Dowd agrees: "Black families characteristically demonstrate greater flexibility in gender roles, rely upon extended family and community support systems, and have strong work and religious orientations. Key characteristics ... include collectivism, cooperation, obligation, sharing, and reciprocity" (1997:106). More recent writers about African-American families describe the strengths, responsibilities, and power of the mother's role (Burton, 1996; Dowd, 1997:105; and see our discussion of feminist viewpoints, later), but as Dowd points out, African-American mothers have been blamed for the violence of young African-American men: Dowd takes strong exception to that viewpoint, describing it as a "myth": "There is no empirically based argument or developmental need for elevating the heterosexual, nuclear two-parent family, or denigrating the single-parent family" (ibid.:39).

Society has been slow to recognize the variety and adaptability of family roles, not only in families of color, but in families headed by women, and gay and lesbian couples. Dowd (1997) provides a spirited defense of single-parent families, African-American in particular; Laird and Green (1996) and Suzanne Slater (1995), provide evidence of the strengths of families headed by lesbian and gay couples.

African-American families also incorporate extended family, neighbors, or others (e.g., Shug Avery in *The Color Purple;* another example 'in this case, American Indian' is Louise Erdrich's *Love Medicine;* see also Stack, *All Our Kin,* 1974). The role of the "aunt" in black families is well-known (e.g., Ella's role in *The Autobiography of Malcolm X*).

Parsons did later observe that roles for women broadened from the "pseudo-occupation" of mother-housewife to include such quaint role descriptions as "career pattern," "glamour pattern," and "good companion pattern" (Rodman, 1966). Within the preceding generation, society apparently accepted a feminine role combining these role patterns (see Margaret Adams's comment on this later in this chapter). While Eleanor Roosevelt broke the mold by acting as her handicapped husband's "eyes and ears," Hillary Rodham Clinton was the first First Lady to fully exemplify the "career pattern" while in the White House, and extend it as Secretary of State; and Michelle Obama is the second, e.g., declaring her interest in being a good citizen and resident of Washington, D.C., and contributing to its civic welfare. Both First Ladies, Clinton and Obama, are lawyers. Laura Bush was a teacher, and maintained the narrower, traditional role. The public has held mixed opinions about this change in First Ladies' roles. Shifts in masculine and feminine roles occurred because of societal changes in work roles.

Traditionally, in most (but not all) societies, the family business or family farm consolidated the instrumental functions in the father and reinforced his paternal authority, primarily through inheritance laws passing property from father to son. See, e.g., Engels (1884, 1902) on the importance of bloodlines in capitalist societies.

In "modern" societies, much of a father's authority derives from his financial contribution to the family, usually through employment in a work organization (Bernard, 1997). Relying upon the external work system diffuses and dissipates the traditional authority of the father role, particularly when he is (or is perceived by family members, and perhaps himself) as a functionary in a bureaucracy. In addition, most married women in the United States are employed; the rate of employment increases with the age of the children. When the youngest child is between two and seven years of age, the rate of employment gradually increases to 60 percent as the age of the child increases; there is no further increase until the child reaches about age seventeen. Authority that derives from economic contribution is thus shared by both parents, in a two-parent family.

As of 2006, about 65 percent of American children lived with two parents; 84 percent of Asian children, 76 percent of white (non-Hispanic) children, 66 percent of Hispanic children, and 35 percent of "black" children. In 1970, 11 percent of children lived with mothers only; by 2006, this had grown to 24 percent; the increase of children living with father only rose from 1 percent to 5 percent over the same time span; those living without either parent rose from 3 percent to 5 percent. One factor in the number of children living with mothers only was the employment of women, which has changed significantly over that 36-year period; whether this increase is due to choice or necessity is uncertain, but the relatively low rate of enforcement of child support is clearly significant.

Single-parent families headed by women, many of which result from divorce, provide a model that has further reduced the legitimacy of father-husband dominance of families and reinforced a model of shared power and authority. Another source of the decline of males' authority is loss of employment, often due to "downsizing" and "restructuring"

(Rubin, 1997; Newman, 1997; Wallulis, 1998). Lack of employment and loss of employment affect African-American males more frequently than Caucasian males (O'Hare, *et al.,* 1997).

The family's role as determinant and perpetuator of cultural expectations has long been controversial. Engels argued that the family was a bourgeois device designed to enslave women: "The Modern individual family is founded on the open or concealed domestic slavery of the wife." More recently, C. Wright Mills stated: "In so far as the family as an institution turns women into darling little slaves and men into their chief providers and unweaned dependents, the problem of a satisfactory marriage remains incapable of purely private solution."

Far more attention is devoted to adults' roles in families as being necessary to family integrity and functioning than to children's roles, and these adult roles are largely parental roles. Popenoe suggested that inattention to children results from their subordination not only in the family but in society as well:

> "Individual" means adults and not children; the rights of adults are given considerably more weight in this regard than are any presumed rights of children . . . . It is often pointed out that in virtually every welfare state the growth of benefits for the elderly has far exceeded that for children. If children were involved in formulating welfare-state policies, I have little doubt that the situation would be different. (Popenoe, 1988:336)

One indication of this attitude toward children (and women, as well) is the lack of a national family policy in Great Britain (Muncie, Wetherell, Dallos, and Cochrane, 1995:40) and in the United States. (Hansen and Garey, 1998; Mason, Skolnick, and Sugarman, 1998)

1. *Feminist Views of Women's Roles and Families.* Feminist theories have profoundly affected academic and clinical analysis and popular views of family life. Our discussion of feminist views is indebted to Lynne Segal, a professor of gender studies in England, who describes herself as "a feminist psychologist and political activist who has attempted to map out the theoretical and political significance of different strands of feminist thinking around the nature of sexual difference" (Segal, 1995:295-316). She says the feminist perception of the family may seem to have come full circle; it began with a fundamental critique of women's "dependent, undervalued and frequently isolated and miserable existence inside the family" (ibid.:296). "Radical" feminists stressed the oppression of women in families, which was part of patriarchy, and was the basis for other hierarchies, such as race and class. Segal reports that "social feminists" like herself rejected (in some part, at least)

the "radical" view, instead analyzing racism, sexism, and classism as "hierarchical axes of power currently serving the interests of a global 'patriarchal capitalism' " (ibid.:299). Male dominance of social science was challenged, and new concepts were needed that capably interpreted women's experiences: "a women-centred orientation."

What this meant was that the family should no longer be viewed as an undifferentiated unit. Its subsystems and suprasystems, its wider economic, political and ideological environment, all needed to be analyzed ("deconstructed") to identify the ways in which men held power over women, and the effects upon women. "Feminist solutions ... usually involved extensive social—as well as personal—struggle and transformation" (ibid.:300). In the 1970s, an intense period of research and theorizing focused on the role of the state, and of welfare policies in particular, in subordinating women; this was accompanied by proposals for reforms of policies and programs, including women's work and wages, and reproductive choices. Men were encouraged to broaden their roles to include child care and domestic responsibilities (see Booth and Crouter, 1998). In contrast to the earlier feminist view, this aim in this period was to *reform* the family, not to replace it.

In the late 1970s, Segal says, a shift occurred: some feminists began to celebrate the importance and significance of motherhood and of women's roles as mothers and wives, particularly stressing female bonding and "maternal thinking." This shift was led by Betty Friedan's rethinking of her position in *The Second Stage* in 1981, by Adrienne Rich's *Of Woman Born* in 1976, and Nancy Chodorow's *The Reproduction of Mothering* in 1978. These books "emphasized the overriding importance of women's maternalism" (Segal, 1995:303). Chodorow introduced the theory (later built upon by Carol Gilligan—see Chapter 8) that men and women had different relational styles, which depended upon their need to separate from or identify with *mothers*—that this fundamental fact that *mothers raised children* was centrally significant. Thus, in systems terms, individual women determined all larger social systems, a truly radical feminist viewpoint, but consistent with mutual causation among levels of "nested" systems.

Segal cautions that this shift in thinking occurred amid disputes and theoretical divergences. One of the most significant factors that modified feminist thinking in the early 1980s was the "flowering of Black feminism" which had its own viewpoint on the family, and was critical of the views of white feminists. Other feminists' views evolved; some rejected the earlier negative views of nuclear families, and others advocated for more recognition of diversity among families. Some feminists rejected *any* generalizations about women or women's viewpoints.

These feminist theoreticians were now questioning all types of fixed categories, identities and relationships, stressing what they saw as the complex, shifting and plural nature of the social meanings which construct, and allow us to speak of, our own experiences of gender, sexuality, parenting or any other aspect of our existence. (Segal, 1995:297)

The rethinking of women's roles led to the reexamination of men's roles, as well, and of the psychology of men. By the early 1980s, "'fatherism' was being reclaimed and celebrated by men influenced by feminism" (ibid.:306). Research since then tends to confirm that "fathers who are full-time caregivers display the same type of enhanced sensitivity to their infants as full-time mothers" (ibid.:307). If this is true, men's relational style may change when they are given cultural permission to be "fatherly," and not merely workers. "One study in Britain, for example, found that married men under thirty work four times the amount of overtime as childless men of the same age" (ibid.:307, citing her own work). This might indicate that married men work more to earn more for their families, indicating a conflict between "family time" and "work time." There is accumulating anecdotal evidence that men as well as women are making choices to opt out of the "rat race" and to replace the values of the marketplace with familial values, such as choosing to stay in smaller communities that are "family friendly" rather than climbing the corporate ladder (see the example of a Japanese family in Chapter 5, Organizations). But so far, most men's behaviors regarding child care and domestic chores have not changed significantly, and it is not clear "who benefits" (*cui bono?* as Cato said, millennia ago) from the new emphasis on fathering.

Family roles evolve, and not merely in grand terms. From the viewpoint of the family as subsystem, it makes changes almost daily in its social, marital, personal, and parental choices. Viewed from a role perspective, contemporary work provisions such as flextime, flexiplace (telecommuting, or working by computer from home, e.g.), maternity/paternity/family leaves, and day-care at the work site are family choices designed to relieve role stresses and strains and to accommodate shifts in family structure and role allocations. Feminist theoreticians and activists have greatly influenced society's view of the roles of women (and men); and so have families, one by one, parent by parent, child by child, day by day.

2. *Families Headed by Lesbian or Gay Couples.* Until the 1990s, little was published regarding lesbian and gay families. Recently some

remarkable books have appeared, including Suzanne Slater's *The Lesbian Family Life Cycle* (1995), Laird and Green's *Lesbian and Gays in Couples and Families* (1996), and Drucker's *Families of Value* (1998). Weston describes gays and lesbians as "exiles from kinship"; a common stereotype is that they reject family and exile themselves from family life, but to assert that "gay people are destined to move toward a future of solitude and loneliness, is not only to tie kinship closely to procreation, but also to treat gay men and lesbians as members of a nonprocreative species set apart from the rest of humanity" (Weston, 1995:160). Benkov describes the process and the choices that are made by lesbians and gay men who want to have children, the nature of joint parenting, and how they "reinvent the family" (Benkov, 1997).

Slater says, "Starting from scratch, they look to themselves and to each other to construct their partnerships, devoting tremendous energy to imagining and experimenting with possible ways to proceed" (1995:231). She describes a life cycle of couples somewhat like Erikson's stages, particularly in the use of "generativity" to describe Stage 4. The stages are: (1) *formation,* in which the couple bonds and eventually tells others of their relationship; (2) *ongoing couplehood,* in which the couple makes a commitment and works out aspects of their dyad; (3) the *middle years,* in which the couple makes a deeper commitment, but encounters the possibility of disruption by separation or death; (4) *generativity,* which is similar to Erikson's adult stage, and involves a wider commitment to others (including parenting, perhaps); and (5) *couples over 65,* who are likely (because of women's longevity) to share old age—and to face the same crises of aging as other couples. "Lesbian widowhood" is similar to other spouses' survival, with the exception that "lesbian elders … frequently must do without most or all of the public component of the healing process. Funeral rituals, newspaper and other public announcements … and the public naming of the deceased person's next of kin are critical acknowledgements" (ibid.:223).

B. Family as Cause or Effect

The family as cause or effect is a second major approach. The family can be seen either as a "dependent" variable or as an "independent" variable. In the former, the family is responsive to the demands and dictates of larger social systems (macroperspective). It adapts or, more precisely, *accommodates* to the goal requirements of the society within which it exists. The nuclear, mobile family emerges because of the requirements of the economy; parents relinquish their functions to other social institutions.

Governments influence families by prescriptions and proscriptions, for example, compulsory school attendance, abortion laws, Sweden's law against spanking of children (Popenoe, 1988:199; also see Davis, 1997), and court decisions that place the "welfare of the child" above the rights of the parents. In this way, society determines the family. Although few family theorists opt for either extreme, dependent or independent variable, most do see the family as determined by societal changes rather than the reverse. But, as noted earlier, this is not a universal opinion. Scholars increasingly recognize families as initiators of change.

In the opposing view, family as independent variable, family is seen to be a cause rather than an effect (microperspective). The family initiates change, and society accommodates; in other words, the family determines the society. Popenoe said that the "classical Western family died out in portions of Europe well *before* the Industrial Revolution and, indeed ... the nuclear family is now seen to be as much a cause as a consequence of industrialization" (1988:58). Laslett (1971, 1974) concluded that the nuclear family preceded industrialization in Europe and thus may have caused it. Another example is sociologist Elise Boulding (1972:188), who believed that "the family is a potentially powerful contributor to the generation of alternative images of the future." In this sense of creating alternatives, the family is an independent variable.

The role of women in creating social change through child-rearing and character-building activities has been greatly neglected, except in autobiographies (usually of prominent men) that point out mothers' influences. The influence of the mothers of presidents of the United States, for example, has been noted episodically, including President Obama, whose mother and grandmother were determinative in his life, and President Clinton, whose mother was widowed.

According to Boulding (ibid.), the family is also an independent variable in that it generates social change as a "play community." Play is one means by which culture is created, and alternative societal futures are imagined. The family's position between the person and the society allows it to perform this function. However, Popenoe noted that in Sweden, which he suggests may be the future, contemporary families do less together, including play.

The controversy over abortion laws exemplifies families' initiation of social change that requires social accommodation. Family planning, in order to liberate the parents and maintain their desired living standards for themselves and their offspring, requires that society approve and provide means for birth control. The 1973 Supreme Court decision

Roe v. Wade gave legal sanction to abortion. In December 1988, Nancy Klein was pregnant, and comatose as the result of an auto accident. Physicians believed abortion might increase her chance of survival, and her husband requested an abortion, but prolife advocates sought to prohibit it. Two weeks later, a court affirmed the husband's right to make the decision, the judge remarking that outsiders had no right to interfere in this family tragedy. One columnist observed that Ms. Klein's situation had restored rationality to the controversy over the control a woman, or someone legally responsible for her if she is unable to make decisions, has over her own body (Goodman, 1989b). This is a vivid example of a family as initiator of change. Attempts continue to persuade the Supreme Court to overturn the *Roe v. Wade* ruling, which may be a factor in President Obama's choice of a replacement for Supreme Court Justice Stevens in 2010.

The family is, of course, both an independent and a dependent variable, since it is a holon. Mutual causation between families and society can be seen in all aspects of living. For example, shifts in family structure and roles that are responsive to changes in employment patterns lead to marketplace accommodations. Women are increasingly employed outside the home, and family living standards are increasingly dependent upon their incomes. Employment hours vary, which influences the time available to shop, prepare, and serve meals, and for family dining (feature articles often report that employed mothers rarely have more than half an hour per day to themselves, if that much). All of the following could be construed as societal adaptations to such family changes:

1. Extension of business hours by commercial and retail establishments.
2. "One Stop, Full Service" shopping at convenience stores.
3. Marketing of increased varieties of frozen prepared foods.
4. Fast-food restaurants, that usually portray workers or families in their advertising.
5. Mass production of synthetic fabrics marketed as "wash and wear."
6. The use of fax machines and computers to order from grocery stores and restaurants, to stay in touch with family and friends via e-mail, or to shop online.
7. Cell phones, frequently used for business, but now seen as almost indispensable for many "busy families" (as ads often describe them) to contact their children or other family members, to make health appointments, or to contact their children's schools or other appointments, while one or more parents commute to or from work. How would banning use of all cell phones while driving affect parents, principally mothers?

C. Family as Evolving System

The family as evolving system is a dual approach to family inquiry. One focus is on the developmental cycle of *a family,* while the other is a focus on the evolutionary cycle of *the family* as a social institution.

Family life cycle has sometimes been adopted as an organizing theme in courses in human behavior. The usual conception of the family life cycle is from the point of marriage, to and through expansion stages, then to and through contraction stages. The more thorough formulations of family stages attempt to account for the related growth tasks for all family members, not just the children. Most of these formulations assume a nuclear family, the presence of biological offspring, and a marriage that will continue until the death of a spouse. These assumptions, in fact, describe *only a relatively small minority of actual families,* given the proportion of divorces and female-headed families, of "reconstituted" and "blended" families (remarried couples with children of former marriages), and the increasing number of single, never-married parents (both adoptive and biological); see the 2007 movie, *Juno,* e.g.

Family evolution comprises a series of changes as family members of various ages simultaneously encounter transition stages in the life cycle. The preschooler may face becoming a kindergartner at the same time the parents are dealing with the recognition that the future is not boundless. The preteen enters puberty while parents are taking stock of their own adult identity and grandparents are moving toward retirement. Conflicts between adolescents and their parents are legendary, and are the basis for numerous films (e.g., *Rebel without a Cause*). One book addressed "how your child's adolescence triggers your own crisis" (Steinberg, 1994). As young adults seek a more fully consistent identity, their parents are adapting to the "empty nest" and the grandparents cope with the decline of physical functions. The most frequently cited events that signal role changes and new stages of the life cycle are: forming a couple, birth of the first child, departure of the children, and dissolution of the couple (by divorce or death of one partner, e.g.). Added to these are educational, residential, and occupational changes (which research indicates may be highly stressful events), e.g., moving to a new work location that requires children to change schools.

A related facet of family change that is being studied is *resilience,* the ability of families (and children) to cope successfully with stress (see Hetherington and Blechman, 1996, among others). Three dimensions of family dynamics that have been identified as relevant to stress and change are cohesion, adaptability, and communication. These three are combined in the "circumplex" model of marital and family types, which has demonstrated validity as a predictor of family success (Olson, 1983, 1993; Olson et al, 1988).

Carle Zimmerman, the best known advocate of a cyclical theory of family in society, began with the premise that family and society constantly interact and cause changes, each in the other. Other social institutions (particularly the church and government) vie with the family for control of family members. Drawing on historical data, Zimmerman proposed a three-phase family typology and suggested that it is a repetitive cycle (Leslie, 1967:223-230).

1. The *trustee* family—the living members are trustees of the family name, family property, and family blood. The family itself is immortal; there is no conception of individual rights, and individual welfare is subordinate to the family. To the extent that this type survives in contemporary society, it is most obvious in "royal" families such as the Windsors of England, and in tribal cultures of Asia, Africa, and the Middle East. Dramas have long used the tensions in such families: see Shakespeare's *Romeo and Juliet* and *King Lear,* television's "Brothers and Sisters," e.g., and of course, "soap operas."

2. The *domestic* family—an intermediate type that evolves from the trustee family. As the state gains in power, family control over its members is weakened. The state shares this power and control with the family and creates the concept of individual rights to be maintained against family authority. Popenoe said:

> The modern nuclear family was organized largely to serve the end of child rearing in an environment of stability and love between the married couple. Backed by the unique coercive powers of organized religion, as well as by the laws of the state, the nuclear family unit was culturally held up as the goal of human sexuality combined with romantic love; it was the only acceptable form of adult pair-bond. (1988:329)

3. The *atomistic* family—the power and scope of family authority is reduced to a minimum: The family no longer mediates between its members and society. The state becomes a bureaucracy that deals directly with individual persons, without intermediary systems. "Family" functions are shifted to community or societal institutions; e.g., hospitals, nursing homes, and extended care facilities care for ill family members; foster care and juvenile institutions provide for children needing care or control; domestic courts provide counseling for parents and

children; schools educate with little involvement by parents; and the nation conscripts youth without consulting families about their beliefs.

Zimmerman judged the present-day American family to be well into the third phase, the "atomic age" in yet another sense. He did not find the "present decay of the family" unique. He documented similar family dissolution prior to the fall of the Greek and Roman civilizations. Popenoe suggested that, in Sweden, a new, truly nuclear family has emerged, that of single mother and child (e.g., the child born "out of wedlock" but later adopted by the mother's husband, or mother and child after a divorce). Such a pattern may be emerging in the United States, as well, as evidenced by public concern about public welfare expenditures for single (particularly teenage) women who bear children, and by legislation intended to control the women's behavior, e.g., not allowing the purchase of alcohol with food stamps.

Popenoe identified "the emerging value system of America as 'bureaucratic consumer capitalism' in which expressive individualism overtakes moral commitment" (Popenoe 1988:289, citing Bellah et al., 1985). He speculated, "This style of life could be the wave of the future—the new, individualized, and autonomous individual making a suitable adjustment to a rationalized and affluent world" (Popenoe, 1988:327). United States census data revealed that

> Marriage and family relationships seem to be occupying a shrinking space in our lives. Marriage rates before 25 have declined markedly. ... Parenthood is also being delayed ... [A] substantial proportion of today's youth may never become parents at all. The vast majority will marry and have children, but over half of those who do will experience the breakup of that marriage. Persons who are not currently married ... have progressively chosen to live alone, rather than with other family members. (Sweet and Bumpass, 1987:391)

Zimmerman deplored the popular view of the family as ever evolving to higher and better forms:

> ... [modern] inhumanity lies close, in a basic casual sense, to the decay of the family system. Indeed the familial decline may well be the primary causal agent in the sapping of the universal capacity for human sympathy. Juvenal held this opinion when he wrote of "the decline in the capacity to weep," ... The consequence then of a declining family system is that controls of society come more into the hands of men who, in the words of Bacon, have no "hostages to fortune," and who do not possess judgments biased by an immersion in fundamental humanism. (1947:77)

Consider the discussion of empathy in the Addendum to Chapter 2. Zimmerman recommended open recognition and understanding of the current state of family decline and hoped that a "creative minority" would come forward to reassert the values of familism.

D. The Structural Approach

The structural approach to the family has received the attention of a host of investigators. Any attempt at family analysis addresses itself to certain family forms and excludes others. The majority of Western observers of the family accept the two-generation nuclear family as the norm (two parents and their children). This is particularly true of those interested in the child-rearing aspects of the family. As noted earlier, the nuclear family has been the norm in some parts of European culture for five or six centuries. It is this family structure that serves as the basis for societal policy in support of the family (e.g., welfare and tax structure). It should again be emphasized that this family form is no longer found in the majority of families in the United States, and that there is variation by ethnic group: "African-American children have been most affected by the changes in marital status and family composition. … The share of black children living with two parents declined from 58 percent in 1970 to 38 percent in 1990. … Black children are more likely to live with a grandparent than are white or Hispanic children" (O'Hare et al, 1997:89).

Nearly half a century ago, Parsons characterized the American family as "the isolated family," isolated especially residentially and economically from the extended family, which was a natural consequence of the specialization and differentiation of the complex social system of the United States today. He qualified the degree of isolation, however: "there is much accumulating evidence that the extended family is an exceedingly important resource to fall back on in case of emergency or trouble, for financial support and for emotional support and help in planning" (Parsons, 1964:17). The high cost of living in many areas of the country during the past two decades, and the current (as of 2010) economic crisis has impelled adult (especially young adult) children to return to live with their parents: the "revolving door" phenomenon (the "nest" contracts and expands parallel to the state of the economy).

The extended family may well go beyond the bounds of those related by blood or marriage. Billingsley established a typology of forms for categorizing African-American family structures. The refinements he introduced through his three categories and twelve types have also been applied to the society generally (Billingsley, 1968:15-21):

1. The *nuclear* family includes three types: the *incipient,* consisting of only the marital pair; the *simple,* consisting of the marital pair and minor children; and the *attenuated,* containing only one parent and minor children. The latter seems to imply that the family previously was a "whole" family and was reduced by some circumstance; another

description, such as "single-parent family" might avoid this implication and include the single, never-married parent with children. Dowd notes that *"70 percent of children will spend some time in a single-parent family before reaching age eighteen; for women entering adulthood, the probability that they will maintain a single-parent family for some period of time is 40 percent"* (1997:5). Another form of attenuation is the "bean pole" family, in which there are more generations living at one time, and fewer members are born in each generation (Bengtson, *et al.,* 1995:347).

2. The *extended* family includes types in which other relatives are part of the household. As noted elsewhere, African-American children are more likely than other children to be living with grandparents. "The rise of out-of-wedlock childbearing suggests yet another form of intergenerational family structure. ... Older black women may be called upon more often by their daughters to serve as the 'other parent'" (ibid.:350).

3. The *augmented* family includes types of families wherein unrelated persons are incorporated into the household, and function as family members. Dowd describes this type: "The model of single-parent families is of caretakers within a support structure—whether kin, friends, or paid care ... simply one form of a support structure" (1997:113).

The study of kinship networks and relationships, particularly by social anthropologists, has yielded additional insights into the variety of family forms. Kinship responsibility in the United States has been a neglected dimension in family studies. Cultural guidelines for determination of allegiance to kinsmen are ambiguous and often conflicting. Although the nuclear family norm would seem to dictate that one's primary responsibility is to spouse and children, conflicting claims do arise. The parent of today in an isolated nuclear family might have been the child of yesterday in a closely tied extended or nuclear family. For such a person, the transfer of allegiance and emotional involvement from the family of orientation to the family of procreation may be a monumental task, as indicated by frequent letters to "Dear Abby" from wives and mothers-in-law about the son/ husband's responsibilities to each.

Scholars have studied kinship relationships in "remarried families" and "blended" families and the perceptions of obligations and relationships within them (Hetherington, Law, and O'Connor, 1997; Ahrons and Rodgers, 1997). The term "binuclear" was coined to describe families in which a child is part of two separate nuclear families, formed by the child's divorced parents (Ahrons, 1987). Children must decide (often with strong guidance from one or both parents) who are "kin": Does a stepmother's mother become "Grandma"? Are the noncustodial parent and the new stepparent invited to graduation ceremonies? Divorced parents must decide their relationships to their biological children with whom they no longer live: Do they attend the funeral of the former spouse's parent who is, after all, the children's grandparent? Who "walks the bride down the aisle," the father or stepfather? These are often painful questions to resolve.

Overall, the present generation of elders in the United States is relatively fortunate compared to earlier generations regarding health and income, but many live in isolation or in situations of inadequate care. The unenviable status of these aged persons and the guilt felt by their adult children are products of the nuclear family and the nature of the society in which it exists. Women in their fifties often have parents who are over eighty, and with smaller families, these women are less likely to have siblings to share responsibility for care of parents (Bengtson et al, 1997:348).

Alternative family forms have been suggested as possible substitutions for traditional ones, especially to replace the nuclear family norm. In the latter half of the twentieth century in the United States, a new family form has emerged, most easily termed "living together," or cohabitation. Popenoe (1988:303) noted that in the Netherlands it has been carried one step further, and called "living-apart-together." In Sweden, he observed, there are separate names for persons with whom you have a sexual bond, and share a household (a *sämbo),* or do not share a household with (a *särbo*). About a quarter of all couples are sämbos; most sämbo couples marry eventually; such unions have been legalized since 1988, and have most of the rights of married couples; however, the surviving partner does not inherit, unlike married couples. Lesbian and gay couples also have sämbo rights.

Some thoughtful observers, including some feminist authors, argue that the family in its traditional forms is dysfunctional in modern industrial society, and that alternative forms are preferable. Endorsement of the ultimate nuclear form of family—mother and child—by a prominent celebrity indicates that it may have become an accepted social form: Academy Award-winning actress Jodie Foster, in disclosing her pregnancy, said she "plans to be a single mother, 'just like I was raised myself.'" A significant number of women have made a similar choice.

E. The Functional Approach

This is another dominant theme in family studies. Usually, *functions* are looked at in tandem with *structures* because they cannot readily be separated, not even for purposes of objective study. There are inherent difficulties in functional analysis of the family, as in examining the functions of any other social system. The pitfall is, of course, to reason circularly that a pattern or value is "functional" to the given system and the proof of functionality is found in the fact of its existence.

Parsons explained the changing functions of the modern family as examples of differentiation and specialization of the family system. As the macrosystem (society) becomes increasingly complex, the family as a component system (or microsystem) becomes increasingly specialized in the functions it performs for both the larger system and for family components. The core functions remaining in the family are the maintenance of the household and the intimate personal relations of the members of the household, including child rearing and socialization into affective networks (of peers, friends, sexual and marital partners, and communities). Relinquishing of family functions particularly affects women. Margaret Adams, a social worker, described the historical process by which women are channeled into social work, nursing, teaching, secretarial work, and certain other professions, as "the compassion trap":

> The proliferation of the helping professions into a complex array of welfare services took many of the more highly specialized aspects of the nurturing and protective functions out of the home. ... In addition, when one or both parents were out of the home for a substantial part of the day, they had to delegate their acculturating functions. Thus the synthesizing role traditionally discharged by women in the home was translated into a wider sphere and spread its influence through a broader range of activities. Instead of (or in addition to) keeping the family intact and maximally functional, women became involved in housekeeping tasks on behalf of society at large and assumed responsibility for keeping its operation viable. (Adams, 1971:72)

Lasch (1979) deplored the transfer of nurturance and parenting from the family to the burgeoning professional experts. He noted the emergence of specialized peer groupings that evidently have assumed functions previously performed by the family. Popenoe's studies in Sweden showed that "many of these youth were lonely and had few, merely superficial, social contacts. The young people ... inhabit an 'age-stratified world' in which they meet very few adults other than their parents" (1988:320-321). This is graphically portrayed in *A Tribe Apart* (P. Hersch, 1998). Peer groups differentiate and remain separated on the axis of age: examples include senior centers and communities for the aged, adolescent clubs and gangs, and young adult bars and health clubs. A generation ago, Keniston proposed a "new" stage of life, which occurs outside either a family of orientation or a family of procreation, noting

> ... the emergence on a mass scale of a previously unrecognized stage of life ... the stage of youth. ... A growing minority of post-adolescents today ... have not settled the questions whose answers once defined adulthood: questions of relationship to the existing society, questions of vocation, questions of social role and lifestyle. (Keniston, 1970:634-635)

The youthful followers of cults may be a manifestation of this new life phase; those who have received the most notoriety, because of their parents' efforts to regain their allegiance, have been in their twenties, opting for a calling devoid of any kind of family connection; however, not all such followers are youths. The Unification church (followers of Reverend Sun Yung Moon: disparagingly referred to as "Moonies") conducts mass marriages of hundreds of couples at the same time to partners selected by the organization; this is perhaps an example of deliberate attempts to create "family" within an organization and to negate family ties outside it.

This "youth" stage is clearly related to Erikson's sixth "crisis," that of *intimacy vs. isolation* (see Chapter 8). If families are unable to assist in resolving this crisis, then many young adults must look to other institutions, create new ones, or conceivably simply fail to resolve the crisis, in large numbers. Currently, there are many "youth service" programs that would reward teenagers and young adults for participation in volunteer programs with vouchers for housing or education, as well as wages (the armed services offer similar inducements). The most obvious objectives are social control, socialization, and integration into the society in some significant way, either as workers, students, or consumers. Described another way, its purpose is to structure the adolescent (or young adult) "moratorium" (see Erikson's definition in Chapter 8) to reduce the possibility of deviance, when the family is not capable or sufficient to do so. The Peace Corps, or President Obama's proposal for a "youth corps," may provide such opportunities.

Youth gangs are another form of socialization, in this case to a "deviant" subculture:

Dysfunctional families as the cause of gangs … is the theory Armando Morales (1992) uses to explain Hispanic gangs in Los Angeles. Morales maintains that adolescents turn to gang membership to achieve the nurturance, support, and protection denied them in their biological families. Invariably, their families are beset by drug addiction, alcoholism, chronic illness, impoverished housing, physical and emotional abuse, and parental discord. Morales says the gang provides members "affection, understanding, recognition, loyalty, and emotional and physical protection." (Balk, 1995:479-480)

Maruyama (1996) coined the term *monopolarization* to describe the situation in which the child's relationship to adults is confined to a mother or father or, more precisely, to one set of parents. This totality of children's relationships to their parents sets narrow parameters for development and places excessive responsibility in the parents. Maruyama said that this exclusivity was assumed as the norm by theories of personality and of many Western philosophies. He recommended dilution of this relationship through increased interfamily contacts and integration of persons who are not in the family circuit. "Play dates" are a common suburban phenomenon for young children (especially pre-school age). This could be accomplished through the formation of voluntary adult-child communities without any necessity of major reforms in family structure; some religious congregations have attempted this, with mixed success. During the 1960s and 1970s, many communes attempted to create alternative family structures. One writer reported a generation ago that "today's communes seek a family warmth and intimacy, to become extended families. A 50-person commune in California, for example, called itself 'The Lynch Family,' a New Mexico commune 'The Chosen Family,' a New York City group simply 'The Family'" (Kanter 1970:54). Within the last forty years, however, such communal efforts have almost entirely ceased.

II. A Social Systems View of Families

Most professional observers of family now view it as a system (Schutz, 1993). Family therapists are most notable among these, in their relevance to this book. One of the outstanding researchers and pioneers in family therapy, Jay Haley, optimistically stated that

> There is an increasing awareness that psychiatric problems are social problems which involve the total ecological system. ... there is a growing consensus that a new ecological framework defines problems in new ways and calls for new ways in therapy. (Sager and Kaplan, 1972:270)

Analysis of the family system must be from some particular perspective, that is, *from the perspective of some particular person* (and can be from any other family member, as well). If the intent of that perspective is to determine the legal status of a person for inheritance purposes, that is quite different from establishing who are the members of a household. Consistent with our comments about the feedback cycle and system structure, *a family system is best understood as patterns of relatedness as they converge in a specific person*. This is (as discussed in the Introduction to this edition) compatible with a phenomenological viewpoint (see the Addendum to Chapter 2 for this discussion). These patterns may be similar or identical to those of another family member, or they could be unique to this one person. The characteristics of the family system will be grouped under our usual headings of *structure, behavior,* and *evolution*.

A. Structural Aspects

As with any social system, its organization is a fundamental concern. In general, family organization is distinguishable from other systems by a high level of relatedness among its components. Since it is the smallest social and interpersonal system, typically there is intense interdependence among its components. The effectiveness of family organization is the extent to which goals are fulfilled—the goals of its members and the goals of society. If societal goals are not fulfilled, the family may be dissolved by legal decree, as when children are removed or divorces granted; however, the family may persist as an interacting system. However, as Malcolm X clearly described after his family was dispersed by the court after his father's death: "separated though we were, all of us maintained fairly close touch around Lansing—in school and out—whenever we could get together. Despite the artificially created separation and distance between us, we still remained very close in our feelings toward each other" (1966:22).

Society, the family, and its members may all share familial goals of economic independence, intimacy, and affection, and yet be in conflict about the priorities to be assigned to each of these goals. These conflicts may occur when people find it necessary to leave familiar territory to find employment or to maintain family ties. A Kentuckian told this story to one of the authors of this book:

> A man died and was being shown around Heaven by St. Peter. Off in one corner of Heaven they saw a group of people with suitcases. The man asked who these people were and St. Peter replied, "Oh, they're from Kentucky; they go home on weekends."

In the boom times of the 1970s, the greatest "reverse migration" in American history took place as Appalachian coal mining revived and people returned from northern industries to work "at home." African-American families "returned home" to the South:

> By 1990 the South had gained more than half a million black Americans who were leaving the North—or more precisely, the South had *regained* from the cities of the North the half-million it had lost to northward migration during the 1960s. The Census Bureau now predicts that the southward trend will continue "well into the next century." (Stack, 1996:xiv)

Stack says "What people are seeking is not so much the home they left behind as a place they feel they can change, a place in which their lives and strivings will make a difference—a place in which to *create* a home."

In order to achieve goals, the family must, through its organization, secure and conserve energy from both internal and external sources. The members of the family must contribute energy for the family system as well as import energy for their individual purposes. The following dialogue between mother and sons (about the husband-father), from the classic (and prophetic) play, *Death of a Salesman,* illustrates this dependence of family upon energy from its members and from the environment.

LINDA: No, a lot of people think he's lost his—balance. But you don't have to be very smart to know what his trouble is. The man is exhausted.
HAPPY: Sure!
LINDA: A small man can be just as exhausted as a great man. He works for a company thirty-six years this March, opens up unheard-of territories to their trademark, and now in his old age they take his salary away.
HAPPY: (Indignantly) I didn't know that, Mom.
LINDA: You never asked, my dear! Now that you get your spending money someplace else you don't trouble your mind with him.
HAPPY: But I gave you money last—
LINDA: Christmas time, fifty dollars! To fix the water heater it cost ninety-seven fifty! For five weeks he's been on straight commission, like a beginner, an unknown!
BIFF: Those ungrateful bastards!
LINDA: Are they any worse than his sons? (A. Miller, 1955:56-57)

The boundary of a family is behavioral and is evidenced by the intensity and frequency of interaction among its components (see Day, 1995:95-97, for a discussion of family boundaries). Andrew Halloran described the relationships of a international group of gay men who were acquainted with a man called "O":

When he was at home in New York, it was at his place that all of them got together. ... An evening at O.'s involved, above all, conversation—with people one had never met: journalists from Athens, an artist from Mexico City, an old boyfriend of O.'s from Rome. His circle—a circle of friends so constant, so faithful, they had followed one another from city to city and constituted, more than any other I knew, a family—was fixed but fluid, loyal but independent, a function of O.'s affection most of all ... . (Halloran, 2008:70)

The intensity of sentiment interchanges in families is especially distinctive as compared to other small groups. It is within the interactional boundaries of the family that the member participates in a particularly close network of feelings, both positive and negative, with a minimal sense of "needing to put up a front." The common expression, "I feel at home," conveys something of this freedom to be oneself.

Family boundaries change as members come and go. Extended kin, close friends and neighbors, or foster children may be absorbed within the boundary of a given family. Research on "remarried families," especially those with children and stepchildren, found "boundary ambiguity" (Boss, 1987). Whether stepchildren living with an ex-spouse are members of the family, and whether young adults still function as members of the family after they leave home, for example, are important questions for many families. The boundaries are both physical and psychological, and it is particularly stressful when the two definitions do not coincide, for example, when a parent continues to view the adult child who is part of the household as a dependent, and subject to "house rules," but the adult child does not. Boundary ambiguity is found to be highly related to family stress and overall family dysfunction (Pasley and Ihinger-Tallman, 1989).

Even physical presence is not a measure of participation within family boundaries. A person may be related by birth or marriage and live in the same household, yet not be within the family's interactional boundaries. On the other hand, the family member in the hospital, away at school or military service, or incarcerated may well remain within the family boundary as just defined. In the case of families of servicemen who are deployed in war zones for extended periods (one or sometimes more than one "tour"), or are MIAs (missing in action), the difficulty is particularly poignant. Again a quotation from Malcolm X is illustrative:

> I'm rarely at home more than half of any week; I have been away as much as five months. I never get a chance to take her anywhere, and I know she likes to be with her husband. She is used to my calling her from airports anywhere from Boston to San Francisco, or Miami to Seattle, or here lately, cabling her from Cairo, Accra, or the Holy City of Mecca. Once on the long-distance telephone, Betty told me in beautiful phrasing the way she thinks. She said, "You are present when you are away." (Malcolm X, 1966:233)

Maintenance of family boundary occurs on both sides of the boundary. The family frequently excludes others ("this is a family argument," "the family vacation"). Society supports family boundaries by assigning the family priority on occasions highly charged with sentiment such as weddings, illnesses, funerals, and holiday gatherings. Cultures decree special occasions to reinforce family sentiment and interchange, such as Mother's Day and Father's Day (the manufacturers of greeting cards added Grandparents' Day)—is there a "Children's

Day"? Federal policy and the policies of many businesses permit employees leave to care for members of the immediate family who are ill, and for funerals of members of both immediate and extended family. Colleges and universities also recognize and support family boundaries of sentiment through allowing students to absent themselves for such family occasions (one book suggested that exams must be dangerous, since there is such a high correlation between exam days and the deaths of grandparents).

Within the family, boundaries are maintained by differentiation and specialization, as reflected in role allocations. So that the family can meet societal expectations and continue as an economic unit, particular family members are breadwinners by mutual consent of the family members, e.g., the grandfather of one of the authors was killed in a mining accident; the eldest son, not yet in his teens, dropped out of school to work to support his family, and continued to support his mother until her death.

Differentiation is commonly determined by age and sex, but these are uniquely refined in each family system. There is also differentiation of expressive functions, e.g., a family may deposit much of its unresolved or unacknowledged tensions in one family member, who then specializes as the "problem" family member. The concept of the "family scapegoat" or "lightning rod" is a case in point: one of the children

> ... is selected [consciously or not] to symbolize the conflicts and draw off the tension. The emotional disturbance of the child is simply the effect of internalizing the conflicting demands placed on the child by [its] parents. ... The scapegoating mechanism may be functional for the family group through enabling its continued existence but be dysfunctional for the child's development and [its] adaptation outside the family. (Vogel and Bell, 1960:382-397)

Another aspect of family structure is its *territoriality*. Family territory has both a spatial and behavioral dimension. The concept of home territory is especially descriptive of family territory since the occupants have a profound sense of "place" and of "belonging." The family consolidates around, and in part finds its identity through, achieving and maintaining territory. Behavioral territory was earlier described in the discussion of boundary; it is the interactional territory of feeling-closeness. Physically, the family also occupies territory. The architect, the contractor, the city planner, the mail carrier, the garbage collector, "the cable guy," all exist as societally supported occupations to serve and maintain families within their own spatial territory. This territory is signified by an apartment or house number, or by a distinctive name (the grandmother of one of the authors called the family farm "Doomsday"; seaside cottages where family gather often have clever or "cutesy" names, prominently displayed); it may be further marked by posts, fences, and hedges. The family territory may encompass a village, town, or neighborhood. "In ancient imagery, the center of his territory is a man's 'house,' be it a home or a farm, a firm or a family, a dynasty or a church; and his 'city' marks the boundary of all the houses associated with his" (Erikson, 1969:176).

Society requests and requires families to be territorially based, to be oriented in space. Society's most common means of establishing social identifications are the answers to the questions: Name? Address? Or, less formally, Where are you from? which actually means, What was the place of your family of origin? Homeless persons are at a disadvantage to receive services when they cannot state a residential address, despite federal legislation intended to alleviate this difficulty. The societal concern with family territoriality is clearly expressed in this quotation: "Show me a man who cares no more for one place than another, and I will show you in that same person one who loves nothing but himself. Beware those who are homeless by choice" (Southey, 1959:508). Similarly, groups of people who are not identified with a particular or specified "home territory," e.g., nomads, Gypsies (more accurately, "Rom," who originated in India), transients, migrant workers, "hobos," or homeless persons, are often viewed with suspicion by others, and may be subject to expulsion.

B. Behavioral Aspects

Social control and *socialization* are characteristic functions of the family. The family is always a subsystem of its society and, as such, participates in the socialization processes of that society. It would be defensible to classify all families that are socially-defined as dysfunctional as failing to meet the requirements for socialization of its members. A central task of the family is to assure that its members are sufficiently acculturated to participate in other societal subsystems that accomplish societal goals. For example, Project Head Start was instituted to supplement families that were not fulfilling (or *might* not fulfill) this expectation as society defined it—to socialize the children and, if necessary, the parents. Furthermore, the family is expected to control its members in order to prevent them from interfering with attainment of the society's goals; notice the recurring legal efforts to penalize parents for delinquent behavior of their children.

Billingsley's observation that responsibility for socialization is especially difficult for many African-American families continues to be true, four decades later (see also Taylor, Jackson, and Chatters, 1997). Despite the rise of a substantial African-American middle class and increasing integration economically, educationally, and socially, such families still "must teach [their] young members not only how to be human, but also how to be black in a white society" (Billingsley, 1968:28). While the family in television's "The Cosby Show" was portrayed as successful and middle-class, its star, producer, and writer, Bill Cosby, frequently points out the special demands and constraints placed on African-American families and urges African-American parents to fulfill their responsibility for their children's education and social behavior. Two indicators of these stressors are the extraordinarily high number of young African-American men in penal institutions (about 25 percent spend some time in confinement), and the disproportionate number of African-Americans who receive the death penalty. In addition to the pressures that affect all families in America, an African-American family must cope with three additional facts of life (the first applies only to those whose ancestors were forced into slavery):

1. a distinctive historical development;
2. the American stratification system which historically has relegated African-Americans to inferior, caste-like status; and
3. the social class and economic systems that keep most African-Americans in lower socioeconomic classes. (Billingsley, 1968:28)

Power in families is a topic that has received relatively little attention, except from feminist theorists. Kranichfeld stated that earlier research concentrated on men's power derived from outside the family, rather than women's power derived from relationships within the family. Also, research has concentrated on power relations between men and women, neglecting women's power relative to other family members.

> In spite of all the mental, emotional, and physical hardships that women appear to have experienced simply by virtue of their membership in the female gender, they appear to be remarkably resilient and constructive in their approach to human relations. As a group, women continue to struggle for greater equality and justice, but as individuals *almost never do so by choosing to sever the bonds that connect them to other people,* from which they derive tremendous sustenance and reward. (Kranichfeld, 1988:232-233)

She maintains that since men and women experience " 'separate social realities," they wield different types of power. If power is the ability to achieve goals by affecting other systems' functioning, women have great power: "women do not just change the behavior of others, they shape whole generations of families" (ibid.:235). She holds that women's power derives, consistent with Chodorow's (1978) and Gilligan's (1982) views, from *caring* for others in the family, and maintaining deep emotional connections with them. "The message here seems to be that, when it comes to securing the kind of power that exists in the family realm, nothing—not superior physical strength, nor greater economic resources, nor culturally ascribed authority—can substitute for investment, attention, connection, and care" (Kranichfeld, 1988:239). Dowd cites evidence that single-parent families (nearly all headed by women) "are far less hierarchical, and far more cooperative and communal, than most two-parent marital families [and that children] in single-mother families are given more responsibility, and demonstrate higher self-esteem and aspirations than children from two-parent families" (1997:109-110). That is, power is distributed among family members.

Communication is increasingly emphasized as both the keystone of family interaction and the key to understanding family dynamics. Every family's behavior is influenced by the style and effectiveness of its communication. Communication is here used to denote the transfer of energy through meaningful symbols, both vocal and gestural—transfer of energy to accomplish system goals. The discussion of communication in Chapter 2 applies exactly to the family system: each family has a unique combination of communication patterns that strongly influence the behavior of its members. Communication practices are crucial to any understanding of family because of the importance and intensity of exchanges of feeling. Brodey described *the family dance:* "Each family has its own particular game, its rules and regulations. It has its rules of status, its rules of power, its techniques of movement" (1977:41-42). Maturana's concept of *autopoiesis* suggests that a family, as any other social system, strives to continue its existence; its characteristic processes serve to create and to maintain itself. *Change* must also contribute to survival of a system's identity (Maturana and Varela, 1980; see also Adams, 1988:61-64).

Communication in the family is extremely complex and subtle because of the number of functions served by the family. One energy exchange can convey a number of meanings, not all of them congruent. An example is a parent's directive to a child to do what the teacher says. Included in this could be several messages:

1.   You ought to obey authority (to meet societal expectations).
2.   But you should not be required to submit to unjust orders (to meet the child's developmental needs).

3.   Nevertheless, do what the teacher tells you (to avoid conflict with the
     environment).
4.   Keep out of trouble (and avoid conflict between parent and teacher,
     that is, between family system and environment).
5.   Because if you don't you'll get it from me (meet parents' needs for
     societal approval of their parenting, and thus provides for the child's
     security, as well).

The child is expected to understand and comply with all these
messages.

Adaptation is an essential family function. Because the family has
consistently had the capacity to change its structure and function to adapt
to marked changes in its environment, it has survived wars, industrial
and technological revolutions, and traumatic societal disruptions that
made traditional patterns of coping obsolete. The family calls upon the
energies of its components and exchanges energies with the significant
systems in its environment. Many families in Hong Kong are examples
of creative adaptation to a turbulent environment; the family expands to
include nonrelatives, or distantly related relatives, as a means of securing external energy (including money). These members secure jobs or
create businesses, perhaps a new hawker's stall in the streets, or a fish
ball stand. If Hong Kong's economy falters, these "expanded" or "augmented" families share risk by contracting into smaller physical space
and living on less income. The family may send a child to be educated
(or to work) overseas to assure a means of emigration by other family
members, should Hong Kong experience serious economic or political
difficulties.

Another necessary adaptive mode of the family is its assimilation of
external stress as experienced by its members. Although other social
institutions such as religious and fraternal organizations also fulfill the
function, the family is expected to be the primary system wherein a
person can relax ("unwind"), cast off externally adaptable role behaviors, and "be oneself." In some cultures, the coffeehouse, bar, or the
geisha perform this function for men; it is not clear how this function
is performed for women in these societies; perhaps by mutual support
among female family members. Perhaps sensitivity and support groups
are substitutes for this family function, in our culture.

A family is considered maladaptive when it cannot meet the changing
demands placed upon it by its environment and its members. If it cannot or will not change, and devotes an undue proportion of its available
energies to maintenance of existing structures (i.e., morphostasis), it

will not be able to deal with external requirements and the individual development of its members. In essence, it maintains its previous behavior (assimilation; see Piaget in Chapter 8) and is thus dysfunctional. If, on the other hand, it is in a constantly unstable state of transition, it does not furnish the degree of stability its members require for repair of insults to their egos and for the chance to merely be oneself in an atmosphere of affirmative feeling. This leads to the final systems aspects of the family.

C. Evolutionary Aspects

Steady state is an aspect of the family system, which must simultaneously change and remain the same. Throughout its life cycle the family meets ever-changing requirements from its members and from society. The marital dyad, for example, must modify its mode of functioning with the advent of the first child. A family may operate to its satisfaction and to that of society while the offspring are dependent, but run aground when the children need emancipation from the family.

All that was said about steady state in Chapter 2 applies to the family. Often the family in crisis is in a disruptive transition from one steady state to another. At such times, a family may be more open to importing energies, more amenable to interventive efforts (see Erikson's definition of *crisis* in Chapter 8). Some families tend to function only so as to reduce or eliminate pain (equilibrium) rather than to change affirmatively (steady state). It is not easy for its members to achieve a sense of family as a system, an entity in its own right, more than the sum of its members; our Western cultural emphasis on the individual person as the most significant system makes it difficult to conceive of the family as other than matrix, background, or environment. Paradoxically, at the same time, we categorize families as good or bad as measured by the social performance of their members. This leads to the pernicious doctrine, often heard in speeches by legislators, that all problematic or antisocial behavior is rooted in the family, in a cause-effect relationship. Of course, families may to some degree be responsible, but as society blames its families, it denies society's part in personal and social dysfunction. In the past, the "broken home" was especially maligned. This process is similar to family scapegoating, in which a family member is loaded with the responsibility for family pain and dysfunction; thus the family both scapegoats and *is* scapegoated.

Human services professions are coming to understand the distinctive systemic qualities of family. Tolstoy's observation that all happy families resemble each other and each unhappy family is unhappy in its own way suggests that the resemblance may be more apparent than real. Perhaps each happy family, too, is happy in its own way. Each family is like others in having rules, games (sequences of events governed by rules), secrets, and ghosts. Each family is unique in that its rules, games, secrets, and ghosts are its own. Often, work with families is best conceived as aiding a family to discover what its own unique patterns are, how they disguise their unique patterns, and how the patterns operate.

Summary

The family is best defined from the viewpoint of the person within it, consistent with the phenomenological perspective discussed in the Addendum to Chapter 2. The definition should include those relationships that are "family" to that person: those with whom the person interacts and performs family functions within that society. In many ways, the family is the crucial intersection between culture and the persons within the culture, the point of most interaction and change. While particular aspects of the family may be better explained by one of the approaches we have discussed, a systems view best explains overall family system behavior, the changes the family undergoes, and the relationships that are cause and effect of those changes.

In recent years, family issues have largely been perceived as part of women's issues, and this rethinking and redefinition has broadened the marital and parental role expectations for both women and men. Family issues have moved to the center of the political arena, making it possible for politicians to insert themselves and their beliefs into family concerns (especially family planning and abortion). Legislating family matters diminishes tolerance for pluralism of family forms and functions; this is evident in debates about same-sex marital rights.

What does the future hold for families in the United States? Popenoe waved danger flags:

> Over the course of life the subculture yields what has been called a "community of memory," a special cultural heritage that family members carry with them until death. ... With the weakening of the family unit, the disinvestment in family life, this sub-cultural richness is disappearing. For those who have it, the tie to a rich family subculture is one of the most meaningful things in life. For those who do not, the commercially based cultures of mass societies serve as debased substitutes. (Popenoe, 1988, 312-313)

Since families are interdependent parts of the fabric of society, they will continue to influence, and be influenced by, changes in other social institutions. Families will continue to have their unique position at the point where persons and culture meet: but the fate of the family is not assured.

Suggested Readings

Billingsley, Andrew.
> 1968 *Black Families in White America.* Englewood Cliffs, NJ: New York: Simon and Shuster.
> A systems approach to the family that has been used as the small map text for this chapter. Billingsley drew on the experiences of African-Americans to supplement and revise sociological analyses of the family.

Laird, Joan, and Robert Jay Green, eds.
> 1996 *Lesbians and Gays in Couples and Families: A Handbook for Therapists.* San Francisco: Jossey-Bass.
> Edited by a professor of social work and a professor of family and child psychology and with chapters by psychotherapists, psychologists, educators, and social workers, this is the best source on family treatment for this population.

Miller, Sally R., and Patricia Winstead-Fry.
> 1982 *Family Systems Theory in Nursing Practice.* Reston, VA: Reston.
> An excellent text, recommended for other professions as well as nursing. Family systems theory is well integrated into nursing practice.

Popenoe, David.
> 1988 *Disturbing the Nest: Family Change and Decline in Modem Societies.* Hawthorne, NY: Aldine de Gruyter.
> A comparison of families in the United States, Sweden, Switzerland, and New Zealand, which raises disturbing questions about the future of families in advanced industrial societies.

Skolnick, Arlene and Jerome H. Skolnick, eds.
> 1997 *Families in Transition,* ninth edition. New York: Longman,
> A set of readings that are informative and provocative, covering a very wide range of information. The contributors are among the best and most authoritative writers on the modem family.

Slater, Suzanne.
> 1995 *The Lesbian Family Life Cycle.* New York: Free Press.
> An admirable attempt to portray a modal scheme of development for families headed by lesbian couples. It illustrates features that these families have in common with heterosexual families, and features that are distinct. It depicts the early stages of a lesbian relationship very well, and presents the unique dynamics of the relationship.

Watzlawick, Paul, Janet Helmick Beavin, and Don D. Jackson.
> 1967 *Pragmatics of Human Communication: A Study of Interactional Patterns, Pathologies and Paradoxes.* New York: Norton.
> This text deals with systemic communication in a family context. The analysis of communication patterning in the play *Who's Afraid of Virginia Woolf?* is especially interesting.

Literary Sources

Anderson, Robert Woodruff.
  1968 *I Never Sang for My Father.* New York: Random House.
  Portrays a relatively closed family system and the effects such closure has on
  the children as they deal with becoming adults. The film version, starring Gene
  Hackman, is superb.
Erdrich, Louise.
  1985 *Love Medicine.* Toronto, New York: Bantam.
  Sensitively written novel of a Sioux extended family by a Sioux author. The
  book beautifully illustrates systems aspects of families and tribe, which become
  apparent as layers of meaning and family history are laid one on top of another.
Guest, Judith.
  1976 *Ordinary People.* New York: Viking.
  A family coping with the aftermath of tragedy. Also available as a movie.
Olsen, Tillie.
  1976 *Tell Me a Riddle.* New York: Dell/Laurel Edition.
  A small collection of short stories commenting with sensitivity and insight on
  common human experiences within a context of culture and family.
Pa Chin (or Ba Jin).
  1972 *Family.* Garden City, New York: Anchor.
  The first novel in the trilogy *Turbulent Stream,* probably China's best known
  novel previous to the 1949 revolution. Based on the author's own experience, it
  describes a traditional Chinese family encountering modernization during and
  after the revolution of 1911.
Tan, Amy.
  1989 *The Joy Luck Club.* New York: Putnam.
  Chinese-American mothers and daughters deal with two cultures, two generations,
  and their relationships to each other. Very highly regarded by critics.

Films and Videos

The Double Burden: Three Generations of Working Mothers (1985)
  A documentary about three families—Mexican-American, Polish-American, and
  African-American—each with three generations of working women.
Fanny and Alexander (1983)
  Ingmar Bergman's happiest film, based on his extended family in Uppsala, Swe-
  den, in 1907. In Swedish, with English subtitles.
The Great Santini (1979)
  Robert Duvall is forceful as an Air Force pilot whose family "hangs together"
  despite frequent moves and his dictatorial behavior. Told from the viewpoint of
  the adolescent son who frequently conflicts with the father, but learns family
  solidarity from him.
Home for the Holidays (1995)
  This comedy/tragedy portrays the ambivalence and anger that emerges in a three-
  generation family during a holiday visit: "We don't have to like each other. We're
  family."
Homecomin' (1980)
  This film is about a separated African-American family, and the effects on family
  members. The father grapples with his responsibilities to his son.

I Know Why the Caged Bird Sings (1979; made for television)

Based on Maya Angelou's autobiography, this is a story of survival, child abuse, and the strength of family ties among members of an African-American family.

Juno (2007)

A pregnant teenager makes an unorthodox decision about her child, with the help of her supportive family. Well acted and plausible.

Precious (2009)

Based on the novel *Push*, this acclaimed film won numerous prizes. It was hailed by critics as "grim," but triumphant, and "courageous." Shows life in an inner city slum, and the determination of a girl with multiple negatives in her life.

Rachel Getting Married (2008)

An addict provokes a family crisis in order to resolve her family's relationships, following a tragic accident. Well acted and realistic.

Too Little, Too Late (1987)

Families and friends of AIDS patients are profiled and interviewed. Their pain and isolation are conveyed by a mother whose son died of AIDS, and who is active in AIDS hospice programs.

The Vanishing Family—Crisis in Black America (1986)

This video documentary examines structures of African-American families, and difficulties in forming stable relationships among African-American teenagers.

8

The Person

We live life forward, however perilously, although we retrace it backward, and after each travail we are lucky if we achieve a new equilibrium, never quite the one we left behind.
—Max Lerner

Our whole civilization is a masculine civilization. The State, the laws, morality, religion, and the sciences are the creation of men. ... If we are clear about the extent to which all our being, thinking, and doing conform to these masculine standards, we can see how difficult it is for the individual woman to shake off this mode of thought.
—Karen Horney

I. Theoretical Approaches

This chapter deals with the person as a human system and introduces concepts of human growth and development that are congruent with social systems theory. Some theorists have questioned whether persons can be considered to be social systems; however, without the individual, there would be no society, and without the society, there would be no individual. Each determines the other. Social systems concepts explain this interaction.

Our approach to the person as a human system is developmental and cyclical; we draw from the works of a range of theorists, including Sigmund Freud, Carol Gilligan, Karen Horney, Lawrence Kohlberg, Daniel Levinson, and especially Erik H. Erikson and Jean Piaget. Their formulations are particularly congruent with social systems theory.

A. Psychosocial Approach to Human Behavior

The *psychosocial* approach (represented by Sigmund Freud and Erik H. Erikson) is introduced first, since this general view of human behavior provides the framework for this chapter's content on the human *life cycle*. The central theme of this approach is the interaction of the individual person (*self*) with the *social* environment. From a systems viewpoint, the individual person is a human system who is both cause and effect of social systems. Therefore, when we examine persons' growth and development from psychosocial and systems approaches, it is important to make connections between developmental theories and societal provisions, i.e., social programs and institutions.

As the cycle of life unfolds, persons expand their interaction into systems of ever-larger magnitude. Figure 8.1 shows two of the many possible diagrams of this interaction. In either diagram, a person's growth and development is in a pattern of expansion, a movement outward. This chapter uses the life cycle theory of Erik Erikson as a framework to organize and describe the components and stages of that growth process. The psychosocial approach and Erikson's theory, in particular, are applicable in Western societies, and Erikson tested their applicability in India and in American Indian cultures, as well.

1. *Sigmund Freud.* Sigmund Freud was a physician, a physiologist, and a psychologist who treated persons with personality disturbances, and who originated psychoanalysis. From about the age of forty, he wrote prolifically on many facets of personality; he pioneered the study of many of the subjects he chose. His theories were highly controversial, and continue to be. Whether one accepts his theories, knowledge of them is essential for researchers and students of human personality, not only of psychology and psychiatry, but of literature and religion, because he drew upon and wrote about history, anthropology, and culture. His most influential works are *The Interpretation of Dreams* (1900), *The Psychopathology of Everyday Life* (1901), *Three Contributions to the Theory of Sex* (1905), and *The Introductory Lectures to Psychoanalysis* (1916, 1932-1936). *An Outline of Psychoanalysis,* published posthumously, is the most lucid and concise statement of his general theory. Despite revisions by later psychoanalytic theorists, and devaluation of his ideas by critics, "He was an original thinker who radically altered prevailing views of human nature" (Brome, 1987:586).

We regard Freud's theory as one form of social systems theory. Freud's work must be considered in historical-cultural context. Science inherited the "clockwork," mechanical view of the human organism from Sir Isaac Newton, but Freud broke with that tradition. Based on his therapeutic work with disturbed patients, he defined the human organism as a dynamic, complex system composed of physical energy and *psychic energy.* Freud's model was adapted from the physical sciences and the field of engineering (both hydraulic and electrical), hence his terminology of "forces" and "resistances."

Figure 8.1
Diagrams of a person's interaction with systems of increasing scale.

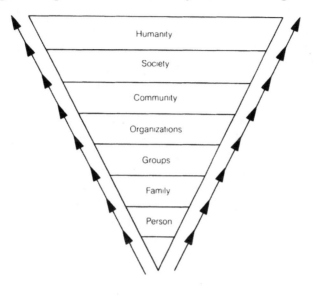

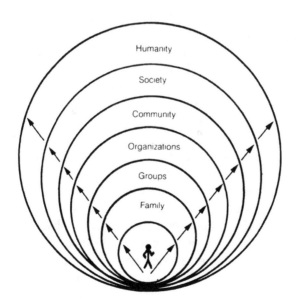

Freud attempted to identify the structure, behavior, and evolution of the human psyche. As a physiologist, Freud identified psychic energies as arising from the "tissue needs" of the body. The *id* is the source of energy for the human personality; it comprises the *libido,* essentially the sexual drive, and other unconscious drives and impulses that derive from human physiology. Its primary functions are the preservation and propagation of life (primarily via the sex drive); it operates on the "pleasure principle." The *ego* and *superego* evolve from the id. The ego's main function is to negotiate between the id and the external world (similar to the function of Piaget's schemas, described later); it operates according to the "reality principle," and controls intellect and perception; it is sometimes referred to as the "manager" of the personality. The superego is composed of social values that the person internalizes, sometimes in a rigid, judgmental way, sometimes in a flexible, tolerant way; it includes what is usually called "conscience." The ego also mediates conflicts between id and superego, employing a variety of *defense mechanisms.* These include (among many others) the sophisticated mechanism of *sublimation* (converting drives into intellectual desires; sex drive emerges as art or music or social power, e.g.), the more primitive *denial* of one's motivations and feelings, and *projection,* in which one's feelings are denied by claiming that it is others who have these feelings (a basic defense mechanism in paranoia). Personality disturbances result when the ego cannot resolve internal conflicts or threats from the external environment (either physical or social), and the person must rely too heavily on defense mechanisms.

Freud theorized that the personality evolves through several stages: *oral, anal, phallic,* and *genital.* Freud was true to his training as a physiologist, anchoring personality development in stages of organic development. Each stage is defined by the body tissues that are emerging and are most sensitive and that "demand attention" at that age. Psychological development might be arrested or fixated at any stage if unconscious conflicts were not sufficiently resolved during that stage.

a. Oral stage, the first year. If the child's personality development was arrested at this stage, it could be characterized by obsessive intake, e.g., eating, smoking, talking, or alcoholism. One's development would be determined by the predominant oral mode: holding onto, biting, spitting out, or shutting out, each with its own specific character traits.

b. Anal stage, the second year. Fixation at this stage would largely be characterized by negative traits, including compulsivity, rigidity, desire to control, possessiveness, or passive resistance, although determination could be considered a positive trait. The reputed characteristics of this stage entered into the popular culture two generations ago, in the expression, "Don't be so anal!"

c. *Phallic stage, ages 2-5.* Freud concluded that this is the stage during which the Oedipal crisis (or its female counterpart, the Electra crisis) is resolved and the child identifies self by gender. He theorized that narcissism, arrogance, flamboyance, and prejudice resulted from fixation, and that homosexuality resulted from arrested development at this stage. This may have ameliorated the view of homosexuality as a moral defect, but created another label, homosexuality as an illness, a failure to develop "normally."

d. *Latency period, ages 6-12.* Freud believed that while children demonstrated sexual behavior from birth, this latency stage is a quiescent time during which sexual curiosity and activity were repressed, after the resolution of the Oedipal crisis. Later psychoanalysts suggest that, instead, libidinal energies are redirected toward cognitive and social developments (compare Erikson's idea of "mastery" at this age, and Piaget's corresponding stage, later).

e. *Genital stage (adolescence and adulthood).* With the arrival of puberty, the person seeks others to love. Freud doubted that the stage of adult genital sexuality could be achieved without resolution of the earlier stages, and devoted his research and theorizing to problematic developments in the earlier stages, in particular internal psychological development, rather than social. That is, he focused on the person's internal structure, behavior, and evolution, and relationship to parents, almost to the exclusion of relationships with wider social systems. Erikson and other psychosocial theorists provide a fuller and more balanced view of adolescent and adult development.

2. *Erik Erikson.* The monumental task that Erikson undertook was to create and extend a conceptual framework for the complete life cycle, based upon Freudian theory, but substantially modified. Erikson's theory was first set forth in *Childhood and Society* (1950, 1985, 1993, 1963). He published major revisions, refinements, and expansions in *Insight and Responsibility* (1964), *Identity, Youth and Crisis* (1968), *Life History and the Historical Moment* (1975), *Identity and the Life Cycle* ([1980] 1994), *The Life Cycle Completed* (1982, 1997), *Vital Involvement in Old Age* (1986; coauthored), and *A Way of Looking at Things* (1987). He applied his theory to the field of psychohistorical biography with two pioneering, monumental works, *Young Man Luther* (1958), and *Gandhi's Truth* (1969), for which he was awarded the Pulitzer prize; he also authored

a study of Thomas Jefferson, *Dimensions of a New Identity* (1974). Each of the three biographical studies was at the same time a study of culture (Germany, India, and the United States), and of a representative individual's interaction with the cultural environment. Erikson's eight stages of the human life cycle are the organizing framework for this chapter for two reasons. First, it encompasses the complete life span. Second, his psychosocial approach to human development is particularly congruent with a systems approach, with its simultaneous attention to the individual and the environment, and with human services, with their emphasis on "person in environment." This chapter will introduce Erikson's thought by presenting a few key ideas from his formulation of the life cycle.

a. Erikson's view of the life cycle. This is based on the *epigenetic* principle. *Epigenesis* (from *epi*—"upon" and *genesis*—"emergence") means that each developmental stage builds upon, and in relation to, preceding stages. It is not merely that one stage succeeds another, but that each stage begins with the building blocks of the preceding stages and rearranges them, adding new elements and creating a structure that is new (at least to some significant degree). The building blocks include the physical, mental, psychological, and social aspects of the person that were created or reshaped in the previous stages.

The *potentials* for growth and development are all present in the human organism at birth; they emerge serially as the human organism matures. The parts arise out of the whole; each component (potential or capacity) has a special time for its emergence, until all the processes have run their course and the person develops into a functioning whole. Thus the human personality is an evolving system that contains its potentials in matrices that arise according to some general sequence. As these matrices emerge, they are interrelated, and in addition, the development of each matrix is dependent upon that which has gone before. Each alters the previously achieved balances. The stages are interrelated and, in systems terms, are synergistic.

Erikson's stages may be pictured simplistically as a set of teeterboards (or seesaws) balanced upon each other (see Figure 8.2). To repeat: Each level (or stage) depends upon the balance achieved in the previous stage, and an adjustment of any level involves a retroactive adjustment of all the preceding stages. The balance of each stage is the ratio of polar qualities that the person possesses at each stage. Bear in mind that it is not static, but a dynamic balance, a steady state subject to change.

b. Erikson's life cycle formulation. The life cycle and its stages are based in human genetic (physiological and psychological) energy but are,

Figure 8.2
One illustration of stages of the life cycle, according to Erikson.

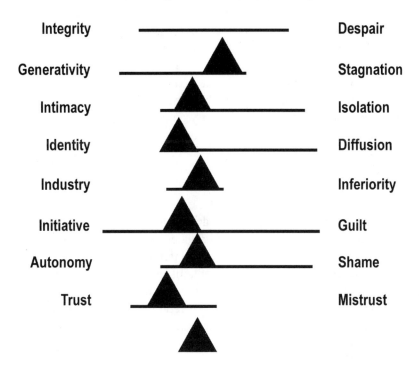

Integrity	Despair
Generativity	Stagnation
Intimacy	Isolation
Identity	Diffusion
Industry	Inferiority
Initiative	Guilt
Autonomy	Shame
Trust	Mistrust

at the same time, dependent on social experiences. Erikson described the life cycle as the product of three processes: (1) *physical,* constitutional (somatic) organization; (2) *ego,* the self as the organizing force, and (3) *social,* self-organization that is responsive to the rules and expectations of society and culture. In other words, the somatic process, the ego process, and the societal process equal the human life. The similarities and differences between this triad and the Freudian triad are important. The observation that Erikson's is an "ego psychology" and Freud's is an "id psychology" has some truth. In Erikson's theory, "A human being ... is at all times an organism, an ego and a member of society and is involved in all three processes of organization" (Erikson, [1950, 1985, 1993] 1963:36). In our view, of course, these are three systems levels, and the person as system simultaneously participates in all three. Within Erikson's scheme, the unfolding of a human system is the intertwining of maturation (organism), education (ego), and socialization (society).

The eight stages of Erikson's life cycle represent a synthesis of developmental (maturation) and social (learning) tasks. *Maturation* is the predictable course of growth for all members of a species, based upon shared physiological structure. *Learning* is unpredictable growth, new behavior based upon the individual experience of the organism and the accumulated learning of the culture. The distinction is similar to that between *genotype,* the inherited characteristics of an organism, and *phenotype,* the characteristics that emerge through the interaction of the organism's heredity with its environment. Growth, then, derives from the constant feedback cycle between maturation and learning. The organism's potentials at any stage of development are determined by maturation, while its learning is a function of social experience.

c. The idea of crisis. This is central to Erikson's theory. *Crisis intervention* is similar to Erikson's use of the term "crisis," which refers to a time of necessary change. The crises during growth and development, as Erikson uses the term, connote a heightened potential for development (or change) accompanied by greater vulnerability; an analogy is that the Chinese character for "crisis" contains elements of both "danger" and "opportunity." Crisis is not necessarily a negative state of affairs, but rather an unavoidable occasion that requires some type of coping. This meaning of crisis has existed since antiquity. Hippocrates described crisis as an occasion of imbalance that required the "constitution" of the person to respond (i.e., cope) (Jones, 1923:ii-iv). In Erikson's view, the crises occur at their scheduled time, arising from the interaction of the organism's maturation and society's expectations. The outcome (not *resolution,* necessarily) is dependent upon the personality resources the individual has accrued up to that point and the opportunities and resources that are available to the person from the social environment.

Erikson wrote most extensively and thoroughly on two of the eight crises of development—the second, *basic trust vs. basic mistrust,* and the fifth, *identity vs. diffusion.* Attention to these particular periods of child development is not unique to Erikson, since infancy and adolescence have attracted the attention of much child development research. In fact, infancy and adolescence *may indeed be* the two most critical phases of personality development. Erikson's theories about the first critical task of life, *trust vs. mistrust,* are compatible with the work of René Spitz (1965) in his studies of maternal deprivation and the establishment of an initial object relationship. Erikson's formulation is also consistent with the extensive literature on infant bonding and maternal deprivation.

Erikson's critical developmental tasks are expressed as bipolarities. This formulation is consistent with general systems theory, that the dynamism of life derives from the existence of negative and positive polarities with tension and movement between them. These bipolarities are not achievement scales to serve as measurable criteria of growth and development; one does not achieve *complete* trust and then move on to the next plateau, autonomy. The outcome of each of the developmental crises is a relative mix (a ratio) of the polar qualities and the developing person must cope with each subsequent task as it emerges at its proper time, as dictated by maturation and social expectations. In one sense, these critical tasks of development are present at all times in each person's life and are directly related to one another; Erikson attempted to illustrate this in his charts of development.

Table 8.1 illustrates the interrelatedness of the various crises. This table focuses on the crisis of adolescence, *identity vs. identity diffusion,* and illustrates how each of the earlier crises contributes to the readiness to cope with this one and how it in turn influences the subsequent crises. It would be possible to take any of the crises represented on the diagonal and fill in the related boxes to show the relationship of that crisis to the preceding and the following stages.

Erikson's worksheet (Table 8.2) illustrates his eight stages of the life cycle on five dimensions. The second dimension (column B, radius of significant relations) indicates the progression of interrelationships from the dyad of the infant and nurturing person on through the broadening hierarchy of social systems. The eighth stage includes all of humanity. Columns C, D, and E concern social order, psychosocial modalities, and psychosexual stages, and indicate the relatedness of these dimensions to the other dimensions.

In our view, Erikson's life cycle scheme is a version of social systems theory, based in the "natural" epigenetic principle. As the individual's life cycle proceeds through successive steady states, it has the maturational potential and the social necessity to be linked to, and be part of, ever-wider social systems and ever-changing social environments. To fulfill their functional destiny, persons must necessarily be engaged in transactions with these other social systems.

In summary then, Erikson's eight stages of the human life cycle represent *necessary* occasions for a person to unite biological, psychological, and social influences. Erikson's theory stresses the adaptive and creative power of a person and respects each person's individual capacity to forge a unique way of life. Erikson's faith in human social creativity is reflected in his optimistic comment, "There is little that cannot be remedied later, there is much that can be prevented from happening at all" (Erikson, 1950:164).

B. Cognitive Theory

1. *Piaget.* Jean Piaget was a biologist as well as a systems theorist, and attended conferences on general systems theory, exchanging ideas with other systems theorists. Maier said:

> Piaget believes in universal order and suggests a single unity of all things biological, social, psychological, and ideational in living as well as nonliving systems. For him, as a biological scientist, "all living forms grow and develop in coherent, logical patterns." ... All science is interrelated, and a theorem established in one branch of science is directly relevant to the laws and principles of other branches. Altogether, Piaget insists upon cosmic unity. (1988:19)

Phillips described Piaget's conception of "the human brain as a vastly complicated system for the storage and retrieval of information; a system that becomes capable of increasingly complex operations; a system that changes in ways that are at least to some degree similar to the constructions that Piaget has given us" (1969:xii).

Piaget was a biologist, and chose to study cognitive development and cognitive theory, which is about the process of knowing and learning. Much of what has been done in this field can be traced to Piaget and his collaborators. With other researchers, he sought to combine biology, philosophy, and psychology in a "psychological and biological epistemology," or theory of knowledge. His greatest influence was on educational theory and practice. Piaget's emphasis on first-hand involvement, experience, and grappling with problems appropriate to the child's intellectual development, were consistent with the educational philosophy of John Dewey, whose influence on American education has been profound. "What [Piaget] found significant is that in every case where acceleration [of learning] takes place, it results from a conflict arising in the child's own mind. It is the child's *own effort* to resolve a conflict that takes him or her on to another level" (Duckworth, 1996:39, emphasis ours). This is an example of self-development of the person as system.

Piaget's research methods were criticized because they were often unorthodox. He used psychoanalytic and qualitative research interviewing (which would be more acceptable today, because of the influence of Piaget, among others), exploring children's responses, especially their mistakes, to discern the rules by which they made them. Piaget questioned children while they were doing various tasks and between tasks, and also silently observed their behaviors; he invented over fifty new research techniques. Here is one example: The child was presented with a group of coins and a bunch of flowers. The child was then asked how many flowers could be purchased if each flower cost one coin.

> Gui (four years, four months) put 5 flowers opposite 6 pennies, then made a one-for-one exchange of 6 flowers (taking the extra flower from the reserve supply). The pennies were in a row and the flowers bunched together: "What have we done?—*We've exchanged them.*—Is there the same number of flowers and pennies?—*No.*—Are there more on one side?—*Yes.*—Where?— *There* (pennies). (The exchange was again made, but this time the pennies were put in a pile and the flowers in a row.) Is there the same number of flowers and pennies?—No.—Where are there more?—Here (flowers).—And here (pennies)—*Less.*" (Phillips, 1969:5)

This exchange illustrates the flexible interview style and search for concepts in the child's thought that was typical of Piaget's methods. In this instance, it appeared to the child that if the objects were spread out there were more of them than if they were bunched up, indicating that the concept of transferability of numbers from one set of objects to another had not yet developed in this child. Piaget also took the "unscholarly" approach of studying his own children and performing small experiments to test their development.

The topics of Piaget's major works include "the construction of reality," "judgment and reason," "language and thought," "logic and psychology," "moral judgment," "the origin of intelligence," and "the psychology of intelligence." His major work is *Genetic Epistemology* (1970).

Piaget is regarded by some as being equal to Freud in his eventual impact on personality theory. "Both Freud and Piaget posited universal, biologically-driven stages of development that scale the individual's changing knowledge and interpretation of the environment" (Bornstein and Lerner, 1987:710). Piaget dealt in concrete detail with the major problems of logic, thought, and philosophy in the twentieth century that hindered our understanding of human behavior. Acceptance of his ideas, and their diffusion among teachers and researchers, have accelerated with the development and use of computers, which mimic the human mind. Piaget's work is important for the human services: he stressed invention, creativity, and the ability of the person to overcome past deficiencies or conflicts. He believed that "every time you teach a child something you keep him from reinventing it" (Phillips, 1969:120) and that

> The principal goal of education ... is to create [persons] who are capable of doing new things ... who are creative, inventive and discoverers. The second goal ... is to form minds which can be critical, can verify, and not accept anything they are

offered ... we need pupils who are active, who learn early to find out by themselves, partly by their own spontaneous activity and partly through materials we set up for them; who learn early to tell what is verifiable and what is simply the first idea to come to them. (Elkind, 1968:80)

Duckworth, Piaget's colleague and translator, echoed both Socrates and Piaget: "You don't want to cover a subject; you want to uncover it" (Duckworth, 1996:7). This is a model of knowledge and learning that is most familiar in Western cultures, which emphasize individual initiative and innovation, as contrasted with, e.g., Chinese education, which traditionally stresses memorization.

The basic ideas of Piaget are relatively easy to understand from a systems viewpoint:

a. Equilibrium. In Piaget's view, equilibrium is a steady state of the cognitive processes. He regarded equilibrium as a dynamic balance between the person and the environment, in which the person's knowledge and self-organization are adequate to understand what is experienced. It is a state of active compatibility between the person and the environment. There is positive feedback that confirms and continues to reinforce the person's developing capacity to understand and master the environment; this is similar to Erikson.

b. Intelligence. As a biologist, Piaget defined intelligence as a form of biological activity. It arises from the person's physiology and is always a part of the individual as a biological being. Its function is the same as that of other system processes: to preserve the organism. According to Piaget, intelligence is *both* the means and the end; it is *both* the activity of coping *and* the end state of compatibility between the organism and its environment. It is the maximum potential of the adaptive capacities; and yet it is never fully realized, because no match of organism (or person) and environment is perfect.

Piaget's view of the structure of intelligence is quite consistent with the systems view. Just as Freud's concepts of id, ego, and superego came from classical mechanical physics, so Piaget's concept of schema comes from Einstein's theory of relativity and is compatible with [Alfred North] Whitehead's and Dewey's philosophies. Piaget specifically refers to physics as being analogous to his own ideas, and many of his experiments deal with children's understanding of such physics concepts as velocity, time, and distance. Piaget has explicitly acknowledged a similarity between his own theories and those of Bertalanffy, the foremost general systems theorist. (Koestler and Smythies, 1971:65)

c. Schemas. The structural units that lie at the heart of Piaget's system are *schemas,* mediating processes that form frameworks onto which information can, indeed must, fit. These frameworks continually change shape, to accommodate to new information. A schema is "like a rule of grammar. Speakers create all sorts sentences they have never before heard, nor even produced themselves before. They have understood the rule of grammar. ... Similarly, once the infant has made the connections, a [schema] is at his disposal, and [the child] uses it in all sorts of different ... manifestations" (Duckworth, 1996:19). Intelligence has a structure and this structure is systematic and orderly; *what Piaget means by intelligence is the same as the operation of consciousness upon phenomena, in phenomenology* (see the Addendum to Chapter 2). At any particular time it maintains an equilibrium that changes—that is, a steady state.

Freud's and Piaget's conceptions of intellectual structure are compatible. Piaget was far less interested in the emotional content of schemas, although he recognized its existence. Piaget believed that thought begins as action; schemas are patterns of internalized actions, ranging from the most elementary reflex pattern to profound philosophical thought. **Schemas are organized action sequences and behavior patterns that arise through associations with each other, again, the same as the operations of consciousness in phenomenology.** Reflexes become associated with other experiences, and such isolated schemas as sucking, grasping, looking, and hearing become larger, more complex and more comprehensive. For example, looking and sucking are coordinated into seeing-grasping-sucking the bottle simultaneously. Progressive refinements of schemes allow the child to see the bottle, hold it, turn it around, tilt it, lay it down, pick it up again, see that it is empty, cry, and so forth.

> Infants begin to act in intelligent ways from the day of their birth, that is, they make connections, seek consistencies and modify their actions.... infants proceed to carry out their reflexes in all possible situations, to modify them as necessary, and to figure out which actions in certain situations give rise to more possible things to do. They more they try to do ... the better they are able to adapt ... and the more they start to differentiate and to coordinate what they can do. They are making refinements and connections in their actions—"thinking" in their actions—long before there is any use of language. (Duckworth, 1996:18-19)

As it matures, the child will conduct these operations mentally—that is, to carry on the action internally, think it through, correct it, then try it, all without picking up the bottle. Piaget said that thought is precisely such actions and schemas, refined and modified endlessly. This is, of course, identical to the *critique carried on by* consciousness as delineated in the Addendum to Chapter 2. Piaget carried this a step further by stressing that reality as we know it can only be this structure of associated and coordinated experiences. In other words, reality is structured by the schemas we have built up. "The totality of your [schemas] is the totality of what you know" (ibid.:19). "Schemas are intellectual structures that organize events as they are perceived and classified into groups according to common characteristics. They are repeatable psychological events" (Wadsworth, 1996:15).

The developing child self-organizes its schemas, and adapts them as new information and experiences are encountered. According to Piaget, adaptation takes two forms: *assimilation* and *accommodation*. The person attempts to fit new information into the old schemas, to interpret it as similar to previous experience; this is assimilation. Accommodation is modification of previous schemas to accept new information.

> Infants take in, incorporate, those parts of the world that enable them to do what they are organized do. In a quite literal sense, this ... is assimilation.
>
> When infants modify their own organization in order to be able to incorporate yet more of the world, they are accommodating. The only food infants can take in at first is milk. Later they manage to *change their own structures,* in order to be able to take in more forms of nourishment. Similarly, they accommodate their mouth movements to a series of different objects, thus becoming able to enlarge the range of things they can suck. The greater the flexibility of the structures for taking things in, the better. (Duckworth, 1996:99, emphasis ours)

Assimilation and accommodation are similar to *morphostasis* and *morphogenesis,* the maintenance or change of a system's structure in order to achieve a new steady state after the input of new energy/ information. These two tendencies, like other polarities, are never mutually exclusive; there is always some balance (ratio) of the two.

d. Stages of growth. Piaget identified four major stages of cognitive growth (ages given here are approximate). "Operations," as Piaget referred to them, mean formal logic, "the manipulation of abstract concepts and the mastery of reasoning" (Bornstein and Lerner, 1987:716), e.g., imagining a concept's opposite, or variations on it, or reversing the sequence in which something occurred, to identify the cause.

(1) *Sensorimotor stage, ages 0-2.* Piaget and Erikson similarly described the infant's profound egocentrism during the initial stage. At birth, the child has no awareness of a self. There is only sensation and reflexes. There is no distinction between self and environment, no consciousness yet to construct a boundary. Duckworth's description, above, is of this stage. The child begins to experience self as an active agent within an environment that is separate from itself, and to influence that environment. This is *coevolution:* the environment changes as the child changes; the parent encourages the child's expanding repertoire, and provides increasingly challenging opportunities for cognitive and

motor development. It is Erikson's *trust vs. mistrust* stage, in which the child develops trust in its own capacities and in the reliability of the environment.

(2) *Preoperational stage, ages 2 to 6 or 7.* In this stage, thought is intuitive rather than deductive or "logical." The child can abstract from experience, but is limited to concrete objects, and to only one aspect of an object at a time. "The beginnings of logic appear in the form of classifications of ideas and an understanding of time and number" (ibid.:716). The capability for reversibility, "running events backward" and to reason back to the beginnings of things, emerges now,

(3) *Concrete operations stage, ages 7 to 11 or 12.* Now that the child can "group" and classify things, the child can manage the logical tasks involved in mathematics, begin to understand scientific method and to understand concepts such as "conservation" (that a volume of water remains the same whether it is in a tall or short glass, e.g.; see the "Gui" illustration, earlier). With these intellectual tools, the child develops an objective certainty about the world, a sense of mastery of it, as Erikson described it in his stage of *industry vs. inferiority.* The child has achieved a temporary *equilibrium* (steady state) in its relationship to the world.

(4) *Formal operations stage, age 12 through adulthood.* Now the person becomes capable of the full range of logical operations; the schemas are fully developed, although they will continue to become more complex throughout life. The adolescent can imagine beyond his or her own experience. In Freudian terms, the ego can now fully idealize, testing reality against ideals. Everything is open to question, parents and authorities included; everything must be analyzed (and reanalyzed). This explains adolescence as the "idealistic" stage of life, and the usefulness of adolescents as the "advance guard" of cultural adaptation. It is no coincidence that the ideal of romantic love is the adolescent pair, Romeo and Juliet. Adolescence, as we discuss later, is a time of crisis (in Erikson's terms) because the person system is physiologically, emotionally, and cognitively in upheaval.

2. *The Development of Moral Judgment: Lawrence Kohlberg*

Piaget hypothesized that all people pass through two phases of moral reasoning. In the first phase an objective and concrete morality is based on the constraints imposed by the powerful (e.g., adults) on the nonpowerful (e.g., children). In the second phase the person develops a subjective morality based on an abstract understanding of the contracts implicit in cooperative and autonomous relationships. Piaget's stress on the universal ordering of moral growth represents an approach that is quite distinct from relativistic, response-centred approaches. As such, it has stimulated considerable interest among developmental researchers. (ibid.:716)

Lawrence Kohlberg (1984, 1987), a psychologist, applied Piaget's theory to the development of moral judgment in children and adults. Piaget's studies of this aspect of human development date from the 1920s; Kohlberg's from the late 1950s. Kohlberg's methodology was to administer verbal and written descriptions of situations that asked children or adults to state what is "right" in each situation. For example, in the "Heinz" case, Heinz's wife is dying and the pharmacist has the rare medicine to cure her but will sell it only at a price that Heinz cannot afford. The respondent must decide what is "right," and why. Should Heinz steal the medicine? If not, why not? If so, why? Because he loves his wife or simply because she is a human being in jeopardy? What are the rights of the pharmacist? Should he be able to set any price he wishes? What of the pharmacist's right to private property that he created? Should Heinz or the pharmacist act according to the "golden rule" or some other universal rule? The answers given in this and other situations indicate the respondent's stage of moral development; Kohlberg's stages are adapted from Piaget.

Kohlberg identified six stages (and later a seventh that seems highly speculative), the first four of which emerge from his research. The fifth and sixth stages are logical extensions of the preceding stages, but they are criticized by other investigators for the lack of empirical evidence.

a. Preconventional moral judgment. Kohlberg identified the majority of the population, which falls in stages 3 and 4, as being "conventional" in their moral judgments. Accordingly, stages 1 and 2 are "preconventional," centering upon self, and stages 5 and 6 are "postconventional," centering upon wider social systems, either societal or universal (all of humanity), in making moral judgments.

Stage 1. In this earliest stage, judgments are based upon the direct consequences the child is likely to suffer. "Will I be punished for this or rewarded?" The child's calculation is simple and straightforward, and it is the first step beyond egocentrism; it represents the ability to take the perspective of another person.

Stage 2. Now the child moves beyond stark reciprocity, it desires to please its nurturers. It anticipates the pleasure or displeasure of these "significant others." The child has differentiated self from other and views self *in relation to* other. The child begins to understand that the will or desires of the other person can change—that they can be changed by the child's actions, and that there is some standard of fairness or reciprocity to which the child can appeal.

b. Conventional moral judgment. According to Kohlberg, stages 3 and 4 comprise the levels of development of most of the population; hence the label "conventional." One could assume that the distribution of the adult population falls within a classic bell-shaped curve, except that the shape of the "bell" would be quite high and quite narrow, since Kohlberg and his fellow researchers estimate that no more than 5 percent of the population have progressed beyond stage 5.

Stage 3. The child now not only understands the other, but is capable of taking the role of the other, and can see the situation (and self) from the other's perspective. "Kohlberg refers to this sometimes as the 'Good-boy/Nice-girl' stage. One is motivated to observe rules in order to maintain relationships. The individual's conception of right at this stage is limited to people within his own circle and does not extend to a broad societal level" (Rosen, 1980:76).

Stage 4. This stage can be called "social system and conscience" (ibid.:77). The child's reference is the entire society. There is a sense of obligation to conform and to obey its laws and fulfill its obligations. Laws are recognized as necessary and legitimate. There is now a conception of a moral code that extends beyond one's family and community systems. Judgments are based upon the rights of society. Vengeance, for example, is the right of society and is interpreted as "paying your debt to society." In a cogent sentence, Kohlberg suggests what underlies the attitude of the general public toward welfare and those who receive it: "Social inequality is allowed where it is reciprocal to effort, moral conformity, and talent, but unequal favoring of the 'idle' and 'immoral,' poor, students, etc., is strongly rejected" (ibid.:77). This, then, is the stage of conventional morality, and is manifested in such current programs as "workfare" and such slogans as "a hand up, not a handout," which were embodied in the 1996 federal welfare reforms and associated policy changes at the state and local levels.

Kohlberg and his collaborators identified a substage (cleverly labeled stage 4B), which is a "moratorium" (Erikson's term; see later in this chapter) or period of limbo. During this substage, the person is in a transition state from stage 4 to stage 5 and, in confusion, alternates between relativism and absolutism in moral judgments. Roughly, this period falls between high school graduation (about age 18) and the mid-twenties, approximately the "college (and perhaps graduate school) years." This poses a question that psychosocial theorists might ask: Is it that the institution of higher education causes such change, or does the developmental change during this period create the institution of higher education, to accommodate this cognitive/moral development? A systems answer might be that this is an example of mutual causation.

Kohlberg said that there are periods of "disequilibrium" between stages (similar to Piaget; we recognize them as phase transformations or transition states) and that the person in substage 4B is in such a disequilibrium. Kohlberg believed that stage 5, if it is achieved, occurs during the mid-twenties, and that stage 6 does not occur until at least the late twenties. If these stages are substantiated by further research, they would tend to confirm Erikson's stages of adulthood as well as Kohlberg's.

   c. Postconventional stages of moral development. Stages 5 and 6 are controversial, since there is less supporting evidence for them. Kohlberg has been accused of deriving these from philosophical premises, rather than empirical research. The person recognizes that societies' rules are relative, that they are sometimes arbitrary and subjective. Postconventional reasoning becomes possible with the arrival of formal logic, and begins at adolescence.

   Stage 5. Now the person entertains the possibility of changing unjust laws and challenging society's practices. The person looks beyond laws to the principles they embody, and questions whether the laws fulfill those principles. According to Kohlberg, the logical outcome of stage 5 is a democratic society. The person becomes aware that there may be two or more valid moral or legal alternatives and must choose between them. In this sense, the person in stage 5 seeks justice as a principle rather than simply obedience to the law. Equity (fairness based on specific criteria) is preferred over absolute equality. It seems clear that Kohlberg has been influenced by a philosophy of justice such as that of John Rawls (Rawls, 1971, 1975, 1999).

   Stage 6. Here are the idealized characteristics of the person who attains stage 6:

> The rare person whose sociocognitive moral development has [progressed] to this stage of moral reasoning is fully autonomous. He is *completely decentered from society's expectations* and bases his resolutions to ethical conflicts upon universal principles of justice. ... Universality, consistency and logical comprehensiveness are the central attributes. ... Respect for the dignity of each individual, regardless of station in life, has reached a zenith. (Rosen, 1980:80-81, emphasis ours)

Kohlberg cited a philosopher's solution to the "Heinz" situation as an example of stage 6 moral judgments:

> IF THE HUSBAND DOES NOT FEEL VERY CLOSE TO OR AFFECTIONATE WITH HIS WIFE, SHOULD HE STEAL THE DRUG? Yes. *The value of her life*

is independent of any personal ties. The value of human life is based upon the fact that it offers the only possible source of a categorical moral "ought" to a rational being acting in the role of a moral agent. SUPPOSE IT WERE A FRIEND OR AN ACQUAINTANCE? *Yes, the value of a human life remains the same.* (Hersh, Paolitto, and Reirner [1979] 1983:80)

Stage 7. Kohlberg identified a seventh stage for which there is no supporting data, as yet. His critics did not find convincing evidence for stages 5 or 6, either. Kohlberg acknowledged being influenced by Erikson and believed that this seventh stage occurs in elderly persons who find meaning in life, despite despair and doubt, by "identifying the self with cosmic perspective of the infinite" (Rosen, 1980:88). Kohlberg does not claim that this is a verifiable stage, but believes that, among the elderly, spiritual growth occurs that is qualitatively different from earlier moral stages. One wonders whether such spiritual growth might also occur among younger persons who face their own imminent death, if given time to ponder its meaning.

Kohlberg's theories have received thorough and sometimes unfavorable reviews; but he has created the largest body of research on moral judgment and for that reason alone is significant. Some observations on his theory may be useful here. Persons do not inevitably progress through either Kohlberg's or Piaget's stages, as contrasted to Erikson's stages; Kohlberg stated that most of the population remains in stage 4.

One serious criticism of Kohlberg's theory is that his idealized persons in stages 5 and 6 (and certainly stage 7) are conceived to be "beyond culture" or "culture-free" (similar to Maslow's theory of the self-actualized person). This contradicts what we have said in Chapter 3 regarding the pervasiveness and power of culture. Socrates, Lincoln, Martin Luther King, Jr. (each of whom Kohlberg cited), and—one could add—Gandhi were certainly not free of their respective cultures. One could maintain (as Erikson did of Luther, Jefferson, and, one could add, Gandhi) that in fact they transformed their cultures through exemplifying certain principles that, in each case, underlay the laws and norms of their societies.

C. Theories Related to Gender and Sexual Orientation

It is extremely important to note criticisms that have been leveled at the preceding theories regarding their focus on men, and Caucasian, heterosexual men in particular. In this and the following section, we will examine some theories of development that begin with other cultural, social, and biological premises. Gender (or more precisely, sexuality) is not solely female; that it is perceived so reveals the male norm in our society. "Masculinity and femininity are not like a set of clothes in a wardrobe which can be put on and off with ease. These identities feel more like a skin which can not be shed" (Wetherell, 1995:250). We will consider some influential theories here.

1. *Women's Development.* Discussion of theories of women's development is placed here because at many points these theories contain critiques of, and advancements on, other theories, including those previously presented. Some views of women's development, particularly within the last generation, may be described as feminist theory. Feminist theory "addresses the invisibility of women's experience and knowledge in domestic and public spheres, and redresses this injustice by reclaiming women's own history and language" (Butler and Wintram, 1991:6). This theoretical field begins with "an underlying feminist assumption" which permeates

> ... our thoughts, behaviour and attitudes ... that patriarchy systematically oppresses women in every sphere of life. (ibid.:8)
> [Therefore,] it is crucial that any theory derived outside of feminism is considered critically for its value *for* women and, in addition, should not preclude the development of woman-based theory. (ibid.:20)

This present book may be evaluated by the same criteria, as well.

At this point, we must look at the reality of women's lives. In the United States, many women are in lower-paid, less-skilled jobs, although there have been increased numbers of women in professional positions. Many have inadequate or no health insurance. Whether the 2010 health insurance reform will positively affect them remains to be seen. Most women will receive a modest pension or none, and will fare better with "spouse" pensions than their own. Typically, employed women work the "second shift" in the home unassisted, with little help in domestic chores or child care, although this seems to be changing somewhat. About half will receive child support payments they are legally entitled to, and when they do, will receive about half the amount specified; again, tighter enforcement of child support orders has improved this a bit in recent years. Women are less often promoted and appear less often on the "fast track" at work, receive lower pay for similar work, and often hit the "glass ceiling." In addition, women are subjected to sexual harassment at the workplace, which includes the military; reports of assaults by their male counterparts are common, and occur far more frequently than officially reported. Women hold a relatively small fraction of executive jobs in work organizations, including higher education, although women are highly represented as creators and executives of small, entrepreneurial firms (see Chapter 5). As Levinson says,

> The level and intensity of gender conflict have risen since 1980. We live in a state of gender warfare—often covert but with flare-ups of overt antagonism. ... Harassment and discrimination take a greater variety of forms, gross as well as subtle. ... There is growing public awareness that many women are abused, discriminated against, and hindered in their personal development.
> ... The conflict is not only between women and men. It exists also among women and among men. Our established customs, laws, and values are in question. (Levinson, 1996:417)

The cultural conflict is not new, of course. As Levinson points out, the writer Virginia Woolf addressed these issues eloquently in 1931 (Levinson, 1996:419-420).

a. Karen Horney. Born in Germany in 1885, Karen Danielson Horney was one of the first psychoanalytic patients (of one of Freud's colleagues), while she was a medical student, and became a psychoanalyst. Her early work elaborated Freud's basic themes, but she proposed a counterinterpretation, using Freud's own ideas. As her theory evolved, she fundamentally diverged from Freud, proposing an alternative "cultural view of human development" rather than a Freudian intrapsychic (instinctual and sexual) view. After she moved to the United States in 1932, she found support among colleagues such as Harry Stack Sullivan and Erich Fromm. She anticipated ideas later advanced by Erikson, regarding the need for basic trust, and Maslow, regarding the need for "safety and satisfaction" (Westkott, 1986:68-71).

Horney's theory of the psychology of women was based upon experience with her female patients, her own experience (as Freud's views grew from his own experience), and her experience as the mother of three daughters. In addition, her view of the impact of culture was influenced by the rise of Nazi ideology. "To understand female psychology, she proposed, one must account for this male-created social subordination of women. Thus, a psychology of women should be a social psychology, an explication of the interaction of psychic and social factors" (ibid.:12). For Horney, "inner conflict is the avoidable consequence of the contradictions and dehumanizing elements of civilization as transmitted by parents to their children" (ibid.). Horney described a "common present-day feminine type" in 1934; she traced its origin to the culture's conflicting definitions of femininity: "a patriarchal ideal of womanhood versus a more independent female identity" (ibid.:14). Women are devalued by the male-dominated culture; they are viewed as sexualized beings from childhood onward. Horney "believed that authentic care for others and mutual love in intimate relationships are possible" (ibid.:165), but recognized that the culture forced women to "overvalue love" as the primary source of self-esteem and validation. In consequence, women compete for the attentions of men (beginning with a rivalry between mother and daughter for the husband/father's affection) and suffer anxiety and self-doubt; other women are seen as "enemies." Thus women's inner conflicts originate in cultural devaluation and dehumanization and *then* are internalized, the converse of Freud's opinion.

Horney intended this analysis to apply to both genders, but feminist interpretations of her work emphasize its particular applicability to women. One author maintains that Horney's analysis explains the "relational traits that subsequent psychologists have more recently identified" (ibid.:5). Among these traits are "female altruism ... the characterological need to care for others" (ibid.: 134), the culturally prescribed imperative to nurture others and to make fewer demands on others for care. This trait has been addressed by Carol Gilligan.

b. Carol Gilligan. Carol Gilligan was a former co-teacher with Erikson, and then collaborator with Kohlberg at Harvard University. She became a full professor at Harvard, then in 2002, moved to New York University. Gilligan applied Kohlberg's technique in her research with women, in particular, the "Heinz" problem. In her book, *In a Different Voice* (1982), Gilligan extended Chodorow's theory of the importance of rearing by mothers, and maintained that the relationship to the mother is crucial to moral development and to a child's later mode of relationships with others. Because males ordinarily separate from their mothers in order to identify with their own gender, and females do not, males employ a mode of relating that is oppositional, separatist, and places more importance upon abstract (rational and impersonal) principles than upon relationships with others. Males' styles of relating are presumably more compatible with bureaucratic (including military) ways of organizing their lives and activities. Conversely, women are presumably more (but not exclusively) compatible with informal styles of organization and communication, even within bureaucracies; "networking" is more characteristic of women as a style of relationship and communication.

Gilligan's statement of the difference is that men and women see attachment and separation differently: men see connection as a threat, while women see separation as a threat. Women view the fundamental issue in relationships as *care* and responsibility, rather than rights and rules (Gilligan, 1982). Gilligan concluded that women's logic is based on equality and reciprocity rather than an abstract conception of justice. "Women ... associate moral behavior with obligation, sacrifice, and inhibitions against hurting others. They are reluctant to make moral judgments about other people and perceive a conflict between power and care" (Westkott, 1986:141). There may be a negative aspect of this role, however:

> The female altruist is not only the selfless caretaker of others but also the great mediator of this vast web of competing needs. Thus the moral paralysis that keeps her from taking a stand which would favor one person over another. (ibid.:143)

Gilligan maintained that women's position will change when "the concept of relationship changes from a bond of continuing dependence to a dynamic of *inter*dependence. Then the notion of care expands ... to an injunction to act responsively toward self and others and thus to sustain connection" (Gilligan, 1982:149). Later research has indicated that moral reasoning does not differ between genders to the degree that Gilligan theorized—that both genders base decisions on justice *and* caring.

Horney stated a similar, existentialist view in *New Ways in Psychoanalysis* in 1939:

> By making self-responsibility her fundamental therapeutic goal, Horney reclaimed judgment as a human capacity that is not reducible to sexuality (libido), guilt (superego), or accommodation to external reality (ego). Freedom and responsibility of choice that draw upon a whole real self, not a segmented and managed self, bring to bear perception, cognition, feeling, and judgment. (Westkott, 1986:207)

Horney's view is highly congruent with a systems view of the relationship of the person and larger systems. Conflict within the person mirrors conflicts in the culture and society, and alteration of the feedback cycle (through locating and validating the "real self") can heal: "From [Horney's] perspective growth is *self-directed* life itself, and at its core is the central inner force that is the real self" (ibid.:71; emphasis ours).

c. Daniel Levinson. Daniel Levinson, a psychologist, began to research women's development shortly after completing his study of men (discussed later in this chapter). The result was *The Seasons of a Woman's Life* (1996), an analysis of homemakers' and career women's experiences during their adult years.

Levinson demonstrates a systems approach: "[T]he primary components of a life structure are the person's *relationships* with various others in the external world" (Levinson, 1996:22). He cautions that

> It is important to distinguish between the development of the life structure and the development of the self. ... The study of adult development inevitably goes beyond the focus on the self. It requires us to examine the life course, to study the engagement of self in the world. (ibid.:29)

"Satisfactoriness of the life structure" is a highly significant factor in his analysis of women's lives:

> [I]t refers to the structure's viability in the external world—how well it works, what it provides in the way of advantages and disadvantages, successes and failures, rewards and deprivations. Internally, it refers to the structure's suitability for the self, that is, what aspects of the self can be lived out within this structure? What aspects must be neglected or suppressed? What are the benefits and costs of this structure for the self? (ibid.:28-29)

Levinson reports that he was surprised by the "extent and power of the differences" between women's and men's lives, and attempts to capture this in the concept of "gender splitting":

> a splitting asunder ... women and men have lived in different worlds: culture, social institutions, everyday social life, the individual psyche. It creates antithetical divisions between women and men, between social worlds, between the masculine and the feminine within the self. It also creates inequalities that limit the adult development of women as well as men. (ibid.:38)

Levinson's research confirmed the effects on women, many of whom experienced what he calls "rock bottom time" during transition periods at about age thirty and age fifty: "a sense of being overwhelmed, of having no way to form a minimally good enough life. ... For some the crisis involved considerable turmoil and conscious suffering; others were not clearly aware of the extent of their difficulties" (ibid.:94). The difficulties arose, in large part, because both societal expectations and women's expectations changed (both macro and microsystems).

> [T]he traditional pattern is difficult to sustain. Most women who tried ... formed structures that were relatively unsatisfactory—not viable in the world, not suitable for the self. The few who were more or less contented paid a considerable price in restriction of self-development. The career women tried to anticipate the future: to reduce the gender-splitting, to enter formerly "male" occupations, to work on equal terms with men, and to establish a family life in which homemaking and provisioning were more equally divided. Their lives attest to the pleasures and problems of innovation, of attempting to realize values not well supported by the current culture and institutions. (ibid.: 415)

2. Theories of Lesbian and Gay Development. Etiology of gay or lesbian sexual orientation is uncertain.

> There is no clear evidence from studies that family of origin relationships contribute to the development of homosexuality. ... The causes of homosexuality remain a mystery, although research is becoming centered increasingly on genetic factors and the prenatal hormonal environment ... as predisposing conditions for subsequent internal and developmental-social processes that lead to self-labeling as lesbian or gay. Most likely, there are multiple routes to adoption of a homosexual identity. (Laird and Green, 1996:7)

Freud believed that homosexuality was due to anal fixation or failure to resolve the Oedipal crisis (note that this applied to males). A behaviorist explanation is that the person finds same-sex experiences reinforcing or less aversive than heterosexual contact. The Kinsey studies in sexuality supported this interpretation: that first sexual experience determined subsequent choices (Kinsey et al., 1948). One study of brain structure indicated similarity between the brains of women and gay males, which might support an organic origin for homosexuality.

There is no clear evidence to suggest patterns of difference between the personality development of homosexuals, heterosexuals, and bisexual persons. However, it was not until 1973 that the American Psychiatric Association removed homosexuality from its list of "pathologies"; in 1991, it officially allowed gays and lesbians admission to its training institutes; and in 1992, it allowed them to teach in these institutes and to become senior analysts (Clark, 1997:30-31). The American Psychological Association agreed in 1975 that homosexuality is not a mental disorder. There have been few studies of personality development among gays or lesbians, certainly not enough to propose a distinct scheme of development with any degree of confidence. However, "coming-out" models suggest four stages of identity development, leading from first awareness to full disclosure. Here is a plausible model:

1. First awareness
    *   An initial cognitive and emotional realization that one is "different" and a feeling of alienation from oneself and others
    *   No disclosure to others
    *   Some awareness that homosexuality may be the relevant issue
2. Test and exploration
    *   Feelings of ambivalence that precede acceptance of homosexuality
    *   Initial but limited contact with gay and lesbian individuals or communities
    *   Alienation from heterosexuality
3. Identity acceptance
    *   Preference for social interactions with other gays and lesbians
    *   Evolution from negative identity to positive identity
    *   Initial disclosure to heterosexuals
4. Identity integration
    *   View of self as gay or lesbian with accompanying anger at society's prejudice
    *   Publicly coming out to many others
    *   Identity stability: unwillingness to change and pride in oneself and one's group (J. Sophie, in Clark, 1997:154-155)

This model indicates the resistance or fear that may justifiably accompany a person's disclosure of gay or lesbian identity. It does not,
however, sufficiently convey the isolation, self-doubt, and negative poles
of Erikson's stages that are experienced by many gays and lesbians, in
response to the fear and hostility they encounter in their social relationships. Most are reluctant to disclose to their families; most will disclose
to friends and to siblings before they disclose to parents; many never
disclose to parents, particularly if their family's culture (Hispanic and
Asian cultures, e.g., are cited) is not receptive to homosexuality. Often,
maintaining psychological defenses and keeping the secret require
massive expenditure of energy, and closing off social exchanges. In
a significant number of instances, the strain is too great; some studies
report that 20-40 percent of gay and lesbian youths have attempted
suicide; half of these have made multiple attempts, and they are two to
three times more likely to commit suicide than other youths (Laird and
Green, 1996:170). Families often find disclosure, or discovery, difficult
to accept; outright rejection may result, or physical or emotional attacks.
Relatively few families handle disclosure affirmatively and supportively,
at least at first.

Homophobia is a word coined by George Weinberg in *Society and
the Healthy Homosexual* in 1972:

> It suggests a phobic, irrational fear of people who are gay or primarily homosexual
> in orientation and, indeed, of anything having to do with homosexuality. ...
> Homophobia may cover a person's fear of his or her own homoerotic feelings. ...
> It is an irrational, illogical pathology driven by simple fear and the awesome power
> of buried anxiety. (Clark, 1997:9)

Whatever its origin, "No other issue taps into such a potential conflict
more than the issue of homosexuality" (Wolfe, 1998:72). Wolfe reported
that while 70 percent of Americans believe that same-sex behavior is
"wrong," most people would live and let live. He believed that public
opinion does not support gays and lesbians teaching in public (elementary
and high) schools, but cited data showing that over 70 percent believe that
it is acceptable for homosexuals to teach in higher education (ibid.:75).
"That support can be explained on the grounds of respect for rights; in
endorsing the right of homosexuals to teach, people are not necessarily
endorsing homosexuality" (ibid.); apparently, they fear for their children.
Homophobia runs deep in American culture, despite respect for privacy
and individual rights, and permeates all systems levels.

Wolfe drew a parallel between this prejudice and American attitudes
toward bilingual education: "It is one thing to say that people's rights

should not be denied and another to say that their identities should be respected" (ibid.:154). The cultural system, with its structure of privilege, and its racial/ethnic and sexual attitudes, strongly resists change. Like all identities, cultural identity contains negative as well as positive elements. Identities change in response to crisis; social work, nursing, education, and other professions have a deep responsibility to assist in the positive resolution of this cultural crisis.

D. Theories of Development: Some Observations

Freud's views were influenced by the *zeitgeist* of his culture: male dominance and the contention of powerful forces (both political and psychological). Feminist views as represented by Horney and Gilligan, and more affirmative views of homosexuality invalidate Freud's chauvinistic opinions. In the long term, Freud's contributions are greatest in his recognition of the unconscious, his introduction of sexuality as a subject of academic and popular discussion, and his attempt to identify stages of human development that are grounded in physiology. History may rehabilitate his reputation as a groundbreaking theorist, but these are precisely the points on which contemporary theorists of women's development take issue, and on which advances in theory have occurred:

1. The unconscious is not an isolated subsystem; it is social as well as instinctual, and inner conflicts result from cultural conflicts.
2. Gender identification is a more complex (and social) process than Freud envisioned; while biology and sexuality are important components of identity, they are not the only, nor necessarily the *most* significant elements. The dynamics of the cultural system and family system are vitally important, and stages of growth (as demonstrated by Erikson and Piaget) are not solely determined by physiology but by feedback cycles between the culture, society, family, and person; description of the stages must (as Erikson's does) include the characteristics and expectations of the cultural system, to be complete.

Summing up from a systems perspective

Freud posited the self, or personality, as a nearly closed system, with the exception of the intimate ties to parents during the initial stages; once the Oedipal crisis was resolved, the structure of the system underwent no further change. Each of the other theorists discussed here described the person as an open system, interacting with its environment throughout the life cycle. Erikson and Piaget viewed physiology as setting some parameters and general timetable within which growth occurred; there was a degree of inevitability about the stages of development. Kohlberg appeared to agree, but did allow for some exceptional persons to surpass the constraints of the social environment.

Horney, Gilligan, and Erikson seemed to agree about the openness of the person to other systems, although it appears that Erikson's description of male and female modalities of relationships is rejected by many feminists as too Freudian, too *essentialist* in the importance he gave to biological determinism. Among these theorists, Horney and Gilligan offer a ' "deep theory" of culture, maintaining that the cultural system penetrates the person system to the level of the unconscious self, creating an "idealized self" that obscures and displaces a "real self" (an "authentic" self, in Sartre's terminology). An objective view of homosexuality recognizes the role that culture plays in shaping the experiences of gays and lesbians, and the defenses they must employ in order to withstand the systematic homophobia of our society; in this respect, they are forced to be *too open* to the dictates of the culture. It is only in recent decades that gay and lesbian subcultures in the United States have been able to sustain sufficient autonomy and self-development to maintain permeable but protective boundaries.

II. The Critical Phases of the Life Cycle

A. Establishment of Primary Attachment (Dependency and Trust) in the Parent-Child Dyad—The First Social System

Initially, at least, we should not refer to the infant as an autonomous entity. It is helpless, dependent, and must be cared for; it is "as one" with the other party to the dyad. It is now confined to being merely a component—something that is not true at any later time. It is a component of a system—a two-person system. In the prenatal environment, the developing organism is connected through the umbilical cord; in the first months of life, it is tethered by a "psychological cord" that must be stretched, and later severed (or transformed), to permit the developing personality to make other, wider, less exclusive social connections.

The newborn enters the world in a totally dependent state. Most of the first year is devoted to the effort to survive and to the formation and elaboration of adaptation devices that will achieve survival. During this early period, the infant is helpless and incapable of surviving by its own efforts. The nurturing person (or persons) compensates for, and supplies, what the newborn lacks. The newborn is initially in an *undifferentiated* state; that is, in the world of the newborn, there is no object or object relation (no conception of self, therefore no sense of anything that is not-self). The infant is initially profoundly egocentric; it is aware of nothing but its own internal conditions. Physiological organization is rudimentary, and there is no demonstrated psychic organization (in the sense of self, or ego or superego).

1. *Trust vs. Mistrust.* Erikson described the first crucial social task as a sense of *basic trust vs. basic mistrust.* By this, he meant the necessity to develop a *feeling* of trust in others and in one's self and for healthy (realistic) mistrust of one's environment (and of oneself, perhaps); that is, one learns to distrust snarling dogs, hot stoves, and strangers (and maybe one's jealous older sibling). Spitz referred to this first task as the initiation of an object relationship. In the Erikson formulation of the dimension of trust, the following elements are important:

a. The nurturing person becomes an inner certainty for the child, as well as an outer predictability. This state includes the qualities of consistency, continuity, and sameness of experience. These experiences and qualities become part of the child's identity.

b. The infant develops a sense of being able to trust self and the capacity of its own organs to cope with urges; it learns to control its hands; it learns to control its bladder and bowel functions (the latter are very important social expectations).

c. This sense of trust in self and others forms the foundation for the later development of a sense of identity; this is an example of how Erikson's stages relate to one another.

d. Since the sense of trust/mistrust is essentially social, it is based in communication (particularly tactile, nutritive, and emotional) between the infant and the caring person(s). Bonding relies on the quality of these experiences.

Ever since René Spitz's work in the 1930s on the effects of maternal deprivation, there has been controversy about whether the primary social attachment must be between infant and *mother;* it is accepted that is not necessarily only the biological mother. The necessary continuity, consistency, and predictability must be embodied in *some* particular person (or persons), but it can be a "caring or nurturing person" other than the biological mother, and not necessarily confined to only one person. This continues to be an important question regarding parents' usage of day-care centers for their infants.

The infant's primary needs are the oral, nutritive needs. The mouth is the initial receptor, the most sensitive and demanding tissue in the body at this time. Sensitive tissues develop in other erotogenic zones later; these are the basis of Freud's *oral, anal,* and *genital* stages. Erikson, too,

employed the idea of physical *zones* and identified the zonal sensitivity of
this stage as *oral-respiratory* and *sensory-kinesthetic* (the latter is compatible with Piaget's view). He stressed that these are incorporative modes:
taking in. The child's first social activities focus on incorporation: *getting*
and learning to *get*. During the later portion of this first, critical stage, the
infant begins to give in return. To paraphrase Erikson, as the child evolves
in the first months of life it could well say, "I am what I am given," next
say, "I am what I can get," and finally say, "I am what I can give."

2. *Dysfunctional conditions.* Within the initial dyad, the infant does
not long remain a passive recipient. In her definitive theoretical review
of object relations, dependency, and attachment, Ainsworth emphasized the important role of infants' behaviors both in eliciting parental
responses and in active "proximity seeking" (Ainsworth, 1969:981).
Transactions between a human system and its social environment are
necessary to its definition of boundary of self; it is through the recognition of and interaction with "other" that the boundaries of self can
be defined. If the boundaries of self do not become defined, *infantile
autism* may result, although the cause(s) of autism is not certain. If
self is not differentiated from other, the resulting condition is referred
to as *symbiosis*.

a. *Maternal deprivation.* A number of dysfunctional dyadic systems
were identified and grouped under the rubric of maternal deprivation
(Bowlby, 1962), which can be described both quantitatively and qualitatively. It usually refers to an *insufficiency of interaction* between the
child and the nurturing person(s) and to the conditions in which the
insufficiency seems to develop. The term "maternal deprivation" should
be interpreted figuratively (it may be someone other than a mother, and
may be insufficiency rather than total deprivation) rather than literally.
It describes the effect upon the child more accurately than it describes
the conditions which cause it. Some of these conditions are:

(1)   Absence of relationships: e.g., institutionalization or hospitalization of
       the infant with no provision for substitute nurturing. The danger of this
       was documented by Spitz in his writings and films (1965). This might
       happen in wartime conditions; in a state of widespread disease (such
       as the AIDS epidemic in some African countries, where 25 percent
       are infected); or in extreme poverty or famine in which parents die or
       are severely ill, and social substitutions are unavailable.
(2)   Child's lack of response: sufficient care is available, but the child is unable
       to interact because of previous deprivations, maturational deficiencies,
       or unknown causes. Not infrequently, parents of disturbed pre-school
       children report that almost from birth, an infant was not responsive

to cuddling and "gentling." Frequently, a neurological deficit is suspected, but not always detectable.

(3) Distorted relationships:

    (a) Situations in which the child is *undifferentiated* from the parent, similar to the normal condition that the newborn experiences, but here the normal process of developing a somewhat autonomous self does not occur. The parent, also, does not distinguish between self and child; the boundary is not clear. This may be due to the parent's emotional or psychological difficulties or, in rare instances, the parent's physical limitations.

    (b) Interlocking dependency, a symbiotic relationship wherein the parent "needs" to have a totally dependent infant and the child "needs" to have total mothering. Again, this is the normal circumstance of the new-born, but to prolong this condition distorts the child's development and prevents development of a healthy parent-child relationship. The Munchhausen syndrome, in which a parent induces illness in a child in order to maintain mutual dependency, is an example.

    (c) The parent may assimilate the child as being certain aspects of himself (or herself) or identify the child completely with the qualities of another person. A measure of this is normal and desirable, e.g., seeing the child as having the parent's eyes or grandparent's chin, but when the child is completely viewed as possessing the qualities of another, the child has little opportunity to differentiate self and establish self as a separate, autonomous, and distinct person.

    (d) The parent perceives the child as the embodiment of a single quality, such as stupid, evil, or totally demanding, without justification.

(4) Insufficient relationships:

    (a) A situation in which a mother (or other primary nurturer) provides insufficient opportunity for interaction. Examples are "crack mothers" or other addicts who may be incapable of providing sufficient interaction, or acute mental illness of the primary nurturer.

    (b) The parenting person is unable to give emotionally because of her/his own isolation, coldness, cruelty, or learned inability to relate to others; this may have originated in the parent's own childhood family system.

    (c) The parent may be narcissistic and involved with self so that no more than physical care is provided. The parent's system is so closed toward the child that little or no transaction of feeling is permitted.

    (d) Circumstances exhaust the caring person's energies, and little affection is available for nurturance of the child. These demands may come from within the family system (parental illness, e.g.) or from the environment (e.g., conditions of poverty, war, an epidemic, or systematic repression).

One or more of these distorted or insufficient relationships are often found in cases of child abuse.

  b. Separation. Another form of defective dyad that complicates the child's efforts to establish a basic sense of trust is labeled *separation.* Deprivation refers to insufficiency of relationship; separation refers to interruption of an already established relationship, and to the need for continuity and predictability. Bowlby (1962:205-214) studied the effects of separation and concluded that a separation in the first three months of life is not disturbing to a child *if an adequate parent substitute* is provided. However, by the age of three months, the infant has formed an attachment (a dyadic system) with the nurturing person, and separation at this time is more likely to interfere with its efforts to establish basic trust. Prolonged separation between the ages of six and twelve months is most harmful and may not be reversible (ibid.:117-119). Bowlby described the possible result as an "affectionless character" an inability (or difficulty) to enter into intimate relationships with other persons, and an unfavorable ratio of mistrust to trust, in Erikson's terms. Bowlby also found that juvenile delinquency was highly correlated with separation experiences in the preschool years and suggested that early childhood separation is a causal factor for some delinquents, but this finding has been questioned.

B. Differentiation of Self within the Family System

  The family system is the scene of the second and third of Erikson's crises of psychosocial growth. The mother-child dyad usually expands to become a three-or-more-person system for these tasks; while the third person may be husband/father, it may be grandmother or other nurturing person (see discussion of this in Chapter 7).

  1. *Autonomy vs. Shame and Doubt.* This psychosocial crisis carries the special requirement for the establishment of a sense of self as an entity, distinguished from the environment. This parallels the child's development, which includes the capacity to manage certain physical functions (e.g., ambulation and elimination) as muscles and nerve systems mature. Assertion of self as an autonomous being, and uncertainty about its capacity to do so, compete within the child, who must risk relinquishing some of the comfortable dependency of the primary dyadic system.

  The first assertion of self as an autonomous, self-developing system is through communicating, "No! No, I can *will* not to do what you want me to do." The well-known negativism of the two-year-old expresses this assertion of the will. In middle-class cultures, this negativism defies cultural dictates about toilet habits, neatness, and respect for others' property.

The corollary of negative assertion is self-control and independence, but if the family system places *too few* limits on assertive behavior, the child may be stranded out on a limb, not having internalized the capacity for self-management and direction. If the family system *overly* restricts opportunities to test the limits of its behavior, the child will not have the chance to experience itself as a autonomous and self-developing entity. At either extreme, the child may develop a sense of shame and doubt.

For the most part, these preschool years are centered in the family system, the primary social unit of the culture. It is within this micro-culture that the child becomes a person, a social being. This crisis of *autonomy vs. shame and doubt* occurs within the family system, in which it is critical to resolve the following issues:

a. Sense of self beyond the dyad. An awareness of autonomy, separate from the nurturing persons, must develop. The question, Where do they end and where do I begin? must be provisionally answered now, and is a question that arises again in adolescence, with full force.

b. Order in the social environment. Sensitivity to order is characteristic of this age. Children frequently insist on sameness in their environment and become distraught when important objects are relocated. The predictability, continuity, and consistency that were needed from the nurturing person in the first stage are now required from the physical environment. The environment must be trustworthy because the child now self-constructs from the environment. Learning to name objects provides the perception of stability in the environment (Piaget's concept of *conservation*), and allows the child a degree of control over it (Brown, 1965:267-276). Self-organization is possible only when the environment is sufficiently organized.

c. Assertion of will—self inserted into the environment. This occurs first in negation and then in affirmation. The child diligently attempts to be an autonomous, self-developing entity. First physiologically, then psychologically, and finally socially, children find (as Erikson described) they can will to *hold on* or to *let go.* Physiologically, maturation of sphincter muscles allows the child to hold on to, or let go; this is accompanied by psychological and social qualities of retention or release. If the society is extremely concerned about toilet habits, elimination may provide the child with a proving ground for a conflict of power and a test of weaponry. Toilet training is sometimes referred to as "breaking" the child as in taming a wild amimal. To persuade the child to submit its will to that of the culture as represented by the family becomes crucially important. The child is encouraged to develop a willing capacity (and a capacity to will), congruent with the conformity and self-control that the culture so highly prizes.

Psychologically, a child can hold on to or let go of feelings ("put a cork in it" or "vent"), express frustration and anger directly through behavior or control it to please "others." If others communicate that these feelings are too dangerous to let out, the child may doubt its capacity to control emotions; it may also have a feeling of omnipotent power (a "blow-up" in more ways than one). If others cannot or will not provide ground rules, the child may feel internal anarchy and shame, not having experienced release and the power to control the release. In holding on to feelings, the child may not engage in enough transactions with others and may have insufficient feedback to establish self. In letting go, self-boundaries may not be established, and the environment continues to be indistinguishable from self. Clear but permeable boundaries, with a repertoire of flexible responses that are appropriate to environmental stimuli, would be a positive outcome, of course.

d. Ambivalences—self-expression in the environment. Dichotomies of feeling (ambivalences) are a characteristic of this crisis. A child may alternately express a sense of love and hate, a sense of independence and total dependence, or a sense of pleasure and displeasure. This rapid alternation of strong, opposite feelings must now be coped with for the first time, and how this is resolved will serve as the prototype for future life tasks. Erikson stated that the cultural solution for this dilemma is embodied in the culture's approach to law and order, in attitudes of social justice, punishment, and compassion.

e. Communication. Although language has developed by now, much communication continues to be nonverbal. Approval and disapproval are more important reinforcers of behavior and are conveyed by feeling, more than by word; the sensitive two- or three-year-old may be more responsive to parental feeling than to word meaning. The parent's prohibitive "no-no" may communicate prohibition or protection, approval or disapproval, challenge or censure, dependent upon the feeling behind the words. The child's thoughts tend to be concrete and fragmentary; the concepts grasped are specific and often literal. At any one time, the child may feel all "good" or all "bad." It is essential at these times that the parents not reinforce this.

The child who does not develop a sufficient sense of autonomy may have little sense of self. Manifestations of this include cloying dependence, general anxiety, foolhardy behavior, expecting others always to be in control, and severe withdrawal. Severe and pervasive negativism may also indicate lack of sufficient autonomy. A sense of autonomy is manifest in a measure of self-regulation and a capacity to enter into social transactions as a discrete entity, that is, self-development.

In the latter preschool years, the primary social system continues to be the family, but the child is beginning to establish linkages to systems beyond the family: playmates, neighbors, extended family or family friends, and increasingly, adults and peers in organizational settings such as Head Start, day-care, and preschool. The qualities of self that the child has developed and brings to these new systems are crucially important.

2. *Initiative vs. Guilt.* The child's second psychosocial crisis occurs through its interaction with its social environment, the family system. With the sense of autonomy, shame and doubt, accrued so far, children must now explore who they are, and what their distinctive qualities are. The Oedipal conflict is central, as is the internalization of right and wrong. As Erikson views this task, the modalities are "to make" (to get) and "to make like" (to play). The bisexuality of the child, which has been apparent up to this time, is now directed toward a culturally defined gender. As Erikson viewed it, the masculine "making" is intrusive, the insertion of self into the social world to accomplish purposes, and the feminine form of "making" is inclusion of the social world to accomplish purposes (this implication that "biology is destiny" is viewed as sexist by feminist critics of Erikson). The genital tissue is hypersensitive at this stage, consistent with Freud's "phallic" stage (one may argue that Freud's view displayed gender bias).

In Erikson's view, the child's active insertion of self, or inclusive behavior, is accompanied by fear of rivalry and anticipated threat of punishment. Identification (or imitation) is a frequent method of coping with the child's compulsion to define self and with the culture's expectations that the child will be like the same-sex parent. Erikson stated that the child could say "I am what I can imagine I will be" (Erikson, 1968:122). The outcome of this crisis will be a mixture of a sense of initiative and a sense of guilt. The child with a favorable ratio of initiative will have purpose and direction as part of her/his adult character, will be self-motivating, and will be able to initiate social behavior and transactions.

This "initiative" crisis has certain common issues:

a. Creating the self. The essential psychosocial task now is to create a qualitative sense of self. This exploration begins in the family and then expands outward. Because of the arousal of awareness of genital sensations and the cultural expectations of sex differentiation, much of this is played out in the Oedipal context. The culturally desired outcome of the Oedipal complex ("complex" refers to sets of relationships) is the child's relinquishment of sexual interest in the parent of the opposite sex and identification with the parent of the same sex. Cultural ambiguity about sex-differentiated behaviors affects parents as well as the child. The child may identify with the "stronger" parent regardless of gender, and sometimes does not know with whom to identify. The child may continue to wallow in this task during later crises; energies may be preempted and later crises may be inadequately dealt with. Ideally, however, a favorable resolution is reached, and the child expands its fields of activity to other social systems.

   b. *Creative use of play.* Play is an important mode of behavior during this crisis. As Piaget indicated, cognitive development has now progressed so that imagination can be controlled and used in various ways. Erikson considered play as "autotherapeutic," a rudimentary form of the adult capacity to create models and experiment with alternative behaviors without committing oneself. Erikson described three stages of forms of play:

   (1)   autocosmic: the child's play begins with and centers on its own body;
   (2)   microspheric: the small world of manageable toys; and
   (3)   macrospheric: sharing of play with others, first in parallel fashion (playing together but apart) and then in concert. (Erikson, [1950,1985, 1993] 1963:220-221)

In this crisis, two kinds of play are especially important. One is solitary daydreaming in which the child can fantasize, imagining what she or he would like to do and be. The second is peer play, wherein children together can work on solving their common concerns. Occasionally, play may carry fantasy beyond control or comfort and be frightening. Pretending is a reassuring way to establish the boundaries of reality, especially when adults occasionally share the "let's pretend" activities.

   c. *Consolidation and integration.* This crisis is a time of transitional consolidation and integration. Exertion of self into the social environment with hope and expectation of influencing the environment involves a measure of trust in the predictability of environment and one's own predictability, as well as a measure of self-control or will. To be able to do this enables children to imagine how they might eventually influence the world. Because children are newly aware of, and concerned about, the intactness and integrity of bodies at this stage, they are likely to be sensitive to anything that threatens this (e.g., children being baked in an oven or eaten by wolves, as in fairy tales; but these tales allow children to face these fears and allay them). They may be frightened by their own fantasies of power and hold themselves responsible for any calamity that befalls others close to them. This is reinforced in many cultures by means of tales of what befalls disobedient or willful children, as means of inculcating rules of good behavior. Don't forget what happened to Pinocchio, Little Red Riding Hood, Hansel and Gretel, the Sorcerer's Apprentice, and Jack with his beanstalk. Beware!

Again, it is well to mention that the outcome of this crisis is a *ratio* of initiative and guilt. This is the critical time for the development of conscience, which can be a tolerant guide or a punitive slave master, but a conscience there will be. It is hoped that initiative will be directed toward "making" things work, in the sense of integrated behaviors, but it can be "making" things and people in the exploitative sense. A child who can emerge from these family-centered growth tasks with a robust sense of trust in others and self, a sense of autonomy as a person who is linked to others, and a sense of purpose is well on the way to a fulfilling life plan.

C. Definition of Self within Secondary Social Systems

1. *Industry vs. Inferiority.* Erikson's next psychosocial crisis occurs in interaction with components of the community system: formal organizations (such as the school and the church) and informal organizations (such as the neighborhood and the peer group). As in all stages of development, physiological and cognitive maturation provide the capacities, and the culture furnishes the expectations. This is the period of development that Freud labeled *latency* (in which the sex drive is presumably dormant) and that Piaget called the phase of *concrete operations.* Erikson described this fourth crisis as *industry vs. inferiority.* "Industry" is used here in the sense of "being industrious," productive or competent. The dominant issues of this crisis are:

a. *Mastery.* Now that the child is encountering wider social systems, it seeks to assert control over both its physical self and its environments: physical objects, social transactions, and ideas and concepts. It is the time to learn the technology and ways of one's culture; the institutionalized means to accomplish this are supplied by the culture, whose investment is in its own survival. The school is one such institution charged with transmission of the cultural technology. The Future Farmers of America and 4-H are organizations for communicating the culture of agricultural communities (and for 4-H, increasingly, urban culture as well). The "block gang" exists to transmit the ways of another specialized, local culture, often without "official" societal recognition. Games, contests, and athletics are also examples of institutionalized culture carriers (witness the English proverb, "Wars are won on the playing fields of Eton"). Churches, mosques, temples, and synagogues are other such institutions. The child participates in these organizations, developing a sense of self as competent and incompetent, in some ratio.

Entry into school is an important step to the child, to the parents, and to the culture. One of the very few clearly demarked way stations on the long trail to adulthood (other than religious rituals), it is the occasion when society ensures that each of its young members participates in an organized, institutionalized culture. In the Midwest, the phrase "kindergarten roundup" conveyed the cultural investment in collecting the mavericks and commencing the long process of "breaking" them, of acculturation to technological society. An arbitrary age is set for such entry, two years younger than the legal requirement for compulsory school attendance in most states, and the social expectation exists that the child will be readied by the family. If children are indeed ready, they eagerly look forward to entry into this *new* world. If unready because energies are lacking, the child may have "problems." The child and parent(s) may not be ready for separation. The kindergartner may not be able to distinguish teacher from parent, or may not have self sufficiently organized to comply with the expectations for settled and cooperative behavior.

If the culture transmitted by the school is alien to, or opposed to, the culture of the child's family (as American Indians have often experienced, for example), the young child is in a difficult, indeed untenable, position. The technology and ways of doing things, and the sense of self and other, that the child has learned in that culture have, by this time, become a part of self. To accept a differing way or culture may be felt as an act of betrayal of self, family, and subcuture. If so, the child may continue its efforts toward mastery outside the school, seeking mastery of its own culture, not that of others. The lack of participation in school by significant numbers of American Indian, African-American, and Hispanic youths may, in large part, be explained this way. Various writers have documented this as experienced by people of color in the United States. Acuña explained how the educational system serves to socialize the student into accepting and supporting the ways of the majority culture. He stated that this is accomplished by "erasing the [ethnic or racial group's] culture, language and values and replacing them with Anglo-American culture, language and values" (1972:146). Such socialization is clearly a means of social control.

The school has evolved as an overburdened carrier of culture as changes in technology and family functions have occurred; too much is expected of the schools, and some expectations are inappropriate. As society has been bureaucratized, so has the school. It is charged with preparing the young for participation in the existing cultural ways; hence the child experiences self as a functioning participant in a bureaucratic organization. "Preventive" intervention in schools, and early identification of difficulty, is based on the premise that a child's success in school predicts success in adult life, and that lack of success predicts adult failure; there is minimal evidence for this belief. Many who are unsuccessful in school are successful in other aspects of living, and vice versa.

Nonetheless, society expects the child to demonstrate mastery and competence primarily in the single institution of the school. This includes not only the technology of literacy, but also physical mastery (Phys. Ed., intramurals, and athletic teams), arts and music, social mastery (social dancing, family life education), domestic skills (now often required of both genders), and such other technological competencies as driving an automobile and operating a computer. Public schools find it very difficult to complete all the assignments the culture gives them. The school has even been required to deal with this society's primary problems: racism, sexism, poverty, and the use of drugs, but at the same time, parents and the public are ambivalent about the school's handling of these.

b. Membership and participation in peer groups. Peer group experience is a necessary element of the crucible in which mastery is tested. It provides a social system parallel to adult society (and intersecting with it on some occasions), with its own organization, rules, purposes, and activities. It is with the peer group that the child can test self and grow to mastery in social relationships with equals.

The school is the primary system in which to construct a sense of competence; the other available secondary social system is the peer group. During middle childhood (latency), the child's primary connections continue to be within the family system; it is later in adolescence that the peer group may take precedence over family. The peer group of middle childhood is modeled after the culture within which it exists. At its best, it is not very visible to the adult world and has its own parallel culture passed from generation to generation (two or three years to a generation) with continuity, but with frequent innovations. Less positively, youth gangs can function in defiance of adult norms, although they may provide means of accomplishment (positive or negative) if youths do not have access to constructive means of achievement.

The peer group is likely to be strongest in direct relation to the stability of the population it draws from. The peer group of suburbia is likely to be weak and transitory, whereas the peer group in the small town or urban neighborhood may be stronger. Increasingly, adults have taken control of middle childhood's peer groups: activities are organized and conducted by adults. School functions are part of this control; Little League baseball exemplifies another part; the day camp and "away camp" are others. The attention to individual fulfillment through lessons in swimming, driving, tennis, golf, dancing, music, skiing, and so on, has diminished the availability of child-controlled peer groups. Other factors are the geographic separation of children from their parents who work elsewhere, perhaps in another community, and are not available to transport them, or to be nearby if needed. Adult-managed and supervised activities undoubtedly enable children to develop skills, but minimize opportunities to develop self through interacting freely in a peer culture. This may explain, in part, the phenomenon of "living together" (Popenoe, 1988:303) within a wider peer culture of young adults who are exploring their selves before committing to adulthood.

c. Outcome. Again, the outcome is a ratio of polar feelings. A dominant sense of inferiority may result from a lack of ability, but most frequently it derives from (1) insufficient accrual of resources from previous crises, (2) unclear or unreasonable expectations by adults or peers, or (3) excessively high criteria by which to judge competence and mastery. The idea of a *sense* of industry or inferiority is important. It is *the feeling* the child has about his or her own competence that is crucial, not competence as measured by adult standards. The person who embarks into adolescence with a feeling that she or he can do at least one thing very well is in a favorable position indeed.

Mastery of the ground rules of life is important to children at this stage. Piaget (1932) found that they are quite occupied with "justice" and accept arbitrary or expiatory punishment as sometimes warranted. As they grow older, they favor the idea of retribution connected to the offending act and its natural consequences. Development of schemas for moral judgment forms the basis for organized social relations. Peer groups have fairness, social order, and "the rules of the game" at the core of their reason for existing.

The largest portion of children referred to child guidance clinics and school special services are aged eight to eleven; the problem most often described is "immaturity." Problems of middle childhood can be grouped under these general headings:

(1) Poor school performance. The child's mastery of cultural technology does not measure up to the standards of the school and/or parents, or the child's school behavior disrupts its own learning, or that of others'.

(2) Symptoms not expected at this age, but not unusual in a younger child. Some of these are incontinence, fearfulness, short attention span, hyper activity, daydreaming, and not assuming expected responsibilities.

(3) Social inferiority (in Erikson's sense). This may be the isolated child or the child who consistently associates only with younger children. A sense of social inferiority may be manifested by overcompensatory behavior (e.g., bullying or braggadocio). If societal expectations are excessive or opportunities for development of competence are too limited, a kind of cultural inferiority may result.

(4) Cultural incongruity. As noted earlier, some children are placed in the difficult position of reconciling cultures or rejecting one of two cultures. If social systems in the child's environment (e.g., family, school, or peer group) recognize this and support the child by emotional support, counseling, providing opportunity to vent frustration, and playing out resentments against authority in a safe situation, the child may be able to reconcile conflicting demands.

Summary of the middle years

"The wonder years" are the time for development of a sense of competence—to master self, social relationships, and the technology of the culture. The human system is relatively open to inputs from, and transactions with, the institutions of the community beyond the family system while retaining a primary linkage to the family. The growing person emerges from this crisis with a sense of being somewhere on the continuum from industry to inferiority. Erikson's view was that the child's situation in this stage could be stated, "I am what I can learn to make work" (Erikson, 1968:127).

D. Transitional Self: Self-Development of Identity (Adolescenthood and Youth)

In Erikson's formulation, this is *the* transitional growth crisis. It is the time when biological and social imperatives demand that the evolving person organize and develop an identity that goes beyond an accumulation of roles. In our culture, this more or less coincides with that period referred to as adolescence. We prefer to use the term *adolescenthood* to convey that it is more than a transitory hiatus. The adolescent span of life has become a distinct life phase with its own culture, role expectations, and style, reinforced by cultural expectations (including consumerism). The concept of *identity* has entered into the conventional wisdom, and references are replete to individual identity, group identity, organizational identity, and even national identity. Erikson used the term with precision, and applied it primarily to the individual person. He saw the social-psychological task at this age as one of integration, or more precisely, *re*integration, of the various components of the person into a whole. It is a process of ego synthesis that culminates in *ego identity,* meaning an internal consistency and a continuity of being, as others see the child. This goes beyond the sum of childhood identifications and is not merely a synthesis of social roles. Again the concept is that of *sense* of identity, of which the person is aware. It should be stated here that this is consistent with the phenomenological view of the self; the self is constructed by consciousness—that is, consciousness critiquing the environment while at the same time constructing the self.

This sense of self is a state of being that is not visible to others, and cannot be objectively evaluated by them.

> An optimal sense of identity ... is experienced merely as a sense of psycho-social well being. Its most obvious concomitants are a feeling of being at home in one's body, a 'sense of knowing where one is going' and an inner assuredness of anticipated recognition from those who count. (ibid.:165)

Erikson first labeled the opposite pole *identity diffusion,* later *role confusion,* and in later writings *identity confusion* (Erikson, 1968). The term conveys the antithesis of integration: the dispersion of selves, and the alienation of the self. From a systems viewpoint, one could say that internal and external tensions compel the human system to integrate its components in order to undertake new purposes and responsibilities. If the components of personality are not brought together, the person is fragmented and has no solid sense of self. The person is not capable of putting energy to concerted use—the person is entropic. Schizophrenia, with its disorganization of personality components and particular disparity between thought and feeling, is the extreme form of such fragmentation. Interestingly, the earlier term for schizophrenia was *dementia praecox,* meaning "insanity of the young." Some theorists,

Erikson among them, hold that true schizophrenia cannot appear until adolescence, since it is foremost a condition of pathology of identity and identification. A sensitive expression of this condition is:

> I am learning peacefulness, lying by myself quietly
> As the light lies on these white walls, this bed, these hands.
> I am nobody; I have nothing to do with explosions.
> I have given my name and my day-clothes up to the nurses
> And my history to the anesthetist and my body to the surgeons.
> (Plath, 1966:10)

Erikson focused much of his study and writing on the adolescent crisis, including *Identity, Youth and Crisis* (1968), *Childhood and Society* (1963), and "The Problem of Ego Identity" (1959). Two of the characteristics of adolescence he identified, the *moratorium* and *negative identity,* particularly deserve emphasis.

Moratorium refers to a socially approved period of delay wherein the person is allowed to, or forced to, postpone assumption of the full responsibilities of adult commitments. The culture relaxes its expectations and is more permissive; the person can try out a variety of identifications, modes of behavior, and roles without a commitment to see them through. The moratorium is both necessary and desirable to allow for integration, regrouping of forces, and the setting of life goals, in a culture that places a high value on individuality. The extension of adolescence into the "twenties" in the United States can be viewed as a socially imposed moratorium that may be unnecessarily long for some. Moratoria may occur at times other than adolescenthood for some persons. Often, these are times when important decisions must be made, or major changes in life goals are considered. If the individually determined moratorium is more prolonged than societal expectations allow, there is reason for concern, for example, the son Biff in *Death of a Salesman.*

HAPPY: Well, you really enjoy it on a farm? Are you content out there?

BIFF: *With rising agitation:* Hap, I've had twenty or thirty different kinds of jobs since I left home before the war, and it always turns out the same. ... And whenever Spring comes to where I am, I suddenly get the feeling, my God, I'm not gettin' anywhere! ... I'm thirty-four years old, I ought to be makin' my future. That's when I come running home. And now, I get here, and I don't know what to do with myself. *After a pause:* I've always made a point of not wasting my life, and everytime I come back here I know that all I've done is to waste my life.

HAPPY: You're a poet, you know that, Biff? You're a—you're an idealist!

BIFF: No, I'm mixed up very bad. Maybe I ought to get married. Maybe
         I oughta get stuck into something. Maybe that's my trouble. I'm
         like a boy. I'm not married, I'm not in business, I just—I'm like
         a boy. (A. Miller, 1955:18-19)

Negative identity occurs because any identity is better than no identity at all. Negative identity is "an identity perversely based on all those
identifications and roles which, at critical stages of development, had
been presented ... as most undesirable or dangerous and yet also as most
real" (Erikson, 1968:174). The "opportunity theory" of delinquency is
consistent with this; when denied legitimate opportunity to achieve,
youths will adopt illegitimate means. Confirmation of the person's
identity comes from within ("this is what I feel like") and from without
("this is what you say I am"). This feedback cycle operates similarly
for any identity. Although one's sense of identity may and often does
change subsequent to adolescence, this is the crucial time for initial
identity formulation, the greatest opportunity for such development,
and the time of greatest vulnerability.

    1. *Adolescenthood.* There are more definitions of adolescence than
there are definers. For a time, adolescence was synonymous with the teen
years, but that is no longer an adequate definition. The idea of the "between
years" is frequently encountered, but that has an implication of "floating."
We will employ the following definition, recognizing that it, too, is open
to dispute: "Adolescence is probably in all societies that period which
comes after the biological and hormonal changes of puberty have set in
but before the individual's incorporation into society as an independent
adult" (Ktsanes, 1965:17). *Adolescence, then, begins with biology and
ends by social definition: the beginning is organism, the process is organism interacting with culture, and the termination is culturally determined.*
The seemingly unique element in adolescenthood in the United States is
that adolescence has become a distinct cultural phase of life in the same
sense as childhood and adulthood. The only qualification we would make
is that adolescent *behavior* may begin before puberty, as adolescent culture
is communicated to children in middle childhood (or even younger).

    Rather than reviewing all the elements of this Eriksonian crisis, we
will approach it from a particular viewpoint. Freud is widely quoted as
believing that the two elements of a successful life were the capacities to
love and to work. The task of identity formulation can be viewed as the
prerequisite for loving and working. We will discuss briefly some of
the characteristics of the adolescent and the culture that are important
to development of these capacities.

a. The peer group. The associations of the adolescent with peers are necessary experiences. Typically, peer groups take over some of the parental roles of support and value-giving. Peers absorb much of the youth's available social energy and become a primary reference group. The person can use peers to find self by projecting her/his ego elements onto others. The person can experience and express feelings of tenderness toward others, beyond the family system, in new systems. Various roles are available to be tried and either accepted or discarded. An attitude of respect for competence develops in the peer group. Within the peer society, the adolescent can begin to be a lover and a worker in close interaction with others. This experience occurred within the family system, but only in the person's role as a child. Adulthood requires more of the person than continuing to be a loving, working child within its family.

For some youths, the peer group gains ultimate importance, totally replacing the family. Substitution of one kind of childlike dependency for another does not suffice for the creation of a unique identity. Some youths remain largely separated from peer groups and still manage to pull together an identity. Peers are, however, an essential part of adolescents' struggles to find out who they are, what they value, and what they want to become.

b. Education. The school continues to be the central social institution that it was during middle childhood. Increasingly, occupational choices are centered in the school experience. As students' choices of occupation have broadened and become minimally determined by their parents' occupations, it has become the school's responsibility to assist in this choice. Curricula are constructed to expose the youth to a range of potential occupations. Performance is self-evaluated as well as judged by peers, parents, teachers, and guidance counselors, and the youth is guided in certain directions. A number of factors enter into determining the "real" possibilities for any given youth. Some of these are race, gender, socio-economic status, and "intelligence" (which is usually defined by the narrow criteria of grades and intelligence tests). In a society where persons are signified by what they do, rather than by who they are, one's choice of work role or, more precisely, occupational aspiration becomes central to one's sense of who one is and what one may become (see the discussion of bureaucracy and personality in Chapter 5). While many theorists comment on the absurdity of this institutionalization of identity development, it continues to be, for most youths, the sole societally approved means to acquire a sense of self as a worker and a potential worker.

2. *Adolescenthood and Culture.* The adolescent is an important person in our culture. There are certain clear manifestations of this importance. Economically, the adolescent has the status of a part-time worker and a full-time consumer. The jobs allotted to youth are usually service occupations rather than production, and often are substitutes for parental role performance (e.g., babysitting, food preparation and serving, carrying grocery bags, and home maintenance, such as lawn care). This age group is a primary target of advertising and merchandising (and has cable television channels devoted to its musical tastes). Whole industries in fashion and leisure time facilities cater to an adolescent market. Pop culture, fashion, food, and music styles originate thrive in the youth culture and permeate the broader culture through the impetus of the advertising and distribution industries (which may have generated the innovations in the first place—consider the emergence of the "Lady Gaga" phenomenon in 2010). Expressions that originate among youth are diffused throughout society, along with their use of technology, e.g., texting and twittering. Bloom's controversial book, *The Closing of the American Mind,* emphasized the pervasive influence of rock music in youth culture, stating, "Nothing is more singular about this generation than its addiction to music" (Bloom, 1987:68).

There is a dual ambivalence that exists between adults and adolescents. This manifests itself in the family system, where parents and youths are both torn between wanting the youths to grow up and wanting them to remain children. The ambivalence appears in the community and broader culture as the adult envies the vitality of youth, whereas youth envies the power and control possessed by adults. Adults may covet youthfulness as a denial of death, while increasing evidences of age cause this denial to be more difficult to maintain. Similarly, youth may covet power and control because of the prolonged dependence the culture dictates. This dual ambivalence complicates the forming of a sense of identity because separation into opposing camps may contribute to premature closure of adolescent identity rather than moving on to adult identity. Such identity foreclosure is problematic in a society where choices are many and increasing in scope. The person who made an early commitment to a total, foreclosed identity may later find it necessary to engage in a moratorium in order to experiment with possibilities for change. This may be highly problematic if others (e.g., spouses) are expecting this person to continue with the foreclosed identity.

As Erikson viewed this, adolescenthood requires the culture to make adjustments because the generation coming up has absorbed the past, lives in the present, and must confront the future with new forms of living constructed of knowledge and experience not available to their elders. Mead (1970) pointed out that youth is, in fact, the arbiter of modern cultures. Youths find that construction of both their own life-styles and those of the culture is a bewildering task. Mead helped to explain why youth experiments widely in life-styles. As many writers conclude, each generation has a wide range of characteristics from which the culture can select those best suited to cultural survival.

Each generation of youth can be considered a component of its culture system and, as such, a source of energy and tension: the primary means by which the culture accommodates to change. An example is the amazing speed with which our culture (and most other world cultures) has adapted to electronic media. It is pre-adolescents and adolescents who have been the most avid "consumers" and masters of computers, video gaming, digital communication, and computer graphics. Many are now among the "under-30s" or young adults who create computer programs and adapt them to their worksites and occupations. Incidentally, it is no longer true that young males dominate this field; recent research indicates that women and men use the Internet in equal numbers.

As the cultural system seeks a steady state, its youth component must interact with and exchange energy/information with, other components: age groups, organizations, institutions, communities, and families. In order for this to happen, the culture will change (accommodate) or seek to maintain the status quo (assimilate). Within this dynamic interaction, each person must seek an identity, and the culture must seek its survival.

Ideology is a special concern of persons in the throes of the identity crisis. The adolescent has a special sensitivity toward, as well as a particular vulnerability about, ideology. As Erikson puts it so clearly, "It is through their ideology that social systems enter into the fiber of the next generation and attempt to absorb into their lifeblood the rejuvenative power of youth" (Erikson, 1968:134). Erikson's psychohistorical studies of Martin Luther and Gandhi demonstrate how persons' resolutions of the ideological aspects of their individual identity crises provided creative innovations that profoundly affected their cultures. Malcolm X, Martin Luther King, Nelson Mandela, and Barack Obama are more recent examples of personal identity crises transmuted into the ideology of a culture (Malcolm X, 1966; Garrow, 1986; Branch, 1988; Mandela, 1994).

The special "virtue" that Erikson attached to identity is *fidelity*. The proclivity of youth to invest self in a belief, an idea, or a person with total commitment and faith is well-known: the search for the Holy Grail, the Crusades, the willingness to follow the knight in shining armor, be he Arthur Pendragon, Gandhi, Mao Tse Tung, or Barack Obama. To experience total and complete volitional commitment (in both work and love) seems a necessary element of an emerging identity.

The characteristic troubles of the adolescent identity crisis are legion. They may be grouped under the following headings:

1.   *Psychosis* usually appears in the form of schizophrenia. This is a condition of extreme identity diffusion. The traits may be considered exaggerations of "normal" traits:
     a.   feelings of dislocation and estrangement;
     b.   total docility or exaggerated rebelliousness;
     c.   emotional lability; rapid mood swings;
     d.   feelings that "everyone is against me";
     e.   exaggerated idealism that seems to be a denial of reality; and
     f.   confused body image and sexual identification.
2.   *Neurosis* can also be described as identity confusion, in that there is a conflict between the ideal self and other selves. Neurosis is a conflict between antagonistic ideas, wishes, desires, or impulses that lead to entropy and disrupt psychological functioning. If they are extreme, the alternating excitability and lethargy of adolescents might be examples of this tendency.
3.   *Delinquency* is a socially defined response to inner demands and outer expectations. It may be the result of particular internal conflicts ("acting out" behavior), or it may be an individual or group rejection of cultural values of a larger system. The negative identity previously referred to may be manifested by delinquent behavior. While delinquency might be pathological, it may be better than no identity at all, as said earlier.

Summary of adolescenthood

Self-development, *system emergence*, is the crisis of adolescence. All subsystems of the adolescent personality—physical, cognitive, and emotional—are in rapid flux, an upheaval of the person's previous steady state. At the same time, the environment demands new linkages and energy exchanges with this new person; and the person seeks them, as well. "To be or not to be" states part of the issue confronting the adolescent. *What* to be or *what not* to be is the second part of the question.

The later crises of adulthood are to a large degree dependent upon the outcome of this crisis. A person must be fairly certain and comfortable with self before successfully entering into a sustained, intimate, and constructive relationship with another.

E. Perpetuation and Sharing of Identity (Adulthood)

When does adulthood begin? The University of Chicago's National Opinion Research Center reported that

> The law may imply that you're a grown-up when you're old enough to vote, serve in the military or drink legally. But most Americans really believe adulthood begins at age 25. ..." There's a much more gradual transition than was traditionally there."
> Take marriage for example. In the 1950s the most common age for brides was 18. "In 2003, when you hear about an 18-year-old bride, the first thing you say is, 'Boy, that's unusual—and boy, that person should have waited'. . ."
> According to those surveyed, the average age someone should marry was 25.7, and the age for having children was 26.2. Most respondents considered parenthood the final milestone needed to reach true adulthood. . . .
> For categories other than marriage and having children, the average ages were: financially independent, age 20.9; not living with parents, age 21.2; finishing school, age 22.3, and being able to support a family, 24.5.
> . . . completing an education was most valued, with 73 percent of those surveyed calling it an "extremely important" step. ...
> Grant Lammersen, a 27-year-old San Franciscan, said it's true that his generation feels less pressure to get married and have kids—perhaps, he said, because so many of their parents are divorced. (Irvine, 2003)

Adulthood has seldom been dealt with in theories of personality development, but perhaps because of the "baby boomer" generation, born post-World War II, more attention has been paid (see, e.g., Sheehy, 1976, 1992, 1993, 1995, 1998, 2006, 2007, 2010; and Levinson, 1978, 1996). Erikson is notable for his attempt to conceptualize the adult period as an integral part of his life cycle formulation. Pertinent here are the sixth crisis, "intimacy vs. isolation," and the seventh, "generativity vs. self-absorption."

The critical task of *intimacy vs. isolation* is to enter in an involved, reciprocal way with others sexually, occupationally, and socially. One's sense of identity is merged with another to form a new primary social system. To put it another way, the person completes the transition from the *family of origin* to the family of procreation (or *family of orientation*). This psychosocial crisis addresses itself to the activities of love and work. If one is not able to merge an intact sense of self with others, the outcome is a sense of isolation and polarization of affect ("I love ... or "I hate ..."). The concept of alienation (discussed later in this section) is another expression of a sense of isolation. The theme of love, genital and reciprocal, is central to this crisis.

These first two adult crises that Erikson delineates are closely related; the second describes the task of *generativity vs. self-absorption*. This involves the task of active participation in establishing the next generation. Erikson explained why he chose to express the quality of feeling as "generativity" rather than creativity or productivity (Erikson, 1959:97). He saw the term *generativity* as being derived from "'genitality" and "genes." This particularly emphasizes responsibility for perpetuation of the species and the culture. The theme of this crisis is *caring:* caring in the sense of nurturance and caring in the sense of concern for others, or "empathy." In his Jefferson Lecture, Erikson further elaborated his notion of the adult virtue of caring (Erikson, 1974). The polar sense of stagnation refers to caring primarily and essentially for one's self, along with pseudointimacy with others and indulgence of one's self. Stagnation can be viewed as the "closed" human system, defending its equilibrium and minimally engaging in transactions of feelings with others.

The adult period requires persons to maintain their own identities while sharing this sense of identity with others. The culture establishes social institutions, particularly procreative and child rearing, through which this task can be accomplished, e.g., schools and colleges, religious organizations, community organizations, and work organizations. At stake is a sense of well-being for the person, continuity for the culture, and survival for the species.

Other approaches to describing personality development in the mature years generally take one of two forms; either an idealized definition of maturity or a listing of the problems to be overcome. Sheehy's popular book *Passages* (1976), supported Erikson's contention that a person can, and does, "go home again," in the sense of redressing the balances of earlier stages. Levinson's view of adult development followed Erikson's (1982, 1997; Erikson et al, 1986), and is highly compatible with a systems view, in that it stressed integration of "self-in-world." Levinson described a "life structure" in which the major components are the person's relationships with others.

There are both external and internal aspects in the total life structure and in every component within it. The external aspects deal with the persons, social systems, and other realities with which the individual is involved. The internal aspects are values, desires, conflicts, and skills—those multiple parts of the self that are lived out in one's relationships. (Herbert, 1989:55)

Levinson identified distinct periods in the lives of men (his subsequent book on women is discussed earlier in this chapter, and again later):

A. The *novice phase of early adulthood.*, ages 17-33: this phase has four tasks: (a) forming a dream, (b) forming mentor relationships, (c) forming an occupation, and (d) forming a marriage and family. Its subphases are:

(1) *Early adult transition,* ages 17-22, the boundary between adolescence and adulthood. Its primary tasks are to terminate preadulthood, to modify previous relationships, and to make steps into the adult world.

(2) *Entry life structure,* ages 22-28; the major task now is to establish a provisional life structure between self and society, involving occupation, love, peer relationships, values, and life style.

(3) *Age thirty transition,* ages 28-33; building a more satisfactory life structure.

B. *Culminating life structure,* ages 33-40; the two major tasks are to find a place in society and to strive to "make it."

Becoming One's Own Man—"BOOM" (ages 36-40) is a distinctive phase of the ... period. The major developmental tasks of this phase are to accomplish ... goals ... to become a senior member in one's world, to speak more strongly with one's own voice, and to have a greater measure of authority,

C. *Mid-life transition,* ages 40-45, and Entering Middle Adulthood, ages 45-50, include the tasks of (a) reappraisal of one's life, (b) individuation, and (c) modifying the life structure yet again. Levinson did not study men older than their 40's. (Herbert, 1989:57-63; emphasis ours)

Following Erikson and Levinson, it is possible to group the central social expectations for adults under four related headings:

1. *Sexuality.* Adult sexuality is an important part of intimacy and the sharing of identity. Genitality, in the sense of the capacity for full and mutual consummation of sexual potential, is characteristic only of adulthood. Sexual mutuality forms the foundation of the procreative family system. Sexuality is not confined to sexual activities, but includes generativity and child rearing; it includes social styles (e.g., "Men are from Mars and Women are from Venus") and dress.

2. *Generativity and Child Rearing.* The assumption of responsibility for transfer of the culture and nurturance of the young fulfills the destiny of the adults of the species (or at least most of them). This requirement is particularly stressful for those without a firm sexual identity or the capacity to merge self-interest with the interest of others. Performance of this task, of course, is not confined to being a biological parent who rears a child. It includes participatory, generative roles that are gratifying

to self and others, such as child care (including the health professions), teaching, child welfare and youth work, mentoring, training young employees, volunteering in social services or civic work, and other roles that benefit future generations. These are all generative forms of the adult task of participation in social processes.

3. *Participation in Social Processes.* To further the purposes of society and culture requires a measure of subordination of personal needs to the needs of others. This is particularly stressful to those who are isolated and retain a primarily self-centered orientation. An additional compli-cating factor here is the perpetual cultural conflict between the values of individualism and social responsibility. One of the most important aspects of social participation is work.

4. *Work.* As Freud said, a work function is required for adulthood; work that is gratifying to self and to society. In our society (more than most, apparently), work is an organizing theme (the famous "work ethic"), and we construct our life-styles around it. In such societies, work provides an identification, represents social usefulness, and is a primary means of organizing a life. The usual response of the adult to a "Who are you?" question is more often than not an occupational response. When we meet someone who does not work, it may be difficult to relate to the person until it is determined why she or he does not work: something must be "wrong." Writings on the rehabilitation of schizophrenics have emphasized the necessity of employment if there is to be hope of contin-ued remission. The Personal Responsibility Act of 1996 espouses work as an answer to the problems of low-income families, and allows for benefits such as day care in order to facilitate employment.

Certain work identifications are still tied to the place of work ("I work in the mines" or "I work at Wal-Mart") but other designations are also used. Now most people express work identification as either "I do" or "I am." Traditionally, the "I am" designation belonged to the classic pro-fessions of law, the clergy, and medicine, including nursing. The "I do" description is usually a shorthand job description ("I sell shoes" or "I wire circuit boards"). The push toward professionalization in a wide variety of occupations is an attempt to establish a work identification of the "I am" type, such as "I am a social worker," "I am a teacher," or computer programmer, or stock analyst. There are still symbolic workplace ter-ritories such as "She's in the navy," "He's in bonds and securities," "I'm in government," or "She's in politics." The escalation of occupational titles is another indication of the significance of work as a determinant of status and position. The farmer is now in agribusiness; the undertaker is a mortician or funeral counselor; the barber or beautician is now a stylist, and the salesperson is an account executive.

Erich Fromm (1962) presented a clear and concise exposition of the idea that the marketplace orientation of our society determines and maintains work identity. He suggested that one is valued not for what one is but for what one *seems* to be; this is then related to supply and demand. "Image" becomes crucial and the person must project the "right" image to be successful; the resumé becomes the person. Advertisers are concerned with product image, politicians with their public image, and professional associations with their profession's image. One's value as a person, said Fromm, is not self-defined, but dependent upon value definitions by others using the criteria of the marketplace. Fromm described how this has led to the cult of adaptability, with emphasis on changeability.

Work identification has permeated our social systems to an extent we seldom recognize. Often, "problem" segments of our society are defined and labeled by work status:

a. The nonworkers. These include youth and the aged. These are not "unemployed persons"; they are clearly identified as *nonworkers,* not responsible to work. School is viewed as a kind of work and "student" serves as a work status (and is accepted on application forms as a proper answer to "Occupation?"). Organizations of, and in support of, the elderly (such as the American Association of Retired Persons) have been successful in redefining their status to allow them to continue to be active workers. For example, Social Security recipients may now continue to work, earning up to a certain amount before it reduces their monthly benefit; this amount will steadily increase over the next few years, approaching the nation's average per capita income. This is acceptable not only because elders wish to continue in useful roles, but also because government policy aims to relieve the tax burden that younger workers may have to bear to support the rapidly increasing number of retired workers, particularly the looming population of "baby boomers."

b. Waste persons. Carse said, "Waste persons are those no longer useful as resources to a society for whatever reason, and have become *apatrides,* or noncitizens. Waste persons must be placed out of view—in ghettos, slums, reservations, camps, retirement villages, mass graves, remote territories ...all places of desolation, and uninhabitable" (1986:133). The same could be said, of course, regarding convicted criminals, and persons with certain disabling or disfiguring conditions (such as Hansen's Disease or skin conditions resulting from HIV/AIDS), among others. American Indians were historically viewed as being in this category, as the "vanishing Americans"—a designation that fortunately is not, and never was, true.

c. *The unemployed.* These seem to be society's greatest concern. "Welfare reform" and "workfare" place primary emphasis upon putting the unemployed to work and rewarding persons who make the effort to seek and sustain work. The able bodied, unemployed person violates social prescriptions. That person is without a work identification—in fact, the primary social identity may well be "unemployed." In the absence of demonstrated lack of jobs, or other obvious barriers beyond the person's control, such unemployment is often attributed to individual deficiency.

d. *The unemployable.* By changing the ground rules and expectations regarding work, as Goodwill Industries (note the use of "Industries") and sheltered workshops do, it becomes possible to remove some people from this classification. Youth Service programs (both public and private) serve the same function, converting untrained (and therefore unemployable) youth into apprentices preparing for careers. This provides opportunity structures in which "the right to work" can be realized.

The Americans with Disabilities Act (ADA) and similar legislation at the state level have made it possible for "differently abled" persons to find employment. Adaptation of work environments to accommodate workers with special needs and the use of facilitating technology (including computers and high-tech prostheses) have "opened doors" to many who were formerly considered unemployable. A Supreme Court opinion in June 1998 included persons with HIV/AIDS among those covered by the ADA who must be given opportunities for employment.

e. *Alienation.* Lack of employment is a significant source of alienation. Alienation is a phenomenon of adulthood, since it is a condition of one's identity. Alienation means the absence or insufficiency of those vital, intimate connections with one's social environment that call forth and sustain one's identity. "Structural unemployment" itself fosters alienation as it breaks the connection between the person and the work environment, and between the person and the society. In most definitions, alienation also includes the feelings and perceptions that accompany these lacks, including the following:

(1) There may be lowered self-esteem, a gulf between societal expectations and perceived self. The person may also experience *self-estrangement* and *self-alienation,* a gulf between ideal and actual self, as though one were someone (or something) other than oneself (an *inauthentic* self, as defined by Sartre, earlier).

(2) *Anomie* is a term coined by sociologist Emile Durkheim to convey what, in systems terminology, may be viewed as absent or faulty

linkage with larger social systems. This is experienced as "rootlessness," "normlessness," or "meaninglessness." The person does not experience a culture of shared meanings, or a sense of shared norms of behavior. Recent observers have identified a new "underclass" of those excluded from opportunities for achievement, particularly victims of racism and discrimination (Wilson, 1987). A prime characteristic of this underclass is the abandonment of any expectation of social mobility or approved achievement within the "legitimate" social classes or structures. In such situations, persons may create or join alternative subcultures, e.g., street gangs and criminal organizations, including those involved in drug trafficking.

(3) *Alienated* persons may perceive, correctly or not, that their values are not shared or supported by their social environments, and the converse, that they do not share the society's (or family's) values.

One of the most frequently examined forms of alienation is *work alienation*. Despite many studies that reveal some degree of dissatisfaction with work, research consistently indicates that most workers are largely satisfied with their jobs. Women probably compose the largest group of alienated workers (Levinson, 1996; see our discussion in Chapter 5). In addition to the reasons already mentioned, women face other alienating circumstances. They frequently are not taken seriously as career-minded workers. "Career women" who are mothers with young children have been described as being on the "mommy track," an "alternative" career line in which flexible schedules are a necessity, but in which advancement is slower. Whether this is fair, and whether it promotes or detracts from women's rights at the workplace, is a matter of much debate. Women often are not paid as much as men for performing the same jobs: women earn about 80 percent of men's wages per hour, about 76 percent per week, and 71 percent of men's annual salaries (U.S. Department of Labor, 1997). They report that they are overworked (particularly in the present climate of "downsizing" among corporations and institutions), their abilities are underestimated; they are less frequently advanced, and are less frequently chosen for specialized training.

(4) Demands on time: The average number of hours worked per week has gradually increased over the past few years, as companies have reduced the work force, in the name of "productivity." Women are especially affected by the combination of commuting time, hours worked, domestic chores and child care. Since currently eighty percent of workers laid off are men, the pressures on women to hold their jobs to support their families will only increase.

"Telecommuting," working by computer and telephone from their own homes, is increasingly common among so-called "knowledge" workers, although it is not available to most workers. This practice presumably has the advantages of reducing commuting time, more flexibility in work hours, more likelihood of being able to care for and supervise children at home (with reduced child care costs), and a greater feeling of independence and being trusted (despite some concern about whether employers will be satisfied with the arrangement). Whether this practice truly frees more time (reports indicate that telecommuters may, in fact, put in *more* hours—for example in evenings and on weekends) is not clear. It is also not clear whether the total workload and stress of women telecommuters is reduced or, in fact, increased by not having structured "break times" and opportunities to "schmooze" with fellow workers.

In conclusion, the crises of adulthood are concentrated in the expectation that the person will intimately involve herself or himself deeply with others in the creation and maintenance of the social systems that enable the culture and species to survive. An adult who does not do this may be regarded as isolated, self-serving, and stagnant. To paraphrase Erikson, the adult may say, "I am what I can love and care for, and about" (in other words, a larger, more inclusive and committed self).

F. Conservation of Identity (Elderhood)

This concluding stage of the life cycle can be characterized as the crisis of aging. *Conservation* refers to consolidation, protection, and holding on to the ego integrity one has accrued over a lifetime, in the midst of loss and divestment of usual roles and functions. The positive sense of "conservation" is that identity passes from one social context to another and yet remains the same; the self maintains its continuity and consistency from one social system to another.

Erikson's polarity during the waning years of life is *ego integrity vs. disgust and despair.* This is the culmination of the previous seven crises. Integrity refers to "the ego's accrued assurance of its proclivity for order and meaning—an emotional integration faithful to the image bearers of the past and ready to take, and eventually to renounce, leadership in the present" (Erikson, 1968:139). It is the capacity of persons to accept their life histories, to see the effect they have had upon their world through their relationships, and to accept their mortality. The other pole, the sense of disgust and despair, is characterized by bitterness and refusal to accept death as the finite boundary of the personal life cycle. Halloran described a response to being tested for AIDS:

> You feel as if you are driving not toward the county health department but the Day of Judgment. In my right hand, I give you life, in my left, Death. What will you do, the voice asks, when you find out? How will you live? How do people with AIDS drive the car, fall asleep at night, face the neighbors, deal with solitude? The stupendous cruelty of this disease crashes in upon you. And so you bargain with God. You apologize, and make vows. You ask: How could this have happened? How could I have reached this point? Where did I make the turn that got me on *this* road? (Halloran, 2008:126-127)

This response has similarities to other devastating illnesses or events, and to dying. A positive resolution was expressed by Max Robinson, former ABC television news anchor, the first African-American to hold such a position. Robinson died of AIDS in December 1988. In his last public appearance, Robinson said to students at Howard University: "Try to keep your integrity, because you're going to find out in life, at the end, that's all you've got."

A definition of "aging" or "age" is difficult to formulate to everyone's satisfaction. In one sense, the aging process begins at birth. Socially, age is defined by function, usually work-related. For example, most professional athletes are "old" by the time they are 35 (quarterback Brett Favre, former Green Bay Packer and more recently, Minnesota Viking, was 40 in 2010). The minimum age qualification to become president is 35—set when life expectancy was less than that. Supreme Court justice John Paul Stevens was thought to be still functional as he retired at age 90. Some businesses consider the 50-year-old worker as too old to be hired. Social security currently sets the "standard" age of retirement at 65 (that is, the age at which a retiree receives full benefits, soon to become 67 for Baby Boomers). The "old elderly," age 80 and older, are the fastest growing segment of the American population. Birren suggested a utilitarian definition:

> A person is "old" or, better perhaps, "aging" when [the person] is so regarded and treated by contemporaries and by the younger generation and when [the person] has read the culturally recognized individual and social signs symbolic of membership in the generation of elders. The only matter of individual choice open to the old person has to do with whether [the person] wishes to accept or postpone belief in [the] new identity and act accordingly. (1959:280)

One elder felt labeled "old" when young persons routinely addressed him as "sir."

Erikson commented, "it is perfectly obvious that if we live long enough, we all face a renewal of infantile tendencies—a certain childlike quality, if we're lucky, and senile childishness, if we're not. The main point is again a developmental one: only in old age can true wisdom develop in those who are thus 'gifted'" (cited in Evans, 1967:53-54). The tasks of aging in our culture were nicely summarized by Birren:

- To live as long as possible, at least until life-satisfaction no longer compensates for its privation, or until the advantages of death seem to outweigh the burden of life.
- To get more rest, relief from the necessity of wearisome exertion at humdrum tasks, and protection from too great exposure to physical hazards—opportunities, in other words, to safeguard and preserve the waning energies of a physical existence.
- To remain active participants in personal and group affairs in either operational or supervisory roles—any participation, in fact, being preferable to complete idleness and indifference.
- To safeguard or even strengthen any prerogatives acquired in long life, i.e., skills, possessions, rights, authorities, prestige, etc.
- Finally, to withdraw from life, when necessity requires it, as honorably as possible, without too much suffering, and with maximum prospects for an attractive hereafter. (1959:864-865)

The cultural definition has changed somewhat, however; notice the number of magazines, tours, and educational opportunities (e.g., Elderhostel, recently renamed Exploritas) for active, financially comfortable elderly). "Disengagement," a once-predominant view of the aging process, seems to be only one option among many.

As earlier stated, aging is characterized by the theme of conservation. It involves relinquishing certain patterned investments of self (Levinson's "life structure") and adoption of other patterns. The nature of one's transactions with other human systems is necessarily modified. The elements of identity involved can be discussed under a few general headings:

1. *Work Role and Occupational Identification.* This may have a more profound effect upon those with the "I do" work identification than upon those with an "I am" identification. The retired physician continues to be seen as "Doctor," but the retired shoe salesman is no longer a salesman. Willy Loman ("low man") in *Death of a Salesman* is an example of a person faced by a loss of work identity. Relinquishing the work role may be especially difficult because so much validation of one's worth is tied to this role. Loss of work role often is accompanied by a marked reduction in income and the necessity of readjustment in standard of living. Women

face losses (or at least changes) of role earlier when children leave home (the "empty nest") or their partners die; in addition, since about 60 percent of women are employed, they too face employment-related changes.

On the other hand, many of both genders who retire from their work roles easily make the transition to a more leisurely pace of living. Many women whose husbands take "early retirement" at age sixty-two for example, retire at the same time, though they are typically younger than their husbands. Time is available to pursue other interests; the economic means may or may not be. One of the effects of the current economic crisis is that many retired persons return to part-time or full-time work, usually at lower wages than before they retired; this is often because their retirement savings "took a hit" when pension funds sharply declined in 2007-2010. A common joke is that "I'll be a greeter at Wal-Mart"—not so humorous for many. In view of the large proportion of people who opt for early retirement, it is conceivable that the work identification of "retired" substitutes for an identification as active worker. Many "retired" persons choose to work part time, or become self-employed in new enterprises; see the information about women as entrepreneurs in Chapter 5.

2. *Intimate Ties.* As a person's friends, acquaintances, and spouse die or become incapacitated, the elderly person is again faced with separation experiences faced as a child or young adult. Those who were part of one's personality system are gone. One must undergo the painful process of withdrawing (decathecting) attachments to them at a time when it is probably most difficult to establish new linkages to replace the former ones. One may not be able to modify one's own personality structure sufficiently to accommodate new attachments, and the social environment may not "reach out and touch" elders. One's environment tends to narrow, and perhaps the intensity of the remaining attachments is increased. Such attachments may become "overinvested"; for example, a pet, a formerly casual acquaintance, or grandchildren may become essential sources of social contact. If no replacements or investments are accomplished, the person may turn inward, seeking energy internally, or may "bank the fires," attempting less and seeking equilibrium on a lower level of interaction with the environment.

Such withdrawal or isolation is not inevitable; some elders "blossom" as they are relieved of responsibilities for family and work. They revive latent interests or hobbies, e.g., travel, writing, volunteering, time with grandchildren, genealogy (for the benefit of children or grandchildren, it is often said), or community and political involvement. The American

Association of Retired Persons (for whom one is eligible at age fifty) has an extremely active and politically "savvy" membership. Some elders help others to file their income tax; some volunteer to check elders' qualifications for community services; others offer help elders to avoid fraudulent predators. Ways are found to economize, or expectations are adjusted. This is truly a "golden age" for many elderly, whose involvement in larger systems increases rather than declines.

As noted earlier, the average life span continues to increase modestly (in most of the world) and the health of elders continues to improve. Increased attention to diet and exercise, e.g., quitting smoking, are resulting in an extended period of active, productive retirement for many aged people, and the possibility of a "cure for cancer" (often announced) may have profound effects on this age group. Their continued presence, whether as persons needing care, or as resources for their adult children, e.g., for loans, or a place to live between jobs, and grandchildren as babysitters, can have significant effects on the social systems to which they are linked.

3. *Sexual Interests.* Although little research has been done on the sexual activity of the aged, findings indicate a gradual decline in sexual activity over the entire adult period; as a group there is no sharp decline at any particular age. The advent of Viagra, Levitra, and Cialis have extended the possibilities for sexual activity among the aged. As overt sexual activity declines, aged persons may express or receive tenderness or affection in other ways; grandchildren frequently serve as recipients of affection from grandparents. Because our social stereotypes of the elderly indicate that such needs (for affection or specifically sexual) somehow disappear, we are often unrealistic about the behavior of the aged. Unfortunately, society's understanding of this is blocked by our tendency to deny sexuality in elderly persons. For example, some residences for the elderly prohibit physical manifestations of affection, do not allow the closing of doors when one has a visitor of the opposite sex, and in a few reported instances, prohibit holding hands. The available evidence indicates that sexual companionship (with or without sexual activity) is as important to most elderly persons as it is to those of earlier adult years. Recent newspaper articles report the discomfort that adult children often feel when confronted with their parents' sexual activity, in residences for elderly or nursing homes, or when their elders "date" or remarry. Perhaps when "baby boomers" inhabit such facilities (as they are now beginning to do in significant numbers), stereotypes will change and more realistic perceptions of elders will result.

4. *Physical Abilities.* Physical abilities, particularly sensory and motor abilities, decline with age, although with attention to diet, exercise, and health care, decline may not be great, or rapid. Physiologically, the number of taste buds declines with age, eyesight and hearing may suffer impairment, and walking may become more difficult, and physical injuries (e.g., fractured hips) more common. The person may lose the ability (or the judgment) to drive safely, often a major loss for one's self-esteem and perhaps a loss in usefulness to others (e.g., to provide transportation to shopping or medical appointments), as well. If these limitations occur, they are likely to handicap the aged person in maintaining contact with the accustomed social environment. In the extreme, the person's world may be narrowed to the walls of his or her own home, and to the television set. Even then, elders may adopt a soap opera or sports team to take interest in.

The older person's self-concept may be threatened by these losses. An example is the sixty-year-old man who refuses to be beaten at tennis. The person's reaction may be to deny the losses and demand performance characteristic of an earlier age, or the reaction may be depression and unrealistic refusal to do what one is still capable of. It is common among the aged to make reasonable adjustments to less acute faculties—in other words, to make the best of one's abilities: to drive only in daylight, e.g., or to use a telephone in which the volume can be turned louder, or to wear a hearing aid. Such realistic adjustments are part of the person's integrity and maintenance of self.

5. *Intellectual Abilities.* Borrowing from Piaget, it could be concluded that as one's schemes multiply and more adequately account for one's experience, they become progressively less modifiable. Accommodation declines, while assimilation increases. The aged may exclude stimuli from awareness, to limit the energy exchange with those in their environment. The aged person may become less concerned with interpreting and storing new information and more concerned with preserving previous information, sometimes literally in the form of scrapbooks, possessions of a deceased spouse, or a house that was the family dwelling. These intellectual patterns, either becoming more closed or remaining open (or becoming *more* open), may be exercised to maintain integrity. Incidentally, the belief that we lose brain cells as we age has been called into question by recent research—keeping mentally active is one key factor.

6. *Life Review.* A review of one's life might include the feeling that time is running out, that there are no alternatives possible "at this late date." In *Death of a Salesman,* Willy depends upon his son Biff to

reassure him of his own integrity, but Biff has neglected to write to his father:

> BIFF: I was on the move. But you know I thought of you all the time. You know that, don't you pal?
> LINDA: I know, dear, I know. But he likes to have a letter. Just to know that there's still a possibility for better things. (A. Miller, 1955:55)

With our society's cultural emphases on youth, external appearance, and robust health, to the neglect of wisdom, experience, and the ability to cope with travail, the elderly may find themselves disadvantaged and their integrity unnoticed and uncelebrated. As human systems, elders must find their steady state, their identity, their self, among the social systems with which they are linked. Erikson said that a person "as a psychosocial creature will face, toward the end of ... life, a new edition of an identity crisis which we may state in the words, 'I am what survives of me'" (1968:141). What survives are the human systems one has been related to and part of: persons, families, groups, organizations, communities, societies, and cultures. These human systems in turn affect other persons who are being born and who are developing. This is why Erikson calls it a life cycle—not the life of an individual, alone, but the cycle of life itself: the human system. He commented:

> Webster's Dictionary is kind enough to help us complete this outline in circular fashion. Trust (the first of our ego values) is here defined as "the assured reliance on another's integrity," the last of our values. ... It seems possible to further paraphrase the relation of adult integrity to infantile trust by saying that healthy children will not fear life if their elders have integrity enough not to fear death. ([1963] 1993:269)

Conclusion

In this book, we have examined and speculated upon social systems—human systems. We state in Chapter 7, "Families," that a family is best understood as patterns of relatedness *as they converge in a particular person.* We can say the same about all social systems: systems are patterns of relatedness as they converge in individual persons. Systems do not exist without persons; and persons can exist only because of social systems of which they are now a part, or have been at some time in their life. Understanding of the implications of this, and applying that understanding to one's life and practice, are the highest wisdom to which a systems approach can contribute.

Suggested Readings

Ainsworth, Mary D. Salter.
1969 "Object Relations, Dependency and Attachments: A Theoretical Review of the Infant-Mother Relationship," *Child Development,* 40(4):969-1025.
   The definitive review of early attachment; grouped under headings of Psychoanalytic, Social Learning, and Ethological.
Butler, Robert N.
1975 *Why Survive? Being Old in America.* New York: Harper and Row.
   A landmark work on the plight of the aged in U.S. society. Dr. Butler, a psychiatrist, was the first director of the National Institute on Aging. This book was awarded a Pulitzer prize.
Case, Robbie.
1992 *The Mind's Staircase.* Hilldale, NJ: Erlbaum.
   Excellent review of Piaget's theory.
Clark, Don.
1998 *Loving Someone Gay.* Berkeley, CA: Celestial Arts.
   "A pioneering gay therapist [clinical psychologist and professor] offers courageous and compassionate guidance for gay men and lesbians, their families, their loved ones and their counselors."
Duckworth, Eleanor
1996 *The Having of 'Wonderful Ideas' and Other Essays on Teaching and Learning.* Second edition. New York: Teachers College Press.
   An excellent exposition of Piaget's ideas, by his collaborator and American translator. Highly recommended.
Erikson, Erik.
1968 *Identity: Youth and Crisis.* New York: Norton.
   Erikson expanded on the critical task of identity formation; he also discussed the total life cycle. This book has been used as the small-map text for this chapter. For a thorough explanation of his life cycle formulation, see *Childhood and Society,* second edition. (New York: Norton, 1963).
Freud, Sigmund.
1949 *An Outline of Psychoanalysis.* New York: Norton.
   Freud's last book, published posthumously, is a concise explanation of the principles derived from his life's work. It is strongly recommended that the reader be familiar with Freud's expression of his ideas rather than relying on interpretations by latter-day critics.
Kuhmerker, Lisa.
1991 *The Kohlberg Legacy for the Helping Professions.* Birmingham, AL: REP Books.
   An critique of Kohlberg's work; a major addition to the literature on moral development.
Laird, Joan, and Robert-Jay Green, eds.
1996 *Lesbians and Gays in Couples and Families: A Handbook for Therapists.* San Francisco: Jossey-Bass.
   An extraordinary book. It should probably be required reading for every social work student (and for other professions, as well). It would be difficult to surpass in its scope, its scholarship, and its depth.
Levinson, Daniel J.
1978 *The Seasons of a Man's Life.* New York: Knopf.
1996 *The Seasons of a Woman's Life.* New York: Knopf.

Levinson's scheme of adult development has been widely adopted. It is highly compatible with systems ideas and the "person-in-situation" view of the helping professions.

Maier, Henry W.

1988 *Three Theories of Child Development,* fourth edition. New York: Harper and Row.

The author, a social worker, compared and contrasted the theories of Erikson, Piaget, and Sears as bases for social work practice.

Munhall, Patricia, L., ed.

1994 *In Women's Experience,* volume I. New York: National League for Nursing Press.

1995 *In Women's Experience,* volume II. New York: National League for Nursing Press.

These are companion volumes authored by nurses. The readings are insightful and approach the experience of women from a unique perspective that adds depth to the study of human behavior.

Phillips, John L., Jr.

1969 *The Origins of Intellect: Piaget's Theory.* San Francisco: Freeman.

Perhaps the best source for the study of Piaget.

Schuster, Clara Shaw, and Shirley Smith Ashburn.

1992 *The Process of Human Development,* third edition. New York: Lippincott.

Intended for students in nursing and other health professions, social work, and any other profession, this is a comprehensive and invaluable resource It includes a short section on general systems theory.

Sheehy, Gail.

1995 *New Passages.* New York: Random House.

Like her earlier books, this is a popularly written but well-grounded study, in this instance, of "a historical revolution in the adult life cycle. ... People are taking longer to grow up and much longer to die, thereby shifting all the stages of adulthood. ..." The following books by Sheehy (along with any others she has written) are worth reading.

————2006 *Sex and the Seasoned Woman.* New York: Random House.

————2010 *Passages in Caregiving.* New York: William Morrow & Co.

Westkott, Marcia.

1986 *The Feminist Legacy of Karen Horney.* New Haven, CT: Yale University Press.

A long-overdue and impressive assessment of the importance of Horney as a major personality theorist. Fundamental to an understanding of women's development.

Williams, Marie Sheppard.

1996, 2006 *The Worldwide Church of the Handicapped.* Lincoln, NE: Authors Guild Backinprint.com. [www.iuniverse.com]

Written by a retired social worker who has a cat named Albert Einstein, this is a marvel of sensitivity, humor, deep concern, and sometimes despair. Superb writing and brilliant observations about agency clientele and the toll that caring takes on the professionals who serve them.

Literary Sources

Ambrose, Stephen E.

1996 *Undaunted Courage: Meriwether Lewis, Thomas Jefferson, and the Opening of the American West.* New York: Simon and Schuster.

Superb psychological and intellectual biography of Meriwether Lewis, co-leader of the Lewis and Clark expedition. A tale of high personal and intellectual achievement and its tragic aftermath.

Bergman, Ingmar.
1960 *Wild Strawberries*. In *Four Screenplays*. New York: Simon and Schuster. An elderly man reminisces about the past as a means of dealing with the present.

Halloran, Andrew.
2008 *Chronicle of a Plague, Revisited: AIDS and Its Aftermath*. New York: Da Capo.
These essays are an intimate, personal account of the AIDS epidemic; sensitively written and socially profound. Includes graphic descriptions of sexual behavior, as well as acute observations on individual, group, and societal responses to the crisis.

McCullers, Carson.
1940 *The Heart Is a Lonely Hunter*. Boston: Houghton Mifflin.
A man with a severe hearing loss cares for and about others. The movie version is beautifully done.

Miller, Arthur.
1949 *The Death of a Salesman*. New York: Bantam.
Miller's classic play of Everyman caught up in a world of change and attempting to live in the past; prophetic regarding the relationship of corporations and their employees.

Thompson, Ernest.
1979 *On Golden Pond*. New York: Dodd, Mead.
Two elders struggle to maintain their integrity. The interaction between them and the youngster well illustrates Erikson's comment at the conclusion of this chapter, i.e., healthy children will not fear life if their elders have integrity enough not to fear death. The movie, with Henry Fonda and Katherine Hepburn, is marvelous.

Films and Videos

Away From Her (2006)
A poignant, entirely believable story of a middle-aged couple faced with the wife's progressive Alzheimer's disease. Fine acting by Julie Chistie and Tom Wilkinson.

The Color Purple (1985)
From Alice Walker's poignant novel, this illustrates Erikson's principle that much can be remedied later in life. Celie, an African-American girl, is viewed as unattractive and is mistreated by those about her. She finds support from her sister and from her husband's girlfriend, and becomes a strong, self-determining woman who cares for others.

400 Blows (1952)
Francois Truffaut's early film illustrates the process by which a young boy is rejected by family and others, and survives by adopting deviant behavior.

Freud (1962)
This is a credible attempt to present the main tenets of Freud's thought and his life, primarily through his work with one female patient. The television series "Freud" is even better.

The Alzheimer's Project. (2010) HBO (Home Box Office).
This 85-minute film follows the course of this disease in seven persons, as they cope with its effects. Critically acclaimed. It can be viewed on line at hbo.com/alzheimers

Iris (2001)
Award-winning biography of writer Iris Murdoch; portrays her youth and her final days as a victim of 'Alzheimer's disease. Superb cast.

Juno (2007)
Sensitively done story of teen-age pregnancy with an unusual result. The issues are dealt with up front; the young woman is unusually mature and well-grounded, but her supportive family perhaps explains that.

Just Because of Who We Are (1986)
Physical and psychological harassment suffered by lesbians, and violence against them, is shown in this documentary. Personal stories of rejection, arrest, and attempts at "cures" are related.

Longtime Companion (1990)
"Perhaps the first film to put a face on the AIDS epidemic" (Internet Movie Database Ltd., 1998). It follows a group of friends from the beginning of the outbreak to its devastation of their lives. The title refers to the *New York Times'* refusal to acknowledge gay partnerships; instead survivors were called "longtime companions."

Philadelphia (1993)
Tom Hanks received an Oscar for this moving portrayal of a gay lawyer dying of AIDS who sues over dismissal from his firm. One of the first films in which a gay person is the main character, presented sympathetically.

Precious (2009)
Critics praised the film as "courageous," "grim," "triumphant." It is the story of a young, black woman in the inner city who overcomes despite the negative aspects of her environment and family.

The Sum of Us (1994)
An Australian film about a gay son and his straight father who love each other. Each is seeking the "right" partner, respectively. Not a "message" film; "very natural, entertaining story-telling" (Internet Movie Database Ltd., 1998).

The Three Faces of Eve (1957)
The real patient in this case has identified herself, and has told her own story. Joanne Woodward is credible as a tormented woman with multiple personalities who finds a self with the help of a psychiatrist.

To *Live Until You Die: The Work of Elizabeth Kübler-Ross* (1983)
This video shows Dr. Ross working with dying patients, and illustrates the five stages of reaction to dying which she identified.

The United States of Tara (2009-2010)
Originally presented on the Showtime cable channel, this would presumably be X-rated for language. Tara has a dissociative identity disorder, which includes five distinct personalities. Very well portrayed by Toni Collette.

Appendices

These appendices provide further information regarding two additions to the authors who appeared in previous editions, and who are significant to the discussion of phenomenology in the new Addendum to Chapter 2.

Appendix A. Paolo Freire

Paolo Freire was born in 1921, in Recife, in Brazil's northeastern province, one of the poorest regions of Brazil. His father was a member of the military police; his father was religious, and the family was Roman Catholic. Freire became a lawyer, but his primary interest was education for the poor in his region, and concentrated on education for the rest of his life.

One assessment of his work concluded that "he should remain the utopian he is, maintaining his faith in people's ability to have their say and thus to recreate the social world leading to a more just society" (Gerhardt, 2000:12). Given that Freire did not systematically develop or state a political or educational theory, but rather described educational practices that while often successful, were adapted to particular settings, that seems a fair assessment. He wrote prolifically, was a government education official in several nations, and was a popular leader of "leftist" (that is, anti-colonialism, anti-authoritarian) organizations and parties.

He is described as "charismatic," with an "air of mystique" because of his exile from Brazil, his international experiences, and his imprisonment, after which he entered exile in 1964, going first to Bolivia and then Chile. In 1967, he conducted seminars in the United States, and stayed at Harvard University as a professor; following that, he became a consultant to the World Council of Churches.

After 1970, when he published *Education: The Practice of Freedom,* followed by *Pedagogy of the Oppressed,* he was in demand as a consultant internationally. He moved slowly leftward politically. He focused more sharply on cultural and political change, speaking of liberation and revolutionary change. He did not ally himself with Western political views, choosing instead to be eclectic in his theoretical approaches. In all instances, the liberation of the masses through education was his paramount interest. He and other Brazilian exiles created, in Geneva, Switzerland, the IDAC, to offer educational services to poor countries; this became very popular and influential, with marked success in some African countries.

He returned to Brazil with his family in 1980. He was, for two years, Secretary of Education for the city of Sao Paulo; the "Freire" reforms met with mixed success because of societal upheavals. He returned to lecturing and writing. His philosophy and educational "system" has continued to receive international acclaim, and he personally remained an iconic figure in education until his death.

Appendix B. Edith Stein

Edith Stein (1891-1942) was born in Breslau, Silesia, now part of Poland, to a Jewish family. She was enrolled in the university there when she heard of Edmund Husserl's phenomenology and, in 1913, transferred to the University of Göttingen, Germany, to study with him; she undertook doctoral study with Husserl as her advisor. She volunteered during World War I as a nurse to soldiers with communicable diseases, on the Eastern front, near Russia. She was awarded the medal of valor. She returned to the university, completing her doctorate *summa cum laude* in 1917; her topic was "empathy" in phenomenology.

From high school through her later career, she involved herself in feminist activities. She applied to universities, but Germany did not allow women in faculty positions. She appealed, and the government ruled in her favor, but it was thirty years before a woman achieved a university position, after World War II. She worked as an assistant to Husserl, organizing his notes and composing some of his work for publication. She published her own work, which received recognition.

In 1922, she became a Roman Catholic. She took a teaching post at St. Magdalena's College in Speyer, Germany, which prepared women for teaching careers. She formed a close relationship with the Benedictine nuns. She translated theological works, and published work on St. Thomas Aquinas. In 1932, she was finally employed in an institution of higher learning, a school of pedagogy, where she lectured on philosophical anthropology and education. She became more widely known, and did lecture tours in Germany, Austria, and Switzerland.

In 1933, because of Nazi anti-Jewish laws, her appointment was terminated. She entered a monastery in Cologne, Germany, taking the name Teresa Benedicta of the Cross; her assignment was to continue her writing and research on philosophy and theology. Nazi persecution intensified and, in 1939, the Carmelite order sent her to a convent in the Netherlands for safety. The Netherlands' Roman Catholic bishops protested Nazi treatment of Jews; Nazis retaliated by sending Jews who had converted to Christianity to concentration camps. On August 2, 1942, she was arrested and sent to Auschwitz. She was executed in a gas chamber a week later.

Within the last twenty years, her work has received greater scholarly attention and a number of books on her philosophy and theology have been published. Her significance as a contributor to phenomenology is now recognized. The Roman Catholic church beatified her in 1987 and canonized her in 1998.

Bibliography

Acuña, Rodolpho. 1972. Occupied America: The Chicano Struggle toward Liberation. San Francisco: Canfield.

Adams, Margaret. 1971. "The Compassion Trap—Women Only." *Psychology Today,* November.

Adams, Richard. 1988. *The Eighth Day: Social Evolution as the Self-Organization of Energy.* Austin: University of Texas Press.

Adams, Scott. 1996. *The Dilbert Principle.* New York: HarperCollins.

Ahrons, Constance R. 1987. "The Binuclear Family: Two Households, One Family." Paper presented at the Sixth Annual Conference of the Stepfamily Association of America, Lincoln, NE.

Ahrons, Constance R., and Roy H. Rodgers. 1987. *Divorced Families.* New York: Norton.

————. 1997. "The Remarriage Transition." In Arlene S. Skolnick and Jerome H. Skolnick, eds. *Family in Transition,* ninth edition. New York: Longman.

Ainsworth, Mary D. Salter. 1969. "Object Relations, Dependency and Attachment: A Theoretical Review of the Infant-Mother Relationship." *Child Development* 40(4).

Anderson, Walter Truett. 1995. "Moralizing Won't Bring Back Community." *Minneapolis Star-Tribune,* March 3.

Andreski, Stanislav. 1973. *The Prospect of a Revolution in the U.S.A.* New York: Harper Colophon.

Ardrey, Robert. [1966] 1971. *The Territorial Imperative.* New York: Atheneum.

Arendt, Hannah. 1962. *The Origins of Totalitarianism.* Cleveland: World Publishing Company.

Argyris, Chris. 1994. *On Organizational Learning.* Cambridge, MA: Blackwell.

Armour, Stephanie. 1998. "Many Turn to Start-Ups for Freedom." *USA Today,* June 8.

Auger, Jeanine Roose. 1976. *Behavioral Systems and Nursing.* Englewood Cliffs, NJ: Prentice-Hall.

Bailey, Kenneth. 1994. *Sociology and the New Systems Theory.* Albany: State University of New York Press.

Bales, Robert F. 1950. *Interaction Process Analysis.* Cambridge: Addison-Wesley.

Balk, David E. 1995. *Adolescent Development.* Pacific Grove, CA: Brooks/ Cole.

Barnard, Chester I. 1938. *The Functions of the Executive.* Cambridge, MA: Harvard University Press.

Barnes, John. 1954. "Class and Committees in a Norwegian Island Parish." *Human Relations* 7 (February).

Baseheart, Mary Catherine. 1997. *Person in the World: Introduction to the Philosophy of Edith Stein.* Dordrecht: Kluwer.

Bawer, Bruce. 1996. "A Tale of Two Cities." *Advocate,* September 17.

Beer, Stafford. 1981. "Death Is Equifinal." Eighth Annual Ludwig Von Bertala lanffy Memorial Lecture. *Behavioral Science* 26.

Bellah, Robert N., Richard Madsen, William M. Sullivan, Ann Swidler, and Steven M. Tipton. 1985. *Habits of the Heart.* Berkeley, CA: University of California Press.

Bengtson, Vern, Carolyn Rosenthal, and Linda Burton. 1995. "Families and Aging: Diversity and Heterogeneity." In Mark Robert Rank and Edward L. Kain, eds. *Diversity and Change in Families.* Englewood Cliffs, NJ: Prentice-Hall.

Benkov, Laura. 1997. "Reinventing the Family." In Arlene S. Skolnick and Jerome H. Skolnick, eds. *Family in Transition,* ninth edition. New York: Longman.

Bernard, Jessie. 1997. "The Good Provider Role: Its Rise and Fall." In Arlene S. Skolnick and Jerome H. Skolnick, eds. *Family in Transition,* ninth edition. New York: Longman.

Bertalanffy, Ludwig Von. 1967. *Robots: Men and Minds.* New York: Braziller.

Billingsley, Andrew. 1968. *Black Families in White America.* Englewood Cliffs, NJ: Spectrum.

———. 1988. *Black Families in White America.* New York: Simon and Schuster.

Birren, James E. 1959. *Handbook of Aging and the Individual.* Chicago: University of Chicago Press.

Blau, Peter. 1956. *Bureaucracy in Modern Society.* New York: Random House.

Bloom, Allan. 1987. *The Closing of the American Mind.* New York: Simon and Schuster.

Boehm, Werner. 1965. "Relationship of Social Work to Other Professions." *Encyclopedia of Social Work.* New York. National Association of Social Workers.

Boguslaw, Robert. 1965. *The New Utopians.* Englewood Cliffs, NJ: Prentice-Hall.

Booth, Alan, and Ann C. Crouter, eds. 1998. *Men in Families.* Mahwah, NJ: Erlbaum.

Boulding, Elise. 1972. "The Family as an Agent of Change." *Futurist* 6(5).

Bowlby, John. 1962. *Deprivation of Maternal Care.* Geneva: World Health Organization.

Brill, Charles. 1974. *Indian and Free.* Minneapolis: University of Minnesota Press.

Brodey, Warren M. 1977. *Family Dance: Building Positive Relationships through Family Therapy.* Garden City, NY: Anchor.

Brome, Vincent. 1987. "Freud." *Encyclopaedia Britannica,* fifteenth edition, volume 19:582-587.

Brown, Roger. 1965. "How Shall a Thing Be Called?" In Paul Musser, ed. *Readings in Child Development and Personality.* New York: Harper and Row.

Bruner, Jerome. 1968. *Toward a Theory of Instruction.* New York: Norton.

Buber, Martin. [1937] 1947. *I and Thou.* Edinburgh: Clark. [Originally in German, 1923.]

———. 1965. *The Knowledge of Man.* New York: HarperCollins.

Buchwald, Emilie, Pamela R. Fletcher, and Martha Roth, eds. 1993. *Transforming A Rape Culture.* Minneapolis: Milkweed.

Bull, Chris. 1994. "Suicidal Tendencies." *Advocate,* April 5.

Burr, Wesley R. 1995. "Using Theories in Family Science." In Randal D. Day, Kathleen R. Gilbert, Barbara H. Settles, and Wesley R. Burr, eds. *Research and Theory in Family Science.* Pacific Grove, CA: Brooks/Cole.

Burton, Linda M. 1996. "The Timing of Childbearing, Family Structure, and the Role Responsibilities of Aging Black Women." In E. Mavis Hetherington and Elaine Blechman, eds. *Stress, Coping and Resiliency in Children and Families.* Mahwah, NJ: Erlbaum.

Business Week. 1998. Quoted in Teresa McUsic, "Biography Shows GE's Welch Is Admired and Hated." *Minneapolis Star-Tribune,* June 12.

Butler, Sandra, and Claire Wintram. 1991. *Feminist Groupwork.* London: Sage.

Bütz, Michael R. 1997. *Chaos and Complexity: Implications for Psychological Theory and Practice.* Washington, DC: Taylor & Francis.

Calcagno, Antonio. 2007. *The Philosophy of Edith Stein.* Pittsburgh: Duquesne University Press.

Caplow, Theodore, Howard M. Bahr, Bruce A. Chadwick, Reuben Hill, and Margaret Holmes Williamson. 1982. *Middletown Families: Fifty Years of Change and Continuity.* Minneapolis: University of Minnesota Press.

Capra, Fritjof. 1996. *The Web of Life.* New York: Anchor.

Carter, Irl. 1975. *Industrial Social Work: Historical Parallels in Five Western Nations.* Unpublished dissertation, University of Iowa.

Carse, James P. 1986. *Finite and Infinite Games.* New York: Free Press.

Case, Robbie. 1992. *The Mind's Staircase.* Hillsdale, NJ: Erlbaum.

Caudill, Harry M. 1963. *Night Comes to the Cumberlands.* Boston: Little, Brown.

Chodorow, Nancy. 1978. *The Reproduction of Mothering: Psychoanalysis and the Sociology of Gender.* Berkeley, CA: University of California Press.

Clark, Don. 1997. *Loving Someone Gay.* Berkeley, CA: Celestial Arts.

Cohen, Ira J. 2000. "Theories of Action and Practice." *Blackwell Companion to Social Theory.* books.google.com

Coleman, Joseph. 1998. "Some Say Corporate Transfers Tear Apart Japanese Families." St. *Paul Pioneer Press,* June 9.

Coser, Lewis. 1964. *The Functions of Social Conflict.* New York: Free Press.

———. 1974. *Greedy Institutions.* New York: Free Press.

Cox, Fred M., et al. 1987. *Strategies of Community Organization: Macro Practice* Itasca, IL: Peacock.

Coyle, Grace. 1948. *Group Work with American Youth.* New York: Harper and Row.

Curtis, Bruce. 2008. *Like Ordinary People.* East Lansing, MI: Little Stronach Press.

Dahl, Robert A. 1957. "The Concept of Power." *Behavioral Science 2.*

Day, Randal D. 1995. "Family Systems Theory." In Randal D. Day, Kathleen R. Gilbert, Barbara H. Settles, and Wesley R. Burr, eds. *Research and Theory In Family Science.* Pacific Grove, CA: Brooks/Cole.

De Kerckhove, Derrick. 1995. *The Skin of Culture: Investigating the New Electronic Reality.* Toronto: Somerville House.

Dowd, Nancy E. 1997. *In Defense of Single-Parent Families.* New York: New York University Press.

Drucker, Jane. 1998. *Families of Value: Gay and Lesbian Parents and Their Children Speak Out.* New York: Insight.

Drucker, Peter. 1982. *The Changing World of the Executive.* New York: Truman Talley.

Duckworth, Eleanor. 1996. *"The Having of Wonderful Ideas" and Other Essays on Teaching and Learning,* second edition. New York: Teachers College Press.

Dunn, Edgar. 1980. *The Development of the U.S. Urban System,* volume 1. Baltimore: Johns Hopkins University Press.

Durkheim, Emile. 1968. "Division of Labor and Interdependence." In Robert Dubin, ed. *Human Relations in Administration,* third edition. Englewood Cliffs, NJ: Prentice-Hall.

Earnshaw, Steven. 2006. *Existentialism: A Guide for the Perplexed.* New York: MJF Books.

Elliot, Faith Robertson. 1986. *The Family: Change or Continuity.* London: Macmillan.

El Nasser, Haya. 1998. "Ruling Puts Workplace Behavior under a Harsher Spotlight." USA *Today,* March 5.

Erikson, Erik H. 1950. In M. S. E. Senn, ed. *Symposium on the Healthy Personality.* New York: Josiah Macy, Jr. Foundation.

———. 1958. *Young Man Luther.* New York: Norton.

———. 1959. "The Problem of Ego Identity." In *Psychological Issues,* edited by George S. Klein. New York: International Universities Press.

———. 1963. *Childhood and Society.* First edition, 1950; 35th anniversary edition, 1985; latest edition, 1993. New York: Norton.

———. 1964. *Insight and Responsibility.* New York: Norton.

———. 1968. *Identity, Youth and Crisis.* New York: Norton.

———. 1969. *Gandhi's Truth.* New York: Norton.

———. 1974. *Dimensions of a New Identity.* New York: Norton.

———. 1975. *Life History and the Historical Moment.* New York: Norton.

———. [1951] 1985. *Childhood and Society,* 35th anniversary edition. New York: Norton.

———. 1987. *A Way of Looking at Things: Selected Papers from 1930 to 1980.* New York: Norton.

————. [1980] 1994. *Identity and the Life Cycle.* New York: Norton.

————. [1982] 1997. *The Life Cycle Completed: A Review.* New York: Norton.

Erikson, Erik H., Joan Erikson, and Helen Q. Kivnick. 1986. *Vital Involvement in Old Age.* New York: Norton.

Etzioni, Amitai. 1964. *Modern Organizations.* Englewood Cliffs, NJ: Prentice-Hall.

Evans, Richard. 1967. *Dialogue with Erik Erikson.* New York: Harper and Row.

Farb, Peter. [1968] 1978. *Man's Rise to His Civilization as Shown by the Indians of North America from Primeval Times to the Coming of the Industrial State.* New York: Dutton.

Fellin, Philip. 1995. *The Community and the Social Worker.* Itasca, IL: Peacock.

Ford, Donald H., and Richard M. Lerner. 1992. *Developmental Systems Theory.* Newbury Park, CA: Sage.

Freire, Paolo. 1983. *Education for Critical Consciousness.* New York: Continuum.

Freud, Sigmund. 1949. *An Outline of Psychoanalysis.* Translated by James Strachey. New York: Norton,

Fromm, Erich. 1942. *The Fear of Freedom.* London: Routledge and Kegan Paul.

————. 1955. *The Sane Society.* New York: Rinehart.

————. 1962. "Personality and the Market Place." In Sigmund Nosow and William H. Form, eds. *Man, Work, and Society,* New York: Basic Books.

Gemmill, Gary, and George Kraus. 1988. "Dynamics of Covert Role Analysis: Small Groups." *Small Group Behavior* 19.

Gilligan, Carol, 1982. *In a Different Voice: Psychological Theory and Women's Development.* Cambridge, MA: Harvard University Press.

Gladwell, Malcolm. 2000. *The Tipping Point.* New York: Little, Brown.

Glassman, Urania, and Len Kates. 1990. *Group Work: A Humanistic Approach.* Newbury Park, CA: Sage.

Gleick, James. 1987. *Chaos: Making a New Science.* New York: Viking Penguin.

Glennon, Lynda M. 1979. *Women and Dualism.* New York: Longman.

Goffman, Erving. [1961] 1973. *Asylums: Essays on the Social Situations of Mental Patients and Other Inmates.* New York: Doubleday.

Hall, Edward T. 1969. *The Hidden Dimension.* Garden City, NY: Doubleday.

————. 1977. *Beyond Culture.* Garden City, NY: Doubleday Anchor Press.

Hall, Richard H. 1996. *Organizations: Structures, Processes, and Outcomes,* sixth edition. Englewood Cliffs, NJ: Prentice-Hall.

Halloran, Andrew. 2008. *Chronicle of a Plague: AIDS and Its Aftermath.* New York: Da Capo.

Handy, Charles. 1985. *Understanding Organizations.* Harmondsworth, England: Penguin.

————. 1993. *Understanding Organizations.* New York: Oxford University Press.

Hansen, Karen V., and Anita Ilta Garey, eds. 1998. *Families in the U.S.: Kinship and Domestic Politics.* Philadelphia: Temple University Press.

Hardcastle, David A., Stanley Wenocur, and Patricia R. Powers. 1997. *Community Practice.* New York: Oxford University Press.

Hasenfeld, Yeheskel. 1983. *Human Service Organizations.* Englewood Cliffs, NJ: Prentice-Hall.

Hearn, Gordon, ed. 1969. *The General Systems Approach: Contributions toward an Holistic Conception of Social Work.* New York: Council on Social Work Education.

Hersch, Patricia. 1998. *A Tribe Apart.* New York: Fawcett Columbine.

Hersh, Richard H., Diana Pritchard Paolitto, and Joseph Reimer. [1979] 1983. *Promoting Moral Growth: from Piaget to Kohlberg.* New York: Longman.

Hetherington, E. Mavis, and Elaine A. Blechman, eds. 1996. *Stress, Coping, and Resiliency in Children and Families.* Mahwah, NJ: Erlbaum.

Hetherington, E. Mavis, Tracy C. Law, and Thomas G. O'Connor. 1997. "Divorce: Challenges, Changes, and New Chances." In Arlene S. Skolnick and Jerome H. Skolnick, eds. *Family in Transition,* ninth edition. New York: Longman.

Hillery, George A., Jr. 1968. *Communal Organizations: A Study of Local Societies.* Chicago: University of Chicago Press.

Hine, Virginia. 1982. *Tarrytoum Newsletter.*

Homans, George. 1950. *The Human Group.* New York: Harcourt, Brace and World.

Huxley, Julian. 1964. *Man in the Modern World.* New York: Mentor.

Irvine, Martha. 2003. "Peter Pan lives! Americans put adulthood at 26." Associated Press, Minneapolis Star-Tribune, May 16.

Jacobs, Jane. 1989. *The Life and Death of Great American Cities.* New York: Vintage.

Johnson, David W., and Frank P. Johnson. [1982] 1991. *Joining Together: Group Theory and Group Skills.* Englewood Cliffs, NJ: Prentice-Hall.

Johnson, Steven. 2001. *Emergence: The Connected Lives of Ants, Brains, Cities, and Software.* New York: Scribner.

Kauffman, Stuart. 1995. *At Home in the Universe: The Search for Laws of Self-Organization and Complexity.* New York: Oxford University Press.

Kimball, Meredith M. 1995. *Feminist Visions of Gender Similarities and Differences.* New York: Harrington Park.

Koestler, Arthur. 1967. *The Act of Creation.* New York: Dell.

———. 1979. *Janus: A Summing Up.* New York: Random House.

Koestler, Arthur, and J. R. Smythies, eds., 1971. *Beyond Reductionism: New Perspectives in the Life Sciences.* Boston: Beacon.

Kohlberg, Lawrence. 1984. *The Psychology of Moral Development.* San Francisco: Harper & Row.

———.1987. *Child Psychology and Childhood Education: A Cognitive-Developmental View,* New York: Longman.

Kosko, Bart. 1993. *Fuzzy Thinking: The New Science of Fuzzy Logic.* New York: Hyperion.

Kranichfeld, Marion L. 1988. "Rethinking Family Power." In Norval D. Glenn and Marion Tolbert Coleman, eds. *Family Relations.* Chicago: Dorsey.

Kuhmerker, Lisa. 1991. *The Kohlberg Legacy for the Helping Professions,* Birmingham, AL: REP.

Kuhn, Thomas S. 1970. *The Structure of Scientific Revolutions,* second edition. Chicago; University of Chicago Press.

Laird, Jean, and Robert Jay Green. 1996. *Lesbians and Gays in Couples and Families.* San Francisco: Jossey-Bass.

Larwood, Laurie. 1984. *Organizational Behavior and Management.* Boston: Kent.

Lasch, Christopher. 1979. *Haven in a Heartless World: The Family Besieged.* New York: Basic Books.

Laslett, Peter. 1971. *The World We Have Lost,* second edition. New York: Charles Scribner's Sons.

———. ed. 1974. *Household and Family in Past Time.* Cambridge: Cambridge University Press.

Laszlo, Ervin. 1972. *The Systems View of the World.* New York: Braziller.

Levinson, Daniel J. 1978. *The Seasons of a Man's Life.* New York: Knopf.

———. 1996. *The Seasons of a Woman's Life.* New York: Knopf.

Lichterman, Paul. 1996. *The Search for Political Community.* Cambridge: Cambridge University Press.

Lind, Christopher. 1994. "When the System Farms the Farmers: What Can We Do About the Saskatchewan Farm Crisis?" In Eleanor M. Godway and Geraldine Finn, eds. *Who is This "We"? Absence of Community.* Montreal: Black Rose.

Lynd, Robert S. and Helen Merrell Lynd. 1929. *Middletown.* New York: Harcourt, Brace and World.

———. 1937. *Middletown in Transition.* New York: Harcourt, Brace and World.

Maier, Henry W. 1988. *Three Theories of Child Development,* fourth edition. Lanham, MD: University Press of America.

Malcolm X (with Alex Haley). 1966. *The Autobiography of Malcolm X.* New York: Grove.

Mandela, Nelson. 1994. *Long Walk to Freedom: The Autobiography of Nelson Mandela.* Boston: Little, Brown.

Marrow, Alfred. 1969. *The Practical Theorist: The Life and Work of Kurt Lewin.* New York: Basic Books.

Marshall, T. H. 1964. *Class, Citizenship, and Social Development.* New York: Doubleday.

Maslow, Abraham. 1968. *Toward a Psychology of Being.* Princeton: Van Nostrand. Mason, Mary Ann, Arlene S. Skolnick, and Stephen D Sugarman, eds. 1998. *Our Families: New Policies for a New Century.* New York: Oxford University Press.

Maturana, Humberto R., and Francisco J. Varela. 1980. *Autopoiesis and Cognition.* Dordrecht, Holland: D. Reidel.

Mayer, Milton, 1969. *On Liberty: Man vs. the State.* Santa Barbara, CA. Center for the Study of Democratic Institutions.

Mayo, Elton. 1945. *The Social Problems of an Industrial Civilization.* Boston: Harvard University Press.

McClure, Bud A. 2005. *Putting a New Spin on Groups: The Science of Chaos.* Mahwah, New Jersey: Lawrence Erlbaum.

McDonald, Catherine. 2006. *Challenging Social Work: the Context of Practice.* Houndmills and New York: Palgrave Macmillan.

McKnight, John. 1995. *The Careless Society.* New York: Basic Books.

McLuhan, Marshall. 1965. *Understanding Media: The Extensions of Man.* New York: McGraw-Hill.

Mead, Margaret. 1970. *Culture and Commitment.* Garden City, NY: Natural History Press.

————. 1972. *Blackberry Winter.* New York: Simon and Schuster.

Menninger, Karl. 1963. *The Vital Balance.* New York: Viking.

Merton, Robert K., 1957. *Social Theory and Social Structure.* New York: Free Press.

Miller, Arthur. 1955. *Death of a Salesman.* New York: Bantam.

Miller, James G., 1972. "Living Systems: The Organization." *Behavioral Science* 17(1).

————. 1978. *Living Systems.* New York: McGraw-Hill.

Miller, Sally R., and Patricia Winstead-Fry. 1982. *Family Systems Theory in Nursing Practice.* Reston. VA: Reston.

Mills, Theodore. 1967. *The Sociology of Small Groups.* Englewood Cliffs, NJ: Prentice-Hall.

Minati, Gianfranco, Eliano Pessa, and Mario Abram, eds. 2006. *Systemics of Emergence: Research and Development.* New York: Springer Science+Business Media, Inc.

Mingers, John. 1995. *Self-Producing Systems: Implications and Applications of Autopoiesis.* New York: Plenum.

Monane, Joseph H. 1967. *A Sociology of Human Systems.* New York: Appleton-Century-Crofts.

Monge, Peter R. 1977. "The Systems Perspective as a Theoretical Basis for the Study of Human Communication." *Communication Quarterly* 25(1).

Mumford, Lewis. 1970. *The Myth of the Machine: II. The Pentagon of Power.* New York: Harcourt Brace Jovanovich.

Muncie, John, Margaret Wetherell, Rudi Dallos, and Allan Cochrane, eds. 1995. *Understanding the Family.* London: Sage.

Munhall, Patricia, L., ed. 1994. *In Women's Experience,* volume I. New York: National League for Nursing Press.

————. 1995. *In Women's Experience,* volume II. New York: National League For Nursing Press.

Northen, Helen. [1969] 1988. *Social Work with Groups.* New York: Columbia University Press.

O'Hare, William P., Kelvin M. Pollard, Taynia L. Mann, and Mary M. Kent. 1997. "African-Americans in the 1990s." In Arlene S. Skolnick and Jerome H. Skolnick, eds. *Family in Transition,* ninth edition. New York: Longman.

Olsen, Marvin. 1968. *The Process of Social Organization.* New York: Holt, Rinehart, and Winston.

Oshry, Barry. 1995. *Seeing Systems: Unlocking the Mysteries of Organizational Life.* San Francisco: Berrett-Koehler.

Ouchi, William G. 1981. *Theory Z: How American Business Can Meet the Japanese Challenge.* Reading, MA: Addison-Wesley.

Papademetriou, Marguerite. 1971. "Use of a Group Technique with Unwed Mothers and Their Families." *Social Work* 16(4).

Parsons, Talcott. 1960. *Structure and Process in Modern Societies.* New York: Free Press.

Pasley, B. Kay, and Marilyn Ihinger-Tallman. 1989. "Boundary Ambiguity in Remarriage: Does Ambiguity Differentiate Degree of Marital Adjustment and Integration?" *Family Relations* 38(1).

Pel, Mario. [1966] 1984. *The Story of Language.* New York: Mentor.

Perrow, Charles. 1986. *Complex Organizations,* third edition. Glenview, IL: Scott, Foresman.

Phillips, John L., Jr. 1969. *The Origins of Intellect: Piaget's Theory.* San Francisco: Freeman.

Piaget, Jean. 1932. *The Moral Judgment of the Child.* Translated by Marjorie Gabian. London: Kegan Paul.

———. 1987. *Possibility and Necessity.* Minneapolis: University of Minnesota Press.

Piaget, Jean (with E. Ackerman-Vailadao et al.). 1970. *Genetic Epistemology,* Translated by Eleanor Duckworth. New York: Columbia University Press.

Plath, Sylvia. 1966. "Tulip." In *Ariel.* New York: Harper and Row.

Popenoe, David. 1988. *Disturbing the Nest.* Hawthorne, NY: Aldine de Gruyter.

Prigogine, Ilya, and Isabelle Stengers. 1984. *Order out of Chaos.* New York: Bantam.

Putnam, Robert. 1995. "Bowling Alone, Revisited." *Responsive Community,* spring.

———. 1996. "The Strange Disappearance of Civic America." *American Prospect.*

Ramsoy, Ødd. 1962. *Social Groups: As System and Subsystem.* Oslo: Norwegian Universities Press.

Rawls, John. 1971, 1975, 1999. *A Theory of Justice.* Cambridge, MA: Belknap.

Reardon, Kathleen Kelley. 1995. *They Don't Get It, Do They? Communication in the Workplace—Closing the Gap between Men and Women.* Boston: Little, Brown.

Reid, Kenneth E. 1997. *Social Work Practice with Groups.* Pacific Grove, CA: Brooks/ Cole.

Reik, Theodor. 1948. *Listening with the Third Ear.* New York: Farrar Strauss.

Richards, Stan, and Associates. 1974. *Hobo Signs.* Dallas, TX: by author.

Richardson, George P. 1991. *Feedback Thought in Social Science and Systems Theory.* Philadelphia: University of Pennsylvania Press.

Roethlisberger, F., and W. L. Dickson. 1947. *Management and the Worker.* Cambridge, MA: Harvard University Press.

Rogers, Carl. 1970. *Carl Rogers on Encounter Groups.* New York: Harper and Row.

Rose, Reginald. 1955. *Twelve Angry Men.* Chicago: Dramatics Publications.
Royce, Graydon. 2009. "Inside the Mind of An Activist." *Minneapolis Star-Tribune*, September 16.
Sager, Clifford, and Helen Singer Kaplan, eds. 1972. *Progress in Group and Family Therapy.* New York: Brunner/Mazel.
Sandburg, Carl. 1955. "Chicago." In Oscar Williams, ed. *The New Pocket Anthology of American Verse.* New York: Pocket Library.
Sawicki, Marianne. 1997. *Body, Text, and Science: The Literacy of Investigative Practices and the Phenomenology of Edith Stein.* Dordrecht: Kluwer.
Sawicki, Marianne. 2005. "Edmund Husserl (1859-1938)." In *Internet Encyclopedia of Philosophy.* http:wws.iep.utm.edu/Husserl/
Schwartz, David B. 1997. *Who Cares? Rediscovering Community.* Boulder, CO: Westview.
Schwartz, Ed. 1996. *Net Activism: How Citizens Use the Internet.* Sebastopol, CA: Songline Studios.
Scott, W. Richard. 1998. *Organizations: Rational, Natural, and Open Systems,* fourth edition, Upper Saddle River, NJ: Prentice-Hall.
Scott, William G., and David K. Hart. 1980. *Organizational America.* Boston: Houghton Mifflin.
Segal, Lynne. 1995. "A Feminist Looks at the Family." In John Muncie, Margaret Wetherell, Rudi Dalos, and Allan Cochrane, eds. *Understanding the Family.* London: Sage.
Sheehy, Gail. 1976. *Passages.* New York: Dutton.
———. 1992. *The Silent Passage.* New York: Random House.
———. 1995. *New Passages.* New York: Random House.
Shilts, Randy. 1988. *And the Band Played On: Politics, People and the AIDS Epidemic.* New York: Penguin.
Simon, H. A. 1945. *Administrative Behavior.* New York: Macmillan.
Skyttner, Lars. 2005. *General Systems Theory.* Singapore: World Scientific.
Skolnick, Arlene S., and Jerome H. Skolnick. 1997. *Family in Transition,* ninth edition. New York: Longman.
Slater, Philip. 1974. *Earthwalk.* New York: Anchor.
Slater, Suzanne. 1995. *The Lesbian Family Life Cycle.* New York: Free Press.
Smith, David Woodruff. 2008. "Phenomenology," in *Stanford Encyclopedia of Philosophy.* http://plato.stanford.edu/entries.phenomenology
Spitz, Rene. 1965. *The First Year of Life.* New York: International Universities Press.
Stack, Carol B. 1974. *All Our Kin: Strategies for Survival In Two Black Families.* New York: Harper and Row.
———1996. *Call to Home: African Americans Reclaim the Rural South.* New York: Basic Books.
Stegner, Wallace. 1992. *Where the Bluebird Sings to the Lemonade Springs.* New York: Random House.
Tönnies, Ferdinand. 1957. *Community And Society,* Translated by Charles P. Loomis. East Lansing: Michigan State University Press.
Taylor, Robert Joseph, James S. Jackson, and Linda M. Chatters, eds. 1997. *Family Life in Black America.* Thousand Oaks, CA: Sage.

Tuckman, Bruce W. 1965. "Developmental sequence in small groups." *Psychological Bulletin* 63.

Van Geert, Paul. 1994. *Dynamic Systems of Development.* New York: Harvester Wheatsheaf.

Van Maanen, John. 1988. *Tales of the Field.* Chicago: University of Chicago Press.

Veninga, Robert, and James P. Spradley. 1981. *The Work-Stress Connection.* Boston: Little, Brown.

Wadsworth, Barry J. 1996. *Piaget's Theory of Cognitive and Affective Development.* White Plains, NY: Longman.

Watzlawick, Paul, Janet Helmick Beavin, and Don Jackson. 1967. *Pragmatics of Human Communication: A Study of Interactional Patterns, Pathologies, and Paradoxes.* New York: Norton.

Weisman, Celia B. 1963. "Social Structures as a Determinant of the Group Worker's Role." *Social Work* 8(3):87-94.

Weiss, Penny A. 1995. "Feminism and Communitarianism." In Penny Weiss and Marilyn Friedman, eds. *Feminism and Community.* Philadelphia: Temple University Press.

Westkott, Marcia. 1986. *The Feminist Legacy of Karen Horney.* New Haven, CT: Yale University Press.

Whorf, Benjamin Lee. 1956. *Language, Thought and Reality.* New York: Wiley/Technology Press.

Whyte, William Foote. [1955] 1981. *Street Corner Society,* second edition. Chicago: University of Chicago Press.

Wilbers, Stephen. 1998. "Of Ego-Surfing Body Nazis and Other New Office Jargon." *Minneapolis Star-Tribune,* January 23.

Wilson, William Julius. 1987. *The Truly Disadvantaged: The Inner City, the Underclass, and Public Policy.* Chicago: University of Chicago Press.

Wolfe, Alan. 1995. "Human Nature and the Quest for Community." In Amitai Etzioni, ed. *New Communitarian Thinking.* Charlottesville: University Press of Virginia.

————. 1998. *One Nation, After All.* New York: Viking.

Wood, Julia T. 1994. *Who Cares? Women, Care, and Culture.* Carbondale: Southern Illinois University Press.

Woodruff, John. 1989. *China In Search of Its Future: Years of Great Reform: 1982-1987.* Seattle: University of Washington Press.

Wuthnow, Robert, James Davison Hunter, Albert Bergesen, and Edith Kurzweil. 1984. *Cultural Analysis.* Boston/London: Routledge and Kegan Paul.

Yahoo News. March 14, 2010. "Culture Clash: European Art provokes Muslims."

Zelazo, Philip David, Morris Moscovitch, and Evan Thompson. 2007. *The Cambridge Handbook of Consciousness.* Cambridge: Cambridge University Press.

Zimmerman, Carle. 1947. *Outline of the Future of the Family.* Cambridge: Phillips Book Store.

Glossary

Accommodation. Modification of the system to adapt to environmental conditions. See ADAPTATION, ASSIMILATION.

Adaptation. Action by the system to secure or conserve energy from the environment. Parsons's use of this term includes such action as well as the achievement of goals in the environment. See ACCOMMODATION, ASSIMILATION, FUNCTIONAL IMPERATIVES.

African-American. This is the preferred term for Americans of African descent, in that it refers to geographic origin rather than skin color, similar to "Caucasian," "European-American" (or "Euro-American") and "Asian-American." "Black" is used in this text in quotations from other sources, and in a historical context.

Alienation. This term has a wide variety of definitions. We consider that, fundamentally, it describes a state in which a person does not experience a synergistic linkage with a system (or component) that is significant to the person.

American Indian. This term refers to indigenous peoples of North America, specifically those within the United States. It is often used interchangeably with "Native American," although the latter also denotes other indigenous peoples such as Pacific Islanders. Other terms, such as "Natives," "First Nations" (in Canada), pueblos, Inuits (formerly referred to as "Eskimos") and Aleuts, and other specific tribes' names are also used. "Indians" is, of course, inaccurate, but some indigenous Americans hold that "American Indian" appears in treaties between the United States and the sovereign tribal governments and thus has historical value.

Assimilation. A form of adaptation in which incoming information is interpreted as being similar to previous information (i.e., fitted into old schemas). See ACCOMMODATION, ADAPTATION.

Autonomy. Independence from other components within a system. The components are related to a common suprasystem but are largely or entirely separate from each other. See AUTOPOIESIS.

Autopoiesis. Literally (from Greek), "self-made"; self-development and self-creation. There is theoretical disagreement about the degree of autonomy implied; Maturana and Varela seem to imply complete control of reproduction by the system; we caution that there is interdependence between part and whole, and perhaps between parts, along with significant autonomy and separateness.

Behavior. Short-term exchanges between components or systems that accomplish specific goals for the system. This includes socialization, communication, and social control. See EVOLUTION, STRUCTURE.

Body Language. Nonvocal communication expressed through touch, posture, facial expression, and movement.

Bond. The common interest, identification, or feeling of "we-ness" among members of a group (which can be as small as a dyad) that permits the group to exist as a system. See BOUNDARY, NETWORK, AND LINKAGE.

Boundary. The limits of the interaction of the components of a system with each other or with the environment. It is usually defined by intensity or frequency of interaction between systems and components. See DENSITY.

Bureaucracy. A distinct form of organization in which there is a relatively high degree of administrative centralization, hierarchical control, specificity of roles, and clearly identified role expectations. This form of organization is usually found in cultures that are highly elaborated, and it serves social control functions and goal achievement in the society.

Caste. A fixed, distinctive and disadvantaged social status based upon the circumstances of one's ancestry, occupation, skin color, or cultural tradition. Hindu "untouchables" are the most frequently cited example, but any relatively rigid social class structure may have one or more groups with low social status and impermeable boundaries.

Chaos and Order. In chaos theory (see below), "chaos" is defined as a completely entropic situation in which there is no exchange, relationship, or structure present. Any structure that arises is an example of "order." These definitions are counterintuitive, in that they seem to contradict usual meanings of these terms. It might be clearer to think of chaos as "unorganized" and order as "structured," but we may be stuck with these terms, for the near future at least. See CHAOS THEORY.

Chaos Theory. This conception of natural events holds that events occur in nonlinear fashion, due to extreme sensitivity to prevailing conditions, and that variations (or perturbations) are random, but occur within some identifiable parameters. The infinite variations of snowflakes, e.g., and of human events, have brought the natural and social sciences closer in recognizing and accounting for complexity and uncertainty. See LINEARITY AND NONLINEARITY, FEEDBACK CYCLE, and LOOP; See also ORDER, COMPLEXITY and STEADY STATE.

Class. A scheme of classification of a particular society. Usually ordered by indices such as income, occupation, and education. See ROLE, STATUS AND CASTE.

Coevolution. This concept has gained importance recently. It is a modification of previous conceptions of the relationship between systems and their environments. The concept means that as systems evolve, so do their environments; in other words, that systems do not simply "adapt" or "adjust" to their environments, but influence the environments, as well, through feedback cycles. This has highly significant implications for the modification of the Darwinian view of evolution. In a broad sense, it redefines systems (particularly living systems) as active, and *autopoietic;* that is, self-developing. See FEEDBACK CYCLE.

Communication. In a narrow sense, the transportation of information between or within systems; in a broader sense, the transportation of energy, also. In this broader sense, information is considered a special form of energy. See INFORMATION.

Complexity. This has less to do with being complicated, or having numerous parts, than with unpredictability and spontaneity. To the extent that feedback loops are are not centrally controlled, interaction between parts, or between system and environment, may create new, unexpected patterns of behavior. Fractal dynamics are a literal illustration of this unpredictability.

Component. Synonymous with "part" (a part of a system). It may or may not be a system in itself, in contrast to a subsystem. See SUBSYSTEM.

Density. The degree to which energy/information can pass through a boundary; permeability of the boundary. (See Day, in Day, Gilbert, Settles, and Burr, 1995.)

Differentiation. Selectivity of function or activity among components of a system. "Division of labor" is one example. A function or activity is performed by one, or some, components and not others. This differs from specialization in that the component may perform other functions or activities in addition to the assigned, differentiated one. See SPECIALIZATION.

Disintegration. This means systemic death; components *desystematize.* "It is a movement away from organization into entropy and randomness" (Monane, 1967:159). See ENTROPY, ORGANIZATION.

Ecological Approach. This is an approach that is virtually synonymous with a systems approach. Specifically, it refers to "nested" systems, that is, from component to subsystem to suprasystem, and specifically to relationships between humans and their environments. Like systems theory, it calls for an analysis and specification of the context of the focal system.

Ecological Systems. A term used by some systems writers in the broad sense of systems that are hierarchically related. In biology and ecology, the term refers to the interactions of organisms and between organisms and their environments. See ECOLOGICAL APPROACH.

Elaboration. Used in reference to evolution of groups, this denotes increasing complexity and multiplication of parts of the system. We also use it to describe similar processes in other systems.

Emergence. The creation, definition, or development of a new system (or all three of these; the term is, itself, still being defined). Some systems theorists raise the issue of *who* recognizes the emergence, and stress the phenomenological nature of this judgment: in other words, "Do you see what I see?" See TRANSITION STATE, PERSPECTIVISM, and PHENOMENOLOGY.

Empathy. In German (see discussion of Edith Stein's phenomenology), the term translates as "feeling with." It is the capacity to interpret and respond to other persons' emotions and actions based upon one's own experience (schemas).

Energy. Capacity for action, action, or power to effect change. We use this term much as Parsons used "action." As increased interaction occurs, there is greater available energy. Richard Adams (1988) preferred the term "energy forms," which is a useful concept. Information is one form of energy. See ENTROPY, POWER, SYNERGY.

Energy Functions. Parsons specified four functions (or processes) that he saw as necessary in a system: adaptation, goal-directed activity, integration, and pattern maintenance. We identify other functions that we consider to be more descriptive—securing energy (S) and goal-direction (G)—and see these as occurring both externally (E) and internally (I); hence a set of four: SE, SI, GE, and GI. None necessarily takes precedence over the others. See GOAL-DIRECTED ACTIVITY.

Entropy. The tendency of systems to "run down," to distribute (or dissipate) energy randomly so that it becomes less accessible; the system thus becomes less capable of organized work. Prigogine, Maturana, Capra, and others argue that living systems violate this "second law of thermodynamics" by maintaining themselves in a high degree of disequilibrium "on the edge of chaos." See ENERGY, NEGENTROPY, ORGANIZATION, SYNTROPY, ORDER, CHAOS THEORY, EQUILIBRIUM.

Environment. Anything not included within the interactions of the components of a system (that is, within the interactional boundary) that affects the system. It may also be considered as anything that affects the system but over which it has little or no control. *Significant environment* refers to those systems or components that are capable of influencing the system in fundamental (as opposed to tangential) ways.

Equifinality. A systems principle that means that two different systems, if they receive similar inputs, will arrive at similar end states, even though they had different initial conditions. One illustration is that two children may grow differently, one "undershooting" and the other "overshooting" initially, but both will arrive at adulthood in good health and normal size if they are nurtured (both nutritionally and emotionally) similarly and adequately. Given newer ideas about nonlinearity and autopoiesis (see these terms), Equifinality may be strictly a theoretical concept, considering the unpredictability of systems.

Equilibrium. Fixed balance of a relatively closed system, characterized by little interchange with the environment and avoidance of disturbance. Freud's concept of psychological structure fits this definition.

Ethology. The study of animal behavior, especially of innate patterns, by ethologists including Konrad Lorenz, Desmond Morris, Lionel Tiger, and Robin Fox. Edward O. Wilson is the leading theorist of sociobiology, which suggests that human behavior is biologically determined in some significant ways.

Evolution. Longer-term change in a system's structure. The term describes which relationships have altered (and which have remained the same) and in what manner a system's functions are being performed differently at the end of some significant period of time. See BEHAVIOR, STRUCTURE.

Feedback Cycle. The process in which a system receives internal or environmental responses to its behavior and, in turn, reacts to these received responses by accommodating and assimilating the energy/information received, by altering the system's structure, and then engaging in altered exchanges of energy/information. See ADAPTATION, ACCOMMODATION, ASSIMILATION, COMMUNICATION, LOOP.

Focal System. This refers to the system that is the object of attention at a particular moment. It must be specified in order to be consistent with the demand that the perspective of the viewer should be stated. Systems analysts frequently label this the *target system* if the focal system is the system in which change is to be achieved. See HOLON, PERSPECTIVISM.

General Systems Theory (GST). A loosely knit set of theories derived from the natural and social sciences, which has generated useful hypotheses about similar (isomorphic) processes and structures across the range of living entities. GST comprises *social* systems theory, among many other varieties of living systems. This body of theory has evolved from the late nineteenth century to the present; Ludwig Von Bertalanffy in biology and Talcott Parsons in sociology are generally recognized as the progenitors of systems theory. One logical extension of GST is the "Gaia hypothesis" that the earth (and its environment of atmosphere and solar radiation) is a global ecological system that demonstrates the properties of a living system.

Goal. A desired steady state to be achieved by fulfilling a specific function of the system within some relatively short period of time. See PURPOSE.

Goal-Directed Activity (GE and GI functions). One of two kinds of energy functions, the other being *securing and conserving energy.* The process is the expenditure of energy (or distribution of information) to achieve system goals, either internally or externally.

Hierarchy. A form of organization that characterizes all viable systems. Hierarchy is a superordinate-subordinate relationship in systems in which any unit is dependent upon its suprasystem for performance of energy functions and must provide direction to its own subsystems. The hierarchy may be one of power, or simply of sequence (that is, one thing must precede another). This does not imply greater or lesser value to any partner in the hierarchical relationship. See HOLON.

Holon. Arthur Koestler's term, which denotes a system that is both part of a larger suprasystem and is itself a suprasystem to other systems. See FOCAL SYSTEM, SUBSYSTEM, SUPRASYSTEM.

Homeostasis. Fixed balance in a partially open system, characterized by very limited interchange with the environment and by maintenance of the system's present structure. The balance can change within very narrowly defined limits. See EQUILIBRIUM, STEADY STATE, CHAOS.

Id, Ego, and Superego. This is Freud's description of persons' psychological structure. The id includes the physiological processes and unconscious drives. The superego is the process that incorporates the socially derived "dos and don'ts." The ego is the process that mediates between the id and the external environment, and between the id and superego. We view this as a systems conception of the personality that attempted to identify and define the essential functions of the personality system. Freud's system was essentially closed, and the goal of the system was equilibrium.

Identity. Erikson defined this in several versions. The central idea is integration of the components of the personality, along with validation through interaction with the social environment. The result of these is *ego identity,* which is inner assurance of congruence between a person's feeling about self and others' feeling about the person. The concept has been loosely applied to other systems such as "national identity" and "racial identity." Identity is a steady state of the personality system but is richer in meaning than steady state. See STEADY STATE, SYNTALITY, SYNERGY.

Information. In the broadest sense, information is one form of energy. In a narrow sense, information includes signs and symbols that are exchanged. It is the content of feedback and communication. As opposed to "noise," it is *information,* organized so that it can be understood and utilized. See COMMUNICATION, FEEDBACK.

Institutionalization. One form of differentiation in which some component or subsystem is assigned (or assumes) responsibility to perform specific major functions for the system (usually a culture, society, or community, but in a broader sense, in microsystems as well). The differentiated component or subsystem may specialize in this function. A new component or subsystem may carry out the function, or the assignment may be carried out by an existing component or subsystem. See DIFFERENTIATION, SPECIALIZATION.

Integration. One of Parsons's four functional imperatives. A system must ensure the harmonious interaction of its components in order to prevent entropy and in order to secure and conserve internal energy sources.

Isomorphic. Similarity of form between systems or components of systems. "Isomorph" is used in this book to point to similarities of structure, behavior, or evolution between different systems and levels of systems. For example, *feedback cycle* is applicable to all levels of systems from person to culture.

Linearity and Nonlinearity. In systems terminology, linearity means "straight-line" causation, in which "*A* causes *B,* which causes *C.*" Nonlinearity means that causation is at least partially determined *by feedback loops,* in which later developments alter conditions that existed earlier, leading to new events and conditions. Examples include Erikson's stages, in which outcomes of later stages may alter the balances achieved in earlier stages.

Loop. This term is borrowed from cybernetics, computer programming, and engineering. It is a specific form of feedback, in which a system's output becomes input that modifies the system's functioning. That is, the system's own behavior supplies stimuli for system modification. See FEEDBACK.

Macrosystem. See MICROSYSTEM. Larger systems, or suprasystems, including culture and society; may also, in some instances, include large communities or large organizations, such as multinational corporations. "Micro" and "macro" are defined relative to the focal system.

Microsystem. See MACROSYSTEM. Smaller systems, or subsystems, including group, family, or person; may also, in some instances, include smaller-scale communities or organizations.

Mission. See PURPOSE.

Morphogenesis. A system tending toward structural change. In actuality, all systems must simultaneously maintain a dynamic balance between morphogenesis (change) and morphostasis (maintenance) if they are to continue. See MORPHOSTASIS.

Morphostasis. A system tending toward maintenance of its current structure. See MORPHOGENESIS.

Negentropy. The word is a contraction of "negative entropy," meaning the reduction of random, unavailable energy via the importation of energy from outside the system. Recent theorists stress that a high degree of negentropy is the means by which systems maintain themselves "on the edge of chaos." See CHAOS, ENTROPY, SYNERGY.

Network. A set of persons linked together, although not necessarily each to every other. We refer you to the quotation from McIntyre (see Chapter 4, of this book); a network includes indirect links, different from a small group, which has only direct, face-to-face linkage between members. *Networking* is the usage or exploitation of such linkages to achieve specific, desired results. See BOND.

Open or Closed System. "Open" denotes energy exchange across a system's boundaries. "Closed" denotes lack of energy exchange across boundaries.

Order. See CHAOS.

Organization. The process of structuring a system's exchange of energy, both internally and externally. Persistent regularities of relationship between components make up the structure, or organization, of the system. See CHAOS, DIFFERENTIATION, ORDER, SPECIALIZATION.

Pattern Maintenance. One of Parsons's four functional imperatives. This refers to the necessity of the system to regulate and enforce legitimated behaviors in order to conserve energy and to achieve goals. We consider this to include our SI and GI functions. See ENERGY FUNCTIONS.

Perspectivism. In social systems theory, this means that any description or definition of a system must include an explicit statement of one's own position or intention with regard to that system and an explicit identification of the system that one is identifying as the focal system. Philosophically, the term denotes that any viewpoint is relative to one's own perceptions and relations to the system being described or defined, and to its environment. See our discussion of postmodernism in the Introduction to this edition. See PHENOMENOLOGY.

Phase transition. Movement from one steady state to another, marked by significantly altered characteristics. See TIPPING POINT.

Phenomenology. A philosophy first articulated by Edmund Husserl, that is highly influential in European thought. It is a "common sense" view that perception and thought consist of each person's interpretation of reality, based on the structures (schemas) built up from social contact with others. Consciousness is the activity of awareness of external and internal phenomena; it posits a "self" which is not fixed, but which adapts to internal and external stimuli. Edith Stein and Jean Paul Sartre identified affective/emotional schemas (empathy) as fundamental to construction of the self. See PERSPECTIVISM, SELF.

Polarities. Opposite or contrasting qualities. Many of the systems ideas are conceived as polarities at opposite ends of a continuum. However, any system at any time is a mixture or ratio of two polar qualities, such as task *vs.* sentiment, adaptation *vs.* integration, and basic trust *vs.* basic mistrust.

Power. The capacity to achieve goals by the application or deprivation of energy to another system so as to affect its functioning.

Praxis. Putting theory into practice, or the application of skill or talent in carrying out a program (not identical to "action" or "practice"). In Marxian thought, praxis is revolutionary, aimed at fundamental change in values or social arrangements.

Psychosexual. Generally, this refers to the Freudian stages of personality development (i.e., oral, anal, phallic, and genital). See PSYCHOSOCIAL.

Psychosocial. Generally, this refers to Erikson's life cycle formulation of personality development. This is a modification and extension of the Freudian psychosexual stages, with emphasis on social and cultural influences. See PSYCHOSEXUAL.

Purpose. A description or statement of a desired steady state to be achieved by assignment of goal achievement to a component or subsystem, and completion of the goal(s). Systems analysts frequently use "mission" to mean the same as purpose. See GOAL.

Role. A set of expectations about behavior that can be fulfilled by a person. It carries with it expectations of behavior that are defined and approved by systems in the persons' social environment. The role occupant generally has some leeway in interpretations of assigned behaviors. This is analogous to the theater, in which the playwright prescribes the role but the artist interprets through the performance. See STATUS.

Schema. Precisely used, this is Piaget's term for a single complex, or nexus, of associated responses that a person is capable of making. These responses, or behaviors, accumulate through experience, and are integrated into larger wholes as the person develops. We use the term to mean the integrated knowledge, experience, and interpretations that underlie any system's responses.

Securing and Conserving Energy. We designate this as one of two kinds of ENERGY FUNCTIONS in a system; the other is GOAL-DIRECTED ACTIVITY. The process is one of expending energy to secure further energy, or to reduce the expenditure of energy, as in minimizing intrasystem conflict. See ENERGY FUNCTIONS, GOAL-DIRECTED ACTIVITY.

Self. A sense of one's identity, perceived by a person or attributed to the person by others. The content of this identity differs according to various theorists; in some theories, it is a relatively fixed entity, sometimes innate, in others it is fluid and mutable. It comprises value preference, past behavior, and projections of future characteristics of this identity. See ROLE, STATUS, PHENOMENOLOGY.

Social Control. The use of energy by a system to assure that its components fulfill assigned functions (see PURPOSES and GOALS). Such activity includes socialization and enforcement of norms of behavior. The purpose of social control is to permit continued functioning of the system through reducing or preventing deviance (energy-diverting behavior) among the components. See SOCIALIZATION.

Socialization. One form of social control intended to assure the availability of components' energies to the system. The means to achieve this are primarily through assimilating the culture. Hence, education, indoctrination, and enculturation are forms of socialization. See SOCIAL CONTROL.

Specialization. Performance of a function or activity to the exclusion of other functions or activities, by a component of a system. A system may differentiate its components by allocating functions or activities among them; some components perform certain functions exclusively; that is, other components do not perform that function. If the component performs *only* the differentiated function, then it has specialized; if it performs other functions as well, it is differentiated but not specialized. The two are separate. See DIFFERENTIATION.

Status. A vertical dimension of ranking; it may be ascribed (assigned by society) or achieved (attained by dint of individual or group activity). See CLASS, ROLE.

Steady State. A total condition of the system in which it is in balance both internally and with its environment but is at the same time undergoing some degree of change (i. e, is not static). The word *steady* fails to connote the dynamic nature of systems, while the word *state* fails to connote a succession of conditions of the system. "Dynamic balance" or Von Bertalanffy's "flowing balance" connote these characteristics better. As noted earlier, steady state is maintained by a high degree of negentropy (importation of energy) in living systems "on the edge of chaos." Used fairly loosely and somewhat interchangeably with equilibrium and homeostasis, but distinct from them. See EQUILIBRIUM, HOMEOSTASIS.

Structure. The most stable relationships between systems and components (i.e., with the slowest rate of change). "Structure" describes which components or systems are related to each other during a given time period, but does not necessarily give details of the amount of energy exchange, or in what direction, or the functions being performed for each party to the relationship. It is thus a "snapshot," frozen in time, not a "movie." See BEHAVIOR, EVOLUTION, SCHEMA.

Subsystem. A component of a system that is itself a system. It is one kind of component. See COMPONENT, SUPRASYSTEM, SYSTEM.

Suprasystem. A larger system that includes the focal system; a "whole" of which the focal system is a "part." See SUBSYSTEM, COMPONENT.

Symbolic Interaction. A theoretical perspective within social psychology that seeks to understand human behavior through study of the "social act." Such study attends to overt behavior and what the act symbolizes within the social context.

Synergy. Increasing the amount of energy available in a system through increased interaction of the components. Loosely, it may be described as the creation of new energy through compounding the actions of the parts, but this is a moot point in systems theory. See ENERGY, ENTROPY, NEGENTROPY.

Syntality. This is the unique character of a group; analogous to the "personality" of a person.

System. An organized whole made up of components that interact in a way distinct from their interaction with other entities, and that endures over some period of time. See COMPONENT, SUBSYSTEM, SUPRASYSTEM.

Territoriality. Refers to the proclivity of organisms, including humans, to seek, obtain, and defend an area or space of action. This serves to order and stabilize behavioral space. See ETHOLOGY.

Tipping point. A crucial event or factor that disrupts a previous steady state perhaps unexpectedly and instantaneously. See TRANSITION STATE.

Transition State. The condition of a system that is moving from one steady state to another. As discussed in the text of this book, transition states may be more frequent than steady states. However, every steady state is in transition, so it may be a "judgment call" as to whether at certain times a system is in steady state or transition. Like other polarities, it is a ratio: in this instance, of change or maintenance of current structure. See BEHAVIOR, EVOLUTION, MORPHOGENESIS, MORPHOSTASIS, STEADY STATE, STRUCTURE.

Name Index

Subject Index